# Common Core Curriculum

# Other Books by Common Core

**THE WHEATLEY PORTFOLIO**

*Common Core Curriculum: English, Grades 6–8, Second Edition*

*Common Core Curriculum: English, Grades 9–12, Second Edition*

**THE ALEXANDRIA PLAN**

*Common Core Curriculum: United States History, Grades K–12*

*Common Core Curriculum: World History, Grades K–12*

*Common Core Curriculum: United States History, Grades 3–5*

*Common Core Curriculum: World History, Grades 3–5*

**EUREKA MATH**

*Common Core Mathematics, A Story of Units: Grades K–5*

*Common Core Mathematics, A Story of Ratios: Grades 6–8*

*Common Core Mathematics, A Story of Functions: Grades 9–12*

# Common Core Curriculum: English, Grades K–5

## SECOND EDITION

COMMON CORE™ *consider the source*

JB JOSSEY-BASS™
A Wiley Brand

Cover design: Chris Clary
Cover image: Katsushika Hokusai (1760-1849), *The Great Wave*, 1831–33, Japanese color woodblock print.
Photo: V&A Images, London/Art Resource, NY

Published by Jossey-Bass
A Wiley Brand
One Montgomery Street, Suite 1200, San Francisco, CA 94104-4594 www.josseybass.com

Limit of Liability/Disclaimer of Warranty: While the publisher and author have used their best efforts in preparing this book, they make no representations or warranties with respect to the accuracy or completeness of the contents of this book and specifically disclaim any implied warranties of merchantability or fitness for a particular purpose. No warranty may be created or extended by sales representatives or written sales materials. The advice and strategies contained herein may not be suitable for your situation. You should consult with a professional where appropriate. Neither the publisher nor author shall be liable for any loss of profit or any other commercial damages, including but not limited to special, incidental, consequential, or other damages. Readers should be aware that Internet Web sites offered as citations and/or sources for further information may have changed or disappeared between the time this was written and when it is read.

Jossey-Bass books and products are available through most bookstores. To contact Jossey-Bass directly call our Customer Care Department within the U.S. at 800-956-7739, outside the U.S. at 317-572-3986, or fax 317-572-4002.

For more information about Common Core, Inc., visit commoncore.org.

Wiley publishes in a variety of print and electronic formats and by print-on-demand. Some material included with standard print versions of this book may not be included in e-books or in print-on-demand. If this book refers to media such as a CD or DVD that is not included in the version you purchased, you may download this material at http://booksupport.wiley.com. For more information about Wiley products, visit www.wiley.com.

**Library of Congress Cataloging-in-Publication Data**
Common Core Curriculum: English, grades K-5 — Second edition.
        pages   cm. – (Common Core English language arts)
Includes index.
Description based on print version record and CIP data provided by publisher; resource not viewed.
ISBN 978-1-118-81135-1 (pbk.)
ISBN 978-1-118-81249-5 (ebk.)
ISBN 978-1-118-81265-5 (ebk.)
1. Language arts (Elementary–Curricula–United States–Case studies.   2. Language arts (Elementary) – Standards–United States–States.
LB1576.C5785 2014
372.6–dc23

2013045493

Printed in the United States of America
SECOND EDITION
PB *Printing* 10 9 8 7 6 5 4 3 2 1

# Contents

# Foreword

## GOOD SCHOOLS: THE SALT OF SOCIETY

Three hundred years ago Cotton Mather preached, "A Good School deserves to be call'd the very Salt of the Town that hath it." Without a school "wherein the Youth may by able Masters be Taught the Things that are necessary to qualify them for future Serviceableness," a community will founder.[1] Mather's advice to townspeople in Puritan New England reflects one of the philosophical underpinnings of the Common Core Curriculum in English Language Arts: Schools matter. Curriculum matters. Teachers matter.

In order to determine which things should be taught, we must of course first define what it means to be serviceable in a twenty-first-century democratic society. To ensure a capable workforce and build a strong economy, high levels of literacy and numeracy are obviously essential. But what about the need for students to develop empathy and thoughtfulness? It is shortsighted to equate the value of education with economic growth. Like salt, good schools with rich curricula enhance the community by adding depth—and piquancy. Like salt, they are a preservative, ensuring that a society's values endure.

Many of the benefits we've come to demand as our rights in a modern society depend on high levels of employment, but if we shift the discussion of the purpose of school from job training to preparing America's children to lead a worthwhile life, the calculus changes. Is simply working nine to five for forty years what you most aspire to for your children? Or do you want them to have an education that invites exploration of essential questions, inspires challenges to the status quo, and somehow prepares them for what we cannot yet know? Most parents want both.

The conundrum for curriculum developers is to avoid becoming so caught up in preparing students to make a living—which starts with paying attention in kindergarten; earning good grades through elementary school, middle school, and high school; achieving competitive SAT and ACT scores; and winning a place in college or in the workplace—that we lose sight of educating students to enrich their lives.

In *Not for Profit: Why Democracy Needs the Humanities*, philosopher Martha Nussbaum warns that, "With the rush to profitability in the global market, values precious for the future of democracy, especially in an era of religious and economic anxiety, are in danger of getting lost."[2] I share her concern. The movement to reform education primarily in order to make the United States more globally competitive seems wrongheaded and even counterproductive. Maybe I lack a competitive spirit, but I have always wanted more for my students than just coming in first. I want them to learn about and to think about the world—today's world and yesterday's. Nussbaum

---

1  Cotton Mather, "The Education of Children," http://www.spurgeon.org/~phil/mather/edkids.htm.
2  Martha Nussbaum, *Not for Profit: Why Democracy Needs the Humanities* (Princeton, NJ: Princeton University Press, 2010), 6.

explains, "World history and economic understanding must be humanistic and critical if they are to be at all useful in forming intelligent global citizens, and they must be taught alongside the study of religion and of philosophical theories of justice. Only then will they supply a useful foundation for the public debates that we must have if we are to cooperate in solving major human problems."[3] One means of learning about the problems that have beset and continue to bedevil humanity is through the study of the humanities—literature and art, history and philosophy. This is the kind of education the Common Core Curriculum offers. I believe it is the education that every generation of citizens needs.

Unit 3 of grade 1, Life Lessons, offers young children opportunities to explore the kind of education Martha Nussbaum recommends. As they work through the unit, "Students read and listen to fables with morals. They also learn about rules for life in a book of manners. Reading the life story of George Washington Carver, students learn about a man who had to overcome obstacles in life to make important contributions to science and agriculture. Students also learn about Thomas Edison's work with electricity and the rules for its safe use. Students write narratives focused on life lessons and create informative/explanatory posters about electricity. Finally, students focus on descriptive words while studying the artwork of Georgia O'Keeffe." This interdisciplinary approach integrates the study of science and builds students' background knowledge. In so doing, it strengthens their reading comprehension and develops their facility with reading informational texts—a key expectation of the Common Core State Standards. It also invites children to investigate Georgia O'Keeffe's paintings and build their cultural literacy.

Some readers of the Common Core Curriculum may argue that their students won't read nineteenth-century novels, that twenty-first-century students raised on Twitter need a faster pace and different kinds of text. I say language arts classrooms may be the last place where young people can unplug themselves from the solipsism of Facebook postings and enter a milieu different from their own. "But my students won't do the homework reading I assign," teachers wail. It isn't as though students don't have the time. A 2010 study by the Kaiser Family Foundation reports that children ages eight to eighteen spend an average of seven-and-a-half hours daily "consuming entertainment media."[4] And this does not include the hour-and-a-half a day they spend texting friends. Today's students have the time to read; many of them simply choose not to.

To those who look at the suggested works for the high school Common Core Curriculum and think, "Our students could never read those books," I urge perusal of the primary grade curriculum. If children were immersed in rich literature and nonfiction from the first days of kindergarten and engaged in classroom conversations that encouraged them to think deeply about what they read, then negotiating Ralph Ellison's *Invisible Man* in eleventh grade and Jane Austen's *Sense and Sensibility* in twelfth is certainly possible. Though such books pose textual challenges for young readers, as part of a continuum and under the tutelage of an "able Master," the work is achievable. In our effort to provide students with readings that they can relate to, we sometimes end up teaching works that students can read on their own at the expense of teaching more worthwhile texts that they most certainly need assistance negotiating.

We need to remind ourselves that curriculum should be aimed at what Lev Vygotsky calls students' zone of proximal development. Writing in 1962, Vygotsky said, "the only good kind of instruction is that which marches ahead of development and leads it."[5] Classroom texts should pose intellectual challenges for readers and invite them to stretch and grow. Students also need

---

3 Ibid., 94.
4 Ulla G. Foehr, Victoria J. Rideout, and Donald F. Roberts, "Generation M[2]: Media in the Lives of 8- to 18-Year-Olds" (Menlo Park, CA: Kaiser Family Foundation, January 2010), http://www.kff.org/entmedia/8010.cfm.
5 Lev Vygotsky, *Thought and Language*, trans. Eugenia Hanfmann and Gertrude Vakar (Cambridge, MA: MIT Press, 1962), 104.

books that feed their personal interests and allow them to explore "the road not taken." Reading a broad range of books makes students stronger readers and, over time, stronger people. Rigor versus relevance doesn't need to be an either-or proposition. With artful instruction by able masters, students can acquire the literacy skills they need—not only to meet the Common Core State Standards, but also to meet the challenges this brave new world is sure to deal them.

Reading literature also helps students explore hypothetical scenarios and consider the ramifications of what might prima facie seem to be a good or profitable idea. Consider the Common Core Curriculum's final grade 7 unit, Literature Reflects Life: Making Sense of Our World. Addressing Common Core Reading Standard RL.7.6, "Analyze how an author develops and contrasts the points of view of different characters or narrators in a text," the curriculum recommends that students read Robert Louis Stevenson's *The Strange Case of Dr. Jekyll and Mr. Hyde*. This nineteenth-century novella invites young readers to reflect on their own conflicting natures and offers a cautionary tale regarding experimentation. When we consider how best to prepare tomorrow's doctors, scientists, programmers, and engineers for the twenty-first century, it seems to me that reading stories about investigations that go very wrong is quite a good idea.

Later in his sermon, Cotton Mather states that "the Devil cannot give a greater Blow to the Reformation among us, than by causing Schools to Languish under Discouragements." The Common Core Curriculum offers hope to discouraged teachers. It offers a plan for developing young minds, a plan that is both rigorous and more relevant than ever before. It may seem odd to be taking guidance from a seventeenth-century Puritan, but I know I couldn't say it better. "Where schools are not vigorously and Honourably Encouraged, whole Colonies will sink apace into a Degenerate and Contemptible Condition, and at last become horribly Barbarous. If you would not betray your Posterity into the very Circumstances of Savages, let Schools have more Encouragement." Amen.

Carol Jago
Associate Director of the California Reading and Literature Project
at UCLA; Former President of the National Council of Teachers
of English; and Trustee, Common Core, Inc.

# From the Writers

To My Fellow Teachers:

Creating this curriculum has been, by far, the most exciting project I have been part of in my twenty-two-year teaching career. As a classroom teacher, I (like many of you) have hung on to the pendulum as it has swung back and forth from prescriptive, mandatory educational initiatives to long periods with no guidance at all—always trying to find a way to provide students with a rich and rigorous education. This curriculum presented us with a perfect opportunity to strike a new balance.

We have brought excellent literary and informational texts alive in new ways by pairing them with the skills and expectations in the Common Core State Standards (CCSS). This curriculum offers terrific new choices to teachers who wish to use the CCSS to create classes that are rich not just with great literature and literary nonfiction but also with art, history, mythology, and science.

If you were to peek into my fifth-grade classroom, you would see me enjoying the difference this curriculum makes. I see poetry brought into a new light with the guidance of our sample lesson plans. I am amazed by students who are working hard to read a book like *Walk Two Moons* because they have been lured by the study of a complex plot and the enticing "coming of age" genre. Teaching has become fun again!

We have worked as a team. Cyndi Wells wrote the units for the fourth and fifth grades, providing a seamless entry into the middle grades' curricula. Ruthie Stern masterfully wrote the sample lesson plans, giving the curriculum articulated lessons aligned vertically as the standards progress from kindergarten toward college and career readiness.

And so we—along with all those who wrote, critiqued, wrote again, revised, rewrote, and edited—give this gift to you! And we can't wait to see it interpreted in classrooms by creative teachers, with new twists and turns, evolving into an even richer and more rigorous curriculum that suits your students, your school, and your community.

Lorraine Griffith
Fifth-grade teacher, Asheville, North Carolina
Lead writer, kindergarten through third grade
Common Core Curriculum: English

To My Fellow Teachers:

Participating in the development of this curriculum has been an eye-opening and incredibly rewarding professional development experience for me. Since my first years as a classroom teacher, I've witnessed the powerful results that come from a marriage between rich content and literacy instruction; I wanted the curriculum to exhibit this component. As an administrator, I approached this project from the perspective of creating resources that provide enough support for you without taking away your creative freedom. As a mother, I've thought about what an impact this curriculum could and will—I hope—have on the education my children receive.

The new Common Core State Standards Initiative presented my colleagues and me—now close friends—with an ideal opportunity for twenty-first-century collaboration: we live in three different states, yet developed this curriculum together. After much trial and error regarding our approach, we decided to pair the best literary and informational texts we know into meaningful thematic units, allowing students to develop literacy in a humanities-rich environment. We hope that the closely related components of this curriculum will give you confidence to use them in various permutations in your classroom. We also hope you will collaborate with your colleagues to refine and create new activities that will not only ensure that the standards are taught and learned but also yield deeper levels of student work and satisfaction.

In the middle school curriculum, we have worked to provide the perfect juxtaposition of substantive and challenging content with engaging and interesting instructional approaches for middle school students. We have made every effort to engage students in a variety of age-appropriate and social ways, encouraging them to take complex ideas and apply them to their daily experiences inside *and outside* of class.

Our own collaboration on this curriculum has been intellectually gratifying and joyful, and we hope it provides you with a similarly rewarding experience. The curriculum is our gift to you, and we sincerely hope you enjoy the journey of making it your own.

Cyndi Wells
Lead coach and fine arts facilitator,
Charlottesville, Virginia
Lead writer, fourth through eighth grade,
Common Core Curriculum: English

To My Fellow Teachers:

For years we have been deluged with reform initiatives from on high that claimed they would improve student achievement. Few have actually brought progress. I joined the Common Core team of teachers out of conviction that the Common Core State Standards (CCSS) would make a difference and have a positive impact on our work in the classroom. The standards provide a framework for composing a rich, well-planned curriculum that guides our instruction.

Classroom teachers know that imaginative planning is at the heart of any successful lesson. The seventy-six sample lesson plans (SLPs), one for each of the units, are instructional road maps. The purpose of each SLP is to demonstrate how to create the necessary link between the literary and informational texts and the CCSS. The SLPs vary in focus and content—from a novel or selection of poems to a play or informational text. Each has a clear topic, a set of objectives, and suggested activities, as well as helpful guides for differentiated instruction. Consider these plans as a place to start. Use them directly or as a model for developing your own lessons.

Writing the curriculum and the SLPs has been both intellectually rewarding and joyful to us as classroom teachers. I hope you find that working with these volumes becomes equally joyful and useful in your own classrooms.

Dr. Ruthie Stern
High school teacher, New York City
Lead writer, sample lesson plans
Common Core Curriculum: English

# Introduction

Few educators or policymakers would have guessed, even a year or so ago, that nearly all states would jettison their standards and embrace new, largely uniform standards for the teaching of ELA and math. Fewer still would have expected all of this to happen as quickly as it has.

The wide adoption of the Common Core State Standards (CCSS) is an unprecedented event at the national level—and, more important, at the school level, where its implications are profound. For educators in most states, the CCSS raise the bar for what students should know and be able to do.[1] If you are reading this, you are probably responsible for implementing the CCSS in your school, district, or state. You will find that the CCSS-ELA contain explicit guidance about the reading, writing, speaking, listening, and language skills students are expected to master. Almost any single standard in the CCSS illustrates this. Here's one of the reading standards from seventh grade:

> Determine two or more central ideas in a text and analyze their development over the course of the text; provide an objective summary of the text. (RI.7.2)

The CCSS call for the new standards to be taught within the context of a "content-rich curriculum." But the CCSS do not specify what content students need to master, as this fell outside the scope of the standards-setting project. Here is how this is explained in the introduction to the CCSS:

> [W]hile the Standards make references to some particular forms of content, including mythology, foundational U.S. documents, and Shakespeare, they do not—indeed, cannot—enumerate all or even most of the content that students should learn. The Standards must therefore be complemented by a well-developed, content-rich curriculum consistent with the expectations laid out in this document.[2]

Responsibility for developing such a curriculum falls to schools, districts, and states. Common Core's Curriculum for English is designed to meet the needs of the teacher, principal, curriculum director, superintendent, or state official who is striving to develop, or to help teachers to develop, new ELA curricula aligned with the CCSS. The curriculum can also serve as a resource for those endeavoring to conduct professional development related to the standards.

The curriculum provides a coherent sequence of thematic curriculum units, roughly six per grade level, K–12. The units connect the skills outlined in the CCSS-ELA with suggested works of literature and informational texts and provide activities teachers can use in their classrooms. You will also find suggested objectives in each unit, along with lists of relevant terminology and links to high-quality additional online resources. *Every standard in the CCSS is covered in the curriculum*, most more than once. Standards citations are included after each sample activity/assessment to indicate alignment. Each grade includes a "standards checklist" showing which standards are covered in which unit. And most of the works that the CCSS lists as "exemplar texts" are included in the curriculum.

---

1 Sheila Byrd Carmichael, Gabrielle Martino, Kathleen Porter-Magee, and W. Stephen Wilson, "The State of State Standards—and the Common Core—in 2010" (Washington, DC: Thomas B. Fordham Institute, July 2010), 13.

2 *Common Core State Standards for English Language Arts & Literacy in History/Social Studies, Science, and Technical Subjects* (Washington, DC: Common Core State Standards Initiative), 6.

Moreover, each unit in this print edition of the curriculum features a sample lesson plan, a road map showing how to use one or more of the suggested texts in that unit to meet specific standards. Each sample lesson plan includes step-by-step guidance for classroom activities tied to the lesson, questions that engage students in a deeper analysis and appreciation of the texts, and even suggestions for differentiated instruction. Many of the sample lesson plans, particularly in the earlier grades, also include detailed guidance for connecting ELA lessons to other subjects, including math, science, history, geography, music, and art.

An important feature of Common Core's Curriculum is its attention to building students' background knowledge of a diverse array of events, people, places, and ideas. Cognitive science has demonstrated that students read better if they know something about the subject they are studying.[3] With this in mind, Common Core incorporated into its curriculum themes, texts, and activities that teach students about "The Great Big World," as one of the kindergarten units is called. The content cloud shown in Figure I.1 includes much of the key content knowledge in the curriculum. The larger an event, name, or idea appears in the cloud, the more emphasis it receives in the curriculum. As you examine this cloud, do keep in mind that the curriculum contains much that is not included here.

Figure I.1

Common Core's Curriculum was written by teachers for teachers. More than three dozen public school teachers had a hand in drafting, writing, reviewing, or revising the curriculum. Collectively, these teachers brought dozens of years of experience to the curriculum project. Each of the lead writers is deeply knowledgeable about the CCSS; some even served as feedback providers to the standards' writers. These teachers looked to model curricula, including the International Baccalaureate, and at excellent, content-specific standards, such as the Massachusetts English Language Arts Curriculum Frameworks, for suggestions of what topics and titles to include at each grade. Most important, the teachers drew on their own considerable experience of what students enjoy learning about, and infused the curriculum with that knowledge.

---

3  Daniel T. Willingham, *Why Don't Students Like School? A Cognitive Scientist Answers Questions About How the Mind Works and What It Means for the Classroom* (San Francisco: Jossey-Bass, 2009).

The curriculum also reflects the contributions and perspective of the many teachers who reviewed them. Twice, the American Federation of Teachers convened the same panel of teachers that reviewed the CCSS to review Common Core's Curriculum. The Milken Family Foundation connected us with a dozen winners of the Milken Educator Award. These teachers, nationally recognized for excellence in the classroom, provided invaluable input and insight. And the National Alliance of Black School Educators identified superintendents, teachers, and content area specialists from across the country who reviewed the curriculum in draft form. A public review of our draft curriculum, conducted in fall 2010, elicited numerous helpful comments.

And the curriculum has continued to evolve and improve. Our work in *The Alexandria Plan* cultivated our expertise in guiding students through close reads of complex texts. We carried this expertise over to *The Wheatley Portfolio* with the addition of the text studies. Each text study includes text dependent questions, assessments, and opportunities for vocabulary instruction that draw out the richness of a carefully selected text. We invite you to explore our study of *Amos & Boris* by William Steig (grade 3) located at the end of this book. Please visit our website to access our ever expanding list of additional text studies. The online edition of the curriculum is open to public comment twenty-four hours a day, seven days a week. Anyone is able to critique any aspect of the curriculum—any essential question, any student objective, any text suggestion. Viewers can rate each unit as a whole, and many other curriculum elements, such as suggested works and sample activities. Comments on the curriculum are open for public view. Also, teachers can submit sample lesson plans that will be reviewed by a committee of teachers who will decide which ones to add to the official curriculum website. In these ways and more, Common Core's Curriculum for English are living documents, expanding and improving over time as they absorb and reflect the experience and perspective of educators across the nation.

We are thrilled that, as of this writing, the online version of this curriculum, which can be found at commoncore.org, has over eighteen thousand users. If you find this volume of interest, we hope you will follow our project as we develop more inspiring and instrumental curriculum-related resources for America's educators.

*March 2014*

Lynne Munson
President and Executive Director, Common Core

# How to Use the Common Core Curriculum: English

Common Core's Curriculum for English is built around the Common Core State Standards (CCSS) in English Language Arts (ELA). The CCSS dictated both the goals and contours of our curriculum. The "exemplar texts" listed in Appendix B of the CCSS figure significantly in our curriculum, which breaks down each grade, K–12, into a series of themed units. Each unit pairs standards with suggested student objectives, texts, activities, and more.

The curriculum is intended to serve as a "road map" for the school year, as an aid for jump-starting the lesson planning process. As common planning tools, this curriculum can facilitate school and districtwide collaboration. It also can become the backbone of rich, content-based professional development as teachers work together to create and then refine curricula for their particular schools and classrooms.

The units are designed to be taught in sequence (particularly in elementary school), but teachers could certainly modify the units if they need to be taught in a different order. We do not expect teachers to use every text or to do every sample activity or assessment. The suggested texts simply offer a range of rich and relevant materials from which teachers may choose. The suggested activities or assessments are neither prescriptive nor exhaustive. Teachers can select from among them, modify them to meet their students' needs, and/or use them as inspiration for creating their own activities.

Each unit contains the following elements:

*Overview.* This is a brief description of the unit. It explains the unit's theme and provides a summary of what students will learn. It explains the structure, progression, and various components of the unit. It may offer some guidance regarding the selection of texts. The unit descriptions illuminate the connections between the skills identified in the standards and the content of the suggested works.

*Essential question.* The essential question highlights the usefulness, the relevance, and the greater benefit of a unit. It is often the "so what?" question about material covered. It should be answerable, at least to some degree, by the end of the unit, but it should also have more than one possible answer. It should prompt intellectual exploration by generating other questions. Here's an example from eighth grade: "How does learning history through literature differ from learning through informational text?"

*Focus standards.* These standards are taken directly from the CCSS and have been identified as especially important for the unit. Other standards are covered in each unit as well, but the focus standards are the ones that the unit has been designed to address specifically.

*Suggested objectives.* These are the specific student outcomes for the unit. They describe the transferable ELA content and skills that students should possess when the unit is completed. The objectives are often components of more broadly worded standards and sometimes address content and skills necessarily related to the standards. The lists are not exhaustive, and the objectives should not supplant the standards themselves. Rather, they are designed to help teachers "drill down" from the standards and augment as necessary, providing added focus and clarity for lesson planning purposes.

*Suggested works.* These are substantial lists of suggested literary and informational texts. In most cases (particularly in the middle and high school grades), these lists contain more texts than a unit could cover; they are meant to offer a range of options to teachers. Several permutations of the lists could meet the goals of the unit. The suggested texts draw heavily from the "exemplar texts" listed in the CCSS. Exemplars are works the CCSS identified as meeting the levels of complexity and rigor described in the standards. These texts are identified with an (E) after the title of an exemplar text. An (EA) indicates a work by an author who has another work cited as an exemplar text.

**Art, music, and media.** These sections list works of visual art, music, film, and other media that reflect the theme of the unit and that a teacher can use to extend students' knowledge in these areas. Each unit includes at least one sample activity involving the works listed under this heading. ELA teachers who choose to use this material may do so on their own, by team teaching with an art or music teacher, or perhaps by sharing the material with the art or music teacher, who could reinforce what students are learning during the ELA block in their classroom. The inclusion of these works in our curriculum is *not* intended to substitute for or infringe in any way upon instruction that students should receive in separate art and music classes.

**Sample activities and assessments.** These items have been written particularly for the unit, with specific standards and often with specific texts in mind. Each activity addresses at least one standard in the CCSS; the applicable standard(s) are cited in parentheses following the description of each activity. The suggested activities or assessments are not intended to be prescriptive, exhaustive, or sequential; they simply demonstrate how specific content can be used to help students learn the skills described in the standards. They are designed to generate evidence of student understanding and give teachers ideas for developing their own activities and assessments. Teachers should use, refine, and/or augment these activities as desired, in order to ensure that they will have addressed all the standards intended for the unit and, in the aggregate, for the year.

**Reading Foundations.** To help kindergarten through second-grade students master the skills necessary to become strong readers, Common Core offers a consolidated pacing guide of instructional goals for the teaching of the CCSS reading Foundational Skills. This guide complements our curriculum and was prepared by reading expert Louisa Moats, who also helped develop the reading standards for the CCSS.

**Additional online resources.** These are links to lesson plans, activities, related background information, author interviews, and other instructional materials for teachers from a variety of resources, including the National Endowment for the Humanities and ReadWriteThink. The standards that could be addressed by each additional resource are cited at the end of each description.

**Terminology.** These are concepts and terms that students will encounter—often for the first time—over the course of the unit. The list is not comprehensive; it is meant to highlight terms that either are particular to the unit, are introduced there, or play a large role in the work or content of the unit. These terms and concepts are usually implied by the standards, but not always made explicit in them.

**Interdisciplinary connections.** This is a section included only in our curriculum for the elementary grades. Here we very broadly list the content areas the unit covers and then suggest opportunities for making interdisciplinary connections from Common Core's Curriculum for English to other subjects, including history, civics, geography, and the arts. We hope this section will be particularly helpful for K–5 teachers, who typically teach all subjects.

**Sample lesson plans.** Each unit includes a supplementary document that outlines a possible sequence of lessons, using one or more suggested unit texts to meet focus standards. Many of the texts used in the sample lesson plans are also CCSS exemplar texts. These sample lessons include guidance for differentiated instruction.

o o o

**Standards checklist.** Each grade includes a standards checklist that indicates which standards are covered in which unit—providing teachers an overview of standards coverage for the entire school year.

**Addressing all of the CCSS.** The curriculum writers worked carefully to ensure that the content and skills in each unit would build on one another so that in the aggregate, all standards would be addressed in a coherent, logical way. They grouped standards that they could envision fitting together in one unit. For example, if a unit were focused on asking and answering questions in informational text, then standards for shared research and expository writing were included in that unit as well. *All standards are addressed at least once*, if not a number of times, in the activities/assessments sections.

**Interpreting CCSS citations.** Our citations for the standards follow the format established by the CCSS (found in the upper right-hand corners of the pages in the CCSS-ELA document):

strand.grade.number

For example, the first Reading Literature (RL) standard in grade 4 would be cited as RL.4.1. You will find our citations in the front of each focus standard and at the end of each sample activity/assessment. Where standards clearly corresponded to lessons listed under Additional Online Resources, standards also have been cited.

**Understanding unit themes.** The unit themes grew organically out of the process of selecting which standards would be the focus of each unit and consulting the list of exemplar texts. The teachers who wrote the curriculum intentionally chose themes that would resonate with students, as well as lend coherence to the skills and content addressed. Some of the themes introduced in the early elementary grades, such as courage, reemerge in later years. We have done so in a deliberate attempt to invite students to wrestle with some of the "great ideas," a hallmark of a liberal education. We hope that as students progress through school, they will consider the themes at greater levels of depth.

**Teaching reading.** The Reading Foundations guide, located in the front of the print edition for elementary grades and embedded in resources for third through fifth grades, is a pacing guide for reading instruction. This guide is aligned with the CCSS reading Foundational Skills. The guide paces instruction in Foundational Skills logically across kindergarten through second grade. Concepts of print, phonological awareness, phonics, and text reading fluency are all addressed and woven into a developmental progression that leads to word recognition and text reading. Accomplishment of these milestones can be achieved with daily practice and brief activities that would require thirty to forty minutes of instructional time per day. A sample of those activities is also provided. Explicit, sequential, and cumulative teaching of these skills should in no way detract from, substitute for, or prevent the teaching of the oral language, comprehension, and literature-focused instruction described in the units.

The curriculum is not tailored for any specific reading instruction method or management technique. *It is up to local school districts and teachers to determine how reading will be taught.* The sample activities and assessments reflect a mix of teacher- and student-centered instruction, but emphasize eliciting evidence of student understanding through authentic assessments.

**Selecting materials.** Most of the texts listed as exemplars in the CCSS Appendix B are included in our curriculum. These texts take priority in our units and indeed shape unit themes. Like the exemplar texts themselves, the additional texts suggested in our curriculum include literary works and informational texts that have stood the test of time, as well as excellent contemporary titles. The suggested texts include novels, short stories, poetry, essays, speeches, memoirs, biographies, autobiographies, fables, folktales, and mythology. Teachers will find texts written by authors of wide-ranging diversity: young and old, living and dead, male and female, American and foreign.

In the early grades, the curriculum gives priority to traditional stories and poetry, Mother Goose rhymes, and award-winning fiction and nonfiction chosen for quality of writing and relevance to themes. They also emphasize concepts of print, phonological awareness, phonics, and text reading fluency. In upper elementary and middle school grades, students read a variety of fiction and nonfiction on science and history topics, as well as diverse selections of classic and contemporary literature. High school begins by establishing in ninth grade a common understanding of literary and informational genres, subgenres, and their characteristics. Grades 10 through 12 each focus on a different literary tradition, both American and international. Along the way, the curriculum highlights numerous points of connection with history, science, and the arts.

Much consideration has been given to readability. Whenever possible, we have used Lexile level ranges, as described in the CCSS Appendix A, as a guide. We realize that there still will be a range of texts within each grade span. We also recognize that simple texts may be read at upper grades with more nuanced analysis. For this reason, some texts appear in more than one grade. Texts that fall outside the CCSS-recommended grade span are noted.

At the elementary and middle school levels, the text availability and readability levels also were cross-checked with the Scholastic Reading Wizard Reading Levels section, Amazon.com, and the Lexile levels (as available) on the Barnes & Noble website.

**Evaluating student work.** Aside from the inclusion of a scoring rubric for high school seminars, the curriculum does not provide sample student work or scoring rubrics. The interactivity feature of the online edition of the curriculum enables teachers to submit these kinds of materials, if they so desire. We offer an online forum that serves as a space for teachers and curriculum developers to share lesson materials inspired by our curriculum. We also anticipate sharing teacher-generated resources from our upcoming professional development sessions.

**Differentiating instruction.** The sample lesson plans provide specific guidance for differentiated instruction for advanced and struggling students. As with student work and scoring rubrics, we expect to develop further guidance on differentiation as the curriculum is implemented and customized.

**Incorporating art, music, and media.** Although literature is of course a vital component of the standards, some standards in the CCSS address the arts as well. Because Common Core promotes the importance of all students studying the arts, we have highlighted places where ELA instruction could be enhanced by connecting a work of literature or an objective of the unit to art, music, or film. For example, students might compare a novel, story, or play to its film or musical rendition. Where a particular period of literature or the literature of a particular region or country is addressed, works of art from that period or country may also be examined. We suggest, for example, that students study self-portraiture when they are encountering memoirs. In each case, connections are made to the standards themselves.

**Promoting student understanding through recitation and memorization.** Recitation requires close reading and therefore nurtures deeper levels of students' understanding. Students also benefit from the satisfaction of making a poem or piece of prose one's own for life. In addition, many teachers observe that memorization and recitation help develop a student's experience and confidence in public speaking, which could help students marshal evidence and make effective arguments in other contexts. Keep in mind that our suggestions for memorization activities are not meant to be mandatory in every unit.

# Reading Foundations: A Pacing Guide for Reading Instruction

The Pacing Guide for Reading Instruction begins at a level appropriate for students who do not already know how to read. This will be the majority of students in most school systems, including those who enter school with limited language and/or literary experience and those who simply lack the phonological, decoding, and encoding skills needed for beginning reading and spelling. The pacing of code-emphasis instruction and the amount of time allotted to it will vary according to student skill levels, as measured on early screening, diagnostic, and progress-monitoring assessments. Nevertheless, all students need to master these essential building blocks.

Some students enter school having already learned the alphabetic principle and basic word recognition and are reading above expectation for these early grades. Those students should be allowed to progress more quickly through the Foundational Skills sequence, as long as they demonstrate mastery of the concepts. It is conceivable that in the same class, one group of students may be just finishing Level One at the end of the first kindergarten unit, but another group of students could be finishing Level Three if the pace is accelerated.

At times, the content might seem incongruent with the skills in the Reading Foundations. An important fact about our curriculum is that the activities are simply sample activities. They represent a *range* of activities. Also, in keeping with the CCSS, we continually use developmental options for writing such as "using a combination of drawing, dictating, and writing."

Differentiated instruction is at the heart of effective classroom management. Teachers may need to deliver the literature-focused and content-focused part of the lesson by reading to and dialoguing with the students, taking care to ensure that they also teach a code-emphasis, explicit, and systematic program to all those who need it.

## Kindergarten, Levels One Through Three

| Kindergarten | Level One | Level Two | Level Three |
|---|---|---|---|
| Reading Objectives for Print Concepts (RF.K.1a,b,c,d) | Identify and track single-syllable printed words in short sentences; identify examples of *word, sentence,* and *letter* on a printed page. (RF.K.1a,b,c) Match letters to templates; match manipulative upper- and lowercase letters; and point to letters that the teacher names. (RF.K.1d) | Listen for word length: identify longer and shorter words in print. (RF.K.1b,c) Using a printed alphabet template, match plastic or wooden letters to the model and name them in sequence. (RF.K.1d) Identify capital letter, period, and specific printed words on sentence strips. (RF.K.1b) | Listen and point to (track) printed words from left to right, top to bottom, and page by page as text is read aloud. (RF.K.1a) Identify features of a book (title page, author, illustrator, left-to-right and top-to-bottom arrangement of print). (RF.K.1a) Independently match upper- and lowercase letters while naming them. (RF.K.1d) |
| Model Activities for Print Concepts | As you read a short nursery rhyme (or poem) from a chart, ask students to point to words as they are read (RF.K.1a,b,c) With movable letters, word cards, and sentence strips, demonstrate the meaning of *letter, word,* and *sentence.* Then ask students to identify examples of each in a printed phrase from a familiar rhyme. (RF.K.1a,b,c) Students trace letters in sand trays, on carpet squares, or on sandpaper while naming them; trace letter shapes written in large font on a chalkboard; or match manipulative upper- and lowercase letters or letters written on cards until they can point to any letter you name. (RF.K.1d) | Write two words, one long and one short. Ask children to guess which one is a match for the word you say: *Ann, Anthony; Kate, Katherine; ball, basketball; elf, elephant; hip, hippopotamus.* (RF.K.1b,c) Write a four- to five-word sentence from a familiar rhyme or story. Ask students to point to each word as they read aloud with you, and point to and name the end punctuation and the capital letter(s). (RF.K.1a,b,c) | Using a big book, point to words as text is read; then ask students to point to words going left to right and top to bottom, matching voice to print. (RF.K.1a,b,c) After explaining *author* and *illustrator,* have students point to names on book covers and explain the role of each in making the book. (RF.K.1a,b,c) Using individual alphabet mats with uppercase letters printed in order, have students match lowercase plastic letters to the uppercase, in order, and name them. (RF.K.1d) |
| Reading Objectives for Phonological Awareness (RF.K.2a,b,c,d) | Listen to and participate in recitation of nursery rhymes, rhyming books, finger plays, songs, and poems. (RF.K.2a) Listen for specific words embedded in rhymes or stories. (RF.K.2a) | Orally identify rhyming words and understand that rhymes have the same last rime (i.e., the vowel and any consonants that follow). (RF.K.2a,c) Count, segment, and delete parts of compound words and words with two and three syllables. (RF.K.2b) | Recite familiar rhymes and poems; play with alliteration; create words with sound substitutions (e.g., "silly" words). (RF.K.2a) Orally segment, delete, and substitute syllables in compound words and multisyllable words. (RF.K.2b) |

| Kindergarten | Level One | Level Two | Level Three |
|---|---|---|---|
| | | Identify the distinguishing features of voiced and voiceless consonant phonemes; orally produce individual consonant phonemes after correct teacher modeling of the voicing distinction: /p/, /b/; /k/, /g/; /t/, /d/; /f/, /v/; /sh/, /zh/; /th/, /th/; /ch/, /j/; /s/, /z/ (RF.K.2d) Classify vowel sounds as open sounds and consonants as closed sounds; locate the vowel sound in every syllable. (RF.K.2d) With teacher modeling and a picture or gestural cue from a key word, pronounce the short vowel sounds and the long vowel sounds (orally—no print). (RF.K.2d) | Explore the way related groups of phonemes are pronounced: stops /p/, /b/, /t/, /d/, /k/, /g/; hissy sounds /f/, /v/, /th/, /th/, /s/, /z/, /sh/; nasals /m/, /n/, /ng/; glides /h/, /w/, /wh/, /y/; and liquids /l/ and /r/. (RF.K.2d) Blend onsets and rimes; orally match the first phonemes in spoken words; delete an initial phoneme from a word; substitute an initial phoneme. (Begin with continuants: /m/, /s/, /f/, /r/, /l/, /v/, /th/, /th/, /z/, /sh/). (RF.K.2c) Attend to short vowel-sound placement in the mouth, with the jaw dropping for /ĭ/, /ĕ/, /ă/, /ŭ/, /ŏ/. Identify whether the short vowel sounds in spoken words are the same or different. (RF.K.2d) Orally blend two or three phonemes into simple words and segment two- to three-phoneme words by moving tokens into sound boxes while the phonemes are being pronounced. (RF.K.2d) |
| Model Activities for Phonological Awareness | While reading (reciting) "Humpty Dumpty," snap your fingers on a word at the end of a line (e.g., wall). The children will snap when they hear the word that rhymes with it (i.e., fall). Continue with various rhymes and poems. (RF.K.2a) After recitation of a favorite rhyme or song, present a puppet that has trouble remembering his words. Students hold up their thumbs if they hear the puppet make a mistake: "Jack and Jill went up the pill." Call on individuals to say the right word. (RF.K.2a) Using felt rectangles to represent four to five spoken words (e.g., "Jack went up the hill"), ask students to change the color of the rectangle standing for the word that is changed in a spoken sentence (e.g., "Jill went up the hill." "Jill climbed up the hill." "Jill climbed up the ladder."). (RF.K.2a) | Using different colored index cards representing three common rimes (/-ill/, /-ock/, /-ate/) and other colored cards for first sounds (/l/, /d/, /m/), show in a pocket chart that the first sound(s) might change, but if the last part is the same, the words rhyme (d-ock and l-ock do rhyme; l-ock and l-ate do not rhyme). (RF.K.2a,c) Say a word slowly in syllables and have students say the whole word: tooth-paste: bath-tub; but-ter-fly: ba-na-na-bread. (RF.K.2b) With students looking in mirrors and putting their hands over their ears to hear vocal resonance, model and describe the difference between /p/ and /b/; /f/ and /v/; /k/ and /g/; and so forth. With students, classify spoken consonant sounds as voiced or unvoiced. (RF.K.2d) | Play "Willaby Wallaby Woo" with students' names. (RF.K.2a) With a picture cue, ask students to help a puppet who only says words in parts. After the puppet speaks the syllables, students blend them into a whole word: Sep-tem-ber; di-no-saur; cin-na-mon; tel-e-vis-ion. (RF.K.2b) Play the speech-sound guessing game. Students imitate the sounds and/or look in a mirror to answer questions such as, "Which sound is made with the lips—/p/ or /k/? Which sound is made with the mouth wide open—/ŏ/ or /w/? Which sound is made with the tongue between the teeth—/f/ or /th/?" and so forth. (RF.K.2d) |

| Kindergarten | Level One | Level Two | Level Three |
|---|---|---|---|
| | | Describe vowels as open sounds and consonants as closed off by the lips, teeth, and tongue; categorize the first sounds of spoken words as vowels (open sounds) or consonants (closed sounds): *o-ver*; *m-ouse*; *sh-ower*; *a-lligator*. (RF.K.2d) <br><br> With puppets, pictures, or gestures, associate each short vowel sound with its keyword and letter name: <br><br> /ĭ/ – itch – i <br> /ĕ/ – edge – e <br> /ă/ – apple – a <br> /ŏ/ – octopus – o <br> /ŭ/ – up – u (RF.K.2d) <br><br> With puppets, pictures, or gestures, practice associating a long vowel sound with its keyword and letter name: <br><br> /ā/ – apron – a <br> /ē/ – eagle – e <br> /ō/ – oval – o <br> /ū/ – unicorn – u <br> /ī/ – ice cream – i (RF.K.2d) | Show three picture cards, such as *milk, bed,* and *moose,* or *fan, feather,* and *thimble.* Students say the words, match the pictures that start with the same sound, isolate the target sound, and then find the sound-symbol card with that sound. Vary the difficulty by monitoring the confusability of the first sounds (i.e., /m/ and /n/ are harder to discriminate than /m/ and /t/). (RF.K.2d) <br><br> Ask students to listen carefully for a specific vowel sound in the words you say. They repeat the sound only if they hear it in the word: /ē/ –*me, eat, sleep, pie, snow, east, team, fast.* (RF.K.2d) |
| Reading Objectives for Phonics and Word Recognition (RF.K.3a,b,c) | With the teacher leading, recite an alphabet song that includes the letter name and a key word (picture or gesture) and sound associated with each letter. (RF.K.3a,b) <br><br> *Note:* A set of sound-symbol cards that includes most of the forty-four speech sounds of English should be displayed and learned in segments. <br><br> High-frequency symbols (graphemes) for each of the consonant and vowel phonemes that are only represented by letter combinations (such as /sh/, /th/, /ch/, /ng/, and /aw/) can be gradually introduced before the end of the kindergarten year. | Name the key word that goes with a letter; say the sound that goes with a key word; and say the letter(s) that represent a sound. <br><br> Given a sound-symbol card, say the keywords and consonant phonemes that are represented with two letters: *th, sh, ch, ng, wh.* (RF.K.3a,b) | Say the alphabet song (as described in Level One) and a short vowel song or rhyme, with minimal teacher prompting. (RF.K.3a,b) <br><br> Demonstrate accuracy and fluency in sound-key word-symbol association for most consonants and short vowels. (RF.K.3a,b) <br><br> Identify the letters *c* and *k* as both representing /k/; *c* and *s* as both representing /s/; *qu* as a team that represents /kw/; and final *x* as the symbol for /ks/ (as in "box"). (RF.K.3a,b) <br><br> Read common words such as *I, the, a.* (RF.K.3c) |

| Kindergarten | Level One | Level Two | Level Three |
|---|---|---|---|
| Model Activities for Phonics and Word Recognition | Teach an alphabet song or rhyme by daily repetition. As you lead recitation of the alphabet song, point to the sound-symbol cards, and pause on occasion so that students can fill in a known letter name/sound (e.g., r, rabbit, /r/) on their own. (RF.K.3a,b) | Play the sound-symbol game with known vowels and consonants: You say a keyword (or make a gesture); students say the sound. Or, you say the sound, and students make the gesture and say the letter name. (RF.K.3a). (Suggested order for introduction and mastery through a 12–18 week period: /m/, /s/, /f/, /a/, /t/, /p/, /n/, /i/, /h/, /k/ spelled c, /u/, /b/, /j/ spelled j; initial /r/, /o/, /k/ spelled k, /d/, /g/ spelled g, /e/, /y/ spelled y, /z/, /ks/ spelled x, /u/, /kw/ spelled qu, /v/, /w/.) Once the students have practiced the sound-symbol associations by recitation, hand out sound-symbol cards to students seated in a circle. Toss a beanbag to students randomly and have them say the letter name, keyword, and/or sound on their card. (RF.K.3a, b) | Play a sound-symbol guessing game, focusing on the end of the alphabet, lower-frequency letter-sound correspondences, and subtle contrasts: "I'm thinking of a letter that stands for the sound combination /ks/"; "I'm thinking of a sound that's made with the lips closed and the voice off (/p/)"; and so forth. (RF.K.3a,b) Make a few simple words with letter tiles (no blends) and leave off the first letter. Say the whole word and ask students what sound is missing. Students find the missing sound in the sound-symbol cards and then supply the missing letter for the beginning of each word: (b)ear; (w)ent; (s)ing. Shift to ending sounds as students become proficient with first sounds: we(t), mu(d), su(n). (RF.K.3a,b) Encourage students to read "first step" books with rebuses for content words by pointing to each word. Ask students to identify high-frequency irregular words I, the, a, in the text. (RF.K.3c) |
| Reading Objectives for Fluency (RF.K.4) | n/a | n/a | Recognize a few familiar words as wholes. (RF.K.4) |
| Model Activities for Fluency | n/a | n/a | Students can collect favorite words with a specific consonant sound (e.g., /s/, /b/, or /r/) and illustrate each word in a word book. Reread the word books many times to pick up fluency. (RF.K.4) |
| Writing, Handwriting, and Spelling Objectives (LK.1a,c,d) | Demonstrate pencil grip and posture for writing; trace, copy, and write lines and circles with large motor and small motor control. (LK.1a) | Copy and write first name: write circle letters (a, c, o, d, g, q) within lines. (LK.1a) | Form letters that are made with a downward line first: b, f, h, i, j, k, l, m, n, p, r, t, u. (LK.1a) Directed writing: write letters for sounds given by the teacher; write high-frequency words I, the, a. (LK.2c) Attempt phonetic spellings of unknown words; copy and/or complete words in simple printed sentences (e.g., "I like to _____."). (LK.2d) |
| Model Activities for Writing, Handwriting, and Spelling | Draw large shapes (circle: horizontal line; cross, etc.) on the chalkboard. Count or provide a rhythm as students trace the shape with the whole arm and pointer fingers on the board or in the air. "Trace" with eyes open and closed. (LK.1a) | As a "writing warm-up," transfer rhythmic writing of shapes and lines to paper with lines; then combine circles and lines for first letters. (LK.1a) | Before students practice tracing and copying, number the pencil strokes and draw arrows to show how the pencil moves. (LK.1a) Encourage students to pay attention to what their mouths are doing when they spell by sound, and to look at the sound-symbol cards to remember the letters as they try to spell new words. (LK.2d) |

## Kindergarten, Levels Four Through Six

| Kindergarten | Level Four | Level Five | Level Six |
|---|---|---|---|
| Reading Objectives for Print Concepts (RF:K.1d) | Increase fluency in naming randomly ordered upper- and lowercase letters to benchmark level. (RF.K.1d) | Increase fluency in accurately naming randomly ordered upper- and lowercase letters. (RF.K.1d) | n/a |
| Model Activities for Print Concepts | Devote a few minutes of classroom time to simple speed drills several times weekly. Create or find letter-naming practice sheets with randomly ordered upper- and lowercase letters on a page. Have students work in pairs to practice naming the letters as quickly as they can until they can name approximately twenty-seven letters in one minute. Reteach any letters students are missing. (RF.K.1d) | Screen students for letter-naming accuracy and fluency. Reteach unknown letters to students who are making errors. Have students who still need practice spend a few minutes daily on speed drills until they can name approximately thirty-five letters in one minute. (RF.K.1d) | Students should be able to name randomly distributed upper- and lowercase letters at a rate of at least forty correct per minute. (RF.K.1d) |
| Reading Objectives for Phonological Awareness (RF:K.2c,d,e) | Delete and substitute initial sounds and final sounds in spoken words; segment one-syllable words with three to four phonemes, using sound boxes. Isolate and pronounce the vowel sound. (RF.K.2d) Identify and recite the long vowel sounds; learn a long vowel song or rhyme for mnemonic support. (RF.K.2d) | Blend four-phoneme words orally, including words with the most transparent consonant blends (-st, -lk, -ft). (RF.K.2c) Classify phonemes as consonants (closed sounds) and vowel sounds (open phonemes), and syllables as closed (ending in a consonant) or open (ending in a long vowel). Make new consonant-vowel-consonant (CVC) words by substituting an initial phoneme, medial vowel, or final phoneme. (RF.K.2e) Match spoken single-syllable words by the medial vowel sound, including all eighteen vowel sounds of English. (RF.K.2d) | With modeling and support, orally segment and blend any single-syllable word with three to four phonemes, including any of the forty-four vowel sounds and consonants of English. (RF.K.2c) |
| Model Activities for Phonological Awareness | Use a picture clue and a puppet who can't say his last sounds. Ask students to help him say a whole word correctly: peanu(t), butt(er), sandwi(ch); chicke(n) McNugge(ts); vanill(a) i(ce) crea(m). (RF.K.2d) Use a grid (sound box template) in which each box stands for one speech sound. Students work with movable tiles or chips. Say a word with two (zoo), three (fog), or four (fast) phonemes. Model, then lead students as they segment each sound, moving a chip into a box as they say the sounds in order. Say the whole word after it is segmented. Ask, "Which is the first sound? the second sound? the last sound?" and so forth. (RF.K.2d) | Model blending words with four sounds. Hold up your fist; raise a finger as you say each sound (e.g., /m/, /a/, /s/, /k/), then blend the whole word (mask) as you sweep your hand from left to right. Students follow your lead. (RF.K.2c) Create "vowel houses" where words with the same vowel sound live together. Using picture cards for one-syllable words with three or four different vowel sounds, students find the house where they live (e.g., saw, paw, dawn; blue, moon, chew; snow, bow, oak; star, art, mark). (RF.K.2d) | Continue matching spoken words to "vowel houses" and be sure that all the vowel houses have some words living in them, even the less frequent: toy, boy, oil; book, hoof, bush; cow, brow, ouch. (RF.K.2d) Segment three- and four-phoneme spoken words by tapping head, shoulders, waist, and toes as you say the sounds (/h/ /ou/ /se/, etc.). Then ask, "What was the waist sound? What was the head sound?" and so forth. (RF.K.2c) |

| Kindergarten | Level Four | Level Five | Level Six |
|---|---|---|---|
| | Ask students to listen for two long vowels (e.g., /ā/ or /ū/) in the words you say. After you say a word, students say the vowel sound: cape, soon, say, blue, stew, sail, and so forth. Or ask students to hold up the sound-symbol card with the correct sound. (RF.K.2d) | Explain that consonant sounds are closed off by the lips, teeth, and tongue, and vowel sounds are open and sustained. Say a sound and ask students to hold up a response card: V for vowel and C for consonant.<br>Using colored squares to represent speech sounds, show which sound has changed when a spoken word is changed, one sound at a time: sun, ton, shun, shut, shout, out, oat, own, shown. (RF.K.2e) | Ask students to help you blend words you are reading in a story. As you read aloud, say a short word in phonemes and have students blend the whole word (e.g., "Because the rabbit ran so /f/ /ă/ /s/ /t/, the /f/ /ŏ/ /k/ /s/ fell way behind."). (RF.K.2c) |
| Reading Objectives for Phonics and Word Recognition (RF.K.3a,b,c,d) | Using manipulative cards, blend initial letter-sounds /f/, /l/, /m/, /n/, /r/, /s/, final sounds /d/, /g/, /p/, /t/, and short vowels /a/, /i/, /o/ into VC and CVC combinations. (RF.K.3a,b)<br>Read up to ten of the most common words by sight, using multisensory or manipulative props as necessary. (RF.K.3c) | Build simple short vowel (closed) syllables with letter-sounds used in Level Four, plus vowels /ŭ/ and /ĕ/, and consonant grapheme cards including b, sh, h, j, c, k, ck, v, w (as in wet), x (as in fox), y (as in yes), z, ch, th, qu, and wh. (RF.K.3a,b)<br>Read up to twenty of the most common words by sight. (RF.K.3c)<br>Recognize the change of meaning when plural -s is added to a noun. (RF.K.3d)<br>Read long vowel (open) syllables he, she, we, so, no, hi, my. (RF.K.3c,d) | Increase fluency and accuracy in reading any CVC syllable that uses the letter-sound correspondences practiced in Levels Four and Five. (RF.K.3a,b)<br>Read twenty-five or more of the most common words by sight. (RF.K.3c)<br>Recognize some common words with the VCe (vowel-consonant-silent e) long vowel spelling pattern (like, ate, home, cute). (RF.K.3a,b,d) |
| Model Activities for Phonics and Word Recognition | Teach blending of simple words with letter tiles or letter cards. Students watch and follow: For example, with the word sat, (1) point to the spelling of the first sound (s) and say "sound" as you point to it; (2) point to the second spelling (a) and say "sound" as you point to it; (3) sweep your hand from left to right under the letters as you say "blend it"; (4) point to the third spelling (t) and say "sound" as you point to it; (5) sweep your hand from left to right under the letters as you say "blend it." Then say, "What's the word?" Quickly use it in a sentence. (RF.K.3a,b)<br>Give students letter cards or tiles with a few consonants and one or two short vowels. Model, then lead them in building words with two to three sounds. (RF.K.3a,b)<br>Progress to sound substitution: Change at to an: an to man: mat to man, man to fan, fan to fin, and so forth. (RF.K.3a,b)<br>Explain that some words in English do not play fair or follow the rules. Introduce five to ten of the most frequent irregular words. | Teach blending of simple words with three to four sounds–on a chalkboard or whiteboard–as students watch and follow: For example, with the word fox, (1) write the spelling of the first sound (f) and say "sound" as you point to it; (2) write the second spelling (o) and say "sound" as you point to it; (3) sweep your hand from left to right under the letters as you say "blend it"; (4) write the third spelling (x) and say "sound" as you point to it; (5) sweep your hand from left to right under the letters as you say "blend it." Then say, "What's the word?" Quickly use it in a sentence. (RF.K.3a,b)<br>Give students letter cards or tiles with more consonants and two or three short vowels. Model, then lead them in building words with three to four sounds. Continue sound substitution games. (RF.K.3a,b)<br>To a familiar word (e.g., rock, zip, jam) have students add –s, pronounce the new word, and use it in a sentence. (RF.K.3d)<br>Practice new irregular or "red" words by tracing them, saying the letters, and saying the whole word before reading in context. (RF.K.3c) | Using a pocket chart or letter tiles, introduce students to the VCe long vowel pattern by adding "magic e" to familiar CVC words and noting the change of vowel sound:<br>hop–hope<br>cap–cape<br>hat–hate<br>pin–pine<br>shin–shine<br>can–cane<br>cut–cute (RF.K.3a,b,d)<br>Practice reading phrases with the learned VCe words, plus like, home, and came. (RF.K.3a,b,d)<br>Underline all irregular words as you read phrases and beginner texts. Ask students to tell you why they are underlined. (RF.K.3c) |

| Kindergarten | Level Four | Level Five | Level Six |
|---|---|---|---|
| Reading Objectives for Fluency (RF.K.4) | After previewing, read simple, decodable texts with words and sound-symbol correspondences that have been taught. (RF.K.4) | After previewing, read simple, decodable texts with words and sound-symbol correspondences that have been taught. (RF.K.4) | After previewing, read simple, decodable texts with words and sound-symbol correspondences that have been taught. (RF.K.4) |
| Model Activities for Fluency | Use simple "first step" stories with high-frequency words and decodable words that have been taught and practiced. Preview the book: What (who) is it about? Where is the title? What might happen? Let students read to a partner and then retell the story. (RF.K.4) <br><br> Have students revisit their predictions. If the prediction was incorrect, explain what was different. | Continue with "first step" stories with high-frequency words and decodable words that have been taught and practiced. Preview the book: What (who) is it about? Where is the title? What might happen? Let students read to a partner and then retell the story. Check predictions and explain any discrepancies. <br><br> Choral-read for variety. (RF.K.4) <br><br> With phonetically regular, unknown words, encourage students to blend each sound into the whole word. (RF.K.4) | Continue with pre-primer stories with high-frequency words and decodable words that have been taught and practiced. Preview the book: What (who) is it about? Where is the title? What might happen? Why? Let students read to a partner and then retell the story. (RF.K.4) <br><br> Encourage rereading of familiar texts, with emphasis on phrasing and expression. (RF.K.4) <br><br> With phonetically regular, unknown words, encourage students to blend each sound into the whole word. (RF.K.4) |
| Writing, Handwriting, and Spelling Objectives (LK.1a,b; LK.2a,c; RF.K.2d) | Form letters with horizontal lines and diagonals: e, s, v, w, x, y, z. (L.K.1a) <br><br> Write the consonant letters, including digraphs th, ch, wh, sh, when the sounds are dictated. Write CVC words to dictation; write simple sentences using CVC words and five to ten of the highest-frequency words in written text. (RF.K.2d; L.K.1f; L.K.2a,c) | Write short, dictated sentences with a capital letter and end punctuation, using a word wall or other reference for high-frequency irregular words. (L.K.2a,b) <br><br> Create short sentences with known words; attempt spellings of unknown/unusual words. (L.K.2c,d) | Using learned words and sound-symbol associations, formulate and transcribe several sentences that tell a narrative sequence or that describe an object, event, or activity. (W.K.3, L.K.1, L.K.2) |
| Model Activities for Writing, Handwriting, and Spelling | Play the sound-symbol game, but with a written response. You say a letter, key word, and/or sound, and students write the symbol. Provide individual sound-symbol cards for reference as necessary. (L.K.1a; RF.K.3a,b) <br><br> Dictate a simple sentence for completion, with unknown words provided and lines for missing words: (He) will (hit) (the) ball; (I) (got) (a) car. Help students segment the phonetically regular words as they write. (RF.K.2d, L.K.1f, L.K.2a,c) | Dictate a simple sentence with a line provided for each word: I hit the pin. He hit his chin. Help students segment the phonetically regular words as they write, referring to sound-symbol cards as necessary. (RF.K.2d; L.K.1f; L.K.2a,c) <br><br> Develop a word wall for easy indexing of irregularly spelled words and encourage correct spelling of words that have been practiced. (L.K.2c,d) <br><br> In shared writing, as students volunteer words for retelling or creating stories, encourage them to provide letters for sounds as you write. (W.K.3, W.K.7, L.K.2d) | After following a storyboard and rehearsing a story orally, encourage students to write several sentences connected by a narrative sequence. Encourage phonetic spelling of unknown words and correct spelling of the highest-frequency words that have been practiced. (W.K.3, L.K.1, L.K.2) |

## Grade One, Levels One Through Three

| Grade One | Level One | Level Two | Level Three |
|---|---|---|---|
| Reading Objectives for Print Concepts (RF.1.1a) | On a printed page, identify examples of first and last letters in a word, first and last words on a page, and first and last words in a sentence. (RF.1.1a)<br>Track print from left to right and top to bottom as the teacher reads the words aloud. (RF.1.1a)<br>On a printed page, point to capital letters and end punctuation in sentences, and match periods, question marks, and exclamation points to sentence types. (RF.1.1a) | Pause and adapt phrasing in response to periods at the ends of sentences. (RF.1.1a) | While orally reading beginning text, notice and respond to all end punctuation by adjusting vocal intonation. (RF.1.1a) |
| Model Activities for Print Concepts | Give students pretend (or real) magnifying glasses to play detective with a simple book they are reading. After each term has been directly taught, play "I Spy" to find examples of first (initial), last (final), middle (medial), top, bottom, left, right, and capital letters, and periods, question marks, and exclamation points. (RF.1.1a)<br>Using a big book or chart with familiar language, ask students to take turns pointing to printed words as you say them. | Before students read sentences or pages aloud, ask them to point to end punctuation. Model vocal phrasing indicated by each mark. Lead the group in choral reading of short sentences, and then call on individuals to reread sentences with appropriate phrasing and intonation. (RF.1.1a) | To practice the inflection required by punctuation, insert punctuation into the alphabet sequence and ask students to choral-read: A, B, C! D, E, F, G, H, I?, K, L, MNO, PQ? R S T, U, V, W! X, Y, Z. (RF.1.1a) |
| Reading Objectives for Phonological Awareness (RF.1.2a,b,d) | Orally segment, delete, and substitute syllables in multisyllable words. (RF.1.2a)<br>Listen for two or three widely contrasting vowel sounds (e.g., /ǐ/ and /ē/) in a series of spoken words; isolate and repeat a target sound when it is heard (RF.1.2a)<br>Say the short vowel sounds in order of placement in the mouth; feel the jaw dropping for /ĭ/, /ĕ/, /ă/, /ŭ/, /ŏ/ and match a word to another with the same short vowel sound. (RF.1.2a) | Orally blend the first part of a word with a final consonant. (RF.1.2b)<br>Substitute an initial or final consonant in a word and blend it into a new word. (RF.1.2b) | Within the context of a simple story, blend two- and three-phoneme words, without consonant blends, that have been orally segmented. (RF.1.2b)<br>Given a two- or three-phoneme word, segment and pronounce the sounds in sequence. (RF.1.2d) |
| Model Activities for Phonological Awareness | Using colored rectangles or cards (distinguished from any manipulative used to mark phonemes), ask students to decide how many rectangles are needed to mark the syllables of a spoken word: detective, investigator, mystery, pilot, adventure. Students put out a card for each syllable, while saying the syllables slowly. Then ask, "Which one is this?" Or ask, "What is left if I take this one away?" (RF.1.2a)<br>Create "vowel houses" where words with the same vowels live. Using picture cards or spoken words, ask students to listen for and pronounce the vowel in the word and then place it in the right vowel house. Start with two vowels per activity; progress to more as the students become skilled. (RF.1.2a) | Using the puppet that has trouble finishing his words (introduced in kindergarten), pronounce words or names (preferably from the stories the students are reading) without the last sound. Ask students to help the puppet say the whole word and say the missing sound clearly in isolation. (RF.1.2b)<br>Play this listening game: "The word is ___ (shop). If I change /sh/ to /ch/, what's the new word?" Students: Chop! "The word is ___ (bake). If I change /k/ to /s/, what's the new word?" Students: Base! (RF.1.2b) | Selecting sentences from stories you've read aloud, segment some words as you read, asking for students' help in putting them together: "This is story about a town /m/ /ou/ /s/ (___) [pause—let students supply whole word] and a country mouse." (RF.1.2d)<br>Using spoken words with all medial vowel sounds (long, short, diphthong, r-controlled), build segmentation fluency with this routine:<br>Say a word.<br>Students repeat.<br>Segment the sounds orally as a finger is raised for each phoneme. |

| Grade One | Level One | Level Two | Level Three |
|---|---|---|---|
| | After demonstrating the jaw dropping as each short vowel is articulated, and providing a visual chart for reference, select the five short vowel sound-symbol cards and give them to students to hold. Say a word with a short vowel. The student with that card holds it up while everyone says the vowel sound and its key word, feeling how open or closed their mouth is and looking in the mirror if necessary. (RF.1.2a) | | Sweep the hand from left to right as the word is blended. (Note: At this stage, students should be fluent and proficient with segmentation of one-syllable words.) (RF.1.2b.d) |
| Reading Objectives for Phonics and Word Recognition (RF.1.3a,b,c.g) | With reference to sound-spelling cards containing a keyword and major spellings for each sound, learn sound-spelling associations by means of a see/hear/say/write sequence: /m/, /ă/, /t/, /h/, /p/, /n/, /k/ spelled c, /d/, /s/, /ĭ/, /b/. (RF.1.3a,b,c) Blend and read simple words containing the taught sound-spellings, in isolation and in connected text. (RF.1.3a,b,c) Using a tracing, oral-spelling, and visual imagery routine, learn approximately three to five common **irregular** new words per week. (Note: Many of the most common words in English do follow regular patterns of phonics and are no longer "irregular" once the patterns have been taught.) (RF.1.3 g) | Learn sound-spelling associations by means of a see/hear/say/write sequence: /r/, /f/, /g/, /ŏ/, /ks/ spelled x, /ar/, /k/ spelled -ck, /ŭ/, /z/, /l/, /ĕ/, spelled e or ea, /y/, /w/, /hw/ spelled wh, /er/ spelled ir, ur, or er. (RF.1.3a,b,c) Blend and read simple words containing the taught sound-spellings, in isolation and in connected text. (RF.1.3a,b,c) Read regular plural nouns formed with -s and pronounced /s/ or /z/ (e.g., cats, dogs) and explain the meaning of the plural. (RF.1.3g) | Learn sound-spelling associations by means of a see/hear/say/write sequence: /sh/ spelled sh; /th/; /ch/; /k/ spelled k; /ā/ spelled a or a_e; /j/ spelled j or –dge: /j/ spelled ge or gi; /ī/ spelled i or i_e; /s/ spelled ce or ci; /ō/ spelled o or o_e; /z/ spelled s; /v/; /ū/ spelled u or u_e; /ē/ spelled e or e_e; /ē/ spelled ee or ea; /kw/ spelled qu; long vowels + r; /ē/ spelled y or _ie_; /ā/ spelled ai or ay; /ī/ spelled igh; /ī/ spelled y or ie; /ng/ spelled -ng (RF.1.3a,b,c) Apply associations to blending and reading simple words in isolation and in connected text. (RF.1.3a,b,c) Read plural nouns with -s and -es and verbs with -ing. (RF.1.3 g) |
| Model Activities for Phonics and Word Recognition | (Note: Introduce about two new sounds per week.) As each new sound-symbol card is introduced, teach a simple story or rhyme about the sound (e.g., "This is Leo the Lion: he loves to lick lollipops . . ."). With learned associations, play "I'm thinking of . . ." (e.g., the letter that represents /h/; a sound that letter c can represent; a vowel that begins the word apple). (RF.1.3a,b,c) Teach sound-by-sound blending of simple words with two to four sounds on a chalkboard or whiteboard, as students watch and follow: For example, with the word pin, (1) write the spelling of the first sound (p) and say "sound" as you point to it; (2) write the second spelling (i) and say "sound" as you point to it; (3) sweep your hand from left to right under the letters as you say "blend it"; (4) write the third spelling (n) and say "sound" as you point to it; (5) sweep your hand from left to right under the letters as you say "blend it." Then say, "What's the word?" Quickly use it in a spoken sentence. (RF.1.3a,b,c) | (Note: Introduce about two to three new sounds per week.) Conduct daily quick drills with learned sound-symbol associations: You say the sound, students say the letter(s); you say the letter(s), students say the sound; you say the sound, students write the letter(s). Automaticity is the goal. (RF.1.3a,b,c) Teach blending of whole words with three to four sounds, as students watch and follow: (1) write the whole word fast; (2) point to each letter-sound and say "sound," cuing students to say the sounds in order–/f/ /a/ /s/ /t/; (3) sweep your hand from left to right under the letters, saying "blend it"; students say the whole word. Quickly use the word in a sentence. (RF.1.3a,b,c) Blend fifteen to thirty words per day with sound-symbol associations that have been taught; then read in phrases, sentences, and books. Include nouns with the nonsyllabic plural -s. (RF.1.3a,b.c.g) | (Note: Introduce about two to three new sounds per week.) Conduct daily quick drills with learned sound-symbol associations. Give students letter (or grapheme) tiles, including digraphs and vowel teams (ng, th, ck, ee, etc.) written on one tile. Students can practice one-minute speed drills in pairs, naming the sounds for the graphemes. (RF.1.3a,b,c) To teach the VCe pattern for long vowels, use letter tiles to show how "magic e" changes words:<br><br>mad–made<br>hop–hope<br>pet–Pete<br>cut–cute<br>hid–hide.<br>(RF.1.3a,b,c) |

| Grade One | Level One | Level Two | Level Three |
|---|---|---|---|
| | Blend fifteen to thirty words per day with sound-symbol associations that have been taught; then read in phrases, sentences, and books. Underline or color-code the irregular words that don't follow the learned patterns. (RF.1.3a,b,c,g) | | Ask students to underline target letter combinations before blending whole words with a new letter pattern: *close, cent, nice: dodge: high*. (RF.1.3a,b,c) With letter (grapheme) tiles, construct whole words with three to four learned sounds. You say a word; students repeat the word, build it, blend it, and use it in a sentence. (RF.1.3a,b,c) Use a pocket chart to add inflections *-ing, -s,* and *-es* to base words that do not require doubling or dropping silent e (*walk-ing, shout-s, pick-ing; pass-es, fox-es*). Challenge students to use an inflected word in spoken sentences, and discuss how the ending changes the word's meaning. (RF.1.3g) |
| Reading Objectives for Fluency (RF.1.4a,b,c) | Discriminate between sense and nonsense, and expect that printed words (if accurately read) will generally make sense. (RF.1.4c) | After teacher or partner modeling, reread phrases and sentences to improve phrasing and intonation. (RF.1.4a,b,c) | By midyear, read twenty to thirty words correctly per minute in unrehearsed grade-level text with 96% accuracy or better, and demonstrate comprehension through retelling. (RF.1.4a) Given printed phrases or phrase markers, reread a familiar passage, adjusting intonation and expression to convey meaning. (RF.1.4b) On encountering an unknown word, the reader (1) looks carefully at the letter sequence, (2) sounds out the word, and (3) checks the sense within the whole sentence or passage. If it does not make sense, he or she rereads or asks for assistance. (RF.1.4c) |
| Model Activities for Fluency | Play with "sense" and "nonsense." Read a sentence, deliberately changing a key word or two. Ask students if it makes sense; if not, ask them to say why. (RF.1.4c) Categorize words as "sense" or "nonsense." Explain that reading, in general, should make sense. (RF.1.4c) | Tell students that reading aloud should sound like talking. After they have read a sentence or passage for accuracy, ask them to read with you and follow your voice. (RF.1.4a,b,c) | Using an overhead projector or large-print book, mark the phrases and read them aloud as you sweep your hand under the groups of words. Encourage students to sweep their fingers under the groups of words as they "smush" them together. (RF.1.4a,b,c) Structure partner reading: Assign one person to be "reader" and the other to be "coach." The coach can say, "Try that again" if an error is made. At the end of the book, the coach asks the reader to tell what each page or part of the book was about. Students then change roles for the next book reading. (RF.1.4a,b,c) |

| Grade One | Level One | Level Two | Level Three |
|---|---|---|---|
| Writing, Handwriting, and Spelling Objectives (L.1.1a,j; L.1.2b,d,e; W.1.3) | Form the upper- and lowercase versions of the letters m, a, t, h, p, n, c, d, s, i, b; spell one-syllable words with those letters and twenty of the most often used words in writing. (L.1.1a, L.1.2d)<br><br>Complete sentences in which one part of the "who" "is doing/did what" "to whom or what" is missing. (L.1.1j)<br><br>Identify, then generate, words or phrases that answer the questions who, what, where, when, or how. (L.1.1j) | Form the upper- and lowercase versions of the letters r, f, g, o, x, k u, z, l, e, y, w: spell one-syllable words with sound-spellings that have been taught. (L.1.1a; L.1.2d,e)<br><br>Change statements into questions and questions into statements, with end punctuation. (L.1.1j; L.1.2b) | Recall and write all the alphabet letters with accuracy. (L.1.1a)<br><br>Spell one-syllable words with sound-spellings that have been taught. (L.1.2d,e)<br><br>Elaborate "bare bones" sentences by describing the subject (the who/what part) and saying more about the predicate (the doing part). (L.1.1j)<br><br>Write several sentences telling events in a narrative sequence. (L.1.1j; W.1.3) |
| Model Activities for Writing, Handwriting, and Spelling | Given directional arrows, lined spaces, and verbal cues, students trace and then write the letters they are learning to read. (L.1.1a)<br><br>Explain that each complete sentence must have basic parts. With a sentence frame representing who or what – is doing or did – to whom or what, where, when, or how, students write words to create a complete sentence: *Sid hid the mat.* (L.1.1j)<br><br>Given a simple statement, such as "The bat hit Sid on his cap," students identify which words answer the basic questions who, what, when, where, and how, as they write the sentence in the sentence frame. (L.1.1j) | Given directional arrows, lined spaces, and verbal cues, students trace and then write the letters they are learning to read. (L.1.1a)<br><br>As you dictate words and sentences for writing, say the whole sentence and have students make a line for each word. Then help students segment the sounds in each word as they write, checking against the sound-spelling cards. (L.1.2d,e)<br><br>Pass out question–word cards to students. Give a simple statement, then call on students to create questions with their question words (who, what, when, where, how). Enlist their help as you transcribe the words onto a chart or board. (L.1.1j; L.1.2b) | Challenge students to write the alphabet accurately and fluently from memory, including j, q, and v. (L.1.1a)<br><br>Use a grid to map graphemes to phonemes during spelling practice; one box contains the letters for one sound: *sh-a-ck; d-o-dge; th-i-ng; ch-i-ll.* (L.1.2d.e)<br><br>Have students expand kernel sentences by answering any three of the question words: who, what, when, where, why, how. (For example, "She rode" becomes "Tina rode her bike into the shrub.") (L.1.1j) Provide a visual frame marked *beginning, middle, and end,* with sequence words such as *first, then, next, and finally;* ask students to write a simple narrative with one or more illustrations. (L.1.1j; W.1.3) |

## Grade One, Levels Four Through Six

| Grade One | Level Four | Level Five | Level Six |
|---|---|---|---|
| Reading Objectives for Print Concepts (RF.1.1) | While orally reading beginner text, adjust intonation and phrasing in response to all punctuation used at first-grade level. (RF.1.1) | n/a | n/a |
| Model Activities for Print Concepts | Extract a passage from a mid–first-grade reader: omit end punctuation and commas, and place on an overhead or chart. Read aloud, pausing where punctuation occurs. Ask students to supply what is missing. Or, mix up the punctuation and see how it changes meaning. (RF.1.1) | | n/a |
| Reading Objectives for Phonological Awareness (RF.1.2c,d) | After segmenting a word, isolate and pronounce the first, second, third, or fourth phoneme. (RF.1.2c) Given a word with up to four phonemes, segment and pronounce the sounds in sequence. (RF.1.2d) | Using sound-spelling cards for reference, match any isolated phoneme with its sound-spelling card. (RF.1.2c) Given a word with up to five phonemes, segment and pronounce the sounds in sequence. (RF.1.2d) | Demonstrate phoneme segmentation fluency and accuracy with any one-syllable word. (RF.1.2d) |
| Model Activities for Phonological Awareness | Give students about six colored squares, including two of the same color. Say a word with a blend: "clock." Students move a square for each sound—/k/ /l/ /ŏ/ /k/—into sound boxes or a grid. Ask, "What was the vowel sound?" (/l/) "What was the second sound?" (/l/) And so forth. Finish by blending the whole word and checking its meaning. (RF.1.2c,d) | Hand out the sound-spelling cards to the whole group. Conduct a quick drill: You say a sound, and the student with the right card holds it up or stands up. Then you say four to five sounds that will build a word: "sleeps"—/s/ /l/ /ē/ /p/ /s/—and students with those cards stand in order to create the word. (RF.1.2c,d) Delete a sound (remove the card holder) and ask students to make the new word: seeps, sleep, or leap." (RF.1.2c,d) | If students are accurate, emphasize fluency with those who are still slow. As students segment a word, have them raise a finger for each sound they say, then sweep the whole hand left to right as they blend the word. (RF.1.2d) |
| Reading Objectives for Phonics and Word Recognition (RF.1.3a,b,c,e.f,g) | Learn sound-spelling associations by means of a see/hear/say/write sequence: /ō/ spelled oe; /ō/ spelled ow; /ō/ spelled oa; /ū/ spelled ew or ue; / ow/ spelled ow; /ow/ spelled ou; /aw/ spelled aw or au; /ū/ spelled oo, ue, u_e, u, or ew; /oo/ spelled oo; /n/ spelled kn; /oi/ spelled oi or oy. (RF.1.3a,b,c) Apply sound-symbol associations to blending and reading simple words in isolation and in connected text. (RF.1.3a,b,c) Identify the vowels in words with two simple closed syllables (e.g., rabbit, humbug, basket, catnip, napkin, webcast, hobnob) before sounding out the words. (RF.1.3e) Apply word-reading skills out of context and in the context of connected text. (RF.1.3e) Read comparative adjective forms with –er and –est and illustrate the effect on meaning. (RF.1.3g) Read verbs with –ed and illustrate or explain the meaning of the past tense. Pronounce the three sounds of the –ed inflection: /d/, /t/, and /ed/ (spelled: missed; mended). (RF.1.3g) | Learn sound-symbol associations for /r/ spelled wr and /f/ spelled ph. (RF.1.3a,b,c) Apply associations to blending and reading simple words in isolation and in connected text. (RF.1.3a,b,c) Count the vowels in words with two open, closed, vowel-r, or VCe syllables (e.g. robot, wiper, compete, dateline) before sounding out the words. (RF.1.3f) Apply word-reading skills out of context and in the context of connected text. (RF.1.3f) Identify the base word and ending in inflected forms with no orthographic change in the base word (e.g., wish+ed, wish+ing, wish+es; dark+er, dark+est). (RF.1.3g) | Read two-syllable words with learned syllable patterns, and compound words with recognizable base words (e.g. backpack, flashlight), by first identifying the vowel in each syllable and then decoding the words. (RF.1.3f) Apply word-reading skills out of context and in the context of connected text. (RF.1.3f) Identify learned inflectional word forms in connected text, reading them with accuracy and fluency. (RF.1.3g) |

| Grade One | Level Four | Level Five | Level Six |
|---|---|---|---|
| Model Activities for Phonics and Word Recognition | Continue sound-symbol drills and whole-word blending as before, incorporating new sounds into the repertoire. (RF.1.3a,b,c)<br><br>Explain that closed syllables have short vowels spelled with one letter and end in one or more consonants; the consonants close off the syllable and keep the vowel contained. Using a pocket chart and/or syllable cards, play a matching game with sets of closed syllables. Start with compounds (back + pack; back + log; hot + dog) and then work with two-syllable words (bas + ket; nap + kin; rab + bit; hum + ming) and longer words for those who are ready (fan + tas + tic; ac + com + plish + ment). (RF.1.3e)<br><br>Put roughly fifteen to twenty words with different spellings for the same long vowel (e.g., /o/) on index cards. Sort words by the spelling for the sound (i.e., snow, blow, know, flow; vote, home, chose; boat, moan, load; toe, floe, doe; no, so, go). Then complete written sentences with the words. (RF.1.3a,b,c)<br><br>With the class, create verbal and/or pictorial illustrations of comparative forms of descriptive words: green, greener, greenest; fast, faster, fastest. Point out that -ed has meaning, is added to verbs, and is pronounced three ways. Write the sounds /d/, /t/, and /ed/ above three columns. As you read past tense words extracted from reading material, ask students to decide in which column a word's past tense ending belongs (e.g., mended = /ed/; picked = /t/; filled = /d/). (RF.1.3g) | Continue blending words with all learned sound-spellings, but delete "sound-by-sound" cues; just sweep your hand under the word from left to right. After reading single words, read phrases, sentences, and decodable texts that use the words. (RF.1.3a,b,c,f)<br><br>Explain that open syllables end in a vowel letter that is free to sing its name. Explain also that vowel-r syllables have vowel sounds affected by "bossy" r. With manipulative word cards, sort single-syllable words by vowel spelling and syllable type: open (so), closed (drop), VCe (slope), and vowel-r (fork). (RF.1.3f)<br><br>As students approach unknown longer words, have them identify or underline the vowel in each syllable, using knowledge of syllable spelling patterns, before sounding out the word. Then use meaning and context to adjust pronunciation as necessary. (RF.1.3a,b,c,f)<br><br>Construct a flip chart with two parallel parts: base words (e.g., dark, fight, peep) and inflections (e.g., -ing, -ed, -est, -er, -s). Combine items from the two columns and ask students to judge if the word makes sense before they try to use it in a sentence. (Note: At this point, avoid base words that require spelling changes.) (RF.1.3g) | Sort sets of single-syllable words by vowel spelling and syllable type: open (so), closed (drop), VCe (slope), vowel-r (fork), and vowel team (boat). Students highlight or color-code the vowel before sorting. (RF.1.3f)<br><br>To decode unknown longer words, use a routine: Underline the vowel in each syllable, say the vowel sound, and underline familiar endings. Sweep a pointer or finger under each syllable as you sound out the word, then use meaning and context to adjust pronunciation as necessary. (RF.1.3f,g)<br><br>Conduct daily one-minute speed drills on irregular words. Distribute six to eight irregular words, repeated randomly over a page, and challenge students to read them accurately at a rate of forty to sixty per minute. (RF.1.3f) |
| Reading Objectives for Fluency (RF.1.4a,b,c) | With text at the instructional level (90–95% accuracy), reread to improve accuracy, phrasing, and intonation. (RF.1.4a,b,c)<br><br>On encountering an unknown word, the reader (1) sounds carefully at the letter sequence, (2) sounds out the word, and (3) checks the sense within the whole sentence or passage. If it does not make sense, he or she rereads or asks for assistance. (RF.1.4c) | Read aloud a familiar text to a peer partner or adult so that the listener will comprehend the text. (RF.1.4a,b,c)<br><br>On encountering an unknown word, the reader (1) looks carefully at the letter sequence, (2) sounds out the word, and (3) checks the sense within the whole sentence or passage. If it does not make sense, he or she rereads or asks for assistance. (RF.1.4c) | By year's end, read fifty to sixty words correctly per minute in unrehearsed grade-level text with 97% accuracy or better and demonstrate comprehension through retelling. (RF.1.4a)<br><br>Read aloud a familiar text to a peer partner or adult so that the listener will comprehend the text. (RF.1.4a,b,c)<br><br>On encountering an unknown word, the reader (1) looks carefully at the letter sequence, (2) sounds out the word, and (3) checks the sense within the whole sentence or passage. If it does not make sense, he or she rereads or asks for assistance. (RF.1.4c) |

Reading Foundations: A Pacing Guide for Reading Instruction (Grade One, Levels Four Through Six)

| Grade One | Level Four | Level Five | Level Six |
|---|---|---|---|
| Model Activities for Fluency | Using a text the students have read once, revisit it for some "detective work." Ask students to read a sentence or page to find words that tell why something happened, who did something, how something was done, and so forth. When students have pointed to those words in their books, choral-read that section with appropriate phrasing. (RF.1.4a,b,c)<br><br>Remind students of the "look at the whole word, sound it out, and check it" routine for unknown words. If they are stuck on a sound, ask them to check the sound-symbol cards—which should be posted in a place easy to see—to solve the problem. (RF.1.4c) | Model an alternate oral reading procedure for students to use as partners: Students sit facing opposite directions, shoulder to shoulder. The first reader reads a page; then the second reader reads the same page (for the less skilled) or reads the next page. After reading, students take turns retelling what was read. (RF.1.4a,b,c)<br><br>Remind students of the "look at the whole word, sound it out, and check it" routine for unknown words. (RF.1.4c) | Conduct daily one-minute speed drills on irregular words. Distribute six to eight irregular words randomly repeated over a page, and challenge students to read them accurately at a rate of forty to sixty words per minute. (RF.1.4a)<br><br>Ask students to keep reading logs, recording about twenty minutes daily of time spent reading with a peer, parent, or other volunteer. (RF.1.4a,b,c) |
| Writing, Handwriting, and Spelling Objectives (L.1.1j; L.1.2d,e; L.1.4c; W.1.2) | Spell accurately and in context sixty to seventy of the most often-used words in writing. (L.1.2d)<br><br>Write sentences with compound subjects and compound predicates. (L.1.1j)<br><br>Given a topic, write several sentences that tell about the same thing. (L.1.1j, W.1.2) | Spell one-syllable words with inflections in a structured context. (L.1.4c)<br><br>Use simple and compound sentences in writing and vary the position of adverbial phrases. (L.1.1j) | Spell accurately and in context one hundred of the most often used words in writing. (L.1.2d)<br><br>Spell one-syllable, regular-pattern words with long and short vowels. (L.1.2d,e)<br><br>Recognize the difference between topic sentences and details. (W.1.2) |
| Model Activities for Writing, Handwriting, and Spelling | Rehearse mnemonic cues and sentences for irregular, high-frequency words: *Mom said, "Sally's apple is delicious."* (L.1.2d)<br><br>Model, then lead students in combining simple sentences: *The hungry snake ate the rat. The snake ate the chipmunk. The hungry snake ate the rat and the chipmunk.* (L.1.1j)<br><br>After selecting a topic for description, brainstorm with students the kinds of descriptive words that could be used in writing about that topic. Encourage them to formulate sentences orally before writing. Provide the target words in a word bank, and ask students to write several sentences using those words and others they know while writing their descriptions. (L.1.1f, L.1.1j, W.1.2) | Complete written sentences with the correct inflected forms of nouns and verbs: *The (tree, trees) are (grow, growing) on the steep slope. That is the (taller, tallest) of three (pine, pines).* (L.1.4c)<br><br>Complete compound sentences using the connectives *and, but, so, because:*<br><br>*"I liked that book because . . ."*<br>*"I liked that book, but . . ."*<br>*"I liked that book, so . . ."*<br><br>(L.1.1j, W.1.1)<br><br>Lift sentences with adverbial clauses from familiar text or student writing. Ask students to rewrite them, moving the adverbial clause if appropriate, and adding a comma if needed:<br>*We went home after the play and ate supper.*<br>*After the play, we went home and ate supper.*<br>*We went home and ate supper after the play.*<br><br>Encourage students to change phrase position when they revise their own writing. (L.1.1j) | To commit the most common hundred words to memory, students can make an index card for each word they need to practice. If they can write the word quickly and accurately three days in a row, the word can be "retired" to a word bank. (L.1.2d)<br><br>Play "What Pattern Am I?" Given three columns for long vowel syllable types—open (*me, she, no, so, hi*), VCe (*spoke, slime, robe, quake*) and vowel team (*seem, sail, play, boat, right, meat*)—write words in the correct category. (L.1.2d)<br><br>Write three to five sentences on sentence strips, including a topic and a few details. Mix them up and give them to pairs of students to put in a sensible order. Then ask students to suggest edits or revisions to the passage, including word choice, elaboration, or word order, as they rewrite the paragraph. (W.1.2, W.1.5, L.1.1j) |

## Grade Two, Levels One Through Three

| Grade Two | Level One | Level Two | Level Three |
|---|---|---|---|
| Reading Objectives for Phonics and Word Recognition (RF.2.3,a,b,c,d,e,f) | Generate symbols (graphemes) for sounds (phonemes) and sounds for symbols, with accuracy and fluency, including short vowels and all common consonant correspondences. (RF.2.3a)<br><br>Identify the syllable units in spoken words; know that each syllable must have a vowel; and when the vowel is short, the syllable will be closed. (RF.2.3c)<br><br>Add and delete common inflectional suffixes (-s, -es, -ed, -ing, -er, -est) from base words that do not require a change of spelling, and recognize how meaning is changed by the suffix. (RF.2.3d)<br><br>Read words with common spelling variations for consonants: double f, l, z after short vowels; -ck, -tch, and -dge after short vowels; soft c and g. (RF.2.3.e)<br><br>Read accurately twenty additional high-frequency, irregular words from the three hundred most common words in written English (e.g., there, where, any, many). (RF.2.3.f) | Accurately associate symbols (graphemes) with sounds (phonemes), and sounds with symbols, including those in Level One and most common spellings for long vowels (/ē/ = e, ee, ea, e_e; /ī/ = i, y, i_e, igh; /ā/ = a, ai, ay, a_e; /ō/ = o, o_e, oa, ow; /ū/ = u, e, oo, ew, ue; /yū/ = u, u_e, ew, eu, ue) (RF.2.3a,b)<br><br>Identify and pronounce the vowel sounds in written closed, open, and VCe syllables (hit, hi, hide). (RF.2.3c)<br><br>Add and delete common inflectional suffixes beginning with vowels (-es, -ed, -ing, -er, -est) from base words that require doubling of a final consonant (running, wettest), and recognize how meaning is changed by the suffix. (RF.2.3d)<br><br>Read words with the -ild, -ind, -old, -ost pattern (finding, kindest, most, unfold) and the -all and -al patterns (fallen, recall; calm, palm, talk). (RF.2.3e)<br><br>Read accurately twenty additional high-frequency, irregular words from the three hundred most common words in written English. (RF.2.3.f) | Fluently and accurately associate symbols (graphemes) with sounds (phonemes), and sounds with symbols, including those in Levels One and Two, diphthongs (/ou/ = ou, ow; /oi/ = oi, oy), and vowel-r correspondences (er, ar, or). (RF.2.3a,b)<br><br>Identify, sort, and pronounce the vowel sounds in closed, open, VCe, vowel team, and vowel-r syllables. (RF.2.3c)<br><br>Add and delete common suffixes beginning with vowels (-es, -ed, -ing, -er, -est, -y) from base words that require deletion of a final silent e (slimy, hoping), and recognize how meaning is changed by the suffix. (RF.2.3d)<br><br>Read and pronounce words with silent letter spellings (knee, wrong, gnaw, comb, ghost) and wo (word, work) and wa (warp, warm; water, was, waffle) patterns. (RF.2.3e)<br><br>Read accurately twenty additional high-frequency, irregular words from the three hundred most common words in written English. (RF.2.3.f) |
| Model Activities for Phonics and Word Recognition | Consolidate students' automatic command of basic sound-symbol associations by including one-minute drills: You say a sound, students write the common spelling(s); or, students look at a series of randomly ordered graphemes and say the sounds. (RF.2.3a)<br><br>Explain that every syllable has a vowel, and the jaw drops open as the vowel is spoken. Ask students to look in a mirror and repeat words with one to four syllables, holding their hand under their chin to feel the jaw drop. To hear the accented syllable, students can pretend that the word is a dog's name. As they "call the dog," they will hold the accented syllable longer. (SUM mer; WIN ter; AU tumn, fan TAS tic) (RF.2.3c)<br><br>Line three students up with large letter cards—h, i, t or b, e, d. Ask the class to read the word and identify the vowel as short. Point out that the last letter is a consonant (a closed sound) that closes in the syllable and keeps the vowel short. Then ask the "last letter" to turn away, leaving an open syllable (hi, be) where the vowel is free to sing its name. Show how two closed syllables can combine: mas-cot; cac-tus; mag-net; ban-dit. (RF.2.3c) | Using manipulative grapheme tiles, create columns for each spelling of one long vowel (i, igh, i_e, y); then have students pronounce and sort single-syllable words with those spellings (my, sight, wipe, pi). (RF.2.3a,b)<br><br>With sets of closed, VCe, and open syllables on cards, ask students to identify the type of syllable and the pronunciation of each syllable; then they can arrange the syllables into words, read and use them in a sentence: prin-cess; grace-ful; life-less; ex-pose; com-pute; e-ven; se-cret; mu-sic; si-lent. (RF.2.3c)<br><br>Practice adding and deleting common suffixes beginning with vowels (-y, -es, -ed, -ing, -er, -est, -ish) from base words that require doubling of a final consonant (running, wettest, fatter, reddish). Explain and illustrate the formula: If the word has one syllable and ends in one consonant, preceded by one vowel, double the consonant before adding a suffix that begins with a vowel. Create cloze sentences to be completed with the correctly suffixed word.<br><br>Example: fatter = fat + (t) + er. (RF.2.3d) | First teach that /er/ has three common spellings: er, ir, ur. Note that /er/ can be treated as one phoneme, because the vowel and consonant are welded together. Also, /ar/ and /or/ are partly welded. (RF.2.3a,b)<br><br>Add vowel-r syllables into the mix (stor-y; black-bird; turn-stile; churn-ing). Practice reading two- and three-syllable words by scooping under each syllable with a pencil, identifying the syllable type, coding the vowel as o (open), c (closed), r (vowel-r), or e (VCe) if necessary. Then play a question game with the words: "Which word means _____?" (RF.2.3c)<br><br>Practice adding and deleting common suffixes beginning with vowels (-y, -es, -ed, -ing, -er, -est, -ish) from base words that require deletion of a final silent e (writing, hoping, skated). Explain and illustrate the formula: If a word ends in a final silent e and the added suffix begins with a vowel, delete the silent e. Create cloze sentences to be completed with the correctly suffixed word.<br><br>Example: slime + y = slimy. (RF.2.3d) |

| Grade Two | Level One | Level Two | Level Three |
|---|---|---|---|
| | Starting with base words that do not require a spelling change (wind, melt, mist, backpack), ask students to combine base words and common inflections, pronounce the result, and use the words in sentences. (RF.2.3d)<br><br>Provide word cards that demonstrate a pattern, such as hard and soft c. Ask students to sort the words by the sound of letter c (/s/ or /k/) and see if they can find the pattern. Confirm that c usually has the sound /s/ before e, i, and y, but the sound /k/ before a, o, and u. (RF.2.3e)<br><br>To introduce an irregular word (does, what, where), contrast the spelling pronunciation and the actual pronunciation. Explain that the oldest words in English have changed their pronunciation over hundreds of years. (RF.2.3f) | Collect words with -ild, -ind, -old, and -ost patterns (finding, kindest, most, unfold, postal). Ask students to underline the base word's vowel, pronounce the words, and describe why the words break the pattern of regular closed or open syllables. (RF.2.3e)<br><br>As students learn an irregular word, provide a written model for the students to trace, copy, and then write from memory. During each step, students say the letter names—not the sounds. Say the word before and after writing. (RF.2.3f) | Collect "wo" words (work, worse, worm, word, worth, worthy, won, wonder) and "wa" words (water, warm, want, was, wash). After explicitly contrasting the expected sound of the vowel with its actual pronunciation, ask students to say what's true about vowels that follow w: W often changes the following vowel. (RF.2.3e)<br><br>Construct one-minute speed drills for centers in which students practice accurate and fluent reading of problematic irregular and/or high-frequency words (because, through, there, where, laugh). Choose six words for each speed drill, randomly distributing them in a 5 × 6 grid. Partners can time one another. (RF.2.3f) |
| Reading Objectives for Fluency (RF.2.4a,b,c) | Orally read grade-appropriate connected text with demonstrated comprehension, at sixty words correct per minute. (RF.2.4a,b,c) | Orally read grade-appropriate connected text with accuracy and demonstrated comprehension, at sixty-five words correct per minute. (RF.2.4a,b,c) | By midyear, orally read grade-appropriate text with 96% accuracy and demonstrated comprehension, at seventy words correct per minute. (RF.2.4a,b,c) |
| Model Activities for Fluency | Using an overhead projector or large-print book, mark phrases and read them aloud as you sweep your hand under the groups of words. Encourage students to sweep their fingers under the groups of words as they "smush" them together. (RF.2.4a,b,c)<br><br>Structure partner reading: Assign one person to be "reader" and the other to be "coach." The coach can say, "Try that again" if an error is made. At the end of the book, the coach asks the reader to tell what each page or part of the book was about. Students then change roles for the next book reading. (RF.2.4a,b,c) | Select a story or poem that students read with 95% accuracy. Practice reading the text in unison until everyone can read it as a chorus. Ask smaller groups of students to perform the reading for other groups or classes. (RF.2.4a,b,c) | Encourage repeated readings of stories that students can read with 95% accuracy. Use a tape-recorded model for students to read along with in a listening center. Then ask individual students to read the same story aloud to a partner, who times them, records words correct per minute, and charts the results. (RF.2.4a,b,c) |

## Grade Two, Levels Four Through Six

| Grade Two | Level Four | Level Five | Level Six |
|---|---|---|---|
| **Reading Objectives for Phonics and Word Recognition** (RF.2.3.a,b,c,d,e,f) | Identify the consonant-*le* final syllable pattern, and accurately read two-syllable words ending in a consonant-*le* syllable (*cradle; paddle; bible; bumble; google, gurgle; steeple; settle*). (RF.2.3a,b,c) Add and delete common suffixes (*-ly, -less, -es, -ed, -ing, -er, -est*) from base words with final *y* (*bunnies, penniless, babying*), and recognize how meaning is changed by the suffix. (RF.2.3d) Read and decompose contractions into their constituent base words (*they'd = they would; should've = should have*). (RF.2.3e) Read accurately twenty additional high-frequency, irregular words from the most common words in written English. (RF.2.3f) | Read two-syllable words with an ambiguous VCV syllable juncture (*e/ven, ev/ery; ra/dar, rad/ish*), adapting pronunciation to make a meaningful word. Identify common prefixes on base words (*un-, mis-, re-, pre-*); recognize how addition or deletion of the prefix changes the word's meaning. (RF.2.3d) Associate spellings of common homophone pairs with their major meanings (*for, four; wear, where; their, there*). (RF.2.3e) Read accurately twenty additional high-frequency, irregular words from the most common words in written English. (RF.2.3f) | Fluently and accurately read two-syllable base words comprising any of the six regular syllable patterns (RF.2.3a,b,c). Read grade-level base words with the most common prefixes (*in-, un-, mis-, dis-, re-, de-, a-*) and suffixes (*-ly, -er, -ion, -less, -ness*) and recognize how meaning of the base is changed by the suffix. (RF.2.3d) Read less common (but predictable) patterns for vowels, such as *eigh* for /ā/ (*neighbor*), *ough* for /ō/ (*though, dough*), and *ei* for /ē/ (*ceiling*). (RF.2.3e) Read accurately twenty additional high-frequency, irregular words from the most common words in written English. (RF.2.3f) |
| **Model Activities for Phonics and Word Recognition** | Give small groups of students sets of cards with closed, vowel-r, vowel team, and open syllables that will combine with a set of -*cle* final syllables to make words. Have students read the syllables before combining them with the -*cle* syllables. Give a point for each real word created, and discuss any unknown meanings (*un-cle; bu-gle; pur-ple; sim-ple; si-dle; nee-dle; net-tle; chor-tle; wad-dle, waf-fle, etc.*). (RF.2.3a,b,c) Introduce the "*y* rule" by comparing word pairs with and without suffixes. Can students determine what happened to the *y*? <br><br> *baby–babies* <br> *dirty–dirtiest* <br> *cry–cried* <br> *jumpy–jumpier* <br> *fry–frier* <br> *story–stories* <br> (RF.2.3d) <br><br> Collect examples of contractions from the texts students are reading. Enlist students' assistance in decomposing the contractions into their base words. Explain that the apostrophe kicks out letters and replaces them when the words are contracted. (RF.2.3e) | Lead students as they practice a routine for reading unknown big words. Find the known parts: Circle a prefix and box a suffix. Identify the vowel(s) in the base word using syllable identification. Scoop under each part as it is pronounced, and then blend the whole word. (RF.2.3a,b,c,d) Explain to students that prefixes and suffixes have meaning, and change meaning of a base word. Define a few of the most common prefixes (*un-, re-, mis-*). Play a question-answer game with the most common prefixes: *If "usable" means you can use an item, what does "unusable" mean? What does "reusable" mean? "Misused"?* Then write the words, circling the prefixes and boxing any suffixes. (RF.2.3d) With the class, gradually create an illustrated homophone dictionary. First introduce the most common and most regular word in a homophone pair or group, ensuring that students have practiced its use in context. Introduce the homophone partner only when students are sure of the most common word of the pair (e.g, *base before bass; there before their; plane before plain*). (RF.2.3e) | Practice the most common syllable division principles: VC/CV (*rab/bit*); VC/CCV (*com/plete*); V/CV (*si/lent*) or VC/V (*mag/ic*) and follow the "big word" routine outlined in Level Five. (RF.2.3a,b,c) Practice using affixed words in cloze exercises (incomplete sentences) where the meaning of the prefix and/or suffix must fit the given context. (*She [remade/remaking/unmade] her bed in the morning.*) (RF.2.3d) After identifying a less common spelling for a vowel (*ā = eigh*), ask students to sort a group of words with several spelling patterns for that vowel: /ā/ = *eigh, ai, ay, a_e*. Then read decodable passages with a heavy concentration of words that contain the spelling patterns just practiced. (RF.2.3e) Continue the irregular word study routine, with emphasis on automatic recognition in the speed drills described in Level Three. (RF.2.3f) |

| Grade Two | Level Four | Level Five | Level Six |
|---|---|---|---|
| | If students have not automatized recognition of common irregular words that have been taught through tracing, copying, and writing, sequence practice so that it moves from single-word recognition, to reading the words in phrases, to reading in sentences and text. Practice only a few words at one time. (RF.2.3f) | Continue study of irregular words, about four to five per week, by first presenting the words out of context. Ask students to trace, say the letters, copy and write the words, examining the parts that are irregular. Then read the words in text that affords many opportunities for practice. (RF.2.3f) | |
| Reading Objectives for Fluency (RF.2.4a,b, c) | Orally read grade-appropriate connected text with demonstrated comprehension, at seventy-five words correct per minute. (RF.2.4a) | Orally read grade-appropriate connected text with accuracy and demonstrated comprehension, at eighty words correct per minute. (RF.2.4a) | By year's end, orally read grade-appropriate text with 97% accuracy and demonstrated comprehension, at ninety words correct per minute. (RF.2.4a) |
| Model Activities for Fluency | Take a simple sentence from a text and change its punctuation. Model accurate reading with a change in prosody indicated by the punctuation. Then ask students to practice similar sequences, explaining the difference in meaning: *Was she lazy! Was she lazy?* (RF.2.4a,b,c) | Including independent reading, partner reading, choral reading, and reading with a taped book, students should document in a reading log that they are spending at least twenty minutes daily with text they can read with sufficient accuracy and comprehension. (RF.2.4a,b,c)  Students at risk should have their progress measured and charted every few weeks. (RF.2.4a) | Encourage students to read several books by the same author, once they discover a series they enjoy. (RF.2.4a,b,c) |

# Kindergarten

Children enter kindergarten with a wide range of knowledge. Some have already learned to read simple books, whereas others have not yet learned the alphabet. Over the course of this year, all students begin to read, write, and advance their existing skills. The kindergarten curriculum consists of a rich array of "read-aloud" stories, nonfiction, and poems, combined with phonics and writing, as well as listening and speaking activities. Teachers of beginning readers are also encouraged to consult the Reading Foundations section found at the beginning of this print edition. This guide is not a comprehensive reading program; rather, it provides guidance for instruction in print concepts, phonological awareness, phonics, word recognition, fluency, and some of the writing and language skills essential to developing foundational reading skills.

Over the course of the six units of kindergarten, students listen to a wide variety of excellent literary and nonfiction texts: poems and informational texts about counting; poems and songs with strong rhythm and rhyme; stories about exploring; books about American symbols and celebrations; and books about plants, insects, and frogs. They learn to retell and discuss what they have learned, putting events in order and explaining why they occurred. By the end of the year, students have learned to decode and encode one-syllable regular words and recognize high-frequency sight words. They have been exposed to historical and biographical nonfiction, as well as fiction, poetry, and fables. In the following year, they will continue to learn to read while building knowledge of an array of topics.

# Standards Checklist for Kindergarten

| Standard | Unit 1 | Unit 2 | Unit 3 | Unit 4 | Unit 5 | Unit 6 |
|---|---|---|---|---|---|---|
| **Reading–Literature** | | | | | | |
| 1 | | A | | | | |
| 2 | | FA | | | A | |
| 3 | | A | FA | A | F | A |
| 4 | | | FA | | | |
| 5 | FA | A | A | | | |
| 6 | | A | | | | |
| 7 | | A | | A | | |
| 8 n/a | | | | | | |
| 9 | | FA | FA | | FA | |
| 10 | | | | A | A | FA |
| **Reading–Informational Text** | | | | | | |
| 1 | | FA | A | FA | | |
| 2 | | | FA | A | | |
| 3 | | | | A | | |
| 4 | FA | | | A | | |
| 5 | A | | A | | | |
| 6 | A | A | | | | |
| 7 | | | A | A | | |
| 8 | | | | A | | FA |
| 9 | | | A | | FA | FA |
| 10 | | | | | A | A |
| **Writing** | | | | | | |
| 1 | F | A | A | | A | |
| 2 | A | A | FA | A | A | A |
| 3 | | FA | A | | A | A |
| 4 n/a | | | | | | |
| 5 | | A | | A | A | A |
| 6 | | | | | FA | FA |
| 7 | | A | | FA | A | A |
| 8 | | A | | | A | FA |
| 9 n/a | | | | | | |
| 10 n/a | | | | | | |
| **Speaking and Listening** | | | | | | |
| 1 | FA | FA | A | A | A | A |
| 1a | FA | A | A | | | A |
| 1b | | FA | | | | A |
| 2 | | | A | A | A | |
| 3 | | | A | A | A | |
| 4 | | | A | FA | A | A |
| 5 | A | A | A | | | |
| 6 | | | A | | A | A |
| **Language** | | | | | | |
| 1 | | | F | F | | |
| 1a | | A | A | A | | |
| 1b | | A | | A | A | A |
| 1c | | A | | A | | |
| 1d | | | FA | | | |
| 1e | | A | | | | |
| 1f | | | FA | | | A |
| 2 | | F | | F | F | |
| 2a | | FA | A | | | A |

| Standard | Unit 1 | Unit 2 | Unit 3 | Unit 4 | Unit 5 | Unit 6 |
|---|---|---|---|---|---|---|
| 2b | | | A | | | |
| 2c | | | A | | | |
| 2d | | | | FA | FA | A |
| 3 | | | | | | |
| 4 | | A | | A | | F |
| 4a | | | | A | | |
| 4b | | | | | | FA |
| 5 | FA | A | | | | |
| 5a | FA | A | | | | |
| 5b | | | A | | A | A | A |
| 5c | | | A | A | | |
| 5d | | | A | A | | |
| 6 | | | | A | A | |

| Reading Foundations (addressed in units) | | | | | | |
|---|---|---|---|---|---|---|
| Standard | Level 1 | Level 2 | Level 3 | Level 4 | Level 5 | Level 6 |
| 1 | A | A | | | | |
| 1a | A | A | | | | |
| 1b | | A | | | | |
| 1c | | A | | | | |
| 1d | | A | | | | |
| 2 | | | | | | |
| 2a | FA | | | | | |
| 2b | | | | | | |
| 2c | | | | | | |
| 2d | | | | | | |
| 2e | | | | | | |
| 3 | | | | | | |
| 3a | | A | | | | |
| 3b | | | | | | |
| 3c | A | | | | | |
| 3d | | | | | A | |
| 4 | | | | | | FA |

| Reading Foundations (addressed in Reading Foundations: A Pacing Guide) | | | | | | |
|---|---|---|---|---|---|---|
| Standard | Level 1 | Level 2 | Level 3 | Level 4 | Level 5 | Level 6 |
| 1 | | A | A | | | |
| 1a | | A | A | | | |
| 1b | | A | A | | | |
| 1c | | A | A | | | |
| 1d | | A | A | A | A | A |
| 2 | F | | | | | |
| 2a | FA | A | A | | | |
| 2b | | A | A | | | |
| 2c | | A | A | | A | A |
| 2d | | A | A | A | A | A |
| 2e | | | | | A | |
| 3 | | | | | A | A |
| 3a | | A | A | A | A | A |
| 3b | | | A | A | A | A |
| 3c | | A | A | A | A | A |
| 3d | | | | | A | A |
| 4 | | A | A | A | A | A |

F = Focus Standard; A = Activity/Assessment

# A Colorful Time with Rhythm and Rhyme

In this first six-week unit of kindergarten, students are introduced to colorful picture books, traditional poetry, and nursery rhymes filled with rhythm and rhyme.

## ESSENTIAL QUESTION

How does rhyme affect the way that we hear and read poetry?

## OVERVIEW

Focusing on phonological awareness, students are challenged to listen for rhythm and rhyming words within the literature. Concepts of print are taught as students read poems on wall charts and in informational books. Descriptions of gathered objects and artworks highlight the secondary focus on color, encouraging rich description, discussion in spoken language, and vocabulary development. In this early stage of writing, students use a combination of drawing, dictation, and writing to give opinions about favorite colors.

## FOCUS STANDARDS

These Focus Standards have been selected for the unit from the Common Core State Standards.

**RI.K.4:** With prompting and support, ask and answer questions about unknown words in a text.

**RL.K.5:** Recognize common types of texts (e.g., storybooks, poems).

**RF.K.2:** Demonstrate understanding of spoken words, syllables, and sounds (phonemes).

**RF.K.2(a):** Recognize and produce rhyming words.

**W.K.1:** Use a combination of drawing, dictating, and writing to compose opinion pieces in which they tell a reader the topic or the name of the book they are writing about and state an opinion or preference about the topic or book (e.g., "My favorite book is . . .").

**SL.K.1:** Participate in collaborative conversations with diverse partners about kindergarten topics and texts with peers and adults in small and larger groups.

**SL.K.1(a):** Follow agreed-upon rules for discussions (e.g., listening to others and taking turns speaking about the topics and texts under discussion).

**L.K.5:** With guidance and support from adults, explore word relationships and nuances in word meanings.

**L.K.5(a):** Sort common objects into categories (e.g., shapes, foods) to gain a sense of the concepts the categories represent.

## SUGGESTED OBJECTIVES

- Recognize the difference between a storybook and a poem.
- Understand that poems (poetry) are written by poets and that they often rhyme.
- Distinguish between a verse (stanza) and a line in a poem.
- Identify the author and illustrator of a storybook and of an informational book.
- Ask questions about unknown words in a text.
- Understand the organization and basic features of print.
- Identify the front cover, back cover, and title page of a book; follow the words from left to right, top to bottom, and page by page.
- Understand that words are separated by spaces in print.
- Use a combination of drawing, dictating, or writing to share an opinion.
- Listen to others and take turns speaking while discussing favorite rhymes.
- Expand vocabulary by sorting objects (e.g., by color, noticing colorful places in school, and describing objects with "color" adjectives).

## SUGGESTED WORKS

(E) indicates a CCSS exemplar text; (EA) indicates a text from a writer with other works identified as exemplars.

### LITERARY TEXTS

*Nursery Rhymes (Read Along)*
- "Diddle, Diddle, Dumpling"
- "Early to Bed"
- "Georgie Porgie"
- "Hey Diddle Diddle"
- "Humpty Dumpty"
- "Jack and Jill"

- "Jack Be Nimble"
- "Little Bo Peep"
- "Little Boy Blue"
- "Little Jack Horner"
- "Little Miss Muffet"
- "Old Mother Hubbard"
- "Pat-a-Cake"
- "Ring Around the Rosey"
- "Rock-a-bye, Baby"
- "Roses Are Red"
- "Simple Simon"
- "Star Light, Star Bright"

## Picture Books (Read Aloud)

- *And the Dish Ran Away with the Spoon* (Janet Stevens and Susan Stevens Crummel)
- *Brown Bear, Brown Bear* (Bill Martin Jr. and Eric Carle)
- *Chicka Chicka Boom Boom* (Bill Martin Jr., John Archambault, and Lois Ehlert)
- *Clang! Clang! Beep! Beep! Listen to the City* (Robert Burleigh and Beppe Giacobbe)
- *Colors! Colores!* (Jorge Lujan and Piet Grobler)
- *Grandmother's Nursery Rhymes: Las Nanas de Abuelita* (Nelly Palacio Jaramillo) (OOP)
- *If Kisses Were Colors* (Janet Lawler and Alison Jay)
- *Itsy Bitsy Spider* (Iza Trapani)
- *Mary Wore Her Red Dress* (Merle Peek)
- *My Many Colored Days* (Dr. Seuss) (EA)
- *Rap a Tap Tap, Here's Bojangles: Think of That!* (Leo and Diane Dillon)
- *The Real Mother Goose* (Blanche Fisher Wright)
- *The Red Book* (Barbara Lehman)
- *Red, Green, Blue: A First Book of Colors* (Alison Jay)
- *Red Is for Dragon: A Book of Colors* (Roseanne Thong and Grace Lin)

## Poems (Read Aloud)

- "Halfway Down" (A. A. Milne) (E)
- "Mary Had a Little Lamb" (Sarah Josepha Hale)
- "Singing Time" (Rose Fyleman) (E) (OOP)
- "Time to Rise" (Robert Louis Stevenson)
- "Twinkle, Twinkle, Little Star" (Ann and Jane Taylor)

## INFORMATIONAL TEXTS

*Nonfiction Books*

- *My Five Senses* (Aliki) (E)

*Nonfiction Books (Read Aloud)*

- *All the Colors of the Rainbow* (Rookie Read-About Science Series) (Allan Fowler)
- *Colors* (Learning with Animals) (Melanie Watt) (OOP)
- *Colors and Shapes: Los colores y las figuras* (Gladys Rosa-Mendoza, Carolina Cifuentes, and Michele Noiset)
- *I Spy Colors in Art* (Lucy Micklethwait)
- *The Magic School Bus Makes a Rainbow: A Book About Color* (Joanna Cole, Carolyn Braken, and Bruce Degan)
- *Matisse: The King of Color* (Laurence Anholt)
- *A World of Colors: Seeing Colors in a New Way* (Marie Houblon)

## ART, MUSIC, AND MEDIA

*Art*

- Diego Rivera, *Flower Day* (1925)
- Helen Frankenthaler, *Mountains and Sea* (1952)
- Henri Matisse, *The Dessert: Harmony in Red* (1908)
- James Abbott McNeill Whistler, *Arrangement in Black and Gray: The Artist's Mother* (1871)
- Pablo Picasso, *Le Gourmet* (1901)
- Paul Gauguin, *The Midday Nap* (1894)
- Pieter Bruegel, *The Hunters in the Snow* (1565)

## SAMPLE ACTIVITIES AND ASSESSMENTS

### 1. READING POETRY, READING COMPREHENSION, VOCABULARY

As students read a nursery rhyme (or poem) from a chart or interactive whiteboard in the front of the class, choose a student to come up and follow the words from left to right with a pointer. Instruct the students that if there is a word they do not understand in this rhyme, they should raise a hand to ask about it. (RF.K.1a, RL.K.4, RL.K.5)

### 2. READING POETRY, READING FOUNDATIONS

While reading (reciting) "Humpty Dumpty," snap your fingers on the word at the end of a line (e.g., "wall"). The children will snap when they hear the word that rhymes with it (e.g., "fall"). Continue with various rhymes and poems. Afterward, put up a second nursery rhyme, but leave out the end word of every other line (i.e., "Humpty Dumpty sat on a wall, Humpty Dumpty had a great _____"). Some students can pick from a list of words the appropriate one to fill in the blank. Once they've mastered that, repeat the exercise without providing the list of words. (RF.K.2a)

## 3. VOCABULARY, LANGUAGE USAGE

Prepare a basket of colored objects. Invite students to come to the basket and choose something to tell the class about. This is the rule: each student must describe the object using at least two "describing words" (i.e., adjectives). Example: a bright red apple, a small green block. Extend this activity by introducing opposites of one of the adjectives. "You showed me a small block. Now find a large block." You could have another vocabulary activity with the same collection by sorting the same objects into color categories such as "red" and "green" or by asking the students to think of rhyming words that describe. (L.K.5a)

## 4. READING INFORMATIONAL TEXT AND LITERATURE, READING COMPREHENSION

As the class reads an informational or literary book, introduce the idea of *author* and *illustrator*. Describe their roles in the creation of a text. Do a "text walk" by carefully showing the front cover, back cover, and title page of the book. As you read an informational text such as *All the Colors of the Rainbow* by Allan Fowler, pause to ask the children questions. Encourage them to ask questions about the text and unfamiliar words. (RI.K.4, RI.K.5, RI.K.6, RL.K.4)

## 5. READING POETRY, SPEAKING AND LISTENING

Arrange small groups of students and place an object (e.g., a block) in the middle of each circle. Instruct the students to discuss which poem in this unit is their favorite. Students pick up the block when ready to share. Ask them to put the block back in the middle when finished. When working with a group, ask the student who has the floor to think of/share a word that rhymes with the last word of a sentence in the chosen poem. (SL.K.1, SL.K.1a)

## 6. ART, SPEAKING AND LISTENING

Show students the Whistler and the Rivera paintings. Ask them to discuss how Whistler used a mostly black-and-white palette, whereas Rivera used a wide range of colors. Then ask them to choose to draw their favorite of the two works, either in black and white or using a wide range of colors. (W.K.2, SL.K.5)

## 7. ART, SPEAKING AND LISTENING

Display the works by Matisse and Picasso. Ask the students what color dominates each work. Ask the students why they think Picasso chose blue whereas Matisse chose red. Ask how the paintings are the same (e.g., both figures are preparing food, and neither is looking at us) and how they are different (e.g., we can see outside in the Matisse, whereas Picasso's is a close-up), preparing the way for literature conversations in comparing and contrasting texts. (SL.K.1, SL.K.5)

## 8. READING POETRY, VOCABULARY

As students read a rhyme, ask them to focus on listening for rhyming words and hearing the rhythm of the lines. By teaching the children to follow along with you on wall charts or an interactive whiteboard, they are able to enjoy rich vocabulary in context and become familiar with sight words and word families. Adding the simple melodies to the nursery rhymes will enhance the students' perception of rhythm. By using musical recordings of the nursery rhymes, students can move to the rhythm of the rhymes in song and recite the words with ease. (RF.K.1, RF.K.2a, RF.K.3c)

# READING FOUNDATIONS: A PACING GUIDE FOR READING INSTRUCTION

Common Core's Reading Foundations begin at a level appropriate for students who do not already know how to read. This will be the majority of students in most school systems, including those who enter school with limited language and/or literary experience and those who simply lack the phonological, decoding, and encoding skills needed for beginning reading and spelling. The pacing of code-emphasis instruction and the amount of time allotted to it will vary according to student skill levels, as measured on early screening, diagnostic, and progress-monitoring assessments. Nevertheless, all students need to master these essential building blocks.

See Kindergarten, Level One, in the Reading Foundations section at the beginning of this book for a complete pacing guide for this unit.

# ADDITIONAL ONLINE RESOURCES

- "Halfway Down" video
- "Rap a Tap Tap" video (Shirley Temple and Bill Robinson)
- "Twinkle, Twinkle, Little Star" video
- *A Rhyme a Week: Nursery Rhymes for Early Literacy* (Webbing into Literacy)
- *Chicka Chicka Boom Boom* video
- *Generating Rhymes: Developing Phonemic Awareness* (ReadWriteThink) (RF.K.2a)
- *Growing Readers and Writers with Help from Mother Goose* (ReadWriteThink) (RF.K.1b, RF.K.2a)
- *Hats Off to Color* (ArtsEdge, the Kennedy Center) (L.K.5a)
- Interview with Eric Carle (RL.K.6)
- *Spicy Hot Colors* video

# TERMINOLOGY

| | | |
|---|---|---|
| Artist | Line | Rhythm |
| Author | Opinion | Stanza |
| Description | Poem | Story book |
| Illustration | Poet | Verse |
| Illustrator | Poetry | |
| Informational book | Rhyme | |

## INTERDISCIPLINARY CONNECTIONS

This unit teaches:

- **Art:** Color in painting (e.g., Matisse, Whistler, Rivera, Bruegel, Frankenthaler, Gauguin, Picasso)
- **Science:** Color in nature (e.g., rainbows), the five senses (e.g., seeing color–eyes; hearing rhythm and rhyme–ears)

This unit could be extended to teach:

- **Art:** Color (e.g., the color wheel, warm and cool colors, and primary and secondary colors)
- **Science:** The five senses (e.g., touch–skin; smell–nose; taste–tongue)
- **Math:** Patterns (e.g., rhyming patterns in Mother Goose rhymes)

## Kindergarten, Unit One Sample Lesson Plan

### "Halfway Down" by A. A. Milne

In this series of four lessons, students read "Halfway Down" by A. A. Milne, and they:

Identify the form of the poem (RL.K.5)

Note the connection between form and content (RL.K.1, RL.K.5)

Examine the theme of the poem (RL.K.1)

Explore a different reading interpretation of the poem (RL.K.1, SL.K.2)

Reflect on the power of a poem to provoke thoughts and feelings (SL.K.1a, SL.K.1b)

### Summary

| Lesson I: Meet A. A. Milne and "Halfway Down" | Lesson II: Kermit the Frog Meets Milne |
|---|---|
| Note the form of Milne's "Halfway Down" (RL.K.5) | Examine Kermit the Frog's performance of Milne's poem "Halfway Down" (SL.K.2) |
| Meet A. A. Milne (RL.K.6) | Note the differences between the reading and the singing of the poem (RL.K.1, SL.K.2) |
| Identify repeating sounds in the poem (rhyming) (RF.K.2a) | Evaluate Kermit's interpretation of the poem (SL.K.2) |
| Identify the setting of the poem (RL.K.3) | (Through memorization) develop ownership of Milne's words |
| Probe the shift from the first to the second stanza | |
| Explore what the poem is about (RL.K.1) | |
| Examine the theme of the poem (RL.K.1) | |
| (Through illustrations) individualize response to the theme (W.K.1, W.K.3, SL.K.5) | |

## Lesson III: We Write Along with Milne

Revisit Milne's "Halfway Down" (RL.K.2)

Revisit Kermit's interpretation of the poem (SL.K.2)

(While citing the poem) revisit its rhymes (RF.K.2a)

Explore the purpose of the rhymes (RF.K.2a)

Compose a new stanza (W.K.2)

## Lesson IV: Halfway Down and Halfway Up

Assimilate the varying components of the unit: Milne's poem; Kermit's song; the students' new stanza and the students' illustrated poems

Reflect on the power of a poem to provoke thoughts and feelings

(SL.K.1a, SL.K.1b)

## Lesson I: Meet A. A. Milne and "Halfway Down"

### Objectives

Note the form of Milne's "Halfway Down" (RL.K.5)

Meet A. A. Milne (RL.K.6)

Identify repeating sounds in the poem (rhyming) (RF.K.2a)

Identify the setting of the poem (RL.K.3)

Probe the shift from the first to the second stanza

Explore what the poem is about (RL.K.1)

Examine the theme of the poem (RL.K.1)

(Through illustrations) individualize response to the theme (W.K.1, W.K.3, SL.K.5)

### Required Materials

☐ Enlarged copy of A. A. Milne's "Halfway Down"

☐ Copies of the poem (free of illustrations) to distribute to the students

☐ Markers and colored pencils

### Procedures

1. Lead-In:

a. The purpose of this part of the lesson (even before reading the poem) is to help the students note the form of the poem.

Point to the enlarged copy of A. A. Milne's "Halfway Down."

Ask the students what they notice.

They will note that it is not very long (i.e., they can count the number of words).

Ask if anyone knows what we call this "grouping of words."

If there is no response from the students, introduce the term *poem*.

You may want to hold up a chapter book to help the students visualize the difference between prose and verse.

b. Continue to probe with students (e.g., "What else do you notice about the poem?")

c. Introduce the word *stanza*.

2. Step by Step:

a. Read the poem aloud (at least twice).

## Halfway Down

### A. A. Milne

*Halfway down the stairs*

*Is a stair where I sit.*

*There isn't any other stair*

*Quite like it.*

*I'm not at the bottom,*

*I'm not at the top;*

*So this is the stair*

*Where I always stop.*

*Halfway up the stairs*

*Isn't up and isn't down.*

*It isn't in the nursery,*

*It isn't in the town.*

*And all kinds of funny thoughts*

*Go running round my head:*

*"It isn't really anywhere!*

*It's somewhere else instead!"*

b. Introduce A. A. Milne (this part can be moved up and become activity a.)

For example, produce a poster with Milne's picture and perhaps a picture of Winnie-the-Pooh. This is a good opportunity to connect with some of the students' prior knowledge.

c. Back to the poem.

Read the poem to the students again; at this point, some of the students may join as you point to the words that you read. The purpose of this step is to emphasize rhyme.

Introduce the term *rhyme* through probing and repeating pairs of words (e.g., sit/it, top/stop).

d. Before reading the poem again (with the help of the students), ask the students to notice the difference between the first and the second stanzas. The students will notice the shift from "halfway down" to "halfway up." Through a series of questions, demonstrate the difference between the two stanzas—for example:

*What does the speaker say in the first stanza?*

—The focus is on the speaker; "I" is repeated four times (point to the "I's"); he sits there because it is "halfway down."

*What does he say in the second stanza?*

—There are no "I's." Instead, the speaker pays more attention to the stairs, especially in the first four lines.

*What happens in the last four lines?*

—The speaker refers to himself again, but he makes a confusing statement: "It isn't really anywhere! It's somewhere else instead!"

e. This is a good time to introduce the students to the idea that sometimes you need to think carefully to figure out what a poet is saying. Provide them with time to discuss their ideas.

3. Closure:

A good way to conclude the lesson is to let the students absorb the information and spend some quiet time, on their own, reflecting. Distribute the individual copies of the poem and ask the students to draw upon their reflections to illustrate the poem.

## Differentiation

### Advanced

- Expand the students' exposure to and enjoyment of more Milne poetry, using poems such as "Solitude," "Waiting at the Window," or "Us Two." Discuss the themes of these poems and ask students to illustrate them. A multistanza poem could be cut into stanzas and glued into a book illustrated by the students.

### Struggling

- If there is a staircase in your school, physically take students to the staircase. Have various students experience going halfway up and halfway down the stairs. If a staircase is not available, draw it on the board and have a student finger-walk up the stairs and down the stairs, stopping at the halfway point.

- Spend some time exploring rhyming sounds by doing rhyming word pairs: red/bed, blue/shoe, yellow/fellow, black/sack, brown/clown, white/kite, and so on.

## Homework/Assessment

N/A

# Tell a Story, 1-2-3

In this second six-week unit of kindergarten, students focus on sequence as they enjoy counting books, both fictional and informational, and stories based on three.

---

## ESSENTIAL QUESTION

How are the beginning, the middle, and the end of a story different from each other?

---

## OVERVIEW

Building on the wide exposure to text types in the first unit, students now focus on the sequence of a text: the beginning, middle, and end of a story. They learn to retell rich stories and, by listening to versions of traditional stories, recognize familiar story lines embedded in different settings with different characters. Counting rhymes and reading a number of counting books will continue the first unit's focus on phonological awareness and listening for more rhythm and rhyme, as well as on sequencing. Students study three paintings, which are used for a creative storytelling activity and are related to the idea of multiple versions of a familiar story.

## FOCUS STANDARDS

These Focus Standards have been selected for the unit from the Common Core State Standards.

**RL.K.2:** With prompting and support, retell familiar stories, including key details.

**RL.K.9:** With prompting and support, compare and contrast the adventures and experiences of characters in familiar stories.

**RI.K.1:** With prompting and support, ask and answer questions about key details in a text.

**SL.K.1:** Participate in collaborative conversations with diverse partners about kindergarten topics and texts with peers and adults in small and larger groups.

**SL.K.1(b):** Continue a conversation through multiple exchanges.

**W.K.3:** Use a combination of drawing, dictating, and writing to narrate a single event or several loosely linked events, tell about the events in the order in which they occurred, and provide a reaction to what happened.

**L.K.2:** Demonstrate command of the conventions of standard English capitalization, punctuation, and spelling when writing.

**L.K.2(a):** Capitalize the first word in a sentence and the pronoun I.

## SUGGESTED OBJECTIVES

- Name the author and illustrator of both the fictional and informational texts in this unit.
- Orally retell familiar stories, including details and events at the beginning, middle, and end.
- Recite and produce rhyming words from nursery rhymes and rhyming texts.
- Use a combination of writing, drawing, and dictating to retell stories with a beginning, middle, and end.
- Distinguish shades of meaning among simple adjectives.
- Recognize the importance of sequence in storytelling, informational and fictional counting books, and nursery rhymes.
- Appreciate the difference between an original story and other versions of the same story.

## SUGGESTED WORKS

(E) indicates a CCSS exemplar text; (EA) indicates a text from a writer with other works identified as exemplars.

### LITERARY TEXTS

*Nursery Rhymes (Read Along)*

- "Baa, Baa, Black Sheep"
- "A Diller, a Dollar"
- "Hickory, Dickory, Dock"
- "Hot Cross Buns"
- "Old King Cole"
- "One, Two, Buckle My Shoe"
- "This Little Pig Went to Market"
- "Three Blind Mice"

*Picture Books (Read Aloud)*

- *Anno's Counting Book* (Mitsumasa Anno)
- *Chicka Chicka 1, 2, 3* (Bill Martin Jr., Michael Sampson, and Lois Ehlert)

- *Grandfather Counts* (Andrea Cheng)
- *One Is a Snail, Ten Is a Crab: A Counting by Feet Book* (April Pulley Sayre, Jeff Sayre, and Randy Cecil)
- *Ten Apples Up on Top!* (Dr. Seuss and Roy McKie) (EA)
- *Ten, Nine, Eight* (Molly Bang) (EA)

### Poems (Read Aloud)

- "Mix a Pancake" in *The Complete Poems* (Christina Rossetti) (E)
- "Three Little Kittens" in *The Oxford Illustrated Book of American Children's Poems* (Eliza Lee Follen)
- "Zin! Zin! Zin! A Violin" (Lloyd Moss and Marjorie Priceman) (E)

### Stories (Read Aloud)

- *Goldilocks and the Three Bears* (Jan Brett)
- *Horrible Harry Bugs the Three Bears* (Suzy Kline and Frank Remkiewicz)
- *Pancakes for Breakfast* (Tomie dePaola) (E)

### Stories (Read Along)

- *Ten Black Dots* (Donald Crews) (EA)
- *The Three Billy Goats Gruff* (Paul Galdone)
- *The Three Cabritos* (Eric A. Kimmel and Stephen Gilpin)
- *Three Cool Kids* (Rebecca Emberley)
- *The Three Little Javelinas: Los Tres Pequeños Jabalies* (bilingual) (Susan Lowell)
- *The Three Little Pigs* (James Marshall)
- *The Three Little Wolves and the Big Bad Pig* (Eugene Trivizas and Helen Oxenbury)
- *The Three Pigs* (David Wiesner)
- *The True Story of the Three Little Pigs* (Jon Scieszka and Lane Smith)
- *The Very Hungry Caterpillar* (Eric Carle)

## INFORMATIONAL TEXTS

### Nonfiction Books (Read Aloud)

- *Arlene Alda's 1-2-3: What Do You See?* (Arlene Alda)
- *Beatrice's Goat* (Page McBrier and Lori Lohstoeter)
- *Can You Count Ten Toes? Count to Ten in Ten Different Languages* (Lezlie Evans and Denis Roche)
- *Farm Animals* (Young Nature Series) (Felicity Everett)
- *Goats* (Animals That Live on the Farm) (JoAnn Early Macken)
- *Moja Means One: Swahili Counting Book* (Muriel and Tom Feelings)
- *One Is a Drummer: A Book of Numbers* (Roseanne Thong and Grace Lin)
- *Our Animal Friends at Maple Hill Farm* (Alice and Martin Provensen) (EA)

- *Pigs (Animals That Live on the Farm)* (JoAnn Early Macken)
- *Pigs* (Gail Gibbons) (EA)
- *The Year at Maple Hill Farm* (Alice and Martin Provensen) (E)

## ART, MUSIC, AND MEDIA

*Art*

- Jean-Francois Millet, *First Steps* (1858–1859)
- Pablo Picasso, *Mother and Child (First Steps)* (1943)
- Vincent van Gogh, *First Steps, After Millet* (1890)

# SAMPLE ACTIVITIES AND ASSESSMENTS

Note: Continue work on rhythm and rhyme from Unit One as more of the students show readiness to hear and see rhyming words. (RF.K.2a)

## 1. READING FOUNDATIONS, INFORMATIVE WRITING

Create a counting book using the letters covered so far this year. Each student will choose a favorite letter and then brainstorm words that begin with that letter. Using the numbers 1 through 5 and five different things that begin with the chosen letter, create a book (e.g., A *Counting Book for T*: 1 Tadpole, 2 Turkeys, 3 Toads, 4 Tigers, 5 Trout). Title each student's book *A Counting Book for* _____. Be sure to write the name of the author and illustrator (student) on the cover of the book. Place the finished books in a basket for other students to enjoy. (RF.K.1a, RF.K.1b, RF.K.1c, RF.K.1d, RF.K.3a)

## 2. ART, READING POETRY, SPEAKING AND LISTENING

"Mix a Pancake" is a poem written by Christina Rossetti. Have students draw illustrations that match the words to show the steps in making pancakes. When finished, they can share the illustrations with a friend and read (recite) the poem together. (RL.K.5, RL.K.7, W.K.2)

## 3. READING LITERATURE, LANGUAGE USAGE

Read the traditional version of a story first. Then read a different version of the story. For example, read the Galdone version of "The Three Billy Goats Gruff" and discuss the beginning, middle, and end of the story. Then read one of the other versions, discussing how the beginning, middle, and end are similar, but also how the setting and characters make it a different story. Note how important the varied shades of meaning for action words (verbs) are crucial to each story. (RL.K.9, L.K.5b)

## 4. READING LITERATURE, NARRATIVE WRITING

Using the book of illustrations *Pancakes for Breakfast* by Tomie dePaola, have students look at the illustrations and note how the pictures tell a story. Point out the importance of looking very closely at the details in the illustrations to tell what happens next. Encourage active thinking by asking what might happen when the page is turned to the next illustration. Because this is a wordless book, point out how the illustrator is telling a story without words. Even picture books with words tell a story through the illustrations. Write the students' dictated stories on sentence strips and place them in a pocket chart. Focus on modeling the capital letter required at the beginning of a sentence and the word I. (Extend this activity by reversing this process: read aloud the text of a simple book without showing the illustrations. Ask students to illustrate the story, creating their own wordless book. The students' illustrations can then be compared to the book.) (RL.K.5, RL.K.6, RL.K.7, L.K.2a)

## 5. READING INFORMATIONAL TEXT, RESEARCH

Because pigs and goats are talking characters who have personalities in these stories, students will enjoy reading about real pigs and goats. Beginning with books and digital resources on pigs or goats, keep a chart of animal needs that are met on the farm. Extend this work by writing a class book about real pigs or real goats. Be sure to talk about their needs and how those needs are met on farms. In an effort to pave the way for focused research, you may want to demonstrate the use of key word searches on an Internet browser with an interactive whiteboard or other projection device. (RI.K.1, RI.K.6, W.K.2, W.K.7, W.K.8)

## 6. NARRATIVE WRITING

Ask students to retell the story of Goldilocks and the Three Bears. Tell them to use illustrations, dictating, and/or writing. Tell them to be sure to focus on the beginning, middle, and end of the story by using transitional words (e.g., ordinal numbers: first, second, . . .). You may use paper folded into three sections to help some students organize their ideas for the beginning, middle, and end. Encourage students to include all the characters in the story and to add as many details as they can remember. You may extend this writing activity for advanced students by asking them to write a new version of Goldilocks and the Three Bears. Be sure to have them change the characters and the setting and to illustrate the new story to create a class book. (RL.K.1, RL.K.2, L.K.1a, L.K.1b, L.K.1c, L.K.2a, L.K.5b, W.K.3, W.K.5)

## 7. READING INFORMATIONAL TEXT, SPEAKING AND LISTENING

Tell students, "Today you will have to think, ask questions, and answer questions while we read an informational counting book titled One Is a Drummer: A Book of Numbers by Roseanne Thong and Grace Lin." (RI.K.1, RI.K.6)

## 8. ART, OPINION WRITING

Ask students to choose the painting they like best and to write (or dictate) a sentence saying why they chose that painting as their favorite. Remind them to begin their sentences with capital letters and to put periods at the end. (W.K.1, W.K.3)

## 9. ART, SPEAKING AND LISTENING

To introduce "versions" of a story to your class, use Millet's First Steps as the original "story." Allow the class to study the painting, giving plenty of time to notice details and create a possible story about the painting. Then show them van Gogh's First Steps, After Millet and have the class note how the "original characters are still in the story," but also that it all looks different (e.g., the Millet is in pencil whereas the van Gogh is an oil painting; in the Millet, the people are prominent, whereas in the van Gogh, other elements—such as the gate, the wheelbarrow, and the tree—are also emphasized). Finally, show them Picasso's Mother and Child (First Steps) to see how another artist expressed the same idea in a completely different way. (RL.K.9)

## 10. SPEAKING AND LISTENING, LANGUAGE USAGE

Arrange small groups of students and place an object (e.g., a block) in the middle of the circle. As a class, tell the story of Goldilocks and the Three Bears (perhaps *Goldilocks and the Three Bears* by Jan Brett), having students take turns telling the events in the story. Students pick up the block when ready to fill in part of the story and put the block back in the middle when finished. Encourage the students to identify all the characters and setting, as well as the major events of the story, when retelling. Encourage the students to note the importance of describing words (adjectives) in the telling of the story. For example, note the different ways the characters are described. Storytelling is shared with all the members of the group. (RL.K.2, RL.K.3, SL.K.1a, SL.K.1b, L.K.5b)

## 11. ART, NARRATIVE WRITING

After looking closely at three paintings with the same title, *First Steps*, choose one of the paintings and imagine it shows the beginning of a story. Pair students to create the middle and end of the story to share with the class. Use the following prompt: "Choose one of the paintings and write (or dictate) a sentence telling why you chose that painting as your favorite. Be sure to begin your sentence with a capital letter and put a period at the end." (W.K.1, W.K.3)

## READING FOUNDATIONS: A PACING GUIDE FOR READING INSTRUCTION

See Kindergarten, Level Two, in the Reading Foundations section at the beginning of this book for a complete pacing guide for this unit.

## ADDITIONAL ONLINE RESOURCES

- Interview with Tomie dePaola (RL.K.6)
- *Poetry Portfolios: Using Poetry to Teach Reading* (ReadWriteThink) (RL.K.5)
- Story Kit (free application available from iTunes) (K.W.1, K.W.2, and/or K.W.3)

## TERMINOLOGY

| | | |
|---|---|---|
| Author | Illustrator | Poem |
| Beginning | Middle | Retelling |
| Characters | Number words | Sequence |
| End | Ordinal number words (*first, second, third*) | Storybook |
| Illustration | | Versions |

# INTERDISCIPLINARY CONNECTIONS

This unit teaches:

- **Art:** Millet, van Gogh, Picasso
- **Science:** Farm animals (e.g., pigs and goats; what farm animals need to live)

This unit could be extended to teach:

- **Science:** Animals and their needs (e.g., farm, pet, and wild animals; what animals need to live) or farming (e.g., crops from field to table)

## Kindergarten, Unit Two Sample Lesson Plan

### Pancakes for Breakfast *by Tomie dePaola*

In this series of two lessons, students examine *Pancakes for Breakfast* by Tomie dePaola, and they:

Explore the story behind the illustrations of *Pancakes for Breakfast* (RL.K.7, SL.K.3)

Note the strength of a story that has few words (RL.K.7, SL.K.3)

## Summary

### Lesson I: *Pancakes for Breakfast*—An Introduction

Identify the author/illustrator of *Pancakes for Breakfast* (RL.K.6)

Note the absence of narration in *Pancakes for Breakfast* (RL.K.5, RL.K.7)

Explore the setting of *Pancakes for Breakfast* (RL.K.3, RL.K.7, SL.K.1, SL.K.4)

Tell the story of *Pancakes for Breakfast* (RL.K.1, RL.K.7, SL.K.1)

### Lesson II: *Pancakes for Breakfast*—The Plot

Examine the characteristics of the protagonist of *Pancakes for Breakfast* (RL.K.3)

Identify additional characters in the story (RL.K.3)

Explore the plot of *Pancakes for Breakfast* (RL.K.1, SL.K.1, SL.K.3)

Probe the moral of the story (SL.K.3)

Note the strength of the story despite the presence of only a few words (RL.K.7, SL.K.3)

### Lesson II: *Pancakes for Breakfast*—The Plot

#### Objectives

Examine the characteristics of the protagonist of *Pancakes for Breakfast* (RL.K.3)

Identify additional characters in the story (RL.K.3)

Explore the plot of *Pancakes for Breakfast* (RL.K.1, SL.K.1, SL.K.3)

Probe the moral of the story (SL.K.3)

Note the strength of the story despite the presence of only a few words (RL.K.7, SL.K.3)

*Required Materials*

☐ *Pancakes for Breakfast* by Tomie dePaola

*Procedures*

1. Lead-In:

   Students retell the story of *Pancakes for Breakfast.*

2. Step by Step:

   a. Students reexamine the story's illustrations and describe the protagonist; they notice her looks, her expressions, and her actions.

   b. Students note the role of the cat and the dog in the story.

   c. In a class discussion, with the help of your probes, students identify the story's introduction, the development of its plot, and its conclusion.

   d. Students discuss the moral of the story: "If at first you don't succeed, try, try again."

3. Closure:

   Students evaluate the illustrator's ability to tell a story without words.

Differentiation

*Advanced*

- A small group of students could create a story to accompany the illustrations. After deciding on a sound to indicate to a reader to turn the page, students could record their story on a digital recording device.

*Struggling*

- Before introducing this book to the class, make pancakes from scratch in the classroom. As you are making the pancakes with the students, discuss the verbs related to cooking, such as "mixing," "stirring," "blending," and "cracking." Be sure that the students understand the process of making a pancake, from mixing the batter to pouring the syrup onto the pancake. Incorporate the phrase, "Try, try again" if there is any difficulty with cracking an egg or flipping the pancake.

Homework/Assessment

N/A

# Exploring with Friends in the Neighborhood

In this third six-week unit of kindergarten, students explore fictional characters in literary texts and neighborhoods in informational texts.

## ESSENTIAL QUESTION

How is reading like exploring?

## OVERVIEW

Building on basic retelling of a familiar story, this unit focuses on introducing the differences between literary and informational texts (though not necessarily by name). Students explore characters, settings, and events in both literary and informational texts by asking questions about unknown words, characters, settings, and events. Students compare the first *Little Bear* adventure with other stories in the book. As they read stories of other characters, as in *Frog and Toad Together*, students extend their skills of comparing and contrasting. *Winnie-the-Pooh* provides the context for students to learn to ask questions when they lose their way in following the story or in understanding Pooh's special language, such as the made-up word "expotition." The informational texts offer a comparable opportunity for students to ask questions about real people in their communities, such as firefighters and police officers.

## FOCUS STANDARDS

These Focus Standards have been selected for the unit from the Common Core State Standards.

**RL.K.3:** With prompting and support, identify characters, settings, and major events in a story.

**RL.K.4:** Ask and answer questions about unknown words in a text.

**RL.K.9:** With prompting and support, compare and contrast the adventures and experiences of characters in familiar stories.

**RI.K.2:** With prompting and support, identify the main topic and retell key details of a text.

**W.K.2:** Use a combination of drawing, dictating, and writing to compose informative/explanatory texts in which they name what they are writing about and supply some information about the topic.

**L.K.1:** Demonstrate command of the conventions of standard English grammar and usage when writing or speaking.

**L.K.1(d):** Understand and use question words (interrogatives) (e.g., *who, what, where, when, why, how*).

## SUGGESTED OBJECTIVES

- Use the words *who, what, where, when,* and *why* to explore informational texts.
- Ask questions about unknown words in both fictional and informational texts.
- Locate basic information in a nonfiction text.
- Identify characters, settings, and key events in a story.
- Compare and contrast the adventures of one character in a collection of stories.
- Compare and contrast the adventures of different characters in different books through the use of a graphic organizer.
- Understand the difference between real (nonfiction) and imagined (fiction) explorations.
- Use a combination of drawing, dictating, or writing to compose an informative text.
- Name and identify periods, question marks, and exclamation points.
- Understand and correctly use the prepositions *to/from, on/off,* and *in/out.*

## SUGGESTED WORKS

(E) indicates a CCSS exemplar text; (EA) indicates a text from a writer with other works identified as exemplars.

### LITERARY TEXTS

*Picture Books (Read Aloud)*
- *Blueberries for Sal* (Robert McCloskey)
- *The Complete Tales of Winnie-the-Pooh* (A. A. Milne) (EA)
- *Curious George* (series) (H. A. and Margret Rey)
- *Frog and Toad Together* (Arnold Lobel) (E)
- *Harold and the Purple Crayon* (Crockett Johnson)
- *The Jolly Postman* (Allan and Janet Ahlberg)
- *Knuffle Bunny: A Cautionary Tale* (Mo Willems)
- *Little Bear* (series) (Else Holmelund Minarik and Maurice Sendak) (E)
- *Little Fur Family* (Margaret Wise Brown and Garth Williams)
- *Make Way for Ducklings* (Robert McCloskey)

- *Margaret and Margarita: Margarita y Margaret* (Lynn Reiser)
- *Officer Buckle and Gloria* (Peggy Rathmann)
- *Owl Moon* (Jane Yolen and John Schoenherr)
- *The Snowy Day* (Ezra Jack Keats)
- *The Story About Ping* (Marjorie Flack and Kurt Wiese)
- *Where the Wild Things Are* (Maurice Sendak)

## Poems (Read Aloud)

- "The Swing" in *A Child's Garden of Verses* (Robert Louis Stevenson)
- "Us Two" in *The Complete Tales and Poems of Winnie-the-Pooh* (A. A. Milne) (EA)

## Stories (Read Along, Wordless Books)

- *A Dog, a Boy, and a Frog* (Mercer Mayer) (E)
- *Trainstop* (Barbara Lehman)

# INFORMATIONAL TEXTS

## Nonfiction Books (Read Aloud)

- *Check It Out! The Book About Libraries* (Gail Gibbons) (EA)
- *Community Helpers from A to Z* (Bobbie Kalman and Niki Walker)
- *A Day in the Life of a Doctor* (First Facts: Community Helpers at Work) (Heather Adamson)
- *A Day in the Life of a Firefighter* (First Facts: Community Helpers at Work) (Heather Adamson)
- *A Day in the Life of a Police Officer* (First Facts: Community Helpers at Work) (Heather Adamson)
- *A Day in the Life of a Teacher* (First Facts: Community Helpers at Work) (Heather Adamson)
- *Fire! Fire!* (Gail Gibbons) (E)
- *Jobs Around My Neighborhood: Oficios en mi vecindario* (Gladys Rosa-Mendoza and Ann Iosa)
- *The Post Office Book: Mail and How It Moves* (Gail Gibbons) (EA)
- *Whose Hat Is This?* (Katz Cooper, Sharon Muehlenhardt, and Amy Bailey)
- *Whose Tools Are These?* (Katz Cooper, Sharon Muehlenhardt, and Amy Bailey)

# ART, MUSIC, AND MEDIA

## Art

- Romare Bearden, *The Block* (1972)
- Pieter Bruegel, *Netherlandish Proverbs* (1559)

## Music

- "Do You Know the Muffin Man?"
- "What Shall We Do When We All Go Out?"
- Camille Saint-Saëns, *Carnival of the Animals*, fifth movement, "The Elephant" (1886)
- Henry Mancini, "Baby Elephant Walk" (1961)
- Jeff Moss, "The People in Your Neighborhood"

## SAMPLE ACTIVITIES AND ASSESSMENTS

### 1. READING POETRY, ART, PERFORMANCE

Read a poem such as "The Swing" by Robert Louis Stevenson. Assign the students the task of drawing an illustration for each stanza of the poem. Do the same activity with other poems, such as "Us Two" by A. A. Milne. Using key words such as *who, what, where, why, when,* and *how,* compare and contrast the two poems. Encourage the children to work on the recitation of their favorite poem. (RL.K.9, L.K.1d)

### 2. MUSIC, SPEAKING AND LISTENING

As a musical illustration of comparing and contrasting, use the work of Henry Mancini ("Baby Elephant Walk") and Saint-Saëns (*Carnival of the Animals,* "The Elephant") to compare and contrast two musical compositions that are inspired by elephants. Introduce the activity by telling the students that they are going to hear two different musical pieces that are based on elephants. As they listen to "Baby Elephant Walk" and "The Elephant," ask them to decide which piece reminds them more of an elephant. Extend this activity by having the students move to the music as they listen, deciding whether the music makes them want to dance or lumber like elephants. (L.K.5d, RL.K.9)

### 3. INFORMATIVE WRITING

Tell students, "Write about a community helper in your neighborhood. Be sure to name the community helper and to tell what she/he does to help the community." (For example, "A trash collector picks up stinky garbage all over our city and takes it to the dump.") (W.K.2, L.K.1a, L.K.2a, L.K.2b, L.K.2c, L.K.5c)

### 4. READING LITERATURE, READING COMPREHENSION

After reading the first story in the *Little Bear* collection of stories by Else Holmelund Minarik, use a chart to organize ideas about each of the three stories. Remind students of the *who, what,* and *where* questions to be answered. Create headings for Character, Setting, and Events. Assign students one of the three categories to think about each time you read, encouraging them to write or draw ideas on sticky notes. Fill in the chart each time you read a new *Little Bear* story. (*Extension:* Create a similar chart to compare other fictional explorations and adventures by characters such as Frog and Toad, Curious George, and more.) (RL.K.3, RL.K.9)

### 5. ART, NARRATIVE WRITING, SPEAKING AND LISTENING

Assign students a section from *Netherlandish Proverbs* to work with. Ask them to study it closely. Partner the students to compose one sentence describing what the people seem to be doing or who they might be. Have students share their sentences with the whole group. (W.K.1, W.K.3)

### 6. READING LITERATURE, READING COMPREHENSION

Read *Winnie-the-Pooh* by A. A. Milne aloud to check for student understanding. To be sure that students are following the story and understanding the words, encourage them to monitor their own comprehension. Tell the children that if they lose their way or a word is confusing them, they should put a hand on their own shoulder. If you see a student do so, stop reading at a good stopping place, reread the confusing section, and allow other students to participate in clearing up the confusion. (RL.K.4)

## 7. SPEAKING AND LISTENING, LANGUAGE USAGE

Tell the students that they are going to practice giving and following directions. Create directions that focus on using prepositions, such as *to/from*, *on/off*, and *in/out*. Pull a child's name out of a basket and then give him or her a command. For example, "Tian, walk *from* your desk *to* the teacher's desk." "Jaxton, put your hand *in* the basket and then take it *out*." Extend this activity by placing the prepositions on cards and having the students make up directions using the words. You could also play the game of "Simon Says" as you give the commands. As students develop confidence, increase the commands by two or three additional steps. (L.K.1e)

## 8. READING INFORMATIONAL TEXT, SPEAKING AND LISTENING

Using two books that describe different jobs but are in the same series of informational books (such as the *Community Helpers at Work* series), create a graphic organizer to compare and contrast the days of various community helpers. Discuss the ways the jobs are similar and different. Require each student to dictate, draw, write, or act out something one of the community helpers does (e.g., a postal worker weighs packages). Ask if the other community helper does something similar (e.g., a nurse weighs patients). (RI.K.2, RI.K.9)

## 9. ART, SPEAKING AND LISTENING

View Bearden's collage. Note that the work is four feet high and eighteen feet long. Compare that to the size of a wall in the classroom. Try to get the students to look at the collage for as long as possible. The following questions will help guide a fifteen-minute discussion: What do you notice first in this collage and why? Where do you think this might be? What do you see that makes it look like this place? How did Bearden make the buildings look different (e.g., color and texture)? Do you notice any people? (SL.K.1, SL.K.2, SL.K.4, SL.K.5, SL.K.6)

## 10. READING INFORMATIONAL TEXT, SPEAKING AND LISTENING

While reading informational books about community helpers, create a chart with the following headings: Who, What, Where, When, and Why. Encourage children to listen for answers to those questions as you read the book aloud. Remind the students to pay close attention to the illustrations for details. To ensure each child's participation, give them sticky notes or whiteboards on which to write or draw their ideas. Begin by talking about the author, illustrator, and front, back, and title page of the book. Fill in the chart each time you read a new book about community helpers. Use this chart as inspiration to change the lyrics for "Do You Know the Muffin Man?" for community helpers in your neighborhood (e.g., "Do you know the fireman . . . That works on 12th and Main!"). (RI.K.1, RI.K.2, RI.K.5, RI.K.7, L.K.1d, SL.K.1, SL.K.3, SL.K.4)

## 11. ART, SPEAKING AND LISTENING

Display the Bearden and Bruegel pieces side by side. Note that these works were created more than four hundred years apart. Ask the students to find similarities and differences between the two works. Which place seems like a real place, and which one seems more like a dream or fantasy? Document the answers on a chart for future discussion. (SL.K.1, SL.K.2, SL.K.4, SL.K.5, SL.K.6)

## READING FOUNDATIONS: A PACING GUIDE FOR READING INSTRUCTION

See Kindergarten, Level Three, in the Reading Foundations section at the beginning of this book for a complete pacing guide for this unit.

## ADDITIONAL ONLINE RESOURCES

- *Imagination or Observation: Frog and Toad Are Friends* (Indiana Department of Education) (RL.K.5)
- Explore the "Make Way for Ducklings" statue in Boston Public Garden

## TERMINOLOGY

| | | |
|---|---|---|
| Character | Imaginary | What |
| Compare | Key events | When |
| Contrast | Nonfiction | Where |
| Exclamation mark | Question mark | Who |
| Fantasy | Questioning | Why |
| Fiction | Real | |
| How | Setting | |

## INTERDISCIPLINARY CONNECTIONS

This unit teaches:
- **Music:** *Carnival of the Animals*, fifth movement, "The Elephant" (Camille Saint-Saëns); elements of music (e.g., moving responsively to music)
- **Social studies:** Community helpers (e.g., wide range of careers)
- **Geography:** Community (i.e., town, city, or community)

This unit could be extended to teach:
- **Music:** *Carnival of the Animals*, movements one through fourteen (Camille Saint-Saens) (e.g., recognizing the instruments within the performance); elements of music (e.g., fast/slow, high/low, and loud/quiet)
- **Science:** The human body (e.g., focus on the medical field through health of your body: exercise, cleanliness, healthy foods, rest, and dental care)
- **Geography:** Locate continent, country, and state where the community is located

## Kindergarten, Unit Three Sample Lesson Plan

### Frog and Toad Together *by Arnold Lobel*

In this series of six lessons, students read *Frog and Toad Together* by Arnold Lobel, and they:

Explore the adventures of the two characters, Frog and Toad (RL.K.1, RL.K.2, RL.K.3, SL.K.2)

Identify the differences between the two characters (RL.K.1, RL.K.2, RL.K.3)

Examine the relationship between Frog and Toad (RL.K.1, RL.K.3)

Note the author's use of humor (RL.K.1)

Imagine and share new adventures of Frog and Toad (W.K.1, W.K.2, W.K.3, SL.K.5, SL.K.6)

## Summary

### Lesson I: "A List"

Examine the book cover and identify the two leading characters in the book (RL.K.2)

(Together) spell out their names (RF.K.3)

Note their activity (RL.K.2, RL.K.7, SL.K.2)

Become aware of the author/illustrator's name (RL.K.5, RL.K.6)

Note the purpose of "Contents" and list the five stories in the book (RL.K.5)

(After listening to you reading the story "A List") list all the facts that they have learned about Frog and Toad (RL.K.1, RL.K.2, SL.K.2)

Ponder the ways that Frog and Toad demonstrate their friendship (RL.K.3)

### Lesson II: "The Garden"

Recall details about Frog and Toad from "A List" (RL.K.2, SL.K.2)

(After listening to "The Garden") recall the story's events (RL.K.1, RL.K.2, RL.K.3)

Examine Lobel's illustrations (RL.K.7)

Explore Toad's dedication to his garden (RL.K.1, RL.K.2, RL.K.3)

Note Frog's support of Toad's efforts (RL.K.1, RL.K.2, RL.K.3)

## Lesson III: "Cookies"

Explore the details of Frog and Toad's friendship so far (RL.K.1, RL.K.2, RL.K.3)

(After listening to "Cookies") revisit the term *willpower* and examine its use in the story (RL.K.1, RL.K.2, RL.K.3)

Determine if Frog and Toad are successful in their attempts to exercise willpower (RL.K.1, RL.K.2, RL.K.3, SL.K.1)

Revisit the ending of the story and discuss Toad's statement: "I am going home now to bake a cake." (RL.K.1, RL.K.2, RL.K.3)

## Lesson V: "The Dream"

Consider how this story is different from the others (RL.K.1, RL.K.2, RL.K.3)

Explore Lobel's use of the dream (RL.K.1, RL.K.2, RL.K.3)

Note the purpose of Lobel's use of capital letters

Examine the different expressions on Toad's face (RL.K.7)

Explore what one learns about Frog when he tells Toad: "I always do." (RL.K.1, RL.K.2, RL.K.3)

## Lesson IV: "Dragons and Giants"

Note the way that the story begins when Toad says: "The people in this story are brave." (RL.K.1)

(After listening to "Dragons and Giants") consider whether Frog and Toad are brave (RL.K.1, RL.K.2, RL.K.3)

Determine if their friendship helps them when they try to be brave (RL.K.3)

Discuss the humor in the story (RL.K.1)

Recall other humorous moments in the previous stories (RL.K.1)

## Lesson VI: Our Own Stories

Revisit Frog and Toad and list the lessons that they have learned (RL.K.1, RL.K.2, RL.K.3, RF.K.3)

Explore the details that show they are friends (RL.K.1, RL.K.2, RL.K.3)

Imagine new adventures for the two characters (SL.K.6)

Translate the new adventure into illustrations (W.K.1, W.K.2, W.K.3)

Share Frog and Toad's new adventures (SL.K.5, SL.K.6)

## Lesson VI: Our Own Stories
### *Objectives*

Revisit Frog and Toad and list the lessons that they have learned (RL.K.1, RL.K.2, RL.K.3)

Explore the details that show they are friends (RL.K.1, RL.K.2, RL.K.3)

Imagine new adventures for the two characters (SL.K.6)

Translate the new adventures into illustrations (W.K.1, W.K.2, W.K.3)

Share Frog and Toad's new adventures (SL.K.5, SL.K.6)

*Required Materials*

☐ *Frog and Toad Together* by Arnold Lobel

☐ Markers

☐ Drawing paper

*Procedures*

1. Lead-In:

   Students take turns discussing:

   ○ The plot of each of the five stories

   ○ The characteristics of Frog and Toad

   ○ The nature of their friendship

2. Step by Step:

   a. Imagining new adventures. Students (either individually, in groups, or with the entire class) invent new adventures for Frog and Toad. Students consider what they already know about the two characters.

   b. Students draw pictures of the new adventures of Frog and Toad, labeling the characters' names.

   c. While the students work, they explain their choices, drawing upon their familiarity with the two characters.

   d. Students may share their ideas with their neighbors while they work.

   e. Display the students' work.

   f. Students share the details of their stories and answer questions from their peers.

3. Closure:

   At the conclusion of the lesson, offer specific details regarding the students' work. Point to the students' ability to

   ○ Understand what a plot is

   ○ Differentiate between the two characters

   ○ Apply their understanding as they imagine new adventures

   ○ Describe the stories that they drew

## Differentiation

### Advanced

- Students will create a graphic organizer (such as a Venn diagram or digital organizer that compares and contrasts the two characters, Frog and Toad).

### Struggling

- Students will first act out one of the stories previously read in the unit, showing the difference between the two characters, Frog and Toad, and demonstrating their understanding of the beginning, middle, and end of the story. You will then present a new situation for Frog and Toad. In a small group, students will discuss a story plot and act out the story.

## Homework/Assessment

N/A

# America: Symbols and Celebrations

In this fourth six-week unit of kindergarten, students explore America's symbols and celebrations through literary and informational texts; they begin to write informative/explanatory pieces.

## ESSENTIAL QUESTION

Why are symbols important?

## OVERVIEW

Building on asking questions about neighborhoods, students begin this unit by asking questions about a local symbol. They progress to asking questions for more detailed information in nonfiction texts. Students learn to write informative pieces with richer content. Through shared writing, students also learn to expand complete sentences by using more details about American symbols. To be sure that the content resonates with the children, celebrations from each student's own ethnicity or religion will be encouraged as part of the information gathering.

## FOCUS STANDARDS

These Focus Standards have been selected for the unit from the Common Core State Standards.

**RI.K.1:** With prompting and support, ask and answer questions about key details in a text.

**W.K.7:** Participate in shared research and writing projects (e.g., explore a number of books by a favorite author and express opinions about them).

**L.K.1:** Demonstrate command of the conventions of standard English grammar and usage when writing or speaking.

**L.K.1(f):** Produce and expand complete sentences in shared language activities.

**L.K.2:** Demonstrate command of the conventions of standard English capitalization, punctuation, and spelling when writing.

**L.K.2(d):** Spell simple words phonetically, drawing on knowledge of sound-letter relationships.

**SL.K.4:** Describe familiar people, places, things, and events and, with prompting and support, provide additional detail.

## SUGGESTED OBJECTIVES

- Describe the connection between two events or ideas in a text.
- Recognize cause-and-effect relationships (e.g., the contributions of Martin Luther King Jr. and the holiday celebrating his life).
- Review characters, setting, and key events in fictional stories when retelling them.
- Answer questions about unknown words, details, and events in both fiction and informational texts.
- Gather information from text sources and experiences to answer questions about a given topic (e.g., about holidays).
- Use a combination of drawing, dictating, and writing to compose an informative text on a given topic (e.g., about holidays).
- Ask questions to get information, to seek help, or to clarify something that is not understood.
- Produce and expand complete sentences in shared writing about a given topic (e.g., symbols in America).
- Identify new meanings for familiar words and apply them accurately (e.g., march—verb; March—month; march—musical piece).
- Use newly learned words in conversation (e.g., new words related to celebrations and symbols).

## SUGGESTED WORKS

(E) indicates a CCSS exemplar text; (EA) indicates a text from a writer with other works identified as exemplars.

### LITERARY TEXTS

*Picture Books (Read Aloud)*

- *America the Beautiful* (Katharine Bates and Wendell Minor)
- *Apple Pie and the Fourth of July* (Janet S. Wong and Margaret Chodos-Irvine) (Note: Tailor to represent the cultures in your classroom.)
- *Clifford Goes to Washington* (Norman Bridwell)
- *Duck for President* (Doreen Cronin and Betsy Lewin)
- *Family Pictures/Cuadros de familia* (Carmen Lomas Garza) (E) (Note: Tailor to represent the cultures in your classroom.)
- *I Pledge Allegiance* (Bill Martin Jr., Michael Sampson, and Chris Raschka)

- *My Country, 'Tis of Thee* (Samuel Francis Smith)
- *Pledge of Allegiance* (Scholastic, Inc.)
- *This Land Is Your Land* (Woody Guthrie and Kathy Jakobsen)

## Poems (Read Aloud)

- "Celebration" in *Song and Dance* (Alonzo Lopez) (E)
- *I Am America* (Charles R. Smith) (selections)
- "Thanksgiving Day" in *Flowers for Children*, Vol. 2 (Lydia Maria Child)

## INFORMATIONAL TEXTS

### Nonfiction Books (Read Aloud)

- *The American Flag* (Welcome Books) (Lloyd G. Douglas)
- *The Bald Eagle* (Welcome Books) (Lloyd G. Douglas)
- *Chanukah* (Rookie Read-About Holiday Series) (David F. Marx)
- *Chinese New Year* (Rookie Read-About Holiday Series) (David F. Marx)
- *Christmas* (Rookie Read-About Holiday Series) (Trudi Strain Trueit)
- *Cinco de Mayo* (Rookie Read-About Holiday Series) (Mary Dodson Wade and Nanci R. Vargus)
- *Diwali* (Rookie Read-About Holiday Series) (Trudi Strain Trueit)
- *El Dia de los Muertos: The Day of the Dead* (Rookie Read-About Holiday Series) (Mary Dodson Wade)
- *Giving Thanks: The 1621 Harvest Feast* (Kate Waters and Russ Kendall)
- *Independence Day* (Rookie Read-About Holiday Series) (Trudi Strain Trueit)
- *In Our Country* (Emergent Reader) (Susan Canizares and S. Berger)
- *John Philip Sousa: Getting to Know the World's Greatest Composers* (Mike Venezia)
- *Kwanzaa* (Rookie Read-About Holiday Series) (Trudi Strain Trueit)
- *The Liberty Bell* (Welcome Books) (Lloyd G. Douglas)
- *Martin Luther King Jr. Day* (Rookie Read-About Holiday Series) (Trudi Strain Trueit)
- *Ramadan* (Rookie Read-About Holiday Series) (David F. Marx)
- *The Statue of Liberty* (Welcome Books) (Lloyd G. Douglas)
- *Veterans Day* (Rookie Read-About Holiday Series) (Jacqueline S. Cotton)
- *The White House* (Welcome Books) (Lloyd G. Douglas)

## ART, MUSIC, AND MEDIA

### Music

- George M. Cohan, "You're a Grand Old Flag" (1906)
- John Philip Sousa, "Stars and Stripes Forever" (1896)
- John Philip Sousa, "The Liberty Bell" (1893)

- John Philip Sousa, "The Washington Post" (1889)
- Katharine Lee Bates and Samuel A. Ward, "America the Beautiful"
- Samuel Francis Smith, "America (My Country, 'Tis of Thee)"
- Traditional, "Yankee Doodle"

## SAMPLE ACTIVITIES AND ASSESSMENTS

### 1. INFORMATIVE WRITING

Use the following prompt to direct students to communicate research findings: "Write an informative/explanatory piece about a symbol or holiday from our class research (KWL chart). Write about the symbol or holiday and what it means. Be sure to use the information on your chart as you write. Illustrate your ideas before you write or after you are finished." (W.K.2, W.K.8, SL.K.5, L.K.1a, L.K.2d)

### 2. SPEAKING AND LISTENING

Send a note to parents asking them to find a photograph of the child taken during a family celebration. Ask parents to name the celebration and to tell what makes it special as their family celebrates it. Use this information to create a display of your class's celebrations and to prepare for the shared research project on community celebrations. Scanning the holiday photographs digitally or receiving them in a digital format would enable a slide show presentation (such as PowerPoint) to accompany the sharing time. (SL.K.4, W.K.8)

### 3. LANGUAGE USAGE, VOCABULARY

Create a word bank to collect new words from this unit. These words can be used in discussion and in journal writing to reinforce their proper use. Use the word bank to practice making nouns plural (e.g., statue, statues). (L.K.1b, L.K.1c, L.K.6)

### 4. LANGUAGE USAGE, VOCABULARY

Tell the students that there are words that are spelled the same and sound the same, but have very different meanings. Listen to John Philip Sousa's music and "march" around the room. Explain that in this case, "march" is an action word. The name of this type of song is a "march," because you want to march to it. And you could even do this "march" in the month of "March." The lesson: some words are used differently to mean different things. This activity can be repeated with the word *flag*, using the word as a verb and as a noun. (L.K.1b, L.K.4a, L.K.5d)

### 5. VOCABULARY, SPEAKING AND LISTENING

To introduce the concept of a symbol, choose a symbol well known to the students in your class (e.g., professional sports team logo or school mascot). Discuss why a symbol is important for unifying fans behind a team or school. Go on to discuss the meaning behind the symbol as a source of inspiration. Learning (reciting) the lyrics to the songs featured in this unit will reinforce the inspiration drawn from common songs as symbols. (RI.K.4, SL.K.2, SL.K.3, SL.K.4, L.K.4, L.K.6)

## 6. LANGUAGE USAGE, INFORMATIVE WRITING

Use a theme-related short sentence to begin your unit, such as "The flag waves." Challenge the class to think of details to add to the sentence to make it more interesting (e.g., "The red, white, and blue flag waves"; "The red, white, and blue American flag waves in the strong winds of March"). (W.K.5, L.K.1b, L.K.1c, L.K.1f, L.K.5b)

## 7. READING INFORMATIONAL TEXT, RESEARCH

Create a KWL chart for American symbols and holidays to set the stage for asking questions, answering questions, and gathering information about the main topics. You may need to model the questioning until the students begin to generate research questions on their own. As the class reads an informational book (e.g., *The Liberty Bell* by Lloyd G. Douglas), gather information about the main topic, noting text features of an informational text, such as photographs or text boxes. Remind the students of the importance of also studying illustrations for information. Add the information to the KWL chart. Look for connections between ideas as you add information to the charts. Use sticky notes or whiteboards for students to fully participate in adding information to the charts. (RI.K.1, RI.K.2, RI.K.3, RI.K.7, RI.K.8)

## 8. RESEARCH, INFORMATIVE WRITING

Choose a holiday celebrated in your community. Gather information about the holiday by reading books and asking people in your community to tell you why it is celebrated, when it is celebrated, who celebrates it, and how it is celebrated. Create a large cube for the holiday and assign small groups of students to prepare an illustration for each face of the cube. Use the guiding questions and details from the text that answer the questions to assign the faces of the cube. Repeat this activity with several holidays celebrated by the members of your classroom. Extend this work with the following writing task to communicate findings: "After researching a community holiday and creating an information cube, write a class book about the holiday and illustrate each page." (SL.K.4, L.K.5c, W.K.2, W.K.7, W.K.8)

## 9. READING LITERATURE, READING COMPREHENSION, SPEAKING AND LISTENING

Introduce a book showing a diverse viewpoint of an American holiday, such as *Apple Pie and the Fourth of July* by Janet Wong and Margaret Chodos-Irvine. As you read the book, ask the students to look for ways that the main character sees one of the traditional American holidays. Encourage the students to look closely at the illustrations and to listen closely to the story. When you are finished reading, ask students to discuss how people see holidays and celebrations differently, depending on their family and ethnic experience. Before turning to whole-group discussion, have students draw a picture or "turn and talk" in preparation for sharing ideas. Pay particular attention to whether the students confirm understanding of what they have read. Encourage listeners to ask relevant questions and speakers to answer them carefully. (RL.K.3, RL.K.7, RL.K.10, SL.K.1, SL.K.2, SL.K.3)

## READING FOUNDATIONS: A PACING GUIDE FOR READING INSTRUCTION

See Kindergarten, Level Four, in the Reading Foundations section at the beginning of this book for a complete pacing guide for this unit.

## ADDITIONAL ONLINE RESOURCES

- *Martin Luther King Jr. and Me: Identifying with a Hero* (ReadWriteThink) (W.K.7, W.K.8)
- KWL chart (Reading Quest.org)

## TERMINOLOGY

| | | |
|---|---|---|
| Cause | Informational text | Symbol |
| Composer | KWL chart | |
| Effect | Questioning | |

## INTERDISCIPLINARY CONNECTIONS

This unit teaches:

- **Music:** Patriotic songs (e.g., "America the Beautiful," "America [My Country, 'Tis of Thee]," "Yankee Doodle," "You're a Grand Old Flag"); band music (e.g., marches of John Philip Sousa)
- **Geography:** United States
- **History:** Celebrations of diversity (e.g., Chinese New Year, Cinco de Mayo, Kwanzaa, Chanukah, and Christmas)

This unit could be extended to teach:

- **Art:** Sculpture
- **History:** Native Americans (e.g., a tribe or nation located near your students compared/contrasted to a tribe or nation farther away); voyages of Christopher Columbus; presidents, past and present

## Kindergarten, Unit Four Sample Lesson Plan

### Family Pictures by Carmen Lomas Garza

In this series of three lessons, students read *Family Pictures* by Carmen Lomas Garza, and they:

Explore the stories of Carmen Lomas Garza (RL.K1, RL.K2, RL.K.3)

Generate their own families' stories (W.K.3, W.K.5, W.K.8, SL.K.4, SL.K.5)

Interpret the stories through illustrations (RL.K.7, SL.K.3)

Share their stories (SL.K.6)

### Summary

#### Lesson I: Family Pictures

Examine the family pictures of Carmen Lomas Garza (RL.K.7)

Identify the themes of Garza's pictures (RL.K.7, SL.K.3)

Notice Garza's use of details (RL.K.2)

Explore the power of pictures to depict family events (SL.K.3)

#### Lesson III: Telling Our Families' Stories

Introduce personal stories (SL.K.4, SL.K.6)

Explore classmates' stories (SL.K.1, SL.K.3)

Evaluate the experience (SL.K.1)

#### Lesson II: Our Family Pictures

Revisit Garza's family stories (RL.K.1, RL.K.2, RL.K.3, RL.K.7, SL.K.3)

Generate ideas for their own families' stories (W.K.3, W.K.8)

Explore the details of the stories (W.K.5, SL.K.4)

Interpret the stories through illustrations (W.K.3, SL.K.4, SL.K.5)

## Lesson II: Our Family Pictures

### Objectives

Revisit Garza's family stories (RL.K.1, RL.K.2, RL.K.3, RL.K.7, SL.K.3)

Generate ideas for their own families' stories (W.K.3, W.K.8)

Explore the details of the stories (W.K.5, SL.K.4)

Interpret the stories through illustrations (W.K.3, SL.K.4, SL.K.5)

### Required Materials

☐ Class set of *Family Pictures* by Carmen Lomas Garza

☐ Drawing paper

☐ Pencils and markers

### Procedures

1. Lead-In:

   Revisit Garza's pictures.

2. Step by Step:

   a. In small groups, the students begin to share family stories.

   b. The students select a specific story to tell and begin to think of the details of the event. Some may choose to look at one of Garza's pictures for help. For example, the picture titled "Oranges" includes the tree, a boy in the tree, and the oranges and the leaves. Such an exploration will help the students grasp the meaning of the type of details that they may choose to include in their pictures.

   c. The students draw their families' pictures.

3. Closure:

   With your assistance, students will prepare an exhibition of their pictures.

## Differentiation

### Advanced

- Students will write a narrative including all of the details in their illustration.
- Students will choose one of the Garza illustrations to compare and contrast with their illustration.

### Struggling

- Using key question prompts such as *who*, *what*, *where*, *why*, and *when*, work with the students to elicit their understanding of key details in the story.
- To enhance vocabulary, make a copy of the student's illustration and label all of the details, enabling a stronger retelling of the story during the sharing time. Work with students on learning each detail in the illustration.

## Homework/Assessment

N/A

# The Great Big World

In this fifth six-week unit of kindergarten, students focus on the difference a setting can make in the creation of a story.

---

## ESSENTIAL QUESTION

Why is it important for writers to describe settings carefully?

---

## OVERVIEW

Building on the diversity of family celebrations, students read about the greater world beyond America. By reading *Mr. Popper's Penguins*, students are lured into dreaming of faraway places. Focusing on the pairing of fiction and informational text, students see how fictional settings can reflect real places. By using an atlas, nonfiction books, video, and interactive online media, students also see how different types of texts give us similar and different information. During these activities, students write words using what they know about vowel sounds, beginning and ending sounds, and word families. Viewing landscapes by master painters reinforces the concept of comparing and contrasting settings.

## FOCUS STANDARDS

These Focus Standards have been selected for the unit from the Common Core State Standards.

**RL.K.3:** With prompting and support, identify characters, settings, and major events in a story.

**RL.K.9:** With prompting and support, compare and contrast the adventures and experiences of characters in familiar stories.

**RI.K.9:** With prompting and support, identify basic similarities in and differences between two texts on the same topic (e.g., in illustrations, descriptions, or procedures).

**W.K.6:** With guidance and support from adults, explore a variety of digital tools to produce and publish writing, including in collaboration with peers.

**W.K.8:** With guidance and support from adults, recall information from experiences or gather information from provided sources to answer a question.

**L.K.2:** Demonstrate command of the conventions of standard English capitalization, punctuation, and spelling when writing.

**L.K.2(d):** Spell simple words phonetically, drawing on knowledge of sound-letter relationships.

## SUGGESTED OBJECTIVES

- Describe the connection between the settings of fictional works and informational books about the same place.
- Learn about the similarities and differences between fictional and informational texts on the same topic.
- Compare and contrast characters' adventures that are set in different continents.
- Use a combination of drawing, dictating, and writing to offer an opinion (e.g., about a continent to visit); include details that explain/support the opinion.
- Demonstrate understanding of common verbs and adjectives by relating them to their opposites (e.g., in the context of describing places).

## SUGGESTED WORKS

(E) indicates a CCSS exemplar text; (EA) indicates a text from a writer with other works identified as exemplars.

### LITERARY TEXTS

*Picture Books (Read Aloud)*
- *Mr. Popper's Penguins* (Richard Atwater and Florence Atwater) (E)

*Africa*
- *Shadow* (Blaise Cendrars, translated by Marcia Brown)
- *A Story, a Story* (Gail E. Haley) (E)
- *Why Mosquitoes Buzz in People's Ears* (Verna Aardema, Leo Dillon, and Diane Dillon)

*Antarctica*
- *Eve of the Emperor Penguin* (Mary Pope Osborne and Sal Murdocca)
- *Something to Tell the Grandcows* (Eileen Spinelli and Bill Slavin)

*Asia*
- *The Fool of the World and the Flying Ship* (Arthur Ransome and Uri Shulevitz)
- *Lon Po Po: A Red-Riding Hood Story from China* (Ed Young) (E)
- *Once a Mouse . . .* (Marcia Brown)
- *The Paper Crane* (Molly Bang) (E)

*Australia*

- *Koala Lou* (Mem Fox and Pamela Lofts)
- *Lizzie Nonsense* (Jan Ormerod)
- *Possum Magic* (Mem Fox and Julie Vivas)

*Europe*

- *Little Red Riding Hood* (Trina Schart Hyman)
- *One Fine Day* (Nonny Hogrogian)
- *The Story of Ferdinand* (Munro Leaf and Robert Lawson)

*North America*

- *Arrow to the Sun* (Gerald McDermott)
- *Song of the Swallows* (Leo Politi)
- *The Story of Jumping Mouse* (John Steptoe)

*South America*

- *Morpha: A Rain Forest Story* (Michael Tennyson and Jennifer H. Yoswa)
- *Rain Player* (David Wisniewski)

## INFORMATIONAL TEXTS
### Nonfiction Books (Read Aloud)

- *Africa* (Rookie Read-About Geography) (Allan Fowler)
- *Antarctica* (Rookie Read-About Geography) (Allan Fowler)
- *Asia* (Rookie Read-About Geography) (Allan Fowler)
- *As the Crow Flies: A First Book of Maps* (Gail Hartman and Harvey Stevenson)
- *Australia* (Rookie Read-About Geography) (Allan Fowler)
- *Beginner's World Atlas* (National Geographic)
- *Continents and Maps* (Big Book, Pearson Learning)
- *Count Your Way Through China* (series) (Jim Haskins)
- *Europe* (Rookie Read-About Geography) (Allan Fowler)
- *Me on the Map* (Joan Sweeney and Annette Cable)
- *North America* (Rookie Read-About Geography) (Allan Fowler)
- *The Seven Continents* (Rookie Read-About Geography) (Wil Mara)
- *South America* (Rookie Read-About Geography) (Allan Fowler)

## ART, MUSIC, AND MEDIA
### Art
#### Africa

- J. H. Pierneef, *Trees in Woodland Landscape* (date unknown)
- *The Linton Panel* (eighteenth or nineteenth century)

Asia

- Guo Xi, *Early Spring* (1072)
- Ando Hiroshige, panel from *Famous Views of 53 Stations of the Tōkaidō Road* (1855)

Australia

- Emily Kam Kngwarreye, *Earth's Creation* (1994)
- Emily Kam Kngwarreye, *The Alhalkere Suite* (1993)

Europe

- John Constable, *The Hay Wain* (1821)
- Paul Cézanne, *Straße vor dem Gebirge Sainte-Victoire* (1898–1902)

North America

- Albert Bierstadt, *Valley of the Yosemite* (1864)
- Piet Mondrian, *Broadway Boogie Woogie* (1942–1943)

## Music

- "Geography Songs on the Continents" compiled by Mary F. Higuchi (2000)
- Walt Disney, "It's a Small World"
- Tinkerbell Records, "London Bridge Is Falling Down"

## Film

- Luc Jacquet, dir., *March of the Penguins* (2005)
- Jon Stone, dir., *Big Bird in China* (1983)

## SAMPLE ACTIVITIES AND ASSESSMENTS

## 1. READING LITERATURE, READING INFORMATIONAL TEXT, RESEARCH, SPEAKING AND LISTENING

Throughout this unit, read fictional stories set in a continent and then read informational text (both from books and digital sources) that describe the continent. Students will develop an appreciation for the setting of the story—the connection between a fictional setting and a real place. Require students to record what they have learned on either sticky notes or a whiteboard to prepare for sharing with the whole group. Following each reading, they record new information, using these details to compare one continent to another. Note the opposites, such as *cold* and *hot*, or *rainy* and *dry*. If possible, arrange a conversation via the Internet with a classroom or individual on another continent. Prepare for the conversation by asking specific, child-generated questions about the continent. (RI.K.9, L.K.1b, L.K.5b)

## 2. INFORMATIVE WRITING

Explain that Mr. Popper loved the idea of "dreaming big." Remind them that he daydreamed about faraway places and that he wished he could have visited Antarctica to explore all that was there. Ask the students, "If you could choose to visit any of the continents we studied, which one would you choose? Be sure to support your choice with one or two strong reasons." Allow students to choose one of the continents studied during this unit that they might like to visit someday. To help the children plan their work, use a program such as Kidspiration to create a graphic organizer on each of the continents chosen by the students. Students can draw pictures of animals, people, and objects one might find on that continent. Have them write two sentences about the continent using a combination of drawing, dictation, and writing. Share the work with the class. (SL.K.6, W.K.1, W.K.5, W.K.6, W.K.8, L.K.2d, RF.K.3d)

## 3. READING LITERATURE, NARRATIVE WRITING, VOCABULARY

The literature in this unit is conducive to storytelling. Pair students so that they can practice retelling a favorite story from this unit. Ask them, "Using illustrations and writing, retell _____. Be sure to focus on the beginning, middle, and end of the story." Introduce the concept of major events, and ask them to focus on major events and the most important details. To make the activity more challenging, after they have retold the story, ask if they can retell a similar story with a completely different setting and character. For example, they may retell *The Story of Ferdinand*. How would the story be different if it took place in South America? Which animal would be the main character? Extend this activity by doing a class write: "Write a new version of *The Story of Ferdinand*. Be sure to change the characters and the setting. Illustrate the new story to create a class book." As students volunteer words for creating this story, encourage them to provide letters for sounds as you write. (RL.K.2, W.K.3, W.K.7, L.K.2d)

## 4. READING INFORMATIONAL TEXT, SPEAKING AND LISTENING

Choose two of the books (or maps) of the seven continents. Read the books aloud to the students. Ask students to explain how these two books are the same and how they are different. Students then can work with a partner or in a small group to discuss similarities and differences between the books or maps. Record students' contributions on a compare-and-contrast graphic organizer. (RI.K.9)

## 5. READING LITERATURE, SPEAKING AND LISTENING, PERFORMANCE

After reading two books, *Little Red Riding Hood* and *Lon Po Po*, discuss how the two stories are the same and how they are different. Generate ideas from among the children through writing, drawing, or acting out parts of each story. (RL.K.9, RL.K.10)

## 6. VOCABULARY

*Mr. Popper's Penguins* by Richard and Florence Atwater is filled with alliteration based on the letter *p*. Encourage the children to listen for *p* words that they hear as you read. The vocabulary words will be challenging and fun to use in classroom discussions. (L.K.6)

## 7. VOCABULARY

Create a word bank of all of the words with *r*-controlled vowels (*ar, er, ir, ur, or*) as you find them in this unit. Create active listeners by encouraging the students to listen for the words and act as "sound detectives." Sort the words by their respective spellings, noting how the letter combinations create similar sounds (e.g., "A W*or*ld of W*or*ds"). (L.K.6)

## 8. ART VOCABULARY

View the Bierstadt and Guo Xi paintings. Note that they were painted eight hundred years apart and on opposite sides of the world. Ask the students to describe what they see. Note similarities (e.g., the monumentality of both works) and differences (e.g., different color palettes).

This is an opportunity to extend the idea of comparing and contrasting the settings in stories to comparing and contrasting the settings in paintings. (SL.K.2)

## 9. ART, SPEAKING AND LISTENING

View the Mondrian. Share the title and ask what clues it provides about the painting's subject. Ask the students what they notice first in this work and what place they think this might be. ("What do you see that makes it look like this place?") Ask whether the place looks busy or slow and how the artist made it appear that way. Compare this work to another painting (e.g., the two by Kngwarreye), noticing similarities and differences and focusing on the idea of both place and painting style. Document responses on a chart. (SL.K.1, SL.K.3, SL.K.4)

## 10. ART, NARRATIVE WRITING

Select two or three works to study that include people or hand-built structures (e.g., Cézanne, Constable, Hiroshige, Linton Panel). Ask the students to find the people or structures and discuss how they compare, in scale, to the natural elements in the works. Ask the students to write a new title for the work that interests them the most. Share titles in small groups and possibly post them next to a reproduction of the work of art for future sharing. (W.K.1, W.K.2)

## READING FOUNDATIONS: A PACING GUIDE FOR READING INSTRUCTION

See Kindergarten, Level Five, in the Reading Foundations section at the beginning of this book for a complete pacing guide for this unit.

## ADDITIONAL ONLINE RESOURCES

- *Lon Po Po: A Chinese Fairytale Lesson Plan* (Elizabeth Mazzurco, Scholastic, Inc.) (RL.K.9)
- *Lon Po Po: A Red Riding Hood Story from China Lesson Plan* (Chinese Childbook) (RL.K.9)
- "All About World Geography: World Map with a Continent Matching Puzzle" (Sheppard Software)

## TERMINOLOGY

| | | |
|---|---|---|
| Antonyms | Details (most important) | Opposites |
| Compare | Different | Settings |
| Contrast | Main idea | Similar |

## INTERDISCIPLINARY CONNECTIONS

This unit teaches:

- **Art:** Landscapes from around the world
- **Geography:** Working with maps and globes (e.g., locating and naming the seven continents)

This unit could be extended to teach:

- **Art:** Portraits from around the world
- **Science:** Animal habitat preservation (e.g., Jane Goodall's work with chimpanzees in East Africa or attempts to preserve giant pandas in China)
- **Geography:** Working with maps and globes (e.g., locating oceans, poles, rivers, lakes, and mountains on globes and maps)

## Kindergarten, Unit Five Sample Lesson Plan

Lon Po Po: A Red-Riding Hood Story from China *by Ed Young*

In this series of three lessons, students read *Lon Po Po: A Red-Riding Hood Story from China* by Ed Young, and they:

- Follow the plot of the story *Lon Po Po* (RL.K.1, RL.K.2, RL.K.3)
- Explore Shang's wise scheme (RL.K.10, SL.K.2)
- Revisit the tale of "Little Red Riding Hood" (RL.K.1)
- Juxtapose the stories of "Little Red Riding Hood" and "Lon Po Po" (RL.K.9)

### Summary

Lesson I: *Lon Po Po*

- Meet Shang, Tao, and Paotze (RL.K.3)
- Explore the plot of *Lon Po Po: A Red-Riding Hood Story from China* (RL.K.1, RL.K.2, RL.K.3)
- Examine Shang's plan (RL.K.10, SL.K.2)
- Identify the reasons for the sisters' success (SL.K.2)

Lesson II: "Little Red Riding Hood"

- Retell the story of "Little Red Riding Hood" (RL.K.9)
- Explore the plot of the story (RL.K.3)
- Examine the story's resolution (SL.K.2)

Lesson III: *Lon Po Po* and "Little Red Riding Hood"

- Recall details of *Lon Po Po* and "Little Red Riding Hood" (RL.K.1)
- Chart the recalled details of the two stories (RL.K.9)
- Revisit Shang's scheme (RL.K.10, SL.K.2)
- Explore the climax of each of the two stories (RL.K.9, SL.K.2)
- Juxtapose the two stories (RL.K.9)

## Lesson III: Lon Po Po and "Little Red Riding Hood"

### Objectives

Recall details of Lon Po Po and "Little Red Riding Hood" (RL.K.1)

Chart the recalled details of the two stories (RL.K.9)

Revisit Shang's scheme (RL.K.10, SL.K.2)

Explore the climax of each of the two stories (RL.K.9, SL.K.2)

Juxtapose the two stories (RL.K.9)

### Required Materials

☐ Class set of Lon Po Po: A Red-Riding Hood Story from China by Ed Young

☐ Class set of "Little Red Riding Hood"

### Procedures

1. Lead-In:

   Students recall the details of the two stories.

2. Step by Step:

   a. With assistance, students create charts that will help them note the differences between the two stories.

|  | Lon Po Po | "Little Red Riding Hood" |
|---|---|---|
| List of Characters |  |  |
| Characters' Actions |  |  |
| Climax |  |  |
| Conclusion |  |  |
| Theme of the story |  |  |

   b.  Help the students investigate the dissimilarities between the plots.

   c.  Students will revisit the wisdom and the strength of Shang, as she is the force that drives the plot.

   d.  Provide prompts that will help point to the thematic differences in the two stories.

3.  Closure:

    Reread, aloud, *Lon Po Po: A Red-Riding Hood Story from China* by Ed Young.

## Differentiation

### Advanced

- Students will use a Venn diagram or other compare/contrast graphic organizer.

- Students will use a digital version of a graphic organizer to transfer the information from the chart in this lesson into a different format.

- Students will compare and contrast the artwork of Ed Young in *Lon Po Po* to the artwork in a version of "Little Red Riding Hood," such as the one illustrated by Trina Schart Hyman.

### Struggling

- Divide this lesson into two lessons, dealing with only one story at a time.

- Use a video version of "Little Red Riding Hood" and then allow the students to act out the story before comparing it to *Lon Po Po*.

## Homework/Assessment

N/A

# Wonders of Nature: Plants, Bugs, and Frogs

In this sixth six-week unit of kindergarten, students enjoy reading emergent-reader informational texts and listening as picture books by Eric Carle and Robert McCloskey are read aloud.

## ESSENTIAL QUESTION

How does nature inspire us as readers, writers, and artists?

## OVERVIEW

Students build on the phonological and phonemic work done all year in kindergarten by reading with the support of teachers and peers. Focusing on the relationships among ideas in texts, students recognize that growth and change occur in both fiction and informational texts. Learning about cause and effect, students recognize interactions in nature and note the role that people can play in preserving nature. Students read about Monet, a painter who was inspired by light and the wonder of nature, as an introduction to revision in the creative process.

## FOCUS STANDARDS

These Focus Standards have been selected for the unit from the Common Core State Standards.

**RL.K.10:** Actively engage in group reading activities with purpose and understanding.

**RI.K.8:** With prompting and support, identify the reasons an author gives to support points in a text.

**RI.K.9:** With prompting and support, identify basic similarities in and differences between two texts on the same topic (e.g., in illustrations, descriptions, or procedures).

**RF.K.4:** Read emergent-reader texts with purpose and understanding.

**W.K.6:** With guidance and support from adults, explore a variety of digital tools to produce and publish writing, including in collaboration with peers.

**L.K.4:** Determine or clarify the meaning of unknown and multiple-meaning words and phrases based on kindergarten reading and content.

**L.K.4(b):** Use the most frequently occurring inflections and affixes (e.g., *-ed, -s, re-, un-, pre-, -ful, -less*) as a clue to the meaning of an unknown word.

## SUGGESTED OBJECTIVES

- Articulate cause-and-effect relationships (e.g., as they occur in the natural world).
- Recognize the basic similarities and differences between two texts on the same topic (e.g., when both are informational or when one is fiction and one nonfiction).
- Read emergent-reader texts with purpose and understanding.
- Write, draw, or dictate a narrative (e.g., describing something that happened in nature and a subsequent reaction).
- Relate the idea of writing revision to a visual artist's creative process (i.e., continuously improving the work).
- Use common affixes as clues to the meaning of an unknown word.

## SUGGESTED WORKS

(E) indicates a CCSS exemplar text; (EA) indicates a text from a writer with other works identified as exemplars.

### LITERARY TEXTS

*Nursery Rhymes (Read Along)*
- "Ladybug, Ladybug"
- "Mary, Mary Quite Contrary"

*Picture Books (Read Aloud)*
- *Days with Frog and Toad* (Arnold Lobel) (EA)
- *Fireflies* (Julie Brinckloe)
- *Hi! Fly Guy* (Tedd Arnold) (E) Read Aloud/Independent
- *It's Earth Day!* (Mercer Mayer)
- *Jack and the Beanstalk* (Steven Kellogg)
- *Kate and the Beanstalk* (Mary Pope Osborne and Giselle Potter)
- *One Morning in Maine* (Robert McCloskey)
- *A Tree Is Nice* (Janice May Udry and Marc Simont)

*Picture Books (Read Aloud/Independent)*
- *The Carrot Seed* (Ruth Krauss and Crockett Johnson)
- *The Grouchy Ladybug* (Eric Carle)

- *The Magical Garden of Claude Monet* (Laurence Anholt)
- *There Was an Old Lady Who Swallowed a Fly* (Simms Taback)
- *Time of Wonder* (Robert McCloskey)
- *The Tiny Seed* (The World of Eric Carle) (Eric Carle)
- *The Very Clumsy Click Beetle* (Eric Carle)
- *The Very Lonely Firefly* (Eric Carle)
- *The Very Quiet Cricket* (Eric Carle)

## Poems (Read Aloud)

- "The Caterpillar" in *Rossetti: Poems* (Christina Rossetti) (EA)
- *Insectlopedia* (Douglas Florian) (selections)
- "Little Black Bug" (Margaret Wise Brown)
- *Over in the Meadow* (John Langstaff and Feodor Rojankovsky) (E)
- "Trees" (Sarah Coleridge)
- "Two Tree Toads" in *Orangutan Tongs: Poems to Tangle Your Tongue* (Jon Agee) (E)
- "Wouldn't You?" in *You Read to Me, I'll Read to You* (John Ciardi) (E) (Read Along)

## INFORMATIONAL TEXTS

## Nonfiction Books (Read Aloud)

- *A Blue Butterfly* (Bijou Le Tord)
- *Follow the Water from Brook to Ocean* (Arthur Dorros) (E)
- "Garden Helpers" in *National Geographic Young Explorer!* (September 2009) (E)
- "Our Good Earth" in *National Geographic Young Explorer!* (April 2009) (EA)
- *The Reasons for Seasons* (Gail Gibbons) (EA)
- *Red-Eyed Tree Frog* (Joy Cowley and Nic Bishop)
- *The Seasons of Arnold's Apple Tree* (Gail Gibbons) (EA)
- *Water, Water Everywhere* (Mark Rauzon and Cynthia Overbeck Bix) (E)

## Informational Books (Read Aloud/Independent)

- *Cactuses* (Rookie Read-About Science) (Allan Fowler)
- *Earth Day* (Rookie Read-About Holidays) (Trudi Strain Trueit)
- *Frogs and Toads and Tadpoles, Too!* (Rookie Read-About Science) (Allan Fowler)
- *From Caterpillar to Butterfly* (Let's-Read-and-Find-Out Science) (Deborah Heiligman and Bari Weissman) (E Series)
- *From Seed to Plant* (Rookie Read-About Science) (Allan Fowler)
- *From Seed to Pumpkin* (Let's-Read-and-Find-Out Science) (Wendy Pfeffer and James Graham Hale) (E)
- *From Tadpole to Frog* (Let's-Read-and-Find-Out Science) (Wendy Pfeffer and Holly Keller) (E Series)
- *How a Seed Grows* (Let's-Read-and-Find-Out Science) (Helene J. Jordan and Loretta Krupinski) (E Series)

- *Inside an Ant Colony* (Rookie Read-About Science) (Allan Fowler)
- *It Could Still Be a Flower* (Rookie Read-About Science) (Allan Fowler)
- *It's a Good Thing There Are Insects* (Rookie Read-About Science) (Allan Fowler)
- *Living Sunlight: How Plants Bring the Earth to Life* (Molly Bang and Penny Chisholm) (EA)
- *Maple Trees* (Rookie Read-About Science) (Allan Fowler)
- *Pine Trees* (Rookie Read-About Science) (Allan Fowler)
- *Plants That Eat Animals* (Rookie Read-About Science) (Allan Fowler)
- *Spiders Are Not Insects* (Rookie Read-About Science) (Allan Fowler)
- *Taking Root* (Rookie Read-About Science) (Allan Fowler)
- *A Tree Is a Plant* (Let's-Read-and-Find-Out Science) (Clyde Robert Bulla and Stacey Schuett) (E)

## ART, MUSIC, AND MEDIA

### Art

- Claude Monet, *Water Lilies (The Clouds)* (1903)
- Claude Monet, *Water Lilies* (1906)
- Claude Monet, *Water Lilies* (1916–1923)

### Music (Sing Along)

- "The Ants Go Marching One by One"
- "Itsy Bitsy Spider"

### Media

- Lena Anderson and Christina Bjork, dirs., *Linnea in Monet's Garden* (1999)

## SAMPLE ACTIVITIES AND ASSESSMENTS

### 1. READING INFORMATION TEXT, SPEAKING AND LISTENING

Create a cause-and-effect table (as shown next) to record your class work. Read a book such as *Earth Day* (Trudi Strain Trueit). As you read, encourage the students to think about whether we need Earth Day and how celebrating this special day helps the earth. Build in personal accountability by asking students to draw, write, dictate, or act out their ideas before adding them to the chart. Add a writing dimension to this work by giving students the following whole-class writing prompt: "Write a class book titled *Earth Day: Making a Difference*. Use the cause-and-effect chart to plan each page of the book. Work in teams to illustrate." (RI.K.8, RI.K.10, SL.K.6, W.K.2, W.K.7, L.K.1f)

| Cause | Effect |
|---|---|
| People are careless and throw trash in the water | The water is dirty and fish don't have clean water to swim in. |
| People pick up trash around a stream | Fish have a healthier place to live. Water is cleaner. |

- *Cause* (why we have a problem)
- "Earth Day Activities" (event)
- *Effect* (how we help the earth)

## 2. NARRATIVE WRITING

Give students this prompt: "Write (or draw or dictate) a story about something amazing you have seen in nature. Be sure to include the name of what you saw (e.g., a firefly), the setting (e.g., a dark night in June, in my yard), and two events that happened (e.g., I chased it and caught it). Tell about how you reacted to the events (e.g., I screamed because I had a bug in my hand and didn't know what to do with it!)." (W.K.3, SL.K.4, L.K.2a)

## 3. ART, NARRATIVE WRITING

Claude Monet painted water lilies over and over again. Tell the students to look at his paintings to see how they changed. Explain that one of the reasons for this change was the shifting light in his garden, but also that painters sometimes paint the same subject many times as a way to innovate. Display the three paintings in chronological order, spending time on each individually. What changes did Monet make when he painted the same subject again and again? Relate this idea to the revision process when writing stories. Return the students' nature stories (see Narrative Writing, Activity 2) and ask the students to try writing them again, but to make them a little different this time, perhaps by adding new details. Publish the writing in a digital format by scanning the student work and inserting it into a PowerPoint presentation. Students will present the work to parents as a culminating writing activity for the year. (SL.K.1, W.K.5, W.K.6)

## 4. READING LITERATURE, INFORMATIVE WRITING

After reading a chapter from *Days with Frog and Toad* by Arnold Lobel and *From Tadpole to Frog* by Wendy Pfeffer and Holly Keller, lead the following activity with the students: Work together to make a list of the ways the frog in the fictional book (Lobel) was similar to the frog in the nonfiction book (Pfeffer and Keller). Make a list of how the two frogs are different. Students may be ready to create this list themselves on their personal graphic organizer. (RL.K.3, RL.K.10, RI.K.10, SL.K.6)

## 5. READING INFORMATIONAL TEXT, SPEAKING AND LISTENING

Read a book such as *From Tadpole to Frog* by Wendy Pfeffer and Holly Keller and then read *Red-Eyed Tree Frog* by Joy Cowley and Nic Bishop. (These are both nonfiction books, and they both talk about toads.) Ask what the students noticed about how these books were the same and how they were different. (RI.K.9, RI.K.10, SL.K.6)

## 6. READING INFORMATIONAL TEXT, INFORMATIVE WRITING

After reading an informational text detailing a process, such as the life cycle of a butterfly or frog, give the students the following writing prompt: "Write a four-page booklet explaining the life cycle of a frog or butterfly, using illustrations and sentences." (W.K.2, L.K.2a)

## 7. VOCABULARY, PERFORMANCE

Create a word bank for "Ways Animals Move" (e.g., dart, fly, hop, and swim). Use these verbs to teach the *-ed*, *-s*, and *-ing* suffixes. Act out the words, adding adverbs to make the actions opposite in speed like "hopping slowly" or "hopping fast." Have some fun with the word bank by creating a "wordle" (from the website www.wordle.net) with the verbs describing animal movements. (L.K.1b, L.K.4b, L.K.5b)

## 8. READING INFORMATIONAL TEXT, READING POETRY, PERFORMANCE

Because students are reading, introduce them to the easy science texts in this unit. Spend time having the students read the books aloud with partners or alone. When reading (reciting) poetry, encourage the dramatic expression of poems such as "Wouldn't You?" (RF.K.4)

## READING FOUNDATIONS: A PACING GUIDE FOR READING INSTRUCTION

See Kindergarten, Level Six, in the Reading Foundations section at the beginning of this book for a complete pacing guide for this unit.

## ADDITIONAL ONLINE RESOURCE

- *Animal Study: From Fiction to Facts* (ReadWriteThink) (RI.K.10)

## TERMINOLOGY

Cause

Creative process

Different

Effect

Explanatory writing

Oral presentation

Revision

Similar

## INTERDISCIPLINARY CONNECTIONS

This unit teaches:

- **Art:** Monet (e.g., painting, "Water Lilies" series)
- **Science:** Plants (e.g., what plants need to grow; seeds, flowers, and the parts of a plant); Earth Day (e.g., pollution, recycling, conservation); seasons; bugs and frogs (e.g., habitats and life cycles)

This unit could be extended to teach:

- **Art:** More famous artworks inspired by nature
- **Science:** Weather (e.g., local weather patterns and daily weather changes)

## Kindergarten, Unit Six Sample Lesson Plan

### From Seed to Pumpkin *by Wendy Pfeffer*

In this series of two lessons, students read *From Seed to Pumpkin* by Wendy Pfeffer, and they:

Trace the growth of a plant from a seed to a pumpkin (RI.K.1, RI.K.2, RI.K.4, SL.K.1, SL.K.2, SL.K.5)

Appreciate the growth process by charting the growth of the plant and the passage of time (SL.K.6, RF.K.4)

### Summary

#### Lesson I: From Seed to Pumpkin

Trace the development of the seeds (RI.K.1, RI.K.2, RI.K.4, SL.K.1, SL.K.2, SL.K.5)

Closely observe the illustrations depicting the growth from a seed, to a plant, to a pumpkin (RI.K.6, RI.K.7)

Note the passage of time (RI.K.1, RI.K.2, SL.K.1, SL.K.2)

#### Lesson II: From Seed to Pumpkin–Charting the Process

Identify the steps that begin with the seed and end with a pumpkin (RI.K.1, RI.K.2, RI.K.3, SL.K.2)

Chart the steps identified (W.K.2)

Illustrate the chart (W.K.2)

Revisit the process (SL.K.6)

### Lesson II: From Seed to Pumpkin–Charting the Process

#### Objectives

Identify the steps that begin with the seed and end with a pumpkin (RI.K.1, RI.K.2, RI.K.3, SL.K.2)

Chart the steps identified (W.K.2)

Illustrate the chart (W.K.2)

Revisit the process (SL.K.6)

#### Required Materials

- [ ] *From Seed to Pumpkin* by Wendy Pfeffer
- [ ] Markers
- [ ] Paper

*Procedures*

1. Lead-In:

   Discuss the book *From Seed to Pumpkin* with students. Students revisit the transition of the pumpkin from a seed to a plant.

2. Step by Step:

   a. Introduce the class project.

   - Students chart the growth of the pumpkin plant.
   - Students write about (with your assistance) and illustrate the process.

   b. Collaboratively, returning to the book for details when necessary, students work on the chart.

3. Closure:

   Students reflect about what they have learned from the book *From Seed to Pumpkin*.

*Differentiation*

*Advanced*

- Create an electronic slide for each step of the growth of the pumpkin seed. Create a narration to go with the slides and record it. Share the presentation with another class.
- Using a familiar tune like "The Farmer in the Dell," write verses for a song that show the steps of growth for a pumpkin.

*Struggling*

- Before this lesson set begins, create a KWL chart about pumpkins. If possible, show students what a real pumpkin looks like and what a pumpkin seed looks like.
- Spend some time talking about sequence, reviewing how plants in the classroom have grown from seeds.

*Homework/Assessment*

N/A

# Grade 1

In first grade, students build on the reading, writing, listening, and speaking that they practiced in kindergarten. As in kindergarten, these units also refer to the Reading Foundations sequence included at the beginning of this edition. Although not a comprehensive reading program, this pacing guide provides guidance for instruction in print concepts, phonological awareness, phonics, word recognition, fluency, and some of the writing and language skills. Students should enter first grade with basic decoding skills and familiarity with a range of fiction, nonfiction, and poetry. As their reading and writing skills become more advanced, they begin to apply their knowledge to new topics and situations. Students are exposed to a rich variety of "read-aloud" stories, nonfiction, and poems, including stories about animals, fables, and other life lessons; stories and nonfiction accounts about contributors to America; versions of the "Cinderella" tale from many nations; and more. They have opportunities to draw interesting connections between literature and other subjects; for example, in the unit Winds of Change, they consider changes in nature as well as changes in characters' feelings. They explore the arts throughout the year: in one unit they look at paintings by Matisse, and in another they compare masks from around the world. They start to produce writing—journal entries, brief descriptions, opinion pieces, and stories—and to collaborate on simple research projects (such as finding out about an animal). They learn to create short books with a table of contents and numbered pages. By the end of first grade, they are able to sound out and recognize many one-syllable and multisyllabic words, and they have a strong repertoire of sight words.

# Standards Checklist for Grade One

## Reading–Literature

| Standard | Unit 1 | Unit 2 | Unit 3 | Unit 4 | Unit 5 | Unit 6 |
|---|---|---|---|---|---|---|
| 1 | FA | | | | | A |
| 2 | | FA | FA | | A | A |
| 3 | | | FA | A | | |
| 4 | | | | FA | | |
| 5 | A | F | | | A | A |
| 6 | | A | A | | | |
| 7 | | | A | | A | A |
| 8 n/a | | | | | | |
| 9 | | | A | | | FA |
| 10 | | | | A | | |

## Reading–Informational Text

| Standard | Unit 1 | Unit 2 | Unit 3 | Unit 4 | Unit 5 | Unit 6 |
|---|---|---|---|---|---|---|
| 1 | FA | | | | | |
| 2 | | FA | | | | A |
| 3 | | | | | FA | A |
| 4 | | | | | A | |
| 5 | | A | | | | A |
| 6 | | | FA | | | |
| 7 | A | | | | | |
| 8 | | | | FA | | |
| 9 | | | | | | FA |
| 10 | | A | | | FA | A |

## Writing

| Standard | Unit 1 | Unit 2 | Unit 3 | Unit 4 | Unit 5 | Unit 6 |
|---|---|---|---|---|---|---|
| 1 | | | A | | FA | FA |
| 2 | A | FA | A | | | |
| 3 | | | FA | A | | |
| 4 n/a | | | | | | |
| 5 | A | A | A | FA | A | |
| 6 | | | | | | F |
| 7 | FA | A | A | A | | A |
| 8 | A | | A | A | A | A |
| 9 n/a | | | | | | |
| 10 n/a | | | | | | |

## Speaking and Listening

| Standard | Unit 1 | Unit 2 | Unit 3 | Unit 4 | Unit 5 | Unit 6 |
|---|---|---|---|---|---|---|
| 1 | FA | | | | A | A |
| 1a | | | | | | |
| 1b | | A | | | | |
| 1c | | | | | | |
| 2 | A | FA | | | | |
| 3 | | A | A | A | FA | |
| 4 | | A | | FA | A | A |
| 5 | | | A | | | FA |
| 6 | A | | A | A | A | A |

## Language

| Standard | Unit 1 | Unit 2 | Unit 3 | Unit 4 | Unit 5 | Unit 6 |
|---|---|---|---|---|---|---|
| 1 | FA | | | | | |
| 1a | A | | | | | |
| 1b | | A | | | | |
| 1c | | | A | | | |
| 1d | | | | A | | |
| 1e | | | A | A | | |
| 1f | | | | | | |
| 1g | | | | A | | |
| 1h | | | | | A | |
| 1i | | | | A | | |
| 1j | FA | A | A | | A | A |
| 2 | | F | | | | A |
| 2a | | | | | A | A |
| 2b | A | | FA | | A | A |
| 2c | | | | A | | |

| Standard | Unit 1 | Unit 2 | Unit 3 | Unit 4 | Unit 5 | Unit 6 |
|---|---|---|---|---|---|---|
| 2d | A | | | | A | A |
| 2e | A | | | | A | A |
| 3 n/a | | | | | | |
| 4 | | | | | | |
| 4a | | A | | | | |
| 4b | | | | | | |
| 4c | | | | A | | |
| 5 | | FA | | FA | | F |
| 5a | | A | | | | |
| 5b | | FA | | | | |
| 5c | | | | | A | |
| 5d | | | | FA | | FA |
| 6 | | | | | A | |

## Reading Foundations (addressed in units)

| Standard | Level 1 | Level 2 | Level 3 | Level 4 | Level 5 | Level 6 |
|---|---|---|---|---|---|---|
| 1 | | | | | | |
| 1a | A | | | | | |
| 2 | | | | | | A |
| 2a | | | | | | |
| 2b | | | | | | |
| 2c | | | | | | |
| 2d | | | | | | |
| 3 | | | | | | |
| 3a | | | | | | |
| 3b | | | | | | |
| 3c | | | | | | |
| 3d | | | | | | |
| 3e | | | | | | |
| 3f | | | | | | |
| 3g | | | | | | |
| 4 | A | A | F | | F | A |
| 4a | | A | | | A | |
| 4b | | A | FA | | A | |
| 4c | | A | | FA | | |

## Reading Foundations (addressed in Reading Foundations: A Pacing Guide)

| Standard | Level 1 | Level 2 | Level 3 | Level 4 | Level 5 | Level 6 |
|---|---|---|---|---|---|---|
| 1 | | | | A | | |
| 1a | A | A | | A | | |
| 1b | | | | A | | |
| 1c | | | | A | | |
| 1d | | | | A | | |
| 2 | | | | | | |
| 2a | A | | | | | |
| 2b | | A | A | | | |
| 2c | | | | A | A | |
| 2d | | | A | A | A | A |
| 2e | | | | | | |
| 3 | | | | | | |
| 3a | A | A | A | A | A | |
| 3b | A | A | A | A | A | |
| 3c | A | A | A | A | A | |
| 3d | | | | | | |
| 3e | | | | A | | |
| 3f | | | | | A | A |
| 3g | A | A | A | A | A | A |
| 4 | | A | A | A | A | A |
| 4a | | A | A | A | A | A |
| 4b | | A | A | A | A | A |
| 4c | A | A | A | A | A | A |

# Alphabet Books and Children Who Read Them

In this first six-week unit of first grade, students are welcomed to school as readers and begin reviewing the alphabet and concepts of print through books about the library, friendship, and the ABCs.

---

## ESSENTIAL QUESTION

Why is it important to ask questions while you are reading?

---

## OVERVIEW

By conducting shared research, students learn that investigating is foundational to learning. By using books that require conversation, such as *The Graphic Alphabet*, students understand that ideas are processed through inquiry, thought, and conversation. After the students perform shared research based on a class question, they write a class ABC book about their topic. During this writing, they review the formation of a sentence with proper punctuation. Students respond to a question (prompt) to write what they know about healthy habits (e.g., exercise, healthy eating), focusing on their topic and supporting it with facts. Finally, they apply their knowledge of questioning to poetry and perform the poetry as a choral reading.

## FOCUS STANDARDS

These Focus Standards have been selected for the unit from the Common Core State Standards.

**RL.1.1:** Ask and answer questions about key details in a text.

**RI.1.1:** Ask and answer questions about key details in a text.

**W.1.7:** Participate in shared research and writing projects (e.g., explore a number of "how-to" books on a given topic and use them to write a sequence of instructions).

**SL.1.1:** Participate in collaborative conversations with diverse partners about grade 1 topics and texts with peers and adults in small and larger groups.

**L.1.1:** Demonstrate command of the conventions of standard English grammar and usage when writing or speaking.

**L.1.1(j):** Produce and expand complete simple and compound declarative, interrogative, imperative, and exclamatory sentences in response to prompts.

## SUGGESTED OBJECTIVES

- Use pictures, illustrations, and details in a text to discern and describe key ideas.
- Help shape research questions.
- Gather information on a given topic.
- Listen to one another in conversations and speak one at a time.
- Capitalize names, places, and dates.
- Punctuate sentences correctly with a period and question mark.
- Perform poetry as a choral reading.

## SUGGESTED WORKS

(E) indicates a CCSS exemplar text; (EA) indicates a text from a writer with other works identified as exemplars.

### LITERARY TEXTS

*Stories*

- *A Kiss for Little Bear* (Else Holmelund Minarik and Maurice Sendak) (EA)
- *Little Bear's Visit* (Else Holmelund Minarik and Maurice Sendak) (EA)
- *Morris Goes to School* (Bernard Wiseman)

*Stories (Read Aloud)*

- *Alphabet Mystery* (Audrey Wood and Bruce Wood)
- *Chicka Chicka Boom Boom* (Bill Martin Jr., John Archambault, and Lois Ehlert)
- *Dr. Seuss's ABC: An Amazing Alphabet Book!* (Dr. Seuss) (EA)
- *I Can Read with My Eyes Shut!* (Dr. Seuss) (EA)
- *The Library* (Sarah Stewart and David Small)
- *¡Marimba! Animales from A to Z* (Pat Mora and Doug Cushman) (EA)
- *Our Library* (Eve Bunting and Maggie Smith)
- *Tomas and the Library Lady* (Pat Mora and Raul Colon) (E)

*Poems*

- "Good Books, Good Times!" (Lee Bennett Hopkins)
- "You Read to Me, I'll Read to You" (Mary Ann Hoberman and Michael Emberley)

*Poems (Read Aloud)*

- "Books Fall Open" (David McCord)
- "Books to the Ceiling" (Arnold Lobel) (EA)
- "How to Eat a Poem" (Eve Merriam) (EA)
- "Read to Me" (Jane Yolen)

## INFORMATIONAL TEXTS

*Nonfiction Books*

- *26 Letters and 99 Cents* (Tana Hoban) (EA)
- *Alphabet City* (Stephen T. Johnson)
- *Exactly the Opposite* (Tana Hoban) (EA)
- *Exercise* (Rookie Read-About Health) (Sharon Gordon)
- *Germs! Germs! Germs!* (Hello Reader Science Level 3) (Bobbi Katz and Steve Bjorkman)
- *I Read Signs* (Tana Hoban) (E)
- *Look Book* (Tana Hoban) (EA)
- *School Bus* (Donald Crews) (EA)

*Nonfiction Books (Read Aloud)*

- *An A to Z Walk in the Park* (R. M. Smith)
- *Eating the Alphabet: Fruits & Vegetables from A to Z* (Harcourt Brace Big Book) (Lois Ehlert)
- *A Good Night's Sleep* (Rookie Read-About Health) (Sharon Gordon)
- *The Graphic Alphabet* (David Pelletier)
- *The Hidden Alphabet* (Laura Vaccaro Seeger)
- *I Spy: An Alphabet in Art* (Lucy Micklethwait)
- *Museum ABC* (New York Metropolitan Museum of Art)
- *The Turn-Around, Upside-Down Alphabet Book* (Lisa Campbell Ernst)

## ART, MUSIC, AND MEDIA

*Art*

- Pieter Bruegel, *Children's Games* (1560)

## SAMPLE ACTIVITIES AND ASSESSMENTS

### 1. ART, SPEAKING AND LISTENING

Look at *Children's Games* by Pieter Bruegel. Ask the students to study it closely for a few minutes and write down any questions they have about what they see. When the time is up, have them ask their questions. As the students begin to ask questions aloud, write all of the questions on a chart (e.g., "What are they doing?" "Is that like a hula hoop?" "Was this painted a long time ago?"). Talk about the value of asking questions and how we begin to open our minds to think deeply about something. (The painting was done in the sixteenth century, and the artist was perhaps trying to show all of the games he knew. You may want to note the few toys children had–sticks, hoops, etc.) (SL.1.2)

## 2. READING INFORMATIONAL TEXT, SPEAKING AND LISTENING

Tell the students that just because books are called "ABC books" does not mean they are always easy to understand. Therefore, to understand them, we have to be willing to ask questions and to think deeply and look for key details. Tell the students that they are going to look at *The Graphic Alphabet* by David Pelletier. Using a document camera for viewing this book would be helpful. On each page, there is a letter, but there is something more going on than just that letter. Look at A. Have the students ask questions about the page and try to answer them (e.g., "Why is the letter A crumbling? Could the letter be a mountain? Is that an *avalanche*?"). As you go through the book and throughout the unit, introduce the new vocabulary. (RI.1.1, RI.1.7, L.1.1j, SL.1.2)

## 3. LANGUAGE MECHANICS, SPEAKING AND LISTENING

Introduce the writing of declarative and interrogative sentences by focusing on an informational ABC book, such as *Eating the Alphabet: Fruits & Vegetables from A to Z* by Lois Ehlert. On a chart, write a question such as "What is your favorite fruit?" Teach the students to answer the question with a complete declarative response, such as "My favorite fruit is a strawberry." Discuss the end punctuation. Continue this activity to teach the expansion of sentences to include details, such as "Strawberries are my favorite fruit because they are juicy, sweet, and delicious." (L.1.1j, L.1.2b, W.1.5, SL.1.6)

## 4. READING POETRY, READING FLUENCY, PERFORMANCE

The theme of the poetry in this unit is the love of books and language. By visually displaying the poems (i.e., using an interactive whiteboard, document camera, overhead projector, or chart paper), students will review sight words and see the way the poem is written (i.e., with lines and stanzas). Using a poem such as "Good Books, Good Times!" by Lee Bennett Hopkins or "How to Eat a Poem" by Eve Merriam, encourage the students to read with you repeatedly and to ask questions until they understand the poem. Poetry is easily transformed into choral reading (reciting) by highlighting lines from one punctuation mark to the next, and then assigning groups to read those highlighted sections. (SL.1.2, RF.1.4)

## 5. INFORMATIVE WRITING, LANGUAGE MECHANICS

Give students this prompt: "Children should eat healthy foods, exercise, and take care of their bodies. Name one way to stay healthy. Supply some facts about the topic you chose and provide closure at the end of your writing." As students write, watch closely that they focus on just one way to stay healthy and that they compose an essay supported by facts. Encourage students to write complete sentences and to use the correct end punctuation. (W.1.2, L.1.1j, L.1.2b)

## 6. INFORMATIVE WRITING, RESEARCH

Using the ABC books as a model, generate some ideas for writing a class ABC book. Work together as a class to come up with potential research questions. Begin by asking such questions as, "Is it possible to create an ABC book with *Games to Play* as our title?" Allow the class to give some ideas (e.g., names, authors, books, plants, insects). After ideas have been shaped into a research question, allow the children to vote on a theme for the class ABC book. Once the theme is chosen, gather information from a variety of texts and digital resources for each letter of the alphabet. Decide on a design for the book. Assign each student a letter in the book. Each page should include an upper- and lowercase letter, the key word, an illustration, and a sentence using the key word. Be sure to have students follow rules for spelling and punctuating correctly. (SL.1.1, W.1.2, W.1.7, W.1.8, L.1.1a, L.1.1j, L.1.2b, L.1.2d, L.1.2e, RF.1.1a)

## 7. READING LITERATURE, SPEAKING AND LISTENING

As you read the book *Tomas and the Library Lady*, pause periodically and encourage students to ask questions. By using "I wonder" as the beginning of the question, have students predict what is coming next in the story and clarify understanding. Use sticky notes or whiteboards to keep each child engaged in the questioning. (RL.1.1)

## 8. READING LITERATURE, READING INFORMATIONAL TEXT, READING POETRY, SPEAKING AND LISTENING

Throughout this unit, students read from a variety of texts: stories, poems, and informational texts. When you have a ten-minute block, play "I Spy" with the children (e.g., "I spy an informational book," "I spy a nonfiction book"). The students then have to guess which book you are looking at in the display of unit books. (RL.1.5, L.1.1)

## READING FOUNDATIONS: A PACING GUIDE FOR READING INSTRUCTION

See Grade One, Level One, in the Reading Foundations section at the beginning of this book for a complete pacing guide for this unit.

## ADDITIONAL RESOURCES

- *Book Sorting: Using Observation and Comprehension to Categorize Books* (ReadWriteThink) (RL.1.5)
- *Adventures in Nonfiction: A Guided Inquiry Journey* (ReadWriteThink) (W.1.7, W.1.8)

## TERMINOLOGY

| | | |
|---|---|---|
| Alphabet books | Key details | Research question |
| Author | Periods | Shared research |
| Capitalization | Poems | Sort |
| Illustrator | Question marks | Stories |
| Informational | Questions | Topic |

## INTERDISCIPLINARY CONNECTIONS

This unit teaches:

- **Art:** Pieter Bruegel (*Children's Games*)
- **Science:** Healthy living (e.g., eat fruits and vegetables, exercise, sleep, avoid germs)

This unit could be extended to teach:

- **Science:** Healthy living (e.g., body systems, Jenner, Pasteur)

## Grade One, Unit One Sample Lesson Plan

A Kiss for Little Bear *by Else Holmelund Minarik*

In this series of two lessons, students read *A Kiss for Little Bear* by Else Holmelund Minarik, and they:

Follow the plot of the story as they trace the path of the kiss (RL.1.1, RL.1.2, RL.1.3)

Explore the use of illustrations (RL.1.7, SL.1.2)

### Summary

**Lesson I: A Picture for Grandmother**

Meet Little Bear, the painter (RL.1.3)

Note the use of illustrations (RL.1.7, SL.1.2)

Examine Little Bear's painting (RL.1.1, RL.1.3, RL.1.7, SL.1.2)

Explore Grandmother's response (RL.1.1, RL.1.2, RL.1.3, SL.1.2)

(Begin to) follow Little Bear's kiss (RL.1.1)

**Lesson II: A Kiss for Little Bear**

(Continue to) follow Little Bear's kiss (RL.1.1, RL.1.2, RL.1.3, RL.1.7)

(Continue to) examine the use of illustrations (RL.1.7)

Chart the path of the kiss (RL.1.2)

Explore the ending of the story (RL.1.1, RL.1.2, SL.1.2)

Reread *A Kiss for Little Bear*

### Lesson II: *A Kiss for Little Bear*

*Objectives*

(Continue to) follow Little Bear's kiss (RL.1.1, RL.1.2, RL.1.3, RL.1.7)

(Continue to) examine the use of illustrations (RL.1.7)

Chart the path of the kiss (RL.1.2)

Explore the ending of the story (RL.1.1, RL.1.2, SL.1.2)

Reread *A Kiss for Little Bear*

*Required Materials*

Class set of *A Kiss for Little Bear* by Else Holmelund Minarik

*Procedures*

1. Lead-In:

   The students conclude the reading of *A Kiss for Little Bear*. Depending on the students' reading levels, you may choose to read the story to the students or have them read it.

2. Step by Step:

   a. In several small groups, students chart the path of Little Bear's kiss.

      Little Bear draws the picture→

      Little Bear decides to send his picture to Grandmother→

      Little Bear asks Hen to take the picture to Grandmother→

      Grandmother sends a kiss back with Hen→

      Hen passes it to Frog→

      And Frog asks Cat to deliver the kiss→

      Cat asks Skunk to bring Little Bear the kiss→

      But Little Skunk meets another Little Skunk and gives her the kiss→

      And she kisses him back→

      Hen sees all that kissing→

      And takes the kiss to Little Bear.

   b. Reconvene the students to discuss the story's ending.

   c. Ask students to introduce and explain their groups chart/s.

3. Closure:

   The class rereads *A Kiss for Little Bear*.

Differentiation

*Advanced*

- Allow students to read silently or with a partner.
- Ask the students to work together to find text evidence for each step in the path of Little Bear's kiss.

*Struggling*

- Before you read the story aloud, assign the students to be characters with name cards in front of their seats: Little Bear, Grandmother, Hen, Frog, Cat, Skunk, and Little Skunk.
- When the "kiss" is introduced, physically hand the "kiss" from one character to the next. (You could use a candy kiss or just "blow a kiss" to the next person.)

## Homework/Assessment

N/A

# The Amazing Animal World

In this second six-week unit of first grade, students read informational texts about animals and learn how to strengthen their own informative/explanatory writing.

## ESSENTIAL QUESTION

How can reading teach us about writing?

## OVERVIEW

Building on the informative/explanatory writing in the first unit, students focus on constructing stronger informative/explanatory writing pieces. Then students revise their work with an adult. They also learn about the creative process through studying the artwork of Henry Matisse, and create a piece of art to go with their informative writing. The class explores informative/explanatory writing by explaining the technique used to create their own artistic works. As they read fictional texts, they continue to retell a story using details and focusing on a central message.

## FOCUS STANDARDS

These Focus Standards have been selected for the unit from the Common Core State Standards.

**RL.1.2:** Retell stories, including key details, and demonstrate understanding of their central message or lesson.

**RL.1.5:** Explain major differences between books that tell stories and books that give information, drawing on a wide reading of a range of text types.

**RI.1.2:** Identify the main topic and retell key details of a text.

**L.1.5:** With guidance and support from adults, demonstrate understanding of word relationships and nuances in word meanings.

**L.1.5(b):** Define words by category and by one or more key attributes (e.g., a *duck* is a bird that swims; a *tiger* is a large cat with stripes).

**W.1.2:** Write informative/explanatory texts in which they name a topic, supply some facts about the topic, and provide some sense of closure.

**SL.1.2:** Ask and answer questions about key details in a text read aloud or information presented orally or through other media.

## SUGGESTED OBJECTIVES

- Describe how a text can group information into general categories.
- Write an informative/explanatory text about a given topic (e.g., about an animal), supplying factual information and providing a sense of closure.
- In a revision process, and under the guidance and support of an adult, add details to an informative text.
- Confirming understanding of information, present the information orally by restating key elements and answering questions about key details.
- Write an informative/explanatory text explaining how to do something (e.g., how Matisse created the large-scale cutout *The Snail*).
- Use sentence context clues to help determine word meanings.
- Use common, proper, and possessive nouns in speech and writing.

## SUGGESTED WORKS

(E) indicates a CCSS exemplar text; (EA) indicates a text from a writer with other works identified as exemplars.

### LITERARY TEXTS

*Stories*
- *Are You My Mother?* (P. D. Eastman) (E)
- *Finn Family Moomintroll* (Tove Jansson) (E) (Read Aloud)
- *Mouse Tales* (Arnold Lobel) (EA)
- *Mouse Soup* (Arnold Lobel) (EA)
- *Uncle Elephant* (Arnold Lobel) (EA)

*Poems*
- "Fish" (Mary Ann Hoberman)
- "The Fox's Foray" in *The Oxford Nursery Rhyme Book* (anonymous) (E) (Read Aloud)
- "I Know All the Sounds That the Animals Make" in *Something Big Has Been Here* (Jack Prelutsky) (Read Aloud)
- "The Owl and the Pussycat" in *The Complete Nonsense of Edward Lear* (Edward Lear) (E) (Read Aloud)

- "The Pasture" in *The Poetry of Robert Frost* (Robert Frost) (Read Aloud)
- "The Purple Cow" in *The Burgess Nonsense Book: Being a Complete Collection of the Humorous Masterpieces of Gelett Burgess* (Gelett Burgess) (Read Aloud)

## INFORMATIONAL TEXTS

### Nonfiction Books

- *Big Tracks, Little Tracks: Following Animal Prints* (Let's-Read-and-Find-Out Science) (Millicent E. Selsam and Marlene Hill Donnelly) (E series)
- *An Earthworm's Life* (John Himmelman)
- *Pass the Energy, Please!* (Barbara Shaw)
- *Starfish* (Let's-Read-and-Find-Out Science) (Edith Thacher Hurd and Robin Brickman) (E)
- *Tracks, Scats, and Signs* (Leslie Dendy)
- *What Lives in a Shell?* (Let's-Read-and-Find-Out Science) (Kathleen Weidner Zoehfeld and Helen K. Davie) (E series)
- *Where Are the Night Animals?* (Let's-Read-and-Find-Out Science) (Mary Ann Fraser) (E series)

### Nonfiction Books (Read Aloud)

- *Amazing Whales!* (Sarah L. Thomson) (E)
- *Biggest, Strongest, Fastest* (Steve Jenkins) (EA)
- *Creature ABC* (Andrew Zuckerman)
- *Earthworms* (Claire Llewellyn and Barrie Watts) (E)
- *How Animals Work* (DK Publishing)
- *A Nest Full of Eggs* (Let's-Read-and-Find-Out Science) (Priscilla Belz Jenkins and Lizzy Rockwell) (E series)
- *Never Smile at a Monkey: And 17 Other Important Things to Remember* (Steve Jenkins) (EA)
- *What Do You Do When Something Wants to Eat You?* (Steve Jenkins) (EA)
- *What Do You Do with a Tail Like This?* (Steve Jenkins and Robin Page) (E)
- *What's It Like to Be a Fish?* (Let's-Read-and-Find-Out Science) (Wendy Pfeffer and Holly Keller) (E series)
- *Where Do Chicks Come From?* (Let's-Read-and-Find-Out Science) (Amy E. Sklansky and Pam Paparone) (E series)

## ART, MUSIC, AND MEDIA

### Art

- Albrecht Dürer, *A Young Hare* (1502)
- Henri Matisse, *The Snail* (1953)
- Henri Rousseau, *The Flamingoes* (1907)
- Louisa Matthíasdóttir, *Five Sheep* (no date)
- Marc Chagall, *I and the Village* (1945)
- Paul Klee, *Cat and Bird* (1928)
- Susan Rothenberg, *Untitled (Horse)* (1976)

# SAMPLE ACTIVITIES AND ASSESSMENTS

## 1. READING INFORMATIONAL TEXT, RESEARCH, INFORMATIVE WRITING

While reading a book such as *What Do You Do with a Tail Like This?* by Steve Jenkins, make a chart to record the name of each animal (main topic) mentioned. Record key details, such as where the animal lives (i.e., its habitat), what the animal eats (i.e., whether it is a herbivore, carnivore, or omnivore), and an interesting fact (e.g., its method of adaptation) on the chart. Ask students to supply at least one piece of information on a sticky note when you are finished reading. Create and add to similar charts about animal facts as you read to the children and as they read independently. Use these charts to create oral and written sentences about the animals. (RI.1.2, L.1.1j, L.1.5b)

## 2. READING INFORMATIONAL TEXT, SPEAKING AND LISTENING

Before beginning this lesson, ask students what they are experts at doing (e.g., bike riding, roller skating, or back flips). Allow some time to share. Remind the students that an author is a real person who has worked hard to know the information to fill a book such as *What Do You Do with a Tail Like This?* by Steve Jenkins. Ask the students to think about how authors become experts on a topic, such as the tails of animals. If possible, invite a speaker who has expertise in something. Talk about how he or she became an expert. Talk about why this makes informational texts better and how having good information can help improve one's writing. (RI.1.2, SL.1.3)

## 3. ART, INFORMATIVE WRITING

Using a projector and computer, display the Tate's website for Matisse's *The Snail*. Encourage students to comment about the colors and what they see in the artwork. As you read the background information and move through the site, students will see the process Matisse used to create his work. Students will then create a work of their favorite animal from this unit using torn pieces of painted paper. Later, do a shared writing in which the students explain the steps taken to create an art piece in the style of Matisse. This activity could be a model for a piece of informative/explanatory writing later. (W.1.7, SL.1.2)

## 4. ART, INFORMATIVE WRITING

Because the students have now completed an artistic masterpiece of their favorite animal, extend the work into a writing assignment. Give the students this prompt: "Write about your favorite animal. Be sure to include interesting facts about your animal and include a catchy beginning, some facts, and a strong ending." Allow your students to begin by working in teams to gather information. Using nonfiction texts, remind them to use the index or table of contents to locate more information about the animal. When they have some basic information, have them write the first draft. Ensure that adults are available to help with revision of the writing. Display the published writing with the Matisse-style artwork (see Art, Informative Writing, Activity 3). (W.1.2, W.1.5, RI.1.5, RI.1.10, RF.1.4)

## 5. READING LITERATURE, VOCABULARY

Read a fictional animal story, such as *Are You My Mother?* by P. D. Eastman. Discuss the vocabulary in the story and work on understanding unknown words. Ask the students (if, e.g., discussing *Are You My Mother?*), "What word was funny in the story because of the way it was used?" (Possible answer: "Snort.") Then ask, "How did you know what it meant?" Divide the students into groups of three and have them tell the story to each other, taking turns as each tells a part. Let them know that if they are stuck on a part of the story, you will allow them to use the book to solve the problem. Encourage the students to try to remember as many details as they can for retelling the story because details are what make the story interesting. When they are finished retelling the story, talk about what lesson might be learned from the story and what new words they learned. (L.1.4a, RL.1.2)

## 6.  READING LITERATURE, LANGUAGE USAGE

Follow up on a book read previously in class, such as *Are You My Mother?* by P. D. Eastman. Go back and reread the story. As you read it this time, read for the purpose of finding all of the animals and things that the baby bird thought might be his mother. As students find the words, write them on index cards (e.g., kitten, hen, dog, cow, boat, plane). Sort the words into categories (e.g., animals, modes of transportation). Think of more words for each of the categories. This activity could also be done with a poem such as "The Pasture" by Robert Frost or "I Know All the Sounds That the Animals Make" by Jack Prelutsky. After reading and rereading (reciting) the poem, gather the nouns in the poem and sort them according to categories (e.g., places, animals, sounds). (L.1.1b, L.1.5a)

## 7.  READING LITERATURE, LANGUAGE MECHANICS

As students read independently, remind them that different characters often tell the story at different times in a book. Using a book such as *Mouse Tales* by Arnold Lobel, allow the students to reread parts of the text where the weasel speaks, where the mouse speaks, and where the narrator tells the story. Provide elbow macaroni at each table. Ask students to place the macaroni on the quotation marks in the book, reminding them that quotation marks mean that someone is speaking. Assigning the parts to three readers will show others how dialogue works in literature. (RL.1.6)

## 8.  READING LITERATURE, READING COMPREHENSION, SPEAKING AND LISTENING

Choose a fantasy read-aloud, such as *Finn Family Moomintroll* by Tove Jansson. Continuing to focus on the retelling of fiction, give the children the opportunity to retell the previous chapters by allowing them to choose an object to prompt the retelling. For example, provide a number of props (e.g., a black hat made of construction paper) and ask students to find the appropriate object when it appears in the story and put it into a "retelling basket." Before each reading time, have the students retell the story using the gathered objects as prompts for remembering characters and events. By the time the book ends, you will have an object for each chapter or key event in the book—and the students will be efficient storytellers. (RL.1.2)

## 9.  ART, SPEAKING AND LISTENING

Select three or four works to view (e.g., the Klee, Chagall, and Dürer). Ask the students the following questions:

- What animal do you see in this work? Does anyone see a different animal?
- What color is the animal? Is this the real color of this animal?
- Why do you think the artist chose the color he or she did?

Begin to introduce the concept of abstraction (versus realism) by comparing the Dürer image with either the Klee or the Chagall. Ask questions like:

- Is this exactly what a rabbit looks like?
- What about a cat? A picture of a cow? How can we tell the difference?
- What was the artist trying to do? (SL.1.1b, SL.1.3, SL.1.4)

## 10. ART, INFORMATIVE WRITING

Ask the students to draw an animal of their choice. They will then color it using the animal's real colors, or they can choose to use other colors. Students may also choose to do either a realistic or abstract version of their animal. Ask the students to write an informative/explanatory text based on their drawing, using their choice of realistic or creative coloring. (W.1.2)

## READING FOUNDATIONS: A PACING GUIDE FOR READING INSTRUCTION

See Grade One, Level Two, in the Reading Foundations section at the beginning of this book for a complete pacing guide for this unit.

## ADDITIONAL ONLINE RESOURCES

- *Animal Study: From Fiction to Facts* (National Endowment for the Humanities) (RL.1.5)
- *Investigating Animals: Using Nonfiction for Inquiry-Based Research* (ReadWriteThink) (W.1.7)
- Edward Lear home page
- Robert Frost, "The Pasture" and other poems

## TERMINOLOGY

| | | |
|---|---|---|
| Categories | Lesson | Retell |
| Context clues | Main topic | Revision |
| Informative/explanatory | Message | |

## INTERDISCIPLINARY CONNECTIONS

This unit teaches:
- **Art:** Henri Matisse, Albrecht Dürer
- **Science:** Animals (e.g., habitats, unique adaptations, and the food chain)

This unit could be extended to teach:
- **Geography:** Oceans
- **Science:** Animals (e.g., undersea life, habitat destruction, Rachel Carson)

## Grade One, Unit Two Sample Lesson Plan

### Are You My Mother? by P. D. Eastman

In this series of three lessons, students read *Are You My Mother?* by P. D. Eastman, and they:

Explore the adventures of a baby bird in search of his mother (RL.1.1, RL.1.2, RL.1.3)

Consider the importance of the illustrations in the story (RL.1.7, SL.1.1, SL.1.2)

Appreciate the importance of rereading stories (RL.1.2)

### Summary

| Lesson I: Baby Bird Begins a Search | Lesson II: Continue Baby Bird's Search |
|---|---|
| Explore the reason for the mother bird's decision to leave the nest (RL.1.1, RL.1.3, SL.1.1, SL.1.2) | Note the shift in the narrative when the baby bird begins to run (RL.1.1, RL.1.2) |
| Note the changing facial expressions of the baby bird leading up to his decision to search for his mother (RL.1.3, RL.1.7) | Examine the bird's encounter with the Snort (RL.1.1, RL.1.2, RL.1.3, SL.1.1, SL.1.2) |
| Examine the baby bird's exchanges with the animals that he meets (RL.1.1, RL.1.2) | Explore the meeting between the mother and the baby bird (RL.1.1, RL.1.2, RL.1.3, SL.1.1, SL.1.3) |
|  | Consider the impact of the illustrations on the reader's understanding of the baby bird's emotions (RL.1.7, SL.1.1, SL.1.2) |

## Lesson III: Revisit Baby Bird's Adventure

Recall the baby bird's adventures with the help of passages from the text (RL.1.1, RL.1.2, RL.1.3, SL.1.1, SL.1.2)

Chart the baby bird's adventures (RL.1.1, SL.1.5)

Illustrate the baby bird's adventures (SL.1.5)

Consider what *Are You My Mother?* teaches (SL.1.1, SL.1.2)

## Lesson III: Revisit Baby Bird's Adventure

### Objectives

Recall the baby bird's adventures with the help of passages from the text (RL.1.1, RL.1.2, RL.1.3, SL.1.1, SL.1.2)

Chart the baby bird's adventures (RL.1.1, SL.1.5)

Illustrate the baby bird's adventures (SL.1.5)

Consider what *Are You My Mother?* teaches (SL.1.1, SL.1.2)

### Required Materials

☐ *Are You My Mother?* by P. D. Eastman

☐ Large, blank poster boards

☐ Markers

☐ Colored pencils

### Procedures

1. Lead-In:

   The class rereads *Are You My Mother?* aloud. (Depending on the students' reading levels, you may choose to read the story or have students read it.)

2. In a class discussion, the students recall the details of the baby bird's journey.

a. In small groups, students create a chart (see following sample) where they trace the baby bird's steps. They consult the book whenever they are not sure of the next step. (Because the journey begins and ends at home, a circular chart makes the most sense.)

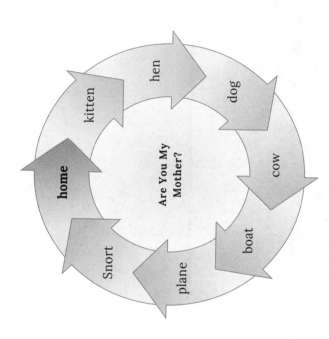

b. Students illustrate the charts. The illustrations will enable students to add individual perspective. In Lessons I and II, the students note the contribution of the illustrations to the presentation of the baby bird, his character, his mood, and his emotions. This is their opportunity to do the same.

3. Closure:

Students will introduce and discuss their groups' charts.

## Differentiation

### Advanced

- When students finish this activity, put them into small performance teams to read the book with expression.
- Arrange for the students to go and read the book to a kindergartener or to a kindergarten class.

### Struggling

- Create a three-by-three table with nouns from the story printed in the table. As you review each noun, have students make a picture of the noun. For example, draw a kitten in the square labeled "kitten." If students need more work with word recognition, play bingo with the words.
- Create the circular chart for the children and allow each child in the group to write two of the words on sticky notes. Have children practice looking at story clues to put the sticky notes in the right place.

## Homework/Assessment

N/A

# Life Lessons

In this third six-week unit of first grade, students read literature and informational texts related to life lessons.

---

## ESSENTIAL QUESTION

How can stories teach us life lessons?

---

## OVERVIEW

Building on the retelling of stories with details, students delve deeper by focusing on the categorizing of story details into the following groupings: characters, key events, and settings. Students read and listen to fables with morals. They also learn about rules for life in a book of manners. Reading the life story of George Washington Carver, students learn about a man who had to overcome obstacles in life to make important contributions to science and agriculture. Students also learn about Thomas Edison's work with electricity and the rules for its safe use. Students write narratives focused on life lessons and create informative/explanatory posters about electricity. Finally, students focus on descriptive words while studying the artwork of Georgia O'Keeffe.

## FOCUS STANDARDS

These Focus Standards have been selected for the unit from the Common Core State Standards.

**RL.1.2:** Retell stories, including key details, and demonstrate understanding of their central message or lesson.

**RL.1.3:** Describe characters, settings, and major events in a story, using key details.

**RI.1.6:** Distinguish between information provided by pictures or other illustrations and information provided by the words in a text.

**W.1.3:** Write narratives in which they recount two or more appropriately sequenced events, include some details regarding what happened, use temporal words to signal event order, and provide some sense of closure.

**L.1.2:** Demonstrate command of the conventions of standard English capitalization, punctuation, and spelling when writing.

**L.1.2(b):** Use end punctuation for sentences.

**RF.1.4:** Read with sufficient accuracy and fluency to support comprehension.

**RF.1.4(b):** Read on-level text orally with accuracy, appropriate rate, and expression on successive readings.

## SUGGESTED OBJECTIVES

- Describe characters, key events, and the setting in a story.
- Identify who is speaking in a story or fable.
- Distinguish between the information provided by the pictures or illustrations in a text and the information provided by the words.
- Using time cue words, providing some details, and ending with a sense of closure, write narratives that include at least two sequenced events.
- With the help of an adult, revise narratives.
- Produce complete sentences with correct past, present, or future verb tenses.
- Use end punctuation for sentences: periods, question marks, and exclamation points.
- Relate the use of punctuation to the way a text should be read expressively.
- Compare and contrast two versions of an Indian fable.
- Create informative/explanatory posters using both text and illustrations (e.g., to teach about electrical safety).

## SUGGESTED WORKS

(E) indicates a CCSS exemplar text; (EA) indicates a text from a writer with other works identified as exemplars.

### LITERARY TEXTS

*Stories*
- *The Blind Men and the Elephant* (Karen Backstein and Annie Mitra)
- *Green Eggs and Ham* (Dr. Seuss) (E)
- *Inch by Inch* (Leo Lionni)
- *The Lion & the Mouse* (Jerry Pinkney)
- *Lousy Rotten Stinkin' Grapes* (Margie Palatini and Barry Moser)
- *Seven Blind Mice* (Ed Young) (EA)
- *Yo! Yes?* (Chris Raschka)

## Stories (Read Aloud)

- *Alexander and the Wind-up Mouse* (Leo Lionni)
- *The Boy Who Cried Wolf* (B. G. Hennessy and Boris Kulikov)
- *Fables* (Arnold Lobel) (EA)
- *The Hare and the Tortoise* (Helen Ward)
- *The Little Red Hen* (Paul Galdone)
- *Punctuation Takes a Vacation* (Robin Pulver and Lynn Rowe Reed)
- *Swimmy* (Leo Lionni)
- *The Tortoise and the Hare* (Janet Stevens)
- *Town Mouse, Country Mouse* (Jan Brett)
- *The Ugly Duckling* (Hans Christian Andersen and Jerry Pinkney)

## Poems

- "By Myself" in *Honey, I Love and Other Poems* (Eloise Greenfield)
- "Ridiculous Rose" in *Where the Sidewalk Ends* (Shel Silverstein)
- "Sharing" in *Falling Up* (Shel Silverstein)

## Poems (Read Aloud)

- *Goops and How to Be Them: A Manual of Manners for Polite Children* (Gelett Burgess)
- "I'm Making a List" in *Where the Sidewalk Ends* (Shel Silverstein)
- "My Mother Says I'm Sickening" in *The New Kid on the Block* (Jack Prelutsky)

## INFORMATIONAL TEXTS

### Nonfiction Books

- *George Washington Carver* (Rookie Biographies) (Lynea Bowdish)
- *Thomas Alva Edison* (Rookie Biographies) (Wil Mara)
- *A Weed Is a Flower: The Life of George Washington Carver* (Aliki) (E)
- *What Is Electricity?* (Rookie Read-About Science) (Lisa Trumbauer)

### Nonfiction Books (Read Aloud)

- *Flick a Switch: How Electricity Gets to Your Home* (Barbara Seuling and Nancy Tobin)
- *Georgia O'Keeffe* (Getting to Know the World's Greatest Artists) (Mike Venezia)
- *Hello! Good-bye!* (Aliki) (EA)
- *Manners* (Aliki) (EA)
- *My Light* (Molly Bang) (EA)
- *Watch Out! At Home* (Claire Llewellyn and Mike Gordon)

## ART, MUSIC, AND MEDIA

*Art*

- Georgia O'Keeffe, *Red Poppy* (1927)
- Georgia O'Keeffe, *Jack in the Pulpit No. IV* (1930)
- Georgia O'Keeffe, *Jimson Weed* (1936)
- Georgia O'Keeffe, *Oriental Poppies* (1928)
- Georgia O'Keeffe, *Two Calla Lilies on Pink* (1928)
- Vincent van Gogh, *Sunflowers* (1888–1889)
- Vincent van Gogh, *Irises* (1890)
- Vincent van Gogh, *Almond Blossom* (1890)
- Vincent van Gogh, *Butterflies and Poppies* (1890)

## SAMPLE ACTIVITIES AND ASSESSMENTS

### 1. READING LITERATURE, LANGUAGE MECHANICS

To introduce the relationship between punctuation and reading expression, use the book *Yo! Yes?* by Chris Raschka. Show the students the cover of the book with its very simple title: *Yo! Yes?* Ask how someone would say those words. As you read the book with the students, have the boys read one page, and the girls the opposite page. As they focus on the illustrations and the way the author ends each sentence, they will know how to read the words, and a story will be created in their minds. Follow this reading with other books so that the children learn how important it is to read with the end punctuation in mind. *Extension:* Reading (reciting) poetry with punctuated lines, such as "Sharing" by Shel Silverstein, would be a way to extend this knowledge of punctuation and dramatic expression into other literary forms. Follow this activity with practice using different kinds of end punctuation. (RL.1.6, RL.1.7, RF.1.4b, L.1.2b)

### 2. READING LITERATURE, READING COMPREHENSION

Tell the students that fables are stories that teach us a lesson. The characters in the story are usually animals and have one main characteristic. Read the familiar fable "The Tortoise and the Hare." Ask students what they can tell you about the tortoise. (He's slow, but steady.) What can they tell about the hare? (He's fast, but undependable.) Create a chart with cells for the title, characters (with one characteristic each), setting, key events (i.e., from the beginning, middle, and end), and the lesson learned (i.e., the moral of the story). As you read each fable in this unit, continue to fill in the chart. Give students more and more responsibility for filling in the characters, setting, and key events of a fable. Assess understanding at the end of the unit by reading a fable and then having each child write or dictate the entries on his or her own chart. (RL.1.2, RL.1.3)

### 3. READING LITERATURE, INFORMATIVE WRITING, SPEAKING AND LISTENING

Tell the students that the Indian fable "The Blind Men and the Elephant" is the original telling of a fable more commonly known in the United States as "Seven Blind Mice." Read the original story first and then read *Seven Blind Mice* by Ed Young. You may want to read the book aloud to students, or they may read on their own if they are able. As the two fables are added to the fable story chart, ask the students to explain how these two stories are the same and how they are different. (RL.1.2, RL.1.9)

## 4. NARRATIVE WRITING, LANGUAGE USAGE

Assign this narrative prompt: "Think of a time when you learned a lesson. Be sure to include at least two sequenced events, use time cue words, provide some details, and include a sense of closure." Encourage the students to think about the lessons learned in the fables as they write their own story. Be sure the students focus on the beginning, middle, and end (where they tell about the lesson learned). Edit to be sure that nouns (singular and plural) match verbs and that verb tenses are correct and consistent. (W.1.3, W.1.5, RL.1.2, L.1.1c, L.1.1e, L.1.1j)

## 5. INFORMATIVE WRITING, LANGUAGE USAGE, SPEAKING AND LISTENING

One of the life lessons focused on in this unit is manners. With the students, create a list of "lunchroom manners" using a book such as *Manners* (Aliki). Students should dictate the sentences while you write them on sentence strips. In this writing lesson, focus on writing complete sentences with subject-verb agreement. To practice handwriting and correct sentence construction, have the students copy some of the sentences. Sentences such as these can be illustrated and compiled in a book titled *Lunchroom Manners*. A follow-up to this lesson would be a humorous list of lunchroom manners inspired by Prelutsky and Silverstein and written in poetic form. (SL.1.6, L.1.1c, L.1.1e, L.1.1j)

## 6. READING INFORMATIONAL TEXT, READING COMPREHENSION, SPEAKING AND LISTENING

Introduce the book *A Weed Is a Flower: The Life of George Washington Carver* by Aliki. Explain that illustrations and text are both very important in a book. Guide students as they read by asking them first to think about what you can learn from the illustrations. Create a two-column chart with the headings Illustrations and Text. When students learn something from studying the illustration, they will write it on a sticky note and put it in the book. When students learn something from the written words of the text, they will also note it on a sticky note. When the students are finished reading the book, use their sticky notes to guide the discussion, focusing on learning from illustrations and learning from the text. (RI.1.6)

## 7. ART, SPEAKING AND LISTENING

Show students images of van Gogh's works in comparison to O'Keeffe's, and discuss the following as a class:

- Both of these artists painted flowers. What is similar and different about their paintings?
- Why do you think each painter chose to paint the flowers as they did? Was it because of their color or shape?
- Do the flowers remind you of anything—like faces or groups of people? (SL.1.3)

## 8. ART, INFORMATIVE WRITING

Consider showing both O'Keeffe and van Gogh works without titles. Have students write a short description of what they see. Which flower can you see actually growing and changing? Which painter chose to make his or her works more abstract? Who painted flowers realistically? (W.1.7, W.1.8)

## 9. INFORMATIVE WRITING, SPEAKING AND LISTENING, ORAL PRESENTATION

After reading several books about electricity, create a list of rules for safety (e.g., avoiding electrical outlets with wet hands). Divide the rules evenly among the students and assign the task of creating a safety poster for each one. Each student will write a rule neatly and show additional information (i.e., the application of the rule) in his or her illustration. Create sets of posters and allow students to present their rules to another classroom or grade level. (W.1.2, RI.1.6, SL.1.5, SL.1.6)

## READING FOUNDATIONS: A PACING GUIDE FOR READING INSTRUCTION

See Grade One, Level Three, in the Reading Foundations section at the beginning of this book for a complete pacing guide for this unit.

## ADDITIONAL ONLINE RESOURCES

- *Building a Matrix for Leo Lionni Books: An Author Study* (ReadWriteThink) (RL.1.9)
- *Aesop and Ananse: Animal Fables and Trickster Tales* (National Endowment for the Humanities) (RL.1.2)
- *The Georgia O'Keeffe Museum*

## TERMINOLOGY

Adjectives
Affixes
Characters
Complete sentences
Declarative
End punctuation
Exclamatory

Fable
Imperative
Interrogative
Key events
Lesson
Message
Moral

Narratives
Period
Revision
Setting
Verbs

## INTERDISCIPLINARY CONNECTIONS

This unit teaches:
- **Art:** Georgia O'Keeffe, Vincent van Gogh
- **Science:** Scientists (e.g., George Washington Carver, Thomas Edison); electricity (e.g., basic principles, safety rules)

This unit could be extended to teach:
- **Science:** Sun (i.e., as a source of energy, light, and heat)

## Grade One, Unit Three Sample Lesson Plan

### A Weed Is a Flower: The Life of George Washington Carver by Aliki

In this series of five lessons, students read *A Weed Is a Flower: The Life of George Washington Carver* by Aliki, and they:

Explore the life of George Washington Carver (RL.1.1, RL.1.2, RL.1.3, RI.1.10)

Trace Carver's successful struggle to get an education (RL.1.1, RL.1.2, RL.1.3, RI.1.10)

Examine the kind of person Carver was (RI.1.2)

Note Carver's contributions to farming (RL.1.2, RL.1.3)

## Summary

### Lesson I: Meet George Washington Carver

Recognize biography as a literary genre

Discuss the function of a biography

Note that Aliki is both the author and the illustrator of the book

Observe the cover and discuss its content

Listen and consider the purpose of the introduction to the book (RI.1.10)

### Lesson III: George Washington Carver Is Free

Trace Carver's struggle to get an education (RL.1.1, RL.1.2, RL.1.3, RI.1.10)

List the jobs he had

(Continue to) list Carver's characteristics (RI.1.2)

Note the point in the story where Carver remembers that his neighbors used to call him "Plant Doctor" (RL.1.2, RL.1.3)

Identify a shift in the plot

### Lesson II: Young George Washington Carver

Note the basic facts of Carver's early years (RL.1.2, RL.1.3, RI.1.10)

Explore Moses Carver's attitude toward the young Carver (RL.1.2, RL.1.3)

(Begin to) list the characteristics of the young boy (RL.1.2, RL.1.3)

Investigate his actions (RL.1.2, RL.1.3)

Consider how his acts reflect who he is

### Lesson IV: The Plant Doctor

Examine Carver's career as the Plant Doctor (RL.1.2, RL.1.3)

Consider how Carver's habit of asking questions helped him to become successful

Investigate Carver's contribution to farming in America (RL.1.2, RL.1.3)

## Lesson V: A Flower for the Plant Doctor

Study the title of the book

Revisit the life of Carver (RL.1.2, RL.1.3, SL.1.1)

Imagine words that describe his life (introduce the concepts of simile and metaphor) (L.1.6)

Consider images that portray the kind of person he was (RL.1.7, RI.1.7, RF.1.3, SL.1.4, SL.1.5)

Reflect on the lessons that Carver's life teaches (SL.1.1a)

## Lesson V: A Flower for the Plant Doctor

*Objectives*

Study the title of the book

Revisit the life of Carver (RL.1.2, RL.1.3, SL.1.1)

Imagine words that describe his life (introduce the concepts of simile and metaphor) (L.1.6)

Consider images that portray the kind of person he was (RL.1.7, RI.1.7, RF.1.3, SL.1.4, SL.1.5)

Reflect on the lessons that Carver's life teaches (SL.1.1a)

*Required Materials*

☐ *A Weed Is a Flower: The Life of George Washington Carver* by Aliki
☐ Large, blank poster board
☐ Construction paper
☐ Scissors
☐ Markers
☐ Colored pencils
☐ Glue

*Procedures*

1. Lead-In:

   Students discuss the life of George Washington Carver.

2. Step by Step:

   a. Following a prompt, the students select words to describe Carver. Students use their imaginations; for example, if a child says "brave," then ask for another word or an image that evokes bravery, such as a lion. The purpose of this activity is to introduce the concepts of simile and metaphor, though students do not need to master those terms at this level. List all the words generated on the board and encourage students to use what they know about phonics and word analysis skills to help with spelling the words.

   b. Once a substantial list has been generated, the students choose words, write them on the construction paper, and illustrate them.

   c. As the students complete their work, place the drawings on a poster board. When the students are done, the final product should be a collection of words and drawings that describe George Washington Carver. (Perhaps place the children's work in the shape of a flower.)

3. Closure:

   Sit with the students and reflect on the following question: Who was Carver, and why was he such a special man?

## Differentiation

### Advanced

- After deciding on metaphors, students will create a graphic representation describing George Washington Carver using an online tool to generate a word cloud or other visualization.

### Struggling

- To pre-teach the concept of simile, students will focus on familiar animal characteristics. Supply the beginning of a phrase and ask students to fill in the name of the animal (e.g., "as hungry as a BEAR," "as fast as a CHEETAH," "as slow as a TURTLE," and "as quiet as a MOUSE").

- To pre-teach the concept of metaphor, explain that these animals can be used to represent a human characteristic, such as a lion representing bravery in the case of George Washington Carver.

## Homework/Assessment

N/A

# Winds of Change

In this fourth six-week unit of first grade, students look at changes in nature through nonfiction, changes in the feelings of characters through fantasy, and changes in their own writing through revision.

---

## ESSENTIAL QUESTION

How do you know what a character is feeling and when these feelings change?

---

## OVERVIEW

Building on the simple characteristics of fable characters, students describe the characters' feelings. Focusing on verbs, students act out the various ways Dorothy in *The Wonderful Wizard of Oz* could "walk" on the yellow brick road. They read an article on wind power to look at how wind can provide energy efficiently. They view the nonfiction in this unit through the lens of cause and effect. Finally, students look at writing as a moldable, changing piece of work that can improve with revision.

## FOCUS STANDARDS

These Focus Standards have been selected for the unit from the Common Core State Standards.

**RL.1.4:** Identify words and phrases in stories or poems that suggest feelings or appeal to the senses.

**RI.1.8:** Identify the reasons an author gives to support points in a text.

**W.1.5:** With guidance and support from adults, focus on a topic, respond to questions and suggestions from peers, and add details to strengthen writing as needed.

**L.1.5:** With guidance and support from adults, demonstrate understanding of word relationships and nuances in word meanings.

**L.1.5(d):** Distinguish shades of meaning among verbs differing in manner (e.g., *look, peek, glance, stare, glare, and scowl*) and adjectives differing in intensity (e.g., *large, gigantic*) by defining or choosing them or by acting out the meanings.

**SL.1.4:** Describe people, places, things, and events with relevant details, expressing ideas and feelings clearly.

## SUGGESTED OBJECTIVES

- Identify words and phrases in stories or poems that suggest feelings and appeal to the senses.
- Identify cause-and-effect relationships in informational text.
- Add details as needed to strengthen writing through revision.
- Distinguish shades of meaning among verbs by defining, choosing, or acting out the meanings.
- Using commas to separate the words, dictate sentences with a series of nouns.
- Write a narrative text with a focus on feelings.
- Revise writing using temporal words, feeling words, and vivid verbs.
- Distinguish between the root and affixes of verb conjugations, such as *walk, walks, walked, walking*.
- Use commas in a series and identify the conjunction (e.g., "I see monkeys, tigers, and elephants at the zoo").

## SUGGESTED WORKS

(E) indicates a CCSS exemplar text; (EA) indicates a text from a writer with other works identified as exemplars.

### LITERARY TEXTS

*Stories*

- *Changes, Changes* (Pat Hutchins)
- *Frog and Toad All Year* (Arnold Lobel) (EA)
- *My Name Is Yoon* (Helen Recorvits and Gabi Swiatkowska)
- *Ten Apples Up on Top!* (Dr. Seuss) (EA)
- *Owl at Home* (Arnold Lobel) (E)
- *When Sophie Gets Angry—Really, Really Angry . . .* (Molly Bang) (EA)
- *The Wind Blew* (Pat Hutchins)

*Stories (Read Aloud)*

- *Alexander and the Horrible, No Good, Very Bad Day* (Judith Viorst and Ray Cruz)
- *Alexander, Who's Not (Do You Hear Me? I Mean It!) Going to Move* (Judith Viorst, Ray Cruz, and Robin Preiss Glasser)

- *The Bat Boy and His Violin* (Gavin Curtis and E. B. Lewis)
- *Goin' Someplace Special* (Patricia C. McKissack and Jerry Pinkney)
- *If You Give a Mouse a Cookie* (Laura Joffe Numeroff and Felicia Bond)
- *Twister on Tuesday* (Mary Pope Osborne and Sal Murdocca) (EA)
- *The Wonderful Wizard of Oz* (L. Frank Baum) (E)

## Poems

- "Covers" in *The Sun Is So Quiet* (Nikki Giovanni) (E)
- "Drinking Fountain" in *Random House Book of Poetry for Children* (Marchette Chute) (E)
- "It Fell in the City" in *Blackberry Ink* (Eve Merriam) (E)
- "Laughing Boy" in *Haiku: This Other World* (Richard Wright) (E)

## Poems (Read Aloud)

- "Blow, Wind, Blow!" (Traditional)
- "Who Has Seen the Wind?" in *Rossetti: Poems* (Everyman's Library Pocket Poets) (Christina Rossetti) (E)
- "The Wind" in *A Child's Garden of Verses* (Robert Louis Stevenson)
- "Windy Nights" in *A Child's Garden of Verses* (Robert Louis Stevenson)

# INFORMATIONAL TEXTS

## Nonfiction Books

- *Storms* (National Geographic Readers) (Miriam Goin)
- "Wind Power" (*National Geographic Young Explorer!*) (November–December 2009) (E)

## Nonfiction Books (Read Aloud)

- *Feelings* (Aliki) (EA)
- *Flash, Crash, Rumble, and Roll* (Franklyn M. Branley and True Kelley)
- *How People Learned to Fly* (Fran Hodgkins and True Kelley) (E)
- *Super Storms* (Seymour Simon)
- *Tornadoes!* (Gail Gibbons) (EA)
- *Tornadoes* (Seymour Simon)
- *Twisters and Other Terrible Storms: A Nonfiction Companion to Magic Tree House #23: Twister on Tuesday* (Will and Mary Pope Osborne, and Sal Murdocca) (EA)

# ART, MUSIC, AND MEDIA

## Art

- Richard Diebenkorn, *Ocean Park No. 38* (1971)
- Richard Diebenkorn, *Ocean Park No. 49* (1972)
- Richard Diebenkorn, *Ocean Park No. 54* (1972)
- Richard Diebenkorn, *Ocean Park No. 115* (1979)

## Music

- Johann Sebastian Bach, Concerto for 2 Violins, Strings, and Continuo in D Minor (Double Violin Concerto) (1730–1731)
- Ludwig van Beethoven, Violin Concerto in D Major, op. 61 (1806)
- Pyotr Ilyich Tchaikovsky, Violin Concerto in D Major, op. 35 (1878)
- Wolfgang Amadeus Mozart, Violin Concerto No. 4 in D Major (1775)

## Film

- Victor Fleming, dir., *The Wizard of Oz* (1939)

## SAMPLE ACTIVITIES AND ASSESSMENTS

### 1. READING LITERATURE, READING COMPREHENSION

Read *The Wonderful Wizard of Oz* by L. Frank Baum aloud to the class. As students meet each character in the text, guide them to think about the character's feelings and how the author shows us how the character feels. Discuss how the author helps us use our senses to see, smell, feel, hear, and even taste while we are reading a book. As you read aloud, model the way you are drawn to use your senses. For example, in the second paragraph of chapter 1, the author describes Kansas so that you can "see" the countryside clearly. Then he goes on to describe Aunt Em, Uncle Henry, Toto, and Dorothy, with a focus on their feelings. (RL.1.3, RL.1.4)

### 2. LANGUAGE USAGE

Choose some verbs that are rather bland, such as "to walk." Ask the students to imagine that they are in the book (*The Wonderful Wizard of Oz*) with Dorothy and that they are walking on the yellow brick road. Have them imagine that they are really happy (e.g., when they see the Emerald City). How would they walk? (Possible answers: *skip, run, dance.*) Allow students to show us how that kind of motion would look. Then have them imagine that they are feeling scared (e.g., when walking through the forest). How would they walk? (Possible answers: *tiptoe, creep.*) Make a list of all the words that could be used as a better choice than *walk*. This lesson on verbs can be extended to cover tenses, roots, and affixes -ed, -s, and -ing. To make the extending lessons more fun, create a "wordle" (from www.wordle.net) for each verb tense (i.e., present tense verbs for "walk," past tense verbs for "walk") (SL.1.4, L1.1e, L.1.4b, L.1.4c, L.1.5d)

### 3. LANGUAGE USAGE, VOCABULARY

To reinforce the idea of a wide range of alternatives for a word like *see*, write the words *look, peek, glance, stare, glare,* and *scowl* on cards. Have the students arrange the cards in order from the most to least cautious (e.g., peek → glance → look → stare → glare → scowl). Use a thesaurus to add other synonyms of "to see" and add them into the range of words. (L.1.5d)

### 4. NARRATIVE WRITING, LANGUAGE USAGE

Give students this prompt: "Write a story about a time you felt happy. Be sure to include at least two sequenced events, use time cue words, provide some details, and include a sense of closure." Combining the focuses of this unit (revision, appealing to the senses with details, and using well-chosen verbs), zero in on details and synonyms while the students revise their stories.

Help the students watch for the proper use of personal, possessive, and indefinite pronouns (e.g., *I, me, my; they, them, their; anyone, everything*) as they are editing. (W.1.3, W.1.5, L.1.1d)

## 5. READING INFORMATIONAL TEXT, INFORMATIVE WRITING, POETRY WRITING

Introduce an informative article such as "Wind Power" (*National Geographic Young Explorer!*). First, ask students to think about what wind causes and brainstorm with the children. Then, have the students read the article independently, with partners, or with you to find out what the wind causes.

| Cause | Effect |
| --- | --- |
| Wind | "Whips up fun" (study illustration for specifics) |
| Wind | Kites fly |
| Wind | Pushes sailboats |
| Wind | Windmills spin, turning wind energy into electricity |

Continue this activity with more nonfiction articles and books, continually giving students more of the responsibility for recording their own ideas. Throughout the unit, continue reading and reciting the poems in the unit to build a love for poetry. Blend the recording of ideas from the nonfiction works into a creative writing activity by creating an illustrated free-form poem using the wind cause-and-effect chart as inspiration. As a class, generate more effects of wind that students may have witnessed. Begin and end the poem with the word *wind*. (RL.1.10, RI.1.8, W.1.7, W.1.8)

## 6. MUSIC, READING LITERATURE, SPEAKING AND LISTENING

Throughout the day, play some violin concerto music in the background. Ask the students how the music made them feel. For example, ask them to finish this sentence: "During the music, I felt _____." Continue to listen to the music at any opportunity. Then read the book *The Bat Boy and His Violin* by Curtis and Lewis, which is the story of a boy who loved to play the violin. After the students listen to the story, go back through the text and have the children talk about how the author used words and phrases to let the reader know how the characters in the book felt. (RL.1.4, L.1.1i)

## 7. LANGUAGE USAGE

To teach the use of a comma in a series, list the five senses on the whiteboard. Give students a "setting" card (e.g., zoo, farm, or beach) and have them dictate a sentence using one of the senses, naming three things they sense in that setting. Explain that when we use the word *and*, we are using a conjunction. For example, "At the zoo, I smell popcorn, elephants, and cotton candy." Write the dictated sentence and then challenge them to write their own sentences using *and* in the sentences. (L.1.1g, L.1.2c)

## 8. READING INFORMATIONAL TEXT, LANGUAGE USAGE

As you read books about the topic of wind or tornadoes, place the word *tornado* in the center of a display board. Look for causes of tornadoes (post on the left) and the effects of tornadoes (post on the right), creating a visual graphic organizer for cause and effect. Have students use the graphic organizer to create sentences showing cause and effect (e.g., "The high winds of the tornado tore the roof from the top of the Civic Center."). Repeat this activity as you read other informational books with a cause-and-effect structure, giving students more of the responsibility for placing sticky notes on the graphic organizer and writing out the sentences. (RL.1.10, RI.1.8)

## 9. ART, LANGUAGE USAGE, SPEAKING AND LISTENING

Show students a sampling of Richard Diebenkorn's *Ocean Park* series, which the painter began in 1967 and worked on for the rest of his life. To help them identify key details, ask students:

- What do you see in these images—the ocean? clouds? sand?
- What techniques has Diebenkorn used to convey the look and feel of these objects? Use adjectives and action verbs to describe what you see. (SL.1.3, L.1.1, L.1.5)

## 10. ART, SPEAKING AND LISTENING

Take time to have students look at each painting closely. What changes in Diebenkorn's series of *Ocean Park* paintings? Where? Discuss together the use of one subject in this selection. What aspects of the paintings stay the same? (SL.1.1, SL.1.3, SL.1.4, SL.1.6)

## READING FOUNDATIONS: A PACING GUIDE FOR READING INSTRUCTION

See Grade One, Level Four, in the Reading Foundations section at the beginning of this book for a complete pacing guide for this unit.

## ADDITIONAL ONLINE RESOURCES

- *The Day Jimmy's Boa Taught Cause and Effect* (ReadWriteThink) (RI.1.8)
- *Lesson Plan on Tornadoes* (National Geographic)

## TERMINOLOGY

Cause

Effect

Revision

Verbs

## INTERDISCIPLINARY CONNECTIONS

This unit teaches:

- **Art:** Richard Diebenkorn
- **Music:** Violin concertos (by Tchaikovsky, Mozart, Bach, and Beethoven)
- **Science:** Weather (e.g., wind and tornadoes)

This unit could be extended to teach:

- **Science:** Changing states of matter (e.g., solid, liquid, and gas)

## Grade One, Unit Four Sample Lesson Plan

### Owl at Home *by Arnold Lobel*

In this series of six lessons, students read *Owl at Home* by Arnold Lobel, and they:

Explore the adventures of Owl (RL.1.1, RL.1.2, RL.1.3, RL.1.4, SL.1.1, SL.1.2)

Note Lobel's use of illustrations to depict Owl's adventures (RL.1.7)

Offer individual perspectives of Owl's character and his understanding of his environment (RL.1.2, RL.1.3, W.1.1, W.1.2, W.1.3)

### Summary

| | |
|---|---|
| **Lesson I: "The Guest"**<br><br>Follow the plot of "The Guest" (RL.1.1, RL.1.2, RL.1.3)<br><br>Identify Owl's guest (RL.1.3, RL.1.3)<br><br>Explore Owl's actions (RL.1.2, SL.1.1, SL.1.2)<br><br>Examine Lobel's use of illustrations to depict the events in the story (RL.1.7) | **Lesson II: "Strange Bumps"**<br><br>Follow the plot of "Strange Bumps" (RL.1.1, RL.1.2, RL.1.3, SL.1.1)<br><br>Probe the mystery of the "strange bumps" along with Owl (RL.1.2, SL.1.1, SL.1.2)<br><br>Examine the use of illustrations to depict Owl's fear (RL.1.7)<br><br>Note the humor in the story |
| **Lesson III: "Tear-Water Tea"**<br><br>Follow the plot of "Tear-Water Tea" (RL.1.1, RL.1.2, RL.1.3)<br><br>Identify the strange idea of the story (RL.1.3)<br><br>Note what you learn about Owl's life (RL.1.1, RL.1.2, RL.1.3)<br><br>Explore what this strange idea reveals about Owl's character (RL.1.2, SL.1.1, SL.1.2) | **Lesson IV: "Upstairs and Downstairs"**<br><br>Follow the plot of "Upstairs and Downstairs" (RL.1.1, RL.1.2, RL.1.3)<br><br>Identify Owl's problem (RL.1.2)<br><br>Probe Owl's attempt to solve his problem (RL.1.2, SL.1.1, SL.1.2)<br><br>Examine the image of Owl at the end of the story (p. 48) (RL.1.7) |

## Lesson V: "Owl and the Moon"

Follow the plot of "Owl and the Moon" (RL.1.1, RL.1.2, RL.1.3)

Explore Owl's view of friendship (RL.1.2, SL.1.1, SL.1.2)

Ponder the reasons for Owl's sadness (RL.1.2. SL.1.1, SL.1.2)

Identify the purpose of the final illustration of the story (p. 64) (RL.1.7)

## Lesson VI: Assessing Owl's Adventures

Revisit Owl's stories (RL.1.1, RL.1.2, SL.1.1)

Select a favorite story

Identify the reason for choosing the story (RL.1.2, RL.1.3)

Articulate a position in support of that choice (W.1.1, W.1.2, W.1.3)

## Lesson VI: Assessing Owl's Adventures

### Objectives

Revisit Owl's stories (RL.1.1, RL.1.2, SL.1.1)

Select a favorite story

Identify the reason for choosing the story (RL.1.2, RL.1.3)

Articulate a position in support of that choice (W.1.1, W.1.2, W.1.3)

### Required Materials

☐ *Owl at Home* by Arnold Lobel

☐ Notebooks

☐ Pencils

### Procedures

1. Lead-In:

    Lead a brief discussion revisiting Owl's stories.

2. Step by Step:

    a.  Students select a favorite story.

    b.  With your assistance, students write paragraphs about the story. Students' paragraphs consist of

    ○ a sentence that identifies the story and the name of the author

    ○ a sentence that offers a point of view about the story

    ○ a sentence (or more, depending on the individual student's ability) that supports the student's opinion

3. Closure:

Student volunteers, taking turns, read their paragraphs aloud.

## Differentiation

### Advanced

- After students complete the best paragraph they can, give them the opportunity to revise and edit with a partner.
- Students may want to type their paragraphs and illustrate their favorite stories.

### Struggling

- Prepare a "fill in the blank" version of the paragraph, giving students a structure for their writing. If time allows, have the students copy the paragraph onto a piece of lined paper. The following is an example:
  - My favorite story in *Owl at Home* by _____ was " _____ ." I chose this story because _____ . I also enjoyed
  
  _____ .

## Homework/Assessment

Students' paragraphs enable you to assess

- Students' basic comprehension of the stories in *Owl at Home*
- Students' ability to take a position
- Students' ability to support their position

# American Contributions

In this fifth six-week unit of first grade, students meet Americans who shaped our nation's history.

---

## ESSENTIAL QUESTION

How does learning about remarkable people help us learn about history?

---

## OVERVIEW

Building on the work with fiction and informational texts in previous units, students meet important Americans in informational books and then hear fictional stories about the same people. Focusing on reading independently and fluently, students read nonfiction to learn about the contributions made by important Americans. By placing events of a similar time period on a time line, students are able to visualize the connections among events and people. Students write and revise an opinion piece. The unit also focuses on vocabulary in context as students learn to read and reread for meaning.

## FOCUS STANDARDS

These Focus Standards have been selected for the unit from the Common Core State Standards.

**RI.1.3:** Describe the connection between two individuals, events, ideas, or pieces of information in a text.

**RI.1.10:** With prompting and support, read informational texts appropriately complex for grade 1.

**RF.1.4:** Read with sufficient accuracy and fluency to support comprehension.

**RF.1.4(c):** Use context to confirm or self-correct word recognition and understanding, rereading as necessary.

**W.1.1:** Write opinion pieces in which they introduce the topic or name the book they are writing about, state an opinion, supply a reason for the opinion, and provide some sense of closure.

**SL.1.3:** Ask and answer questions about what a speaker says in order to gather additional information or clarify something that is not understood.

## SUGGESTED OBJECTIVES

- Read nonfiction independently, proficiently, and fluently.
- See and describe the connection between two key events or ideas within a text and between two texts.
- Use context to confirm or self-correct word recognition.
- Reread when necessary.
- Write an opinion about an interesting person studied in this unit, supporting their choices with reasons.
- Revise opinion writing.

## SUGGESTED WORKS

(E) indicates a CCSS exemplar text; (EA) indicates a text from a writer with other works identified as exemplars.

### LITERARY TEXTS

*Stories (Read Aloud)*

- *Abe Lincoln Crosses a Creek: A Tall, Thin Tale* (Deborah Hopkinson and John Hendrix)
- *A. Lincoln and Me* (Louise Borden and Ted Lewin)
- *George Washington and the General's Dog* (Frank Murphy and Richard Walz)
- *The Hatmaker's Sign: A Story by Benjamin Franklin* (Candace Fleming and Robert Parker)
- *Little House in the Big Woods* (Laura Ingalls Wilder and Garth Williams) (E)
- *Mr. Lincoln's Whiskers* (Karen Winnick)
- *Rockwell: A Boy and His Dog* (Loren Spiotta-DiMare and Cliff Miller)
- *A True Story About Jackie Robinson (Testing the Ice)* (Sharon Robinson and Kadir Nelson)
- *Willie Was Different: A Children's Story* (Norman Rockwell)

*Poems (Read Aloud)*

- "Hope" in *The Collected Poetry of Langston Hughes* (Langston Hughes) (EA)
- "Washington" in *The Random House Book of Poetry for Children* (Nancy Byrd Turner)
- "You're a Grand Old Flag" (George M. Cohan and Norman Rockwell)

## INFORMATIONAL TEXTS

### Nonfiction Books

- *Abraham Lincoln* (Rookie Biographies) (Wil Mara)
- *Benjamin Franklin* (Rookie Biographies) (Wil Mara)
- *George Washington* (Rookie Biographies) (Wil Mara)
- *Jackie Robinson* (Rookie Biographies) (Wil Mara)
- *Laura Ingalls Wilder* (Rookie Biographies) (Wil Mara)
- *Let's Read About . . . Abraham Lincoln* (Scholastic First Biographies) (Sonia Black and Carol Heyer)
- *Let's Read About . . . César Chávez* (Scholastic First Biographies) (Jerry Tello)
- *Let's Read About . . . George Washington* (Scholastic First Biographies) (Kimberly Weinberger and Bob Doucet)
- *The Man Who Walked Between the Towers* (Mordicai Gerstein)
- *Paul Revere* (Rookie Biographies) (Wil Mara)
- *Pocahontas* (DK Readers) (Caryn Jenner)

### Nonfiction Books (Read Aloud)

- *Betsy Ross: The Story of Our Flag* (Easy Reader Biographies) (Pamela Chanko)
- *Dave the Potter: Artist, Poet, Slave* (Laban Carrick Hill and Bryan Collier) (EA)
- *John, Paul, George, and Ben* (Lane Smith)
- *A Picture Book of Benjamin Franklin* (David A. Adler, John Wallner, and Alexandra Wallner)
- *A Picture Book of George Washington* (David A. Adler, John Wallner, and Alexandra Wallner)
- *A Picture Book of Paul Revere* (David A. Adler, John Wallner, and Alexandra Wallner)

## ART, MUSIC, AND MEDIA

### Art

- Ben Wittick, *Geronimo (Goyathlay), a Chiricahua Apache; full-length, kneeling with rifle* (1887)
- *Dr. Martin Luther King Jr. at the Lincoln Memorial* (artist unknown, 1963)
- George P.A. Healey, *Abraham Lincoln* (1869)
- Gilbert Stuart, *Dolley Madison* (1804)
- Gilbert Stuart, *George Washington* (1796)
- John Singleton Copley, *Paul Revere* (1768)
- *Portrait of Harriet Tubman* (artist and date unknown)

### Music

- "Yankee Doodle Boy" (George M. Cohan)
- "You're a Grand Old Flag" (George M. Cohan)

## SAMPLE ACTIVITIES AND ASSESSMENTS

### 1. READING INFORMATIONAL TEXT, SPEAKING AND LISTENING

To help students make visual connections between events and people during early American history, create a simple time line and record events as you read books on this topic together or as students report back on what they read independently. Students should understand that although these informational texts focus on different people or topics, it all happened at the same time in history. By extending the time line to include historical figures, students begin to understand chronology and the connections between events in informational texts. (RI.1.3, RI.1.10)

### 2. READING INFORMATIONAL TEXT, READING FLUENCY, SPEAKING AND LISTENING

Have students choose one of the biographies they enjoyed reading. Have them practice reading the book until they can read it well (i.e., with phrasing and expression). As students read their biographies independently, look for opportunities to use context to confirm or self-correct word recognition and understanding, encouraging the children to reread as necessary. Take the books to a kindergarten class and have students read the books aloud to students there. (RF.1.4a, RF.1.4b, RF.1.4c, RI.1.4, RI.1.10)

### 3. OPINION WRITING

Give students this prompt: "Choose one of the people from this unit who you think is the most interesting. Write about the person. Be sure to name the person and to give two or three reasons why you think he or she is the most interesting." (W.1.1)

### 4. MUSIC, VOCABULARY

Display the lyrics to each of the songs on an overhead projector or interactive whiteboard. After singing the songs together several times, allow the students to choose words that are interesting to them and circle them. Help students look for clues in the text to determine word meanings. Check for the correct definitions in a dictionary. Collect these and other words to add to the word bank from reading throughout the unit. Continue reviewing the songs until the lyrics are well known or memorized. (RF.1.4c)

### 5. INFORMATIVE WRITING, LANGUAGE USAGE, VOCABULARY

Give students this prompt: "Write three sentences about an American person we've read about recently, using at least three new words from our word bank in your work. Illustrate each sentence to demonstrate the meaning of each word." Do a mini-lesson on articles (*a, the*) and demonstrative pronouns (*this, that, these, those*) as the students write their sentences. (L.1.1h, L.1.1j, L.1.2a, L.1.2b, L.1.2d, L.1.2e, L.1.5c, L.1.6)

### 6. READING LITERATURE, INFORMATIVE WRITING, NARRATIVE WRITING

Read and discuss *The Hatmaker's Sign* by Candace Fleming and Robert Parker. Talk about how it relates to revision. Instruct students to take a piece of their writing (such as the "most interesting" piece) and carefully work on revising ideas. Students should edit their pieces and publish them. (W.1.5, RL.1.2)

## 7. READING LITERATURE, READING INFORMATIONAL TEXT, SPEAKING AND LISTENING

Create pairings of books that are literary and informational (e.g., *George Washington and the General's Dog* by Frank Murphy and *George Washington* by Wil Mara). Discuss how reading a story about a character/historic person differs from reading a biography of the same person. Talk about how these two books connect to each other. For example, ask questions like, "How were the books the same?" and "How were they different?" In this unit are numerous potential book pairings among the biographies, fictional stories, and even a fictional story written by the historical person himself (Benjamin Franklin). Pairing the readings presents an opportunity to highlight the different characteristics of each genre. (RI.1.3, RL.1.5, RL.1.7)

## 8. SPEAKING AND LISTENING, INFORMATIVE WRITING

Invite a person from your community who has made a notable contribution to visit your classroom. After the speaker has shared his or her story, invite the students to ask questions to gather additional information or to clarify understanding. Have the students write thank-you notes to the guest speaker, telling the speaker one new thing learned during the presentation. (SL.1.3, W.1.8)

## 9. ART, SPEAKING AND LISTENING

Select several works to view—for instance, you might choose to compare the Copley with the Stuarts. Ask the students to turn to the person next to them and discuss such questions as: "Who is this subject?" and "How did the artist choose to depict/portray this famous American?" Ask students to search the paintings or photographs for important clues to discover who this person really is, and to describe what information they gather simply by looking carefully. (SL.1.1, SL.1.3, SL.1.4, SL.1.6)

## 10. ART, SPEAKING AND LISTENING

Show students Stuart's portrait of Washington, the Martin Luther King Jr. photograph, and the photograph of Geronimo. Ask students to focus on the setting that surrounds each of the subjects. You might ask the following questions to encourage students to deepen their understanding:

- In the case of Washington, how did the painter place his subject in order to convey his importance?
- What does the painter add to the scene?
- How does this differ from the Martin Luther King Jr. photograph, where the photographer had to instantly capture the setting?
- Can you see a merging of these two qualities in the image of Geronimo? (SL.1.1, SL.1.3, SL.1.4, SL.1.6)

## READING FOUNDATIONS: A PACING GUIDE FOR READING INSTRUCTION

See Grade One, Level Five, in the Reading Foundations section at the beginning of this book for a complete pacing guide for this unit.

## ADDITIONAL ONLINE RESOURCES

- *Collaborative Stories 2: Revising* (ReadWriteThink) (W.1.5) Note: Although this is a revision lesson based on a narrative, the technique would work for revising an opinion piece as well.
- Bio-Cube (ReadWriteThink) (RI.1.3)

## TERMINOLOGY

| | | |
|---|---|---|
| Biography | Opinion | Word bank |
| Compare | Reread | Words in context |
| Contrast | Support | |
| Expression | Time line | |

## INTERDISCIPLINARY CONNECTIONS

This unit teaches:

- **Art:** Portraiture, Gilbert Stuart
- **Music:** George M. Cohan
- **Geography:** United States (e.g., thirteen colonies, fifty states, territories)
- **History:** Important Americans (e.g., George Washington, Benjamin Franklin, Harriet Tubman, Geronimo)

This unit could be extended to teach:

- **Geography:** Appalachian Mountains, Rocky Mountains, Mississippi River
- **History:** American Revolution (e.g., Boston Tea Party, Paul Revere's Ride)

## Grade One, Unit Five Sample Lesson Plan

Little House in the Big Woods *by Laura Ingalls Wilder*

In this series of eleven lessons, students read *Little House in the Big Woods* by Laura Ingalls Wilder, and they:

- Explore the life of Laura and her family (RL.1.3)
- Consider scenes to illustrate (RL.1.2)
- Recall details of the scenes (RL.1.1, SL.1.2)
- Write appropriate captions for the illustrations (SL.1.4, SL.1.5, L.1.1, L.1.2)
- Revisit *Little House in the Big Woods* (SL.1.2)
- Explore the life of Laura Ingalls Wilder (RI.1.10, RF.1.4)

## Summary

| Lesson I: *Little House in the Big Woods* | Lessons II–III: Chs. 1–4 |
|---|---|
| Locate Wisconsin on a United States map (RI.1.5, RL.1.5) | Reflect on activities from Lesson I |
| Meet the family members who live in the "little gray house" (RL.1.3) | Proceed to scenes in Ch. 2–Ch. 4 (RL.1.3) |
| Note the author's name | Examine the "substories" in Ch. 2 and Ch. 3 (RL.1.2) |
| Recall details from Ch. 1 (RL.1.1, SL.1.2) | Imagine the family "making pictures" in the snow (RL.1.4) |
| Explore the family's activities (RL.1.3) | Explore Prince's story (SL.1.2) |
| Consider scenes to illustrate (RL.1.2) | Consider scenes to illustrate (RL.1.2) |
| Identify details in assigned scene (RL.1.1, SL.1.2) | Identify details in assigned scene (RL.1.1, SL.1.2) |
| Illustrate scene (RL.1.7, SL.1.2) | Illustrate scene (RL.1.7, SL.1.2) |
| Write appropriate caption for the scene (SL.1.4, SL.1.5, L.1.1, L.1.2) | Write appropriate caption for the scene (SL.1.4, SL.1.5, L.1.1, L.1.2) |

## Lessons IV–V: Chs. 5-7

Explore the lesson of the story about Grandpa (Ch. 5) (RL.1.2)

Probe father's wisdom (RL.1.3)

Examine Ma's courage (Ch. 6) (RL.1.3)

Visualize Grandpa making sugar (RL.1.4)

Consider the mood of the changing seasons (RL.1.4)

Consider scenes to illustrate (RL.1.2)

Identify details in assigned scene (RL.1.1)

Illustrate scene (RL.1.7, SL.1.2)

Write appropriate caption for the scene (SL.1.4, SL.1.5, L.1.1, L.1.2)

## Lessons VI–VII: Chs. 8-10

Explore the setting of the opening scene of Ch. 8 (RL.1.4)

Imagine the smells in Grandma's kitchen (RL.1.4)

Visualize the family dancing (RL.1.3, RL.1.4)

Explore the changing seasons (RL.1.4)

Consider scenes to illustrate (RL.1.2)

Identify details in assigned scene (RL.1.1, SL.1.2)

Illustrate scene (RL.1.7)

Write appropriate caption for the scene (SL.1.4, SL.1.5, L.1.1, L.1.2)

## Lessons VIII–IX: Chs. 11–13

Investigate the harvest season (SL.1.2)

Explore the purpose of storing food (SL.1.2)

Note the customs of autumn (SL.1.2)

Probe why Pa did not kill the deer (RL.1.3)

Consider scenes to illustrate (RL.1.2)

Identify details in assigned scene (RL.1.1, SL.1.2)

Illustrate scene (RL.1.7)

Write appropriate caption for the scene (SL.1.4, SL.1.5, L.1.1, L.1.2)

## Lesson X: *Little House* Revisited

Display the illustrations

Revisit *Little House in the Big Woods* (SL.1.2)

Explore new impressions (SL.1.2)

## Lesson XI: The Life of Laura Ingalls Wilder

(After reading *Laura Ingalls Wilder* by Wil Mara)

Identify biography as a genre

Explore the life of Laura Ingalls Wilder (RI.1.10, RF.1.4)

Probe the similarities between *Little House* and the biography (RI.1.3)

## Lesson I: *Little House in the Big Woods*

### Objectives

Locate Wisconsin on a United States map (RI.1.5, RL.1.5)

Meet the family members who live in the "little gray house" (RL.1.3)

Note the author's name

Recall details from Ch. 1 (RL.1.1, SL.1.2)

Explore the family's activities (RL.1.3)

Consider scenes to illustrate (RL.1.2)

Identify details in assigned scene (RL.1.1, SL.1.2)

Illustrate scene (RL.1.7, SL.1.2)

Write appropriate caption for the scene (SL.1.4, SL.1.5, L.1.1, L.1.2)

### *Required Materials*

☐ Class set of *Little House in the Big Woods* by Laura Ingalls Wilder

☐ Markers/colored pencils

☐ Pencils

☐ Drawing paper

### *Procedures*

1. Lead-In:

   With your assistance, students locate Wisconsin on a United States map.

2. Step by Step:

   a. Introduce the students to the novel *Little House in the Big Woods* by Laura Ingalls Wilder.

   b. Students may read along as you read chapter 1, "Little House in the Big Woods."

c. A class discussion follows the reading. The students list the characters they meet in chapter 1. They note the family's activities. They note the setting of the story.

d. The discussion turns to specific scenes. In small groups, the students explore assigned scenes. They recall details of the scenes and identify moments to illustrate.

e. Students draw details of the scenes.

f. With your assistance, they write captions under their illustrations.

3. Closure:

Back in a large group, reflect on the activities of the lesson with the students.

## Differentiation

*Advanced*

- Students reread the book independently during independent reading time or at home.
- Students take the idea of naming the characters more seriously by also looking for clues as to what each character's personality is like. Assign students a character and look for clues as you read aloud. At the end of each chapter, students report on their assigned character. These inferred character qualities will be used to predict character actions as subsequent chapters are read.

*Struggling*

- Students draw their first illustration together, paying close attention to vocabulary in the story that might need explanation.
- Students label each object and character drawn.
- Guide the class through drawing the setting and characters to solidify these ideas in the students' minds.

## Homework/Assessment

N/A

# Around the World with a Glass Slipper

In this sixth six-week unit of first grade, students compare and contrast multiple versions of "Cinderella" while learning about continents and cultures.

---

## ESSENTIAL QUESTION

What can versions of the same story teach us about different cultures?

---

## OVERVIEW

In the previous unit, students were introduced to writing opinion pieces in the context of studying American contributions. In this unit, students look beyond America, but continue to focus on opinion writing. Students choose a favorite version of a fairy tale, such as "Cinderella," and write about their choices, supporting their opinions with reasons. They continue to focus on similarities and differences in fiction and nonfiction texts. As the unit closes, the students examine artistic masks from various countries and cultures and use descriptive words to describe the masks.

## FOCUS STANDARDS

These Focus Standards have been selected for the unit from the Common Core State Standards.

**RL.1.9:** Compare and contrast the adventures and experiences of characters in stories.

**RI.1.9:** Identify basic similarities in and differences between two texts on the same topic (e.g., in illustrations, descriptions, or procedures).

**W.1.1:** Write opinion pieces in which they introduce the topic or name the book they are writing about, state an opinion, supply a reason for the opinion, and provide some sense of closure.

**W.1.6:** With guidance and support from adults, use a variety of digital tools to produce and publish writing, including in collaboration with peers.

**L.1.5:** With guidance and support from adults, demonstrate understanding of word relationships and nuances in word meanings.

**L.1.5(d):** Distinguish shades of meanings among verbs differing in manner (e.g., *look, peek, glance, stare, glare, scowl*) and adjectives differing in intensity (e.g., *large, gigantic*) by defining or choosing them, or by acting out the meanings.

**SL.1.5:** Add drawings or other visual displays to descriptions when appropriate to clarify ideas, thoughts, and feelings.

## SUGGESTED OBJECTIVES

- Compare and contrast multiple versions of a story (e.g., "Cinderella") by different authors and from different cultures.
- Identify the similarities and differences between two texts on the same topic.
- Write opinions about a favorite version of a story.
- Read nonfiction texts independently with a sense of purpose (e.g., to know about the continents and cultures discussed in a fairy tale version).
- Illustrate an adaptation of a scene from a story and present it to the class in a slide.
- Use vivid words to describe an object.

## SUGGESTED WORKS

(E) indicates a CCSS exemplar text; (EA) indicates a text from a writer with other works identified as exemplars.

### LITERARY TEXTS

*Stories (Read Aloud)*
- *Cinderella* (Marcia Brown)
- *Cinderella* (Charles Perrault, Loek Koopmans, and Anthea Bell)
- *Cinderella Penguin, or, the Little Glass Flipper* (Janet Perlman and John Peterson)
- *Cinderquacker* (Mike Thaler and Dave Clegg)
- *The Egyptian Cinderella* (Shirley Climo and Ruth Heller)
- *Fair, Brown, and Trembling: An Irish Cinderella Story* (Jude Daly)
- *James Marshall's Cinderella* (Barbara Karlin and James Marshall)
- *The Korean Cinderella* (Shirley Climo and Ruth Heller)
- *Little Gold Star: A Spanish American Cinderella Tale* (Robert D. San Souci and Sergio Martinez)
- *Mufaro's Beautiful Daughters* (John Steptoe)
- *Prince Cinders* (Babette Cole)
- *The Turkey Girl: A Zuni Cinderella Story* (Penny Pollock and Ed Young) (EA)
- *The Way Meat Loves Salt: A Cinderella Tale from the Jewish Tradition* (Nina Jaffe and Louise August)
- *Yeh-Shen: A Cinderella Story from China* (retold by Ai-Ling Louie and Ed Young) (EA)

*Poem*

- "Star Light, Star Bright" (Traditional)

## INFORMATIONAL TEXTS

*Nonfiction Books*

- *Africa* (Pull Ahead Books-Continents) (Madeline Donaldson)
- *Antarctica* (Pull Ahead Books-Continents) (Madeline Donaldson)
- *Asia* (Pull Ahead Books-Continents) (Madeline Donaldson)
- *Australia* (Pull Ahead Books-Continents) (Madeline Donaldson)
- *Europe* (Pull Ahead Books-Continents) (Madeline Donaldson)
- *North America* (Pull Ahead Books-Continents) (Madeline Donaldson)
- *South America* (Pull Ahead Books-Continents) (Madeline Donaldson)

*Nonfiction Books (Read Aloud)*

- *Ancient Egypt: A First Look at People of the Nile* (Bruce Strachan)
- *DK First Atlas* (Anita Ganeri and Chris Oxlade)
- *Look What Came from Africa* (Miles Harvey)
- *Look What Came from Australia* (Kevin Davis)
- *Look What Came from China* (Miles Harvey)
- *Look What Came from Egypt* (Miles Harvey)

## ART, MUSIC, AND MEDIA

*Art*

- Africa: mask (Dan, Ivory Coast, ca. early twentieth century)
- Asia: puppet mask (Japan, ca. early twentieth century)
- Australia: display mask (East Sepik, Papua New Guinea, ca. 1980)
- Europe: Captain Scaramouche (Venice, Italy, date unknown)
- North America: shaman's mask (Inuit/Eskimo, Alaska, ca. early twentieth century)
- South America: Devil Dance mask (Aymara, Bolivia, ca. 1974)

# SAMPLE ACTIVITIES AND ASSESSMENTS

## 1. READING LITERATURE, VOCABULARY

As you begin the set of Cinderella stories, create a wall chart to organize the similarities and differences among the versions. Use categories that review the literary terms of this school year, such as characters, setting, beginning, events (middle), and ending. (RL.1.1, RL.1.2, RL.1.9)

## 2.  READING LITERATURE, OPINION WRITING, LANGUAGE USAGE

Read many different versions of "Cinderella." Then give students this prompt: "Choose your favorite version of the Cinderella story. Tell at least two reasons why you liked this version the most." Students should include the title of the book, at least two reasons why they thought it was their favorite, and a strong ending. Revision should focus on word choice, elaboration, or word order as they rewrite the paragraph. (W.1.1, L.1.1j, L.1.2a, L.1.2b, L.1.2d, L.1.2e, RL.1.9)

## 3.  READING LITERATURE, SPEAKING AND LISTENING, ORAL PRESENTATION

Ask the students to think about how all of the Cinderella stories are different because of the time and place in which they happen. Challenge the students to draw the "trying on the slipper" scene as if it were happening right now and in the place where they live. Scan the pictures and create a slide for each image. Students present their drawings to the class, explaining their adaptation of the "slipper scene." (SL.1.5, SL.1.6, RL.1.9)

## 4.  READING INFORMATIONAL TEXT, READING LITERATURE, SPEAKING AND LISTENING

Have students read one of the nonfiction books about a continent or country. After the students finish, have them find and review a fairy tale that is set in a similar place or culture. Discuss what students saw in both books (e.g., geography, people, clothing, food, places, and customs). Discuss how the books are different (e.g., one tells a story; the other gives factual information). (RL.1.5, RL.1.7, RI.1.9)

## 5.  READING INFORMATIONAL TEXT, SPEAKING AND LISTENING

Choose two books about the same continent, such as *Australia* by Madeleine Donaldson and *Look What Came from Australia* by Kevin Davis. Discuss how the books are similar (because they are about the same continent). Determine how they are also different (because they are written by different authors and have different purposes). Then read the books as a class. Make a chart with two columns, one for each book (e.g., *Australia* and *Look What Came from Australia*). Work together to make a list of what is learned in each book and then look for similar information in both books. Challenge the students to do this activity with two books, reading with a partner or reading one independently and having you read the other aloud. (RF.1.4, RI.1.2, RI.1.3, RI.1.9, RI.1.10)

## 6.  READING INFORMATIONAL TEXT, RESEARCH, ORAL PRESENTATION

Partner students to research the contributions/inventions of a country introduced to them in this unit. Tell them to work together to gather information from several different sources. Building on knowledge of the contributions of various countries that is gleaned from informational texts (e.g., the *Look What Came from . . .* series), have students gather actual items that represent the contributions (e.g., for China, writing paper, a compass, and paper money). Ask them to communicate findings by creating a museum of contributions, having the students design information cards to go with each item. Students could stand behind their table to explain the origins of the items as visitors come through the museum. (SL.1.5, RI.1.2, RI.1.5, RI.1.9, RI.1.10, W.1.7, W.1.8, L.1.2)

## 7.  ART, LANGUAGE USAGE, SPEAKING AND LISTENING

Discuss how countries and continents, as depicted in the literature in this unit, are very different. Introduce masks from different continents. As they view each mask, ask the students to think of describing words (i.e., adjectives) they would use to tell someone about the mask. Ask such questions as:

- What materials do you think are used?
- Why do you believe each culture chooses specific colors or textures in their works of art?
- Can you guess how each object was used? (L.1.5d, SL.1.4)

## READING FOUNDATIONS: A PACING GUIDE FOR READING INSTRUCTION

See Grade One, Level Six, in the Reading Foundations section at the beginning of this book for a complete pacing guide for this unit.

## ADDITIONAL ONLINE RESOURCES

- *Cinderella* (Ministry of Education, New Zealand) (RL.1.9)
- *Fairy Tales Around the World* (National Endowment for the Humanities) (RL.1.2)
- *The Meaning Behind the Mask* (National Endowment for the Humanities) (RL.1.2, RL.1.6)

## TERMINOLOGY

| | | |
|---|---|---|
| Act out | Dialogue | Scene |
| Compare | Fairy tales | Setting |
| Contrast | Fantasy | |
| Culture | "Once upon a time, . . ." | |

## INTERDISCIPLINARY CONNECTIONS

This unit teaches:
- **Science:** The Earth's surface (e.g., the seven continents, the four oceans, the two poles)
- **Art:** Masks
- **Geography:** Working with maps and globes (e.g., the seven continents)

This unit could be extended to teach:
- **History:** Ancient Egypt (e.g., Africa, Nile, the Pharaohs, pyramids, mummies, and hieroglyphics)
- **Science:** Inside the Earth (e.g., layers, volcanoes, and rocks)
- **Geography:** Working with maps and globes (e.g., North American countries, the Equator, and cardinal directions)

## Grade One, Unit Six Sample Lesson Plan

### Yeh-Shen: A Cinderella Story from China *retold by Ai-Ling Louie*

In this series of two lessons, students reread *Yeh-Shen: A Cinderella Story from China* retold by Ai-Ling Louie, and they:

Appreciate the history of the tale of Cinderella (RI.1. 1, RI.1.2, SL.1.1.1, SL.1.1.2)

Retell the story of Yeh-Shen (RL.1.2, RL.1.3, SL.1.1, SL.1.2)

Discuss the reasons for choosing Yeh-Shen (SL.1.1, SL.1.2)

## Summary

| Lesson I: Revisiting the Story of Yeh–Shen | Lesson II: Expressing Ideas |
|---|---|
| Locate China on a world map | Revisit previous lesson's talk (RL.1.2) |
| Investigate the historical background of the tale (RI.1. 1, RI.1.2, SL.1.1, SL.1.2) | (Individually) reflect on the choice of Yeh–Shen (W.1.1, W.1.5, W.1.6) |
| Revisit the tale of Yeh–Shen (RL.1.2, RL.1.3, SL.1.1, SL.1.2) | Illustrate written passages (SL.1.5) |
| Explore their choice to revisit Yeh–Shen (RL.1.9, SL.1.1, SL.1.2) | Display and share written reflections (SL.1.1) |

### Lesson I: Revisiting the Story of Yeh–Shen

*Objectives*

Locate China on a world map

Investigate the historical background of the tale (RI.1. 1, RI.1.2, SL.1.1, SL.1.2)

Revisit the tale of Yeh–Shen (RL.1.2, RL.1.3, SL.1.1, SL.1.2)

Explore their choice to revisit Yeh–Shen (RL.1.9, SL.1.1, SL.1.2)

*Required Materials*

☐ Class set of atlases

☐ Multiple copies of *Yeh-Shen: A Cinderella Story from China* retold by Ai-Ling Louie

*Procedures*

1. Lead-In:

    Introduce the students to the class activity.

2. Step by Step:

    a. In a group (where all the students are revisiting Yeh-Shen), students locate China in an atlas or on a world map. They also point to the rest of Asia and the Pacific Ocean. They then locate the United States and note the distance between the two countries.

    b. With your assistance, students investigate the historical origins of the tale. (A brief introduction, containing historical information, is included in the Puffin Books edition of the book.)

    c. In their group, the students retell Yeh-Shen's story.

    d. In their group, the students discuss why, of all the tales, this one might be their favorite.

3. Closure:

    Remind the students that the following day (Lesson II), they will write about the tale of their choice.

*Differentiation*

*Advanced*

- After students have finished the discussion described in this lesson, introduce the book *Beyond the Great Mountains* by Ed Young. Ask students to explore the illustrations of both books by Ed Young. Ask students to use the poem and illustrations of both books to discuss the beauty of China, as seen through the eyes of Ed Young.

*Struggling*

- Mix the groups so that students model good reasons for the selection of a story. Assign one of the confident writers to write the reasons on sentence strips as they are discussed. Allow students to review these reasons during Lesson II, when they write about the tale of their choice. (Even if they choose a different tale, these reasons will serve as a model of statements of support.)

## Homework/Assessment

N/A

The unit Around the World with a Glass Slipper offers students an opportunity to choose a favorite version of the famous fairy tale. This mini-map focuses on the Chinese version of the tale. The mini-map assumes that the students have already read several versions of "Cinderella."

# Grade 2

In second grade, students become independent readers and writers, able to conduct research, write reports, and compare and contrast characters from stories. Now the "read-aloud" works are combined with books that students read for themselves, as they learn about seasons, the Wild West, the African American journey to freedom, and more. In the unit Building Bridges with Unlikely Friends, students learn about bridges—both real and imagined. Later, in Hand-Me-Down Tales from Around the World, students listen to Prokofiev's *Peter and the Wolf* as they consider why tales are passed from one generation to the next. Students learn about the physical world as well; in the final unit, they read about the human body and health. The variety of topics exposes students to rich literature while building their background knowledge of a range of subjects and topics. Students use graphic organizers to clarify their ideas and plan their writing. Their writing includes reports, literary responses, opinion pieces, stories, letters, and explanations. Throughout the year, students build grammatical knowledge and practice reading and speaking with fluency and expression. They engage in discussions about literature and make use of online resources. By the end of second grade, students should be able to read simple storybooks fluently and write in print and cursive. They should be familiar with a repertoire of myths, stories, poems, and nonfiction narratives.

# Standards Checklist for Grade Two

| Standard | Unit 1 | Unit 2 | Unit 3 | Unit 4 | Unit 5 | Unit 6 |
|---|---|---|---|---|---|---|
| Reading–Literature | | | | | | |
| 1 | A | | | | | |
| 2 | | FA | | | FA | A |
| 3 | | | FA | | | |
| 4 | FA | A | A | A | A | FA |
| 5 | FA | | | | A | |
| 6 | | A | | FA | A | |
| 7 | | | FA | | A | |
| 8 n/a | | | | | | |
| 9 | | FA | | | A | |
| 10 | | A | | | A | FA |
| Reading–Informational Text | | | | | | |
| 1 | | A | | | | |
| 2 | FA | | | | | |
| 3 | | | A | FA | A | |
| 4 | | A | | | | A |
| 5 | A | A | | | A | |
| 6 | | FA | FA | | A | |
| 7 | | | A | | FA | A |
| 8 | | | | | | FA |
| 9 | | | | FA | | |
| 10 | | A | | | A | FA |
| Writing | | | | | | |
| 1 | | A | | FA | A | FA |
| 2 | A | FA | FA | | | A |
| 3 | | A | | FA | FA | |
| 4 n/a | | | | | | |
| 5 | | A | A | | | |
| 6 | A | | A | FA | | |
| 7 | FA | A | | | A | |
| 8 | A | A | | | | |
| 9 n/a | | | | | | |
| 10 n/a | | | | | | |
| Speaking and Listening | | | | | | |
| 1 | FA | A | A | | | A |
| 1a | | | | | | |
| 1b | | | | | | |
| 1c | | | | | | |
| 2 | FA | A | | A | A | A |
| 3 | | A | | A | FA | |
| 4 | | A | A | | FA | |
| 5 | | A | A | A | A | F |
| 6 | | A | A | | | A |
| Language | | | | | | |
| 1a | | | | | | |
| 1b | | A | | | A | |
| 1c | | | | | | A |
| 1d | | | | A | | |
| 1e | A | | | | | |

| Standard | Unit 1 | Unit 2 | Unit 3 | Unit 4 | Unit 5 | Unit 6 |
|---|---|---|---|---|---|---|
| 1f | A | | | A | | |
| 2 | A | A | F | | | |
| 2a | A | | | | A | |
| 2b | A | A | FA | | | |
| 2c | A | | | | | |
| 2d | A | | | | | |
| 2e | A | | | | | A |
| 3 | A | A | | | | |
| 3a | A | | | A | | |
| 4 | | A | F | | A | A |
| 4a | | | | | | |
| 4b | | | | A | | |
| 4c | | | | A | | |
| 4d | | | FA | | | |
| 4e | | | A | | | |
| 5 | | | A | | | |
| 5a | | | | | | A |
| 5b | A | | A | A | | |
| 6 | | | | A | | |

| Reading Foundations (addressed in units) | | | | | | |
|---|---|---|---|---|---|---|
| Standard | Level 1 | Level 2 | Level 3 | Level 4 | Level 5 | Level 6 |
| 1 n/a | | | | | | |
| 2 n/a | | | | | | |
| 3 | | | | | | |
| 3a | | | | | | |
| 3b | | | | | | |
| 3c | | | | | | |
| 3d | | | | | | |
| 3e | | | | | | |
| 3f | | | | | | |
| 4 | A | A | | | | |
| 4a | | | | | | |
| 4b | | | | | | |
| 4c | | | | | | |

| Reading Foundations (addressed in Reading Foundations: A Pacing Guide) | | | | | | |
|---|---|---|---|---|---|---|
| Standard | Level 1 | Level 2 | Level 3 | Level 4 | Level 5 | Level 6 |
| 1 n/a | | | | | | |
| 2 n/a | | | | | | |
| 3 | | A | A | A | A | A |
| 3a | A | A | A | A | A | A |
| 3b | | A | A | A | A | A |
| 3c | A | A | A | A | A | A |
| 3d | A | A | A | A | A | A |
| 3e | A | A | A | A | A | A |
| 3f | A | A | A | A | A | A |
| 4 | A | A | A | A | A | A |
| 4a | A | A | A | A | A | A |
| 4b | A | A | A | A | A | A |
| 4c | A | A | A | A | A | A |

F = Focus Standards; A = Activity/Assessment

# A Season for Chapters

In this first six-week unit of second grade, students focus on the beauty of language—in chapter books, informational texts, and poetry—all related to the four seasons.

## ESSENTIAL QUESTION

When is language beautiful?

## OVERVIEW

Focusing on the beauty of language in poetry and fiction, students learn about poetry terms and the beginnings and endings of stories. In preparation for writing informational text, students complete a research project on a seasonal activity from a region of the United States unlike their own. Enjoying the beauty of the language of music through Vivaldi's *The Four Seasons*, students use their own beautiful language when writing "seasonal" poetry. Students review the roles of authors and illustrators, and read about specific authors and poets. This unit could become a weather unit or a solar system unit by adding topic-specific titles to the informational texts.

## FOCUS STANDARDS

These Focus Standards have been selected for the unit from the Common Core State Standards.

**RI.2.2:** Identify the main focus of a multiparagraph text as well as the focus of specific paragraphs within the text.

**RL.2.4:** Describe how words and phrases (e.g., regular beats, alliteration, rhymes, repeated lines) supply rhythm and meaning in a story, poem, or song.

**RL.2.5:** Describe the overall structure of a story, including describing how the beginning introduces the story and the ending concludes the action.

**SL.2.1:** Participate in collaborative conversations with diverse partners about grade 2 topics and texts with peers and adults in small and larger groups.

**SL.2.2:** Recount or describe key ideas or details from a text read aloud or information presented orally or through other media.

**W.2.7:** Participate in shared research and writing projects (e.g., read a number of books on a single topic to produce a report; record science observations).

## SUGGESTED OBJECTIVES

- Independently read chapter books according to ability.
- Distinguish between the roles of author and illustrator in chapter books.
- Ask the questions *who, what, where, when, why,* and *how* after reading fictional books.
- Study the beginnings and endings of chapters and stories.
- Use digital resources to research a seasonal activity.
- Use a computer-generated graphic organizer to organize class research.
- Create an informational class book from this shared research.
- Study art pieces to see the artist's techniques in creating a sense of cold or warmth.
- Create a collection of adjectives and adverbs.
- Expand sentences by adding adjectives and adverbs from the class discussion on art.
- Write a paragraph using complete sentences.
- Write poetry based on music (e.g., Vivaldi's *The Four Seasons*).
- Enjoy and analyze poetry related to the seasons, noting alliteration, rhyme, rhythm, and repetition.
- Study the organization of informational text, specifically the purpose of paragraphs.

## SUGGESTED WORKS

(E) indicates a CCSS exemplar text; (EA) indicates a text from a writer with other works identified as exemplars.

### LITERARY TEXTS

*Stories*

- *The Days of Summer* (Eve Bunting and William Low)
- *Every Autumn Comes the Bear* (Jim Arnosky)
- *Henry and Mudge and the Snowman Plan* (Cynthia Rylant and Sucie Stevenson) (EA)
- *Leaf Man* (Lois Ehlert)
- *The Little Yellow Leaf* (Carin Berger)
- *The Mitten* (Jan Brett) (Read Aloud)
- *Peepers* (Eve Bunting and James Ransome)
- *Poppleton in Fall* (Cynthia Rylant and Mark Teague) (EA)

- *Poppleton in Spring* (Cynthia Rylant and Mark Teague) (EA)
- *Poppleton in Winter* (Cynthia Rylant and Mark Teague) (E)
- *Red Leaf, Yellow Leaf* (Lois Ehlert)
- *Snow* (Uri Shulevitz)
- *Snowballs* (Lois Ehlert)

## Poems

- "Autumn" (Emily Dickinson) (E)
- "Knoxville, Tennessee" (Nikki Giovanni) (E)
- "Something Told the Wild Geese" (Rachel Field) (E)
- "Stopping by Woods on a Snowy Evening" (Robert Frost) (E)
- "Summer Song" (John Ciardi) in *The Seasons* (ed. John N. Serio)
- "Weather" (Eve Merriam) (E)
- "Who Has Seen the Wind?" (Christina Rossetti) (E)

## Poems (Read Aloud)

- "Bed in Summer" (Robert Louis Stevenson)
- "The Locust Tree in Flower" (William Carlos Williams) in *The Seasons* (ed. John N. Serio)
- "The Snowflake" (Walter de la Mare) in *The Seasons* (ed. John N. Serio)
- "A Vagabond Song" (Bliss Carman) in *The Seasons* (ed. John N. Serio)

## INFORMATIONAL TEXTS

### Nonfiction Books

- *Cynthia Rylant: A Writer's Story* (Alice Cary and Susan Spellman)
- *Energy from the Sun* (Rookie Read-About Science) (Allan Fowler)
- *How Do You Know It's Fall?* (Rookie Read-About Science) (Allan Fowler)
- *How Do You Know It's Spring?* (Rookie Read-About Science) (Allan Fowler)
- *How Do You Know It's Summer?* (Rookie Read-About Science) (Allan Fowler)
- *How Do You Know It's Winter?* (Rookie Read-About Science) (Allan Fowler)
- *Look How It Changes!* (Rookie Read-About Science) (June Young)
- *Snowflake Bentley* (Jacqueline Briggs Martin and Mary Azarian) (Read Aloud)
- *Snowflakes in Photographs* (W. A. Bentley) (Read Aloud)
- *Sunshine Makes the Seasons* (Franklyn M. Branley and Michael Rex)
- *A River of Words: The Story of William Carlos Williams* (Jennifer Bryant and Melissa Sweet) (Read Aloud)
- *What Do Authors Do?* (Eileen Christelow)
- *What Do Illustrators Do?* (Eileen Christelow)
- *Why Do Leaves Change Color?* (Betsy Maestro and Loretta Krupinski)

## ART, MUSIC, AND MEDIA

### Art

- Artist unknown, *Snow-Laden Plum Branches* (1098–1169)
- Georges Seurat, *Une Baignade, Asnieres* (1883–1884)
- Gustave Caillebotte, *Paris Street, Rainy Day* (1877)
- Louis Comfort Tiffany, *Dogwood* (1900–1915)
- Maurice de Vlaminck, *Autumn Landscape* (1905)
- Pieter Bruegel, *Hunters in the Snow* (1565)
- Vincent van Gogh, *Mulberry Tree* (1889)
- Vincent van Gogh, *Sunflowers* (1889)

### Music

- Vivaldi, *The Four Seasons* (1723)

## SAMPLE ACTIVITIES AND ASSESSMENTS

Note: Your choice of texts for this unit can be made in a few different ways, such as by completing a few weeks of fiction and then shifting to poetry and finally to nonfiction, or the unit could move along by seasons, with all of the winter materials used during two weeks of the unit before moving on to the other seasons in a logical order.

### 1. READING LITERATURE, SPEAKING AND LISTENING

Ask students to pick a favorite book from the easy section of the library. To introduce the characteristics of a good solid beginning and ending of a story, ask the students to read aloud to a partner just the first paragraph or two and then the last paragraph. Later, allow students to share the books in small groups to see what each child notices about these solid beginnings and solid endings. For example, they may notice things such as a clearly described setting with vivid words at the beginning, the book's coming full circle, and the ending's providing a sense of satisfaction. (RL.2.5)

### 2. READING LITERATURE, SPEAKING AND LISTENING

Introduce and read the first chapter of *Poppleton in Winter* by Cynthia Rylant and Mark Teague. The following day, look at the chapter again. Explain to the class that Cynthia Rylant is an author who knows exactly how to write the beginning of a story and how to wrap it up with a strong ending. Direct the students to look closely at how the story begins. Reread the section where the story is set up. Students will see the setting, characters, and situation/problem in the first two sentences of the story: "Poppleton's house grew very long icicles in winter. Poppleton was proud of them." Create a bulleted list as the students discuss what they see, finishing the sentence "A strong beginning has . . ." Then turn to the end of the story and discuss the attributes of a strong ending. Read Rylant's final sentences: "Poppleton was glad his icicles were knocked down. Icicles always melted. But a new friend would stay." Continue the bulleted list, having students finish the sentence "A strong ending has . . ." As the students read each successive chapter independently, with a partner, or with you, make these charts a focus of discussion. Eventually add a chart for the action in the middle of the story. (RL.2.5, RF.2.4)

## 3. READING LITERATURE, SPEAKING AND LISTENING

After reading the fictional read-aloud picture books for each of the seasons, have students ask and answer questions using *who, what, where, when, why,* and *how.* Challenge students to create questions from these stems that apply directly to the books you are reading. Encourage students to answer the questions on sticky notes under each question on the following chart. (RL.2.1)

| Who? | What? | Where? | When? | Why? | How? |
|------|-------|--------|-------|------|------|
|      |       |        |       |      |      |
|      |       |        |       |      |      |
|      |       |        |       |      |      |
|      |       |        |       |      |      |

## 4. READING INFORMATIONAL TEXT, INFORMATIVE WRITING

This unit contains a wide variety of informational texts. To introduce the work of organizing informational text, choose a book with a variety of text features and strong paragraphs. Explain to the children that as you read for information, you will also be looking at the author's craft. Guide students to look closely at the way each informational book on the four seasons is arranged (e.g., through the use of headings, subheadings, and paragraphs). Choose one page to look for the purpose of paragraphs in organizing the information in the text. You might want to make a copy of the page for the students to examine as you demonstrate the topical chunks of information in paragraphs. Extend this lesson by listing text features in multiple books on seasons and related topics. Focus on the purposes of the text features in the books. Follow this reading lesson by prompting students to write on the following: "Choose one topic related to the book read, and write a paragraph with a strong topic sentence, detailed information, and a satisfying conclusion." (RI.2.2, RF.2.4)

## 5. READING INFORMATIONAL TEXT, LANGUAGE MECHANICS

Use the informational book *How Do You Know It's Fall?* by Allan Fowler to introduce apostrophes. Discuss the concept of contractions by creating sentences starting with "It is . . ." and then contracting the words to "It's." Continue generating lists of contractions for "he is," "she is," "they are," "we are," and so on. Ask the students to create detailed sentences related to the season of fall using a variety of contractions. Extend the lesson by discussing apostrophes used to show possession. Staying with the fall theme, generate a list of possessives focusing on nature's preparation for winter (e.g., a bear's thick coat, a squirrel's collection of acorns, a tree's slow growth). (L.2.2c)

## 6. RESEARCH, INFORMATIVE WRITING

Focus a discussion on the characteristics of seasons in your local climate. Discuss activities that your students might associate with each season. Talk about how one of the season's activities might help the local economy more than others, by generating research questions, such as: "Which season is most important to our community?" Use digital resources and speakers who have visited to gather information. Conclude the research and communicate findings with a class write, such as: "Research a sport or activity in your community that relates to a specific season. Create a nonfiction text about the season, the sport, and the way it affects your community." (RI.2.5, SL.2.1, SL.2.2, W.2.2, W.2.8, L.2.3)

## 7. RESEARCH, INFORMATIVE WRITING

Follow the local community research with a new research challenge. This time, organize small groups to research and write about a community in a contrasting climate and geographical location. Focus on the seasons there, a sport (or activity) that is important, and the way they affect that community. Help students generate the research questions that will guide their work. Ask them to gather information from a variety of online sources and possibly hold a conversation via the Internet with the Chamber of Commerce from the community. Introduce a digital tool for organizing information. Model the organization of gathered information into broad topics through webbing. Use one part of the graphic organizer (web) to demonstrate to the class how to write one well-developed paragraph. Working in small groups, students should use the webbed information to write the remaining paragraphs. When the paragraphs are completed, combine them into books. Students can add illustrations by drawing or by collecting photographs from online sources. (RI.2.2, W.2.2, W.2.6, W.2.7, L.2.2)

## 8. READING POETRY, PERFORMANCE

*The Seasons* (ed. John N. Serio) is a book of collected poems by different poets. Introduce the poem "Summer Song." Ask the students, "What did you notice about the first four lines of the poem?" (*Possible answer*: Repetition of "By the . . .") Note the pattern of rhyme in the first four lines (i.e., ABAB) and how it changes as it progresses through the poem (i.e., AABB). Continue to look at the features of poetry as you read other seasonal poems in this unit. Each of the poems from *The Seasons* exemplifies at least one of the characteristics of the grade 2 standards: rhyme, rhythm, alliteration, and repetition. Encourage students to choose a poem to perform (recite) for the class. (RL.2.4)

## 9. MUSIC, LANGUAGE USAGE, WRITING POETRY

Listen to one of the four concertos in Vivaldi's *The Four Seasons*. Instruct the students to write down words or phrases that come to them as they are listening. After they are finished, tell them to work together as a class to compile a list of words and phrases they thought of while listening. Choose a descriptive word or phrase and then challenge them to think in simile or metaphor (e.g., falling leaves—like what? Like jewels falling from the sky). Use the collection of words and phrases to write a class poem titled "Spring," "Summer," "Autumn," or "Winter." Be sure to use rhythm, rhyme, alliteration, and/or repetition in your class poem. (RL.2.4, L.2.5b)

## 10. ART, LANGUAGE USAGE

View the Bruegel, Caillebotte, and Seurat images. As the class studies each piece, ask the students how the artist creates a sense of warmth or cold, dryness or wetness in the painting. As the students use adjectives and adverbs in the conversation, write them down under the appropriate category on a whiteboard or chart paper. Use these words to create and expand sentences (e.g., "The artist painted snow. The talented artist painted snow with cool colors. Using an icy blue color, the artist painted a snowy scene."). Extend the activity by using the word bank to create free-form poems to go with each painting. (L.2.1e, L.2.1f)

## 11. ART, INFORMATIVE WRITING

Select a work to study—for instance, you might choose the Seurat for a clear depiction of a season. Ask the students to name the season that the artist has painted. Then have students write a two- or three-sentence explanation identifying elements in the work that led them to their observation. (W.2.2)

## 12. ART, SPEAKING AND LISTENING

Artists often convey a sense of season in their depictions of flowers or trees. Ask students to study the Tiffany image, van Gogh's *Mulberry Tree*, and the work titled *Snow-Laden Plum Branches*. Note that these works were created on three different continents at around the same time period. Ask students to discuss similarities and differences in these artists' techniques for depicting the seasons. (SL.2.2)

## READING FOUNDATIONS: A PACING GUIDE FOR READING INSTRUCTION

See Grade Two, Level One, in the Reading Foundations section at the beginning of this book for a complete pacing guide for this unit.

## ADDITIONAL ONLINE RESOURCES

- *English Spelling Rules* (Reading from Scratch) (L.2.2d)
- *All Together Now: Collaborations in Poetry Writing* (National Endowment for the Humanities) (L.2.1e,f)
- The Weather Channel

## TERMINOLOGY

| | | |
|---|---|---|
| Alliteration | Ending | Repetition |
| Author | Illustrator | Research |
| Beginning | Introduction | Rhyme |
| Chapter | Main idea | Rhythm |
| Conclusion | Paragraph | Shared writing |
| Digital graphic organizer | Poet | Spelling patterns |
| Digital sources | Poetry | |

# INTERDISCIPLINARY CONNECTIONS

This unit teaches:

- **Art:** van Gogh, Seurat, Bruegel, Caillebotte, Tiffany
- **Music:** *The Four Seasons* (Vivaldi)
- **Geography:** U.S. landforms (e.g., mountains, coast, plains, hills, and deserts)
- **Science:** Seasonal cycles

This unit could be extended to teach:

- **Geography:** U.S. geography (e.g., the Mississippi River, mountain ranges such as the Appalachian and Rocky Mountains, and the Great Lakes)
- **Science:** Weather, the water cycle, the solar system

## Grade Two, Unit One Sample Lesson Plan

*"Autumn" by Emily Dickinson*

*"Something Told the Wild Geese" by Rachel Field*

*"Who Has Seen the Wind?" by Christina Rossetti*

*"Knoxville, Tennessee" by Nikki Giovanni*

*"Weather" by Eve Merriam*

In this series of six lessons, students read "Autumn" by Emily Dickinson, "Something Told the Wild Geese" by Rachel Field, "Who Has Seen the Wind?" by Christina Rossetti, "Knoxville, Tennessee" by Nikki Giovanni, and "Weather" by Eve Merriam, and they:

Explore the various ways that poets describe the changes in weather (RL.2.1, SL.2.1, SL.2.2, SL.2.3)

Identify several poetic devices that poets use (RL.2.4)

Offer personal reflections on the readings through illustrations and brief passages (W.2.1)

## Summary

| Lesson I: "Autumn" by Emily Dickinson | Lesson II: "Something Told the Wild Geese" by Rachel Field |
|---|---|
| Observe the form of the poem (RL.2.4) | Observe the form of the poem (RL.2.4) |
| Note the name of the poet | Note the name of the poet |
| Conduct first reading of the poem (RL.2.1) | Conduct first reading of the poem (RL.2.1) |
| Identify new vocabulary words | Identify new vocabulary words |
| (After a second reading) explore the dominant colors of the poem (RL.2.1, SL.2.1, SL.2.2, SL.2.3) | (After a second reading) examine the pending changes in nature (RL.2.1, SL.2.1, SL.2.2, SL.2.3) |
| Examine the changes in nature that the speaker depicts (RL.2.1, SL.2.1, SL.2.2, SL.2.3) | Explore what the "something" is, and what it told the wild geese (RL.2.1, SL.2.1, SL.2.2, SL.2.3) |
| Probe the speaker's decision to "put a trinket on" (RL.2.1, SL.2.3) | Consider why the poem is in the past tense (RL.2.1, SL.2.1, SL.2.2) |

## Lesson III: "Who Has Seen the Wind?" by Christina Rossetti

Observe the form of the poem (RL.2.4)

Note the name of the poet

Conduct first reading of the poem (RL.2.1)

Identify new vocabulary words

(After a second reading) note the speaker's repeated question (RL.2.1, RL.2.4, SL.2.3)

Explore the purpose of the repetitions (RL.2.4, SL.2.1, SL.2.2)

Point to and examine the purpose of the two parts of the poem (RL.2.1, SL.2.1, SL.2.2)

## Lesson V: "Weather" by Eve Merriam

Observe the form of the poem (RL.2.4)

Note the name of the poet

Conduct first reading of the poem (RL.2.1)

Note the unusual words that the poet uses (RL.2.4)

(During a second reading) listen to the sounds of the words the poet uses (RL.2.4)

Explore the impact of the sounds on the reader (RL.2.1, RL.2.4, SL.2.1, SL.2.2, SL.2.3)

## Lesson VI: Revisiting the Seasons Poems
*Objectives*

Revisit the poems of Lessons I–V (RL.2.1, RL.2.4, SL.2.1, SL.2.2, SL.2.3)

Individually select a favorite poem

Illustrate the poem

## Lesson IV: "Knoxville, Tennessee" by Nikki Giovanni

Observe the form of the poem (RL.2.4)

Note the name of the poet

Conduct first reading of the poem (RL.2.1)

Identify new vocabulary words

(After a second reading) explore the absence of punctuation in the poem and consider the poet's purpose (RL.2.4, SL.2.1, SL.2.2)

Examine the speaker's list (RL.2.1, SL.2.3)

Explore the objective of the list (RL.2.1, SL.2.1, SL.2.2)

## Lesson VI: Revisiting the Seasons Poems

Revisit the poems of Lessons I–V (RL.2.1, RL.2.4, SL.2.1, SL.2.2, SL.2.3)

Individually select a favorite poem

Illustrate the poem

Explain the purpose of the illustrations (W.2.1)

Assess results (SL.2.1)

Explain the purpose of the illustrations (W.2.1)

Assess results (SL.2.1)

*Required Materials*

☐ "Autumn" by Emily Dickinson

☐ "Something Told the Wild Geese" by Rachel Field

☐ "Who Has Seen the Wind?" by Christina Rossetti

☐ "Knoxville, Tennessee" by Nikki Giovanni

☐ "Weather" by Eve Merriam

*Procedures*

1. Lead-In:

   Student volunteers read the five poems aloud.

2. Step by Step:

   a. A class discussion reminds the students of the uniqueness of each of the five poems:

      ○ The colors in "Autumn"

      ○ The mystery in "Something Told the Wild Geese"

      ○ The repeated question in "Who Has Seen the Wind?"

      ○ The list in "Knoxville, Tennessee"

      ○ The new words and sounds in "Weather"

   b. Students select a favorite poem.

   c. Students illustrate the poems. Their illustrations must reflect the readings. For example, students who choose "Autumn" use warm colors of fall.

   d. Students write two or three sentences explaining their illustrations.

   e. Students, with your help, hang the illustrated poems.

3. Closure:

   Students discuss their work and note the many ways that poets describe the changing seasons.

## Differentiation

### Advanced

- Students choose one of the poems to use as a craft model for writing their own poem. For example, a student could write a winter poem modeled after "Autumn" using the idea of winter colors. A student could choose to write a mystery poem about another seasonal phenomenon.

### Struggling

- Take one of the poems and cut it up. Glue each of the lines on a blank page, making a book out of the poem. Divide the pages to be illustrated among a small group of students. Students illustrate the page after discussing the meaning of their line with other students and/or an adult. Tell students to assemble the pages in order. Encourage students to enjoy reading the picture book they have illustrated.

## Homework/Assessment

N/A

# The Wild West

In this second six-week unit of second grade, students read literature set in the Wild West: chapter books, informational texts, songs, tall tales, and fairy tales.

---

## ESSENTIAL QUESTION

How does setting affect a story?

---

## OVERVIEW

Building on the shared research in the first unit, students research an interesting person from the 1800s in the American Wild West and write an informative/explanatory essay. Students read tall tales and then discuss where the fiction is stretched beyond belief, and why the tale has been told through the years. Students also read their choice of fantasy and chapter books set in different time periods of life in the West. Finally, students will study the art of George Catlin to understand his role in creating historic images of Native Americans.

## FOCUS STANDARDS

These Focus Standards have been selected for the unit from the Common Core State Standards.

**RL.2.2:** Recount stories, including fables and folktales from diverse cultures, and determine their central message, lesson, or moral.

**RL.2.9:** Compare and contrast two or more versions of the same story (e.g., Cinderella stories) by different authors or from different cultures.

**RI.2.6:** Identify the main purpose of a text, including what the author wants to answer, explain, or describe.

**W.2.2:** Write informative/explanatory texts in which they introduce a topic, use facts and definitions to develop points, and provide a concluding statement or section.

## SUGGESTED OBJECTIVES

- Create a list of collective nouns related to topics studied (e.g., *herd*, *flock*, in this unit on the West).
- Read tall tales and learn the distinct characteristics of this type of tale.
- Compare and contrast an original fairy tale with one that has been rewritten in a different setting.
- Read multiple perspectives on a given topic.
- Research the life of a real person.
- Write an informational essay based on research about a real person.
- Read informational texts to answer the questions *who*, *what*, *where*, *when*, *why*, and *how*.
- Read chapter books in the fantasy genre, paying careful attention to the varied voices of the characters.

## SUGGESTED WORKS

(E) indicates a CCSS exemplar text; (EA) indicates a text from a writer with other works identified as exemplars.

### LITERARY TEXTS

*Stories*

- *A Boy Called Slow* (Joseph Bruchac and Rocco Baviera)
- *Buffalo Before Breakfast* (Mary Pope Osborne and Sal Murdocca) (EA)
- *The Cowboy and the Black-Eyed Pea* (Tony Johnston)
- *Cowgirl Kate and Cocoa* (Erica Silverman and Betsy Lewin) (E)
- *Cowgirl Kate and Cocoa: Partners* (Erica Silverman and Betsy Lewin) (EA)
- *Crazy Horse's Vision* (Joseph Bruchac, S. D. Nelson, Curtis Zunigha, and Robert Tree Cody)
- *Dancing with the Indians* (Angela Shelf Medearis)
- *Ghost Town at Sundown* (Mary Pope Osborne and Sal Murdocca) (EA)
- *Gift Horse: A Lakota Story* (S. D. Nelson)
- *The Gingerbread Cowboy* (Janet Squires and Holly Berry)
- *The Gingerbread Man* (Karen Lee Schmidt)
- *Justin and the Best Biscuits in the World* (Mildred Pitts Walter and Catherine Stock)
- *Little Red Cowboy Hat* (Susan Lowell and Randy Cecil)
- *Little Red Riding Hood* (Trina Schart Hyman) (Read Aloud)
- *Little Red Riding Hood: A Newfangled Prairie Tale* (Lisa Campbell Ernst)

- "The Princess and the Pea" in *Fairy Tales from Hans Christian Andersen* (Hans Christian Andersen) (Read Aloud)
- *The Tortoise and the Jackrabbit* (Susan Lowell)
- *The Toughest Cowboy: or How the Wild West Was Tamed* (John Frank and Zachary Pullen) (Read Aloud)

## Tall Tales

- *John Henry* (Julius Lester and Jerry Pinkney)
- *Johnny Appleseed* (Steven Kellogg)
- *Paul Bunyan* (Steven Kellogg)
- *Pecos Bill* (Steven Kellogg and Laura Robb)

## Poems

- "Buffalo Dusk" (Carl Sandburg) (Read Aloud)
- "Home on the Range" (Brewster Higley) (Read Aloud)
- "How I Spent My Summer Vacation" (Mark Teague)

## INFORMATIONAL TEXTS

### Nonfiction Books

- *Cowboys* (Lucille Recht Penner)
- *I Want to Be a Cowboy* (Dan Liebman)
- *The Very First Americans* (Cara Ashrose)

### Nonfiction Books (Read Aloud)

- *B Is for Buckaroo: A Cowboy Alphabet* (Louise Doak Whitney and Sue Guy)
- *Bill Pickett: Rodeo-Ridin' Cowboy* (Andrea D. and Brian Pinkney)
- *Black Cowboy, Wild Horses: A True Story* (Julius Lester and Jerry Pinkney)
- *Cactus Hotel* (Brenda Z. Guiberson)
- *Cowboys and Cowgirls: Yippee-Yay!* (Gail Gibbons) (EA)
- *Wild Tracks! A Guide to Nature's Footprints* (Jim Arnosky) (E)
- *Wild West* (DK Eyewitness Books) (Stuart Murray)
- *You Wouldn't Want to Live in a Wild West Town!* (Peter Hicks, David Salariya, and David Antram)
- Online biographical sources for
  - Annie Oakley
  - Buffalo Bill
  - Kit Carson
  - Wild Bill Hickock
  - Will Rogers

## ART, MUSIC, AND MEDIA

*Art*

- Edward S. Curtis, *Cheyenne Maiden* (1930)
- Edward S. Curtis, *A Smoky Day at the Sugar Bowl–Hupa* (1923)
- Frederic Remington, *Fight for the Water Hole* (1903)
- Frederic Remington, *A Dash for the Timber* (1889)
- George Catlin, *The White Cloud, Head Chief of the Iowas* (1830–1870)
- George Catlin, *A Comanche Family Outside Their Teepee* (1841)

*Music*

- Traditional cowboy ballad, "Git Along, Little Dogies"

## SAMPLE ACTIVITIES AND ASSESSMENTS

### 1. READING POETRY, LANGUAGE USAGE, VOCABULARY

Create a running list of collective nouns in this unit (e.g., a herd or drove of cows; a herd or band of horses; a flock of sheep; and a band, tribe, or nation of Native Americans). Keep a growing word bank of people, vocabulary, and phrases that appear in this unit. Reading (reciting) poetry such as "Buffalo Dusk" and "Home on the Range" will give the students rich opportunities to collect vocabulary and to learn the words in context. These words can be used in later student writing. (RI.2.4, L.2.1b, L.2.4, L.2.4e, RL.2.4, RL.2.10)

### 2. READING LITERATURE, READING COMPREHENSION, SPEAKING AND LISTENING

Introduce the genre of tall tales by explaining that they are stories about a special kind of hero who is bigger than life. Even though the story is based on a real person, the person is exaggerated to be stronger or bigger than any real hero can ever be. Read about a hero from the 1800s named John Henry. As you read the story, challenge the students to think about the part of the story that is so amazing that we know it is not really true. After the students have read the story, go back through the story and have the students write down one thing that might be real and one thing they think is fantasy. Ask such questions as:

- Why do you think we have this tall tale?
- Why do you think the story has a race between a machine and a human?
- Why do you think the man beats the machine? (RL.2.2, SL.2.2)

### 3. READING LITERATURE, INFORMATIVE WRITING

After reading the fairy tale "The Princess and the Pea" by Hans Christian Andersen, introduce another version of the story, *The Cowboy and the Black-Eyed Pea* by Tony Johnston. Before reading the book, challenge the students to think about how the two stories are the same and how they are different. Create a Venn diagram or other graphic organizer to compare and contrast the two stories. Have the students use sticky notes to add their ideas to the Venn diagram. When they are finished, ask them to use the graphic organizer to construct sentences that describe two ways in which the stories are the same and two ways in which they are different. Continue this activity with other traditional stories and their alternative versions. (RL.2.9, SL.2.2)

## 4. READING INFORMATIONAL TEXT, SPEAKING AND LISTENING

*Bill Pickett: Rodeo-Ridin' Cowboy* by Andrea D. and Brian Pinkney is a true story of an African American cowboy. After you have read the story, display the same kind of chart from the Unit One segment on fiction (see the following sample). Again, remind the students that these are only question stems and must be amplified to focus on the story. Ask students to choose two questions to answer and write on their whiteboards. Share the responses from the students and add to the class chart. (RI.2.1, SL.2.2)

| Who? | What? | Where? | When? | Why? | How? |
|------|-------|--------|-------|------|------|
|      |       |        |       |      |      |
|      |       |        |       |      |      |
|      |       |        |       |      |      |
|      |       |        |       |      |      |

## 5. READING INFORMATIONAL TEXT, RESEARCH, SPEAKING AND LISTENING

Remind students that when they are doing research in the classroom, they start with a question. Similarly, authors of informational books also begin their work with a question or the desire to explain something. Have the students read an informational book such as *Cowboys and Cowgirls: Yippee-Yay!* by Gail Gibbons. After they finish the book, ask students to think about what question the author wanted to answer or what she wanted to explain in this book. When they are finished reading and writing down their questions, begin a discussion on how authors base research in asking and answering questions. (RI.2.6)

## 6. INFORMATIVE WRITING, RESEARCH, SPEAKING AND LISTENING

By reading the informational books in this unit, students learn about Native Americans, African Americans, and Caucasians during the 1800s in the American Wild West. Give the students this prompt: "Write about the person most interesting to you from the Wild West days. Be sure to answer the questions *who, what, where, when, why,* and *how* as you write about the person you chose." Using the question stems, students will generate their own research questions. Encourage the use of a variety of sources as they gather additional information using online sources and books. When students are finished with their research, pair them according to related choices to allow sharing of organized gathered information. Have them practice talking through the information to lay the groundwork for writing focused paragraphs. Students write drafts. After the first draft is written, have them spend time revising the work with peers or with you. (RI.2.1, RI.2.5, RI.2.10, W.2.2, W.2.5, W.2.7, W.2.8, SL.2.1, SL.2.2, SL.2.6, L.2.1, L.2.2, L.2.3)

## 7. READING INFORMATIONAL TEXT, READING FLUENCY, PERFORMANCE

Introduce the story about a modern-day cowgirl, *Cowgirl Kate and Cocoa* by Erica Silverman and Betsy Lewin. As they read the first chapter, ask students to think about whether this story could really happen or if it is a fantasy. Ask students to find evidence in the text to support their choices. Use a whiteboard or sticky notes to record their thinking. As they finish reading and writing, pair students to discuss their ideas. After they are finished discussing, ask them to remain partners and to experiment with reading using different voices for different characters in the book. Monitor the reading by listening for reading with expression and character voices. (RL.2.6, RF.2.4)

## 8. ART, SPEAKING AND LISTENING

Explain to the students that George Catlin was a famous artist who traveled west on horseback during the 1800s to paint pictures of Native Americans. Display his works. Ask students what they notice first in these paintings. What do they have in common with other portraits they have seen? (For example, Washington, Revere—see Unit Five in the section on first grade.) Note the titles of the works. Explain that Catlin was unique in his time because he painted Native Americans individualistically. (SL.2.2)

## 9. ART, OPINION WRITING

Select one Curtis and one Catlin artwork to study. Have the students compare Curtis's and Catlin's approaches to depicting Native Americans. Does Curtis's use of the environment expand our understanding of the Native Americans in his photographs? If so, how? (W.2.1, W.2.3)

## 10. ART, SPEAKING AND LISTENING

Have students close their eyes and "turn on" their imaginations. Tell them to imagine traveling back to the nineteenth century as if they were artists studying the Native Americans. Ask questions like: "What do you see? What types of people are there? plants, animals, landscapes?" Have students write a few sentences about their imagined picture, as well as sketch a picture. If time permits, turn the sketched image into a landscape image: add significant aspects, like characters, a setting, and any meaningful details. Use listed artworks as inspiration for students. (SL.2.3, SL.2.4, SL.2.5)

## 11. ART, SPEAKING AND LISTENING

View the two Remington paintings of cowboys. Ask students to look at the individual cowboys and see if they can find many differences in their appearances. Was Remington depicting cowboys individually (like Catlin) or more like types (like Curtis)? What can we learn about cowboy life by looking at these works? (SL.2.3, SL.2.4, SL.2.5)

## READING FOUNDATIONS: A PACING GUIDE FOR READING INSTRUCTION

See Grade Two, Level Two, in the Reading Foundations section at the beginning of this book for a complete pacing guide for this unit.

## ADDITIONAL ONLINE RESOURCES

- *Cowboys and Fairy Tales: Interacting with Fractured Texas Tales* (ReadWriteThink) (RL.2.9, W.2.3)
- *An Interactive Biographical Dictionary Profiling Men and Women Portrayed in* The West (PBS) (W.2.8)
- George Catlin, various paintings of Native Americans (1796–1872)

## TERMINOLOGY

| | | |
|---|---|---|
| Biography | Contrast | Point of view |
| Characters | Expression | Real |
| Collective nouns | Fantasy | Tall tale |
| Compare | Fluency | Venn diagram |

## INTERDISCIPLINARY CONNECTIONS

This unit teaches:

- **Art:** George Catlin, Edward S. Curtis, Frederic Remington
- **Geography:** The western United States
- **History:** American westward expansion (e.g., the role of the railroad) and Native Americans (e.g., Plains Indians and the effect of the railroad on Native American communities)

This unit could be extended to teach:

- **History:** American westward expansion (e.g., the steamboat, wagon trains, the Pony Express) and Native Americans (e.g., Sequoyah and the Trail of Tears)
- **Science:** Simple machines used by the Native Americans and technology related to westward movement (e.g., arrows and wagon wheels)

# Grade Two, Unit Two Sample Lesson Plan

## Cowgirl Kate and Cocoa *by Erica Silverman*

In this series of two lessons, students read Cowgirl *Kate and Cocoa* by Erica Silverman, and they:

Explore the relationship between Kate and Cocoa (RL.2.2, RL.2.3)

Examine the lessons that Kate and Cocoa's experiences teach (RL.2.2, RL.2.3, SL.2.1, SL.2.2)

Identify components of paragraphs (L.2.1)

Compose paragraphs (W.2.1)

## Summary

### Lesson I: Meet Kate and Cocoa

Independently read Cowgirl *Kate and Cocoa* by Erica Silverman (RL.2.10, RF.2.3, RF.2.4)

(In small groups) explore the themes of the stories of Kate and Cocoa (RL2.2, SL.2.1, SL.2.2)

Identify a story to write about (SL.2.1)

### Lesson II: Lessons That Kate and Cocoa Teach Us

Revisit the lessons that we learn from Kate's and Cocoa's stories (RL.2.2, RL.2.3)

Select a story to discuss (SL.2.1, SL.2.2)

Identify the necessary components of a paragraph (L.2.1)

Compose paragraphs (W.2.1)

Edit paragraphs (W.2.5, L.2.1, L.2.2, L.2.3)

Share paragraphs (SL.2.6)

### Lesson II: Lessons That Kate and Cocoa Teach Us

*Objectives*

Revisit the lessons that we learn from Kate's and Cocoa's stories (RL.2.2, RL.2.3)

Select a story to discuss (SL.2.1, SL.2.2)

Identify the necessary components of a paragraph (L.2.1)

Compose paragraphs (W.2.1)

Edit paragraphs (W.2.5, L.2.1, L.2.2, L.2.3)

Share paragraphs (SL.2.6)

*Required Materials*

☐ *Cowgirl Kate and Cocoa* by Erica Silverman

☐ Loose-leaf paper

☐ Pencils

*Procedures*

1. Lead-In:

   Capable student volunteers read *Cowgirl Kate and Cocoa* by Erica Silverman, aloud.

2. Step by Step:

   a. In several small groups, students discuss the content of a story they choose to write about.

   b. Introduce the students to the paragraph template below.

| Sentence I: Identify the story and the author | | | | | |
|---|---|---|---|---|---|
| Topic sentence: State the lesson that the story teaches | | | | | |
| Supporting detail | | | | | |
| Supporting detail | | | | | |
| Supporting detail | | | | | |
| Concluding sentence | | | | | |

   c. Students compose their paragraphs with your support.

   d. Students edit their work based on your comments.

3. Closure:

   Student volunteers read their paragraph aloud.

## Differentiation

### Advanced

- Students will revise and edit, with final editing done by an adult.
- Students will go through each story and create a "six-word lesson" for each one. The six-word lessons will be written on sentence strips for the rest of the class to match to the correct story.

### Struggling

- Students may need modeling of an entire paragraph before they are ready to do this work independently.
- Choose a story, for the class or small group, to do as a modeled lesson before teaching from step b on to the end with an expectation of independent work.
- Using adult volunteers to scribe, allow students to dictate paragraph components into the chart before asking them to write out the paragraph themselves. Students will then be able to focus on the content of the paper. Students will learn from copying the correct spelling and punctuation of their ideas.

## Homework/Assessment

Using a rubric, assess students' compositions.

# Building Bridges with Unlikely Friends

In this third six-week unit of second grade, students explore literal and figurative language through the theme of building bridges.

## ESSENTIAL QUESTION

Why do authors use figurative language?

## OVERVIEW

Students read informational (how-to) texts on building bridges and view these amazing structures on the Internet. Through realistic fiction, they examine the possibility of friendship in conflict-filled settings. Reading fantasy texts that depict animals' experiences with "bridge building" completes their exploration. Building on the writing of previous units, they write a letter to a character in *Charlotte's Web*. Students also gather words from poetry and explore the meanings of idioms and words with common roots.

## FOCUS STANDARDS

These Focus Standards have been selected for the unit from the Common Core State Standards.

**RL.2.3:** Describe how characters in a story respond to major events and challenges.

**RL.2.7:** Use information gained from the illustrations and words in a print or digital text to demonstrate understanding of its characters, setting, or plot.

**RI.2.6:** Identify the main purpose of a text, including what the author wants to answer, explain, or describe.

**W.2.2:** Write explanatory texts in which they introduce a topic, use facts and definitions to develop points, and provide a concluding statement or section.

**L.2.2:** Demonstrate command of the conventions of standard English capitalization, punctuation, and spelling when writing.

**L.2.2(b):** Use commas in greetings and closings of letters.

**L.2.4:** Determine or clarify the meaning of unknown and multiple-meaning words and phrases based on grade 2 reading and content, choosing flexibly from an array of strategies.

**L.2.4(d):** Use knowledge of the meaning of individual words to predict the meaning of compound words (e.g., *birdhouse, lighthouse, housefly; bookshelf, notebook, bookmark*).

## SUGGESTED OBJECTIVES

- Read a how-to book.
- Write an explanatory piece on how to do something.
- Discern the difference between the use of literal and figurative language.
- Discern authors' techniques for describing characters.
- Write friendly letters to one of the characters in a book.
- Use commas correctly in the greeting and closing of a friendly letter.
- Write responses to a letter from a character's point of view.
- Use knowledge of a root word, such as *bridge*, to predict the meaning of compound words and idioms.
- Describe the use of riddles and other language in Haiku poetry.

## SUGGESTED WORKS

(E) indicates a CCSS exemplar text; (EA) indicates a text from a writer with other works identified as exemplars.

### LITERARY TEXTS

*Stories*

- *The Fire Cat* (Esther Holden Averill) (E)
- *George and Martha: The Complete Stories of Two Best Friends* (James Marshall)
- *Henry and Mudge: The First Book* (Cynthia Rylant and Sucie Stevenson) (E)

*Stories (Read Aloud)*

- *Charlotte's Web* (E. B. White and Garth Williams) (E)
- *The Cricket in Times Square* (George Selden and Garth Williams) (E)
- *The Day of Ahmed's Secret* (Florence P. Heide, Judith H. Gilliland, and Ted Lewin)
- *Four Feet, Two Sandals* (Karen Lynn Williams, Khadra Mohammed, and Doug Chayka)
- *The Little Painter of Sabana Grande* (Patricia Maloney Markun and Robert Casilla)

- *Mackinac Bridge: The Story of the Five-Mile Poem* (Gloria Whelan and Gijsbert van Frankenhuyzen)
- *My Father's Shop* (Satomi Ichikawa)
- *One Green Apple* (Eve Bunting and Ted Lewin) (EA)
- *Pop's Bridge* (Eve Bunting and C. F. Payne)
- *Silent Music* (James Rumford)
- *Snow in Jerusalem* (Deborah da Costa, Ying-Hwa Hu, and Cornelius Van Wright)
- *Zen Shorts* (Jon J. Muth)

### Poems (Read Aloud)

- "The Bridge Builder" (Will Allen Dromgoole)
- *I Am the Dog, I Am the Cat* (Donald Hall and Barry Moser)
- *If Not for the Cat* (Jack Prelutsky and Ted Rand)

## INFORMATIONAL TEXTS

### Nonfiction Books

- *Bridges* (See More Readers) (Seymour Simon) (EA)
- *Bridges: Amazing Structures to Design, Build & Test* (Carol A. Johmann, Elizabeth Rieth, and Michael P. Kline) (Read Aloud)
- *Bridges Are to Cross* (Philemon Sturges and Giles Laroche) (Read Aloud)
- *Brooklyn Bridge* (Lynn Curlee)
- *Owen and Mzee: The True Story of a Remarkable Friendship* (Isabella Hatkoff, Craig Hatkoff, Paula Kahumbu, and Peter Greste) (Read Aloud)
- *Owen and Mzee: The Language of Friendship* (Isabella Hatkoff, Craig Hatkoff, Paula Kahumbu, and Peter Greste) (Read Aloud)
- *Tarra and Bella: The Elephant and Dog Who Became Best Friends* (Carol Buckley) (Read Aloud)
- *World's Most Amazing Bridges* (Michael Hurley)

## ART, MUSIC, AND MEDIA

### Art

- Album Quilt, Stanford, New York (1853)
- Album Quilts, Baltimore, Maryland (ca. 1840)

## SAMPLE ACTIVITIES AND ASSESSMENTS

Note: This unit could be taught in three parts. First, start with "bridges" so that students see the bridge as both an architectural structure and a symbolic metaphor for coming together. Students will then see how children are able to bridge cultural gaps through friendship. Then read the fictional works to further the theme of unlikely friends. Students will think about differences in characters such as Charlotte and Wilbur and the way they become friends. Finally, writing a friendly letter to a book character will help the students think deeply about the fictional characters.

## 1. READING INFORMATIONAL TEXT, INFORMATIVE WRITING

Introduce a chapter from *Bridges: Amazing Structures to Design, Build & Test* by Carol A. Johmann, Elizabeth Rieth, and Michael P. Kline. This is an informational book, but it is also a how-to book. It will teach how to build bridge structures in the classroom or at home. Read the text to the children and allow them to note that the how-to section is set up as a series of steps to follow. Gather the supplies and allow the students to follow the directions to experiment with building a bridge. Discuss how diagrams help to explain the directions. Writing prompt: "After building a bridge in the classroom or at home, write an explanatory paragraph telling someone else how you made your bridge." (SL.2.6, W.2.2, RI.2.3, RI.2.6, RI.2.7)

## 2. READING INFORMATIONAL TEXT, INFORMATIVE WRITING, SPEAKING AND LISTENING

Begin a class discussion by asking the students, "If a real hippopotamus had no other companions, what other kind of animal could you imagine her having for a friend?" Be sure to require good reasons for their opinions as they answer. Read the book *Owen and Mzee: The True Story of a Remarkable Friendship* by Isabella Hatkoff et al. aloud. When you are finished reading, have the students discuss what the author (a six-year-old girl) wanted to accomplish by publishing the book, using such questions as: "What did she want to explain? describe? What questions did she want to answer? Why are there so many photographs?" Ask students to write a paragraph explaining how the two animals in the story became friends. Writing prompt: "After reading about these unlikely friends (i.e., Owen and Mzee), write a paragraph explaining how the two animals in the story became friends." (SL.2.6, W.2.2, RI.2.3, RI.2.6, RI.2.7)

## 3. READING INFORMATIONAL TEXT, LANGUAGE USAGE

After reading about bridges, have students predict the meaning of compound words that contain the word *bridge: footbridge, drawbridge, flybridge,* and *bridgework.* Repeat the activity using another root word, such as *water: waterbed, watercolor, watermelon, waterlog, watershed, waterproof, watertight, rainwater, waterway,* and *waterspout.* Extend this lesson by discussing idioms using the word *bridge,* such as "We'll cross that bridge when we come to it," "that's water under the bridge," and "don't burn your bridges." (L.2.4d)

## 4. READING LITERATURE, SPEAKING AND LISTENING

Introduce the idea of a bridge as a metaphor by reading the book *Pop's Bridge* by Eve Bunting. (Help the students think of more metaphors to reinforce the meaning of this important term.) In this book, a group of boys experience the sacrifice involved in bridge building and the joy that comes with friendship. Discuss the literal bridge in the book and the way the bridge served as a link not only between two places but also between two people. Introduce the following Isaac Newton quotation: "We build too many walls and not enough bridges." Discuss what Isaac Newton may have meant by his comment. (RL.2.7)

## 5. READING LITERATURE, SPEAKING AND LISTENING

Introduce a book such as *Snow in Jerusalem* by Deborah da Costa, Ying-Hwa Hu, and Cornelius Van Wright by reviewing the idea that unlikely friends can become friends by finding something in common. Tell the students that they are going to read a book about two children who were not friends, but who found something in common anyway. As they read the story, have the students focus on how the children find something in common to make a friendship. Talk about how these two characters faced a challenge and made a hard choice. (RL.2.3, RL.2.7)

## 6. READING LITERATURE, NARRATIVE WRITING

Read aloud the book *Charlotte's Web* by E. B. White to the class. After you have finished the book, have the students connect with the characters in the book by writing friendly letters. Students should choose one of the characters in *Charlotte's Web* and write the character a letter. You may say, "Write a letter to one of the characters in *Charlotte's Web*. Explain why you chose the character and what you like about him or her, and ask the character a question." Require proper use of punctuation and form for the letters. Revise the letters and edit for spelling and punctuation. Then have the students trade letters and write back to a classmate as if they were the classmate's chosen character. For example, if a child receives a letter addressed to Wilbur, she would write a letter back as if she were Wilbur and answer the question asked. (L.2.2b, RL.2.7, W.2.5)

## 7. NARRATIVE WRITING

To encourage communication among unlikely friends, arrange for your students to communicate with students from another class in a place far away. Begin an email or pen-pal correspondence with students from another class in a contrasting location. Setting parameters for what can be shared, ask students to write letters introducing themselves and asking the other student about himself or herself. The purpose of this activity would be to find ways the students are similar and the ways the students are different from one another. This writing activity could also be done writing from whole class to whole class instead of students writing to one another. (W.2.5, W.2.6, L.2.2b)

## 8. READING LITERATURE, SPEAKING AND LISTENING

As students read the *Henry and Mudge: The First Book* and other books in the series by Cynthia Rylant and Sucie Stevenson, challenge them to look closely at the characters. Before the first chapter, ask the students to be ready to describe Henry and Mudge. Using sticky notes or whiteboards, require each student to write down two characteristics of each character. Although one of the characters is a dog and one is a boy, they have a wonderful friendship. Have students share at least two words to describe Henry and two words to describe Mudge. Discuss what can be learned about friendship through these stories. (RL.2.7, L.2.5b)

## 9. READING POETRY, VOCABULARY, SPEAKING AND LISTENING

As you read from the poetry collection *If Not for the Cat* by Jack Prelutsky and Ted Rand, explain to students the Haiku style of poetry. Point out to the students that these poems are very short, but they make you think. As you read a poem, hide the accompanying illustration until students try to guess the animal being described. These poems are filled with words that may be new to your students. When you are finished reading (reciting) each poem, ask students to choose one new word to save in the word bank. (L.2.4e, L.2.5, RL.2.4)

## 10. ART, SPEAKING AND LISTENING

Use the Philadelphia Museum of Art's and Baltimore Museum of Art's websites to explore the tradition of album quilts. Discuss with students the reasons behind making such quilts by asking such questions as:

- How would quilting build strong friendships?
- What types of images do you see in these quilts?
- What do the images tell us about the people who made these quilts? (SL.2.4)

## 11. ART, SPEAKING AND LISTENING

Divide the class into (unlikely) groupings of three to four students. Hand out paper squares and cutout images. Have students discuss what type of album quilt they would like to produce as a group—what event should they commemorate? Using teamwork, each group should produce a small "quilt" of images. (SL.2.1, SL.2.5)

## READING FOUNDATIONS: A PACING GUIDE FOR READING INSTRUCTION

See Grade Two, Level Three, of the Reading Foundations section at the beginning of this book for a complete pacing guide for this unit.

## ADDITIONAL ONLINE RESOURCES

- *Friendly Letter Mini-Lesson* (L.2.2b)
- Letter Generator (ReadWriteThink) (W.2.6, L.2.2b)
- *Build a Bridge* (RI.2.3)
- *Fun and Learning About Bridges* (RI.2.3)
- Brooklyn Bridge website
- Maryland Historical Society website

## TERMINOLOGY

| | | |
|---|---|---|
| Body | Editing | Haiku |
| Capitalization | Informative/explanatory writing | How-to books |
| Closing | Figurative | Idiom |
| Compare | Friendly letter | Literal |
| Compound word | Greeting | Metaphor |
| Contrast | | Revision |

# INTERDISCIPLINARY CONNECTIONS

This unit teaches:

- **Art:** Structural art (e.g., architecture and symmetry), quilts
- **Geography:** World geography (e.g., as related to settings such as Jerusalem)
- **Science:** Animals (e.g., habitats)

This unit could be extended to teach:

- **Science:** Animals (e.g., classifications)

# Grade Two, Unit Three Sample Lesson Plan

## The Fire Cat *by Esther Averill*

In this series of four lessons, students read *The Fire Cat* by Esther Averill, and they:

Explore the adventures of Pickles, the Fire Cat (RL.2.1, RL.2.3)

Examine the power of friendship (RL.2.3)

Learn the meaning of responsibility (RL.2.3)

Examine the concept of happiness (RL.2.3)

## Summary

### Lesson I: Meet Pickles

Identify and chart the characteristics of Pickles, Mrs. Goodkind, and fireman Joe (RL.2.1, RL.2.5)

Explore the meanings of the names of the leading characters (RL.2.1)

Investigate the main conflict in the first chapter (RL.2.5, RL.2.6)

Recognize the use of foreshadowing (RL.2.5)

### Lesson III: Pickles the Hero

Explore Pickles's new life (RL.2.1, SL.2.1)

Articulate the lessons that Pickles learns and the actions that he takes (RL.2.1, SL.2.1)

Discuss Pickles's courage (RL.2.1, SL.2.1)

Examine the statement that Pickles "rode home . . . a proud and happy cat." (RL.2.1)

### Lesson II: Pickles, the Fire Cat

Examine the role that the fire chief plays in Pickles's evolving character (RL.2.1, RL.2.6, RF.2.4)

Trace the steps that Pickles takes in his desire to become a "good firehouse cat" (RL.2.1, RL.2.5, RF.2.4, SL.2.1)

Compare Pickles's life living with Mrs. Goodkind with his life in the firehouse (RL.2.6, SL.2.1)

Note the power of persistence (W.2.1, W.2.2, RF.2.3)

### Lesson IV: Learning from Pickles

Revisit the Pickles story (RL.2.1, SL.2.1, SL.2.2)

Examine the meaning of responsibility that Pickles's story reveals (RL.2.5, SL.2.1)

Explore the ways that Pickles's story teaches the meaning of friendship (SL.2.1)

## Lesson II: Pickles, the Fire Cat

### Objectives

Examine the role that the fire chief plays in Pickles's evolving character (RL.2.1, RL.2.6, RF.2.4)

Trace the steps that Pickles takes in his desire to become a "good firehouse cat" (RL.2.1, RL.2.5, RF.2.4, SL.2.1)

Compare Pickles's life living with Mrs. Goodkind with his life in the firehouse (RL.2.6, SL.2.1)

Note the power of persistence (W.2.1, W.2.2, RF.2.3)

### Required Materials

☐ Class set of *The Fire Cat* by Esther Averill

### Procedures

1. Lead-In:

   Quietly, students read chapter 2 of *The Fire Cat*.

2. Step by Step:

   a. Students reread *The Fire Cat* (the whole book) aloud with partners.

   b. In a class discussion (where students provide evidence from the text), the students trace Pickles's actions once the fire chief tells him that he will be permitted to stay "IF" he learns "to be a good firehouse cat."

      ○ Pickles does not give up when he falls "with a BUMP." He continues to practice sliding down the pole.

      ○ He says to himself, "I must keep on learning everything I can." He also tells himself that he "must learn to help the firemen with their work."

      ○ He learns how to sit in the fire truck.

      ○ He holds on to the hose.

   c. A discussion about the fire chief follows several prompts:

      How many times does the narrator say, "The chief did not say anything"? Why?

      How does the fire chief help Pickles become a responsible fire cat?

   d. In order to understand Pickles's character, compare his life with Mrs. Goodkind with his life in the firehouse. Students are likely to conclude that Pickles does not search for physical comfort; instead, he wants to have challenges.

3. **Closure:**

   In preparation for the writing assignment (homework), the students explore how Pickles's persistence and determination help him become a fire cat.

## Differentiation

### Advanced

- In a small group, explore the meaning of the word *persistence* by using a cube. Use each face of the cube to do one of the following: write the word, illustrate it, write two antonyms for it, write two synonyms for it, write the name of a person you know who exemplifies it, and write a strong sentence using the word as related to a character in a different book.

### Struggling

- Offer the option of also listening to a recording of *The Fire Cat.*
- Support the students in writing a paragraph by writing the first two sentences of the paragraph together before the students leave school.

## Homework/Assessment

Students write a paragraph that discusses how Pickles's determination helps him become a firehouse cat.

# A Long Journey to Freedom

In this fourth six-week unit of second grade, students read informational text and fictionalized accounts of the African American journey to freedom.

## ESSENTIAL QUESTION

What is challenging about writing a narrative?

## OVERVIEW

Building on Unit Three's focus on building bridges, students recognize the long and multi-faceted effort to break down barriers to racial equality in the United States. By reading the true stories of Henry "Box" Brown, Rosa Parks, Ruby Bridges, the Greensboro Four, and others, students see the links between historical events. Each student writes a narrative "from a box" (i.e., in the style of *Henry's Freedom Box*). They also write an opinion piece that is published digitally in a class presentation and possibly online.

## FOCUS STANDARDS

These Focus Standards have been selected for the unit from the Common Core State Standards.

**RL.2.6:** Acknowledge differences in the points of view of characters, including by speaking in a different voice for each character when reading dialogue aloud.

**RI.2.3:** Describe the connection between a series of historical events, scientific ideas or concepts, or steps in technical procedures in a text.

**RI.2.9:** Compare and contrast the most important points presented by two texts on the same topic.

**W.2.1:** Write opinion pieces in which they introduce the topic or book they are writing about, state an opinion, supply reasons that support the opinion, use linking words (e.g., *because, and, also*) to connect opinion and reasons, and provide a concluding statement or section.

**W.2.3:** Write narratives in which they recount a well-elaborated event or short sequence of events, include details to describe action, thoughts, and feelings, use temporal words to signal event order, and provide a sense of closure.

**W.2.6:** With guidance and support from adults, use a variety of digital tools to produce and publish writing, including in collaboration with peers.

## SUGGESTED OBJECTIVES

- Write a narrative imagining that you are a character in one of the stories.
- Select the correct verb form, particularly of irregular verbs, to show past tense in narrative writing.
- Note links between historical events, including parallel connections and sequential connections.
- Analyze narrative poetry to understand its elements, its meaning, and the use of formal and informal English.
- Compare two texts (a biography and an autobiography) on the life of a famous person.
- Write an opinion piece, citing evidence for the opinion.
- Express an opinion by creating and displaying a PowerPoint slide.
- Record the opinion piece being read aloud to use for a class presentation or web page.

## SUGGESTED WORKS

(E) indicates a CCSS exemplar text; (EA) indicates a text from a writer with other works identified as exemplars.

### LITERARY TEXTS

Note: The date or time period that is captured or discussed in each of these works is included in parentheses for your reference.

#### Stories

- *Dear Mr. Rosenwald* (1920) (Carole Boston Weatherford) (Read Aloud)
- *Finding Lincoln* (1951) (Ann Malaspina and Colin Bootman) (Read Aloud)
- *Freedom on the Menu: The Greensboro Sit-Ins* (1960) (Carole Boston Weatherford and Jerome Lagarrigue) (Read Aloud)
- *Freedom Summer* (1964) (Deborah Wiles and Jerome Lagarrigue)
- *Friend on the Freedom River* (1850) Gloria Whelan
- *The Other Side* (1950s) (Jacqueline Woodson and E. B. Lewis)
- *A Sweet Smell of Roses* (1963) (Angela Johnson and Eric Velasquez) (Read Aloud)

*Poems*

- "Harriet Tubman" (Eloise Greenfield) (Read Aloud)
- "Lincoln" (Nancy Byrd Turner) (Read Aloud)
- "Merry-Go-Round" (Langston Hughes) (EA) (Read Aloud)
- "Rosa" (Rita Dove) (Read Aloud)
- "Words Like Freedom" (Langston Hughes) (EA)

## INFORMATIONAL TEXTS

*Nonfiction Books*

- *Birmingham, 1963* (Carole Boston Weatherford)
- *Henry's Freedom Box: A True Story from the Underground Railroad* (1849) (Ellen Levine and Kadir Nelson)
- *Lincoln: A Photobiography* (1809–1865) (Russell Freedman) (E) (Read Aloud)
- *Martin Luther King, Jr. and the March on Washington* (1963) (Frances E. Ruffin and Stephen Marchesi) (E)
- *Martin's Big Words: The Life of Dr. Martin Luther King Jr.* (1963) (Doreen Rappaport and Bryan Collier)
- *Moses: When Harriet Tubman Led Her People to Freedom* (ca. 1820–1913) (Carole Boston Weatherford and Kadir Nelson) (Read Aloud)
- *A Picture Book of Jesse Owens* (1935) (David A. Adler and Robert Casilla) (Read Aloud)
- *Rosa Parks* (1955) (Rookie Biographies) (Wil Mara)
- *Ruby Bridges Goes to School: My True Story* (1960) (Ruby Bridges)
- *Sit-In: How Four Friends Stood Up by Sitting Down* (1960) (Andrea D. and Brian Pinkney)
- *The Story of Ruby Bridges* (1960) (Robert Coles and George Ford) (E) (Read Aloud)

## ART, MUSIC, AND MEDIA

*Art*

- Norman Rockwell, *The Problem We All Live With* (1963)
- *Working Photograph of Ruby Bridges* (artist and date unknown)
- *Photograph of Ruby Bridges* (AP Photo, 1963)

*Film*

- Euzhan Palcy, dir., *Disney's Ruby Bridges: A Real American Hero* (1998)

## SAMPLE ACTIVITIES AND ASSESSMENTS

Note: The books in this unit can be taught in chronological order, beginning in the middle 1800s with the Underground Railroad, Harriet Tubman, and Abraham Lincoln; moving to Jesse Owens, and then Julius Rosenwald (1920), Rosa Parks (1955), Ruby Bridges and the Greensboro Sit-In (1960); and, finally, Martin Luther King Jr. The connections between historical events (RI.2.3) will be seen as a long journey if each book is linked to the others as related stories.

## 1. LANGUAGE USAGE, VOCABULARY

As you have the students read the literature of this unit, look for words that might lend themselves to a discussion of affixes and roots. Teach the students that by knowing the root word, they can approximate the meaning of another word that they may not know. For example, if the children have learned the meaning of *prejudice* and then come across the word *prejudicial*, they may have an idea of its meaning, especially if they see *prejudicial* in context as they read. Encourage students to use dictionaries to determine accurate meanings and to check spelling while writing. (L.2.4b, L.2.4c)

## 2. READING INFORMATIONAL TEXT, SPEAKING AND LISTENING

Read and discuss the book *Henry's Freedom Box* by Ellen Levine and Kadir Nelson, a true story of a slave's journey to freedom. Be sure to discuss the characters, setting, plot, and message of the book. Students may enjoy listening to the author read the story, noting the way she changes her voice with the different characters. (RL.2.6, RI.2.3, SL.2.2)

## 3. READING INFORMATIONAL TEXT, NARRATIVE WRITING

After reading about Henry's journey to freedom (in *Henry's Freedom Box*), introduce this narrative prompt: "Write a story as if you are in the box headed for freedom. Begin your story as you get into the box and end the story as the box is opened at your destination. Be sure to describe the action in the story, your thoughts, and feelings. Use words to show time order and end with a strong wrap-up." To help prepare students for writing strong paragraphs, plan the writing using a sequential graphic organizer (flow map or trifold paper) showing a beginning, middle, and end. To help the students with thoughts and feelings, you may want to have them journal after spending several minutes in a *well-ventilated, open* box. (W.2.3)

## 4. LANGUAGE USAGE

Revise the "stories from inside a box" (see Narrative Writing, Activity 3) by focusing on action words. Discuss the present tense and past tense of verbs, focusing particularly on irregular verbs, such as "I hide, I hid" and "I sit, I sat." (L.2.1d)

## 5. READING POETRY, SPEAKING AND LISTENING

The poems about Harriet Tubman ("Harriet Tubman," Eloise Greenfield) and Abraham Lincoln ("Lincoln," Nancy Byrd Turner) are narrative poems that tell a story. Read (recite) the poems. Use these questions to discuss the poems:

- How are the poems similar, and how are they different?
- What poetic elements (e.g., alliteration, repetition, regular beats, and rhyme) do you hear/see in the poetry?
- What is the message of each poem? Are they similar or different?
- Which of the poems uses formal English, and which one uses more informal English? (L.2.3a, RL.2.4)

## 6. READING INFORMATIONAL TEXT, SPEAKING AND LISTENING

Read aloud the two suggested texts about Ruby Bridges (*Ruby Bridges Goes to School* and *The Story of Ruby Bridges*). Before reading, explain that one of the books is an autobiography (*Ruby Bridges Goes to School: A True Story*) that Bridges wrote about her own experiences. Explain that the other book, *The Story of Ruby Bridges* by Robert Coles and George Ford, is biographical, which means that an author wrote the book about Bridges's life. When you finish reading each book aloud, have the students choose the most important parts of the story. Then have them compare how the books are similar and how they are different. (There are several other opportunities to do this compare/contrast activity, or assessment, e.g., with the Greensboro Sit-In and Martin Luther King Jr. texts.) (RI.2.3, RI.2.9, SL.2.3)

## 7. ART, LANGUAGE USAGE, SPEAKING AND LISTENING

While the class is focused on Ruby Bridges, show the students some photographs of Bridges and the Rockwell, which was painted after a photograph of her. What can you learn about Bridges and the time in which she lived by looking at these works? Compare the photo of Bridges walking to school with that section of Rockwell's painting. What has Rockwell added or subtracted (e.g., the lunchbox, graffiti)? What tells us more about Bridges's character, the photograph or Rockwell's depiction of her? (Note: You should look for adjectives and character vocabulary in the conversation.) (L.2.5b, L.2.6, SL.2.3)

## 8. OPINION WRITING, LANGUAGE USAGE

Give the students this writing prompt: "Choose one of the people studied in this unit who you think is the greatest hero in this long journey to freedom. Give two or three strong reasons for choosing this person." Students should be moving toward writing paragraphs. Remind them to introduce the person and give strong reasons why the person was chosen, using words like *because* and *also* to link ideas. Encourage the addition of details to strengthen the writing and a strong statement to close. (W.2.1, L.2.1f)

## 9. OPINION WRITING, MULTIMEDIA PRESENTATION

Students can publish their opinion pieces by scanning the drawing and putting it into a slide. Opinion pieces should be recorded and played as the drawing is projected. These slides and recordings could be posted on a web page to be viewed by friends and relatives. Arrange the slides chronologically to reinforce the linking of ideas in this long journey to freedom. (W.2.6, SL.2.5)

## READING FOUNDATIONS: A PACING GUIDE FOR READING INSTRUCTION

See Grade Two, Level Four, in the Reading Foundations section at the beginning of this book for a complete pacing guide for this unit.

## ADDITIONAL ONLINE RESOURCES

- *Inside and Outside: Paradox of the Box* (LearnNC) (RL.2.3)
- *Ellen Levine Reads* Henry's Freedom Box (Scholastic, Author Interviews) (RL.2.6)
- A *Class of One* (PBS, an interview with Ruby Bridges Hall, 1997) (SL.2.2)
- Martin Luther King Jr.'s "I Have a Dream" speech (American Rhetoric: Top 100 Speeches) (SL.2.3)

## TERMINOLOGY

Action
Autobiography
Biography
Conclusion

Linking words
Narrative
Opinion piece

Record
Scan
Time order words

## INTERDISCIPLINARY CONNECTIONS

This unit teaches:

- **Art:** Photography, Norman Rockwell
- **Geography:** Southern states and Canada
- **History:** Slavery (e.g., Lincoln, Tubman), civil rights movement (e.g., Ruby Bridges, Martin Luther King Jr.)

This unit could be extended to teach:

- **History:** Civil War (e.g., slavery, states' rights), civil rights (e.g., Susan B. Anthony)

# Grade Two, Unit Four Sample Lesson Plan

*"Words Like Freedom" by Langston Hughes*

Langston Hughes, *edited by David Roessel and Arnold Rampersad*

In this series of three lessons, students read "Words Like Freedom" by Langston Hughes, and they:

Explore the life and legacy of Langston Hughes (RI.2.1, RI.2.2, RI.2.3, RI.2.6, SL.1.1, SL.1.2)

Explore the theme of "Words Like Freedom" (RL.2.4, SL.1.1, SL.1.2)

Examine a collection of Hughes's poems (RL.2.4, RL.2.10, RF.2.4, SL.1.1, SL.1.2)

## Summary

### Lesson I: Meet Langston Hughes

Meet Langston Hughes–an introduction

Recall key ideas from the introduction (RI.2.1, RI.2.2, RI.2.3, RI.2.6, SL.1.1, SL.1.2)

Explore the role that poets can play in society (RI.2.3)

### Lesson II: "Words Like Freedom"

Examine the use of repetition in the poem (RL.2.4)

Note the use of italics in the poem (RL.2.4)

Explore the theme of the poem (RL.2.4, SL.1.1, SL.1.2)

### Lesson III: The Poems of Langston Hughes

Select (in groups) a different poem from *Langston Hughes*, edited by David Roessel and Arnold Rampersad (RL.2.4, RL.2.10, RF.2.4)

Explore the theme of the new poem (RL.2.4, SL.1.1, SL.1.2)

Note the possible similarities between the new poem and "Words Like Freedom" (RL.2.4, SL.1.1, SL.1.2)

## Lesson I: Meet Langston Hughes

### Objectives

Meet Langston Hughes–an introduction

Recall key ideas from the introduction (RI.2.1, RI.2.2, RI.2.3, RI.2.6, SL.1.1, SL.1.2)

Explore the role that poets can play in society (RI.2.3)

### Required Materials

☐ Class set of "Words Like Freedom" by Langston Hughes

☐ Poster-size copy of "Words Like Freedom"

☐ *Langston Hughes*, edited by David Roessel and Arnold Rampersad

☐ Map of the United States

### Procedures

1. Lead-In:

   Read aloud the poem "Words Like Freedom." Students can read along from the poster-size copy of the poem. After the reading, tell the students that they will return to this and other poems after they learn about the poet and his life.

2. Step by Step:

   a. Before you begin to read excerpts from *Langston Hughes* to the students, tell them to note details about the life of Hughes and his place in the literary history of the United States. (You may choose to use other sources as you introduce Hughes.)

   b. Read excerpts from "Introduction" in *Langston Hughes*.

   c. Lead a discussion about Langston Hughes, his life, and his legacy. Some important facts to highlight:

      o Hughes was born in Missouri in 1902. (Students locate Missouri on the map of the United States.)

      o He was an important African American poet.

      o He wrote about the African American experience.

      o He lived most of his adult life in New York City. (Students locate New York City on the map of the United States.)

      o In the 1920s, Hughes lived and worked in Harlem.

      o This period was known as the Harlem Renaissance.

- ○ Many artists lived and worked in Harlem at that time.
- ○ Hughes incorporated traditions of African American music into his work. (This list includes only a few important facts. You may choose to expand this part of the lesson.)

3. Closure:

   Together, the students read "Words Like Freedom" aloud.

## Differentiation

### Advanced

- Students read through a variety of Hughes's poetry with a partner, noting his craft in creating poetry.
- Students choose another work of art from the Harlem Renaissance period and describe it in writing. After studying the artwork, students create original poetry based on what they see in the art.

### Struggling

- Pre-teach the meaning and discuss the powerful connotations of the words *freedom* and *liberty*.
- Students work through the poem line by line in a small group, looking for connections to the civil rights movement and illustrating each line or stanza.

## Homework/Assessment

N/A

# Hand-Me-Down Tales from Around the World

In this fifth six-week unit of second grade, students practice opinion and narrative writing as they read the poetry of Robert Louis Stevenson and a wide variety of legends, folktales, and informational books from around the world.

## ESSENTIAL QUESTION

How are stories and poems alike? How are they different?

## OVERVIEW

Building on previous units, students write opinions and narratives related to the folktale/world theme of this unit. Students discuss text features as a part of reading informational text. Although students have compared versions of tales in Unit Two, they will now compare a narrative version of a story to a poetry version, using the story of the Pied Piper. Students develop independent reading skills as they read texts on grade level (and beyond) throughout this unit.

## FOCUS STANDARDS

These Focus Standards have been selected for the unit from the Common Core State Standards.

**RL.2.2:** Recount stories, including fables and folktales from diverse cultures, and determine their central message, lesson, or moral.

**RI.2.7:** Explain how specific images (e.g., a diagram showing how a machine works) contribute to and clarify a text.

**W.2.3:** Write narratives in which they recount a well-elaborated event or short sequence of events, include details to describe action, thoughts, and feelings, use temporal words to signal event order, and provide a sense of closure.

**SL.2.3:** Ask and answer questions about what a speaker says in order to clarify comprehension, gather additional information, or deepen understanding of a topic or issue.

**SL.2.4:** Tell a story or recount an experience with appropriate facts and relevant, descriptive details, speaking audibly in coherent sentences.

## SUGGESTED OBJECTIVES

- Read poetry, informational text, and literature on grade and stretch levels.
- Retell folktales from diverse cultures, determining their central message or lesson.
- Write imaginative narratives in which they tell a well-elaborated story.
- Ask and answer questions of a guest speaker.
- Use text features in nonfiction to aid comprehension of the text.
- Compare a variety of versions of the same story (e.g., versions of *Stone Soup*), contrasting the differences in story elements and key details.
- Compare a poetry version and a prose version of the same story (e.g., the Pied Piper legend).
- Learn the irregular forms of plural nouns.
- Memorize a poem and record it.

## SUGGESTED WORKS

(E) indicates a CCSS exemplar text; (EA) indicates a text from a writer with other works identified as exemplars.

## LITERARY TEXTS

### Stories

- *Bone Button Borscht* (Aubrey Davis and Dušan Petričić)
- *Caps for Sale: A Tale of a Peddler* (Esphyr Slobodkina)
- *Cuckoo/Cucú: A Mexican Folktale* (Lois Ehlert and Gloria De Aragon Andujar)
- *The Enormous Turnip* (Alexei Tolstoy and Scott Goto)
- *The Girl Who Wore Too Much: A Folktale from Thailand* (Margaret Read McDonald and Yvonne Lebrun Davis)
- *Itching and Twitching: A Nigerian Folktale* (Patricia C. McKissack, Robert L. McKissack, and Laura Freeman)
- *Liang and the Magic Paintbrush* (Demi)
- *Moon Rope/Un lazo a la luna: A Peruvian Folktale* (Lois Ehlert and Amy Prince)
- *The Pied Piper's Magic* (Steven Kellogg)
- *The Real Story of Stone Soup* (Ying Chang Compestine)
- *Some Friends to Feed: The Story of Stone Soup* (Pete Seeger, Paul Dubois Jacobs, and Michael Hays)
- *Stone Soup* (Marcia Brown)

- *Stone Soup* (Heather Forest and Susan Gaber)
- *Stone Soup* (Ann McGovern and Winslow Pinney Pels)
- *Stone Soup* (Jon J. Muth)
- *Stone Soup* (Tony Ross)
- *The Treasure* (Uri Shulevitz) (E)

## Stories (Read Aloud)

- *The 13 Clocks* (James Thurber and Marc Simont) (E)
- *The Five Chinese Brothers* (Claire Huchet Bishop and Kurt Wiese)
- "How the Camel Got His Hump" in *Just So Stories* (Rudyard Kipling) (E)
- *The Lost Horse: A Chinese Folktale* (Ed Young and Tracey Adams) (EA)
- *Martina the Beautiful Cockroach: A Cuban Folktale* (Carmen Agra Deedy and Michael Austin) (EA)
- *Not One Damsel in Distress: World Folktales for Strong Girls* (Jane Yolen and Susan Guevara)
- *The Village of Round and Square Houses* (Ann Grifalconi)

## Poems

- "At the Seaside" (Robert Louis Stevenson)
- "Foreign Lands" (Robert Louis Stevenson)
- "The Land of Counterpane" (Robert Louis Stevenson)
- "The Land of Story Books" (Robert Louis Stevenson)
- "My Bed is a Boat" (Robert Louis Stevenson)
- "The Pied Piper of Hamelin" (Robert Browning) (E) (Read Aloud)
- "Where Go the Boats?" (Robert Louis Stevenson)

# INFORMATIONAL TEXTS

## Nonfiction Books

- *Art Around the World* (Discovery World) (Heather Leonard) (E)
- *Bread, Bread, Bread* (Around the World Series) (Ann Morris and Ken Heyman)
- *Houses and Homes* (Around the World Series) (Ann Morris and Ken Heyman)
- *How I Learned Geography* (Uri Shulevitz) (EA) (Read Aloud)
- *Hungry Planet: What the World Eats* (Peter Menzel and Faith D'Aluisio) (Read Aloud)
- *If the World Were a Village: A Book About the World's People* (David Smith and Shelagh Armstrong) (E) (Read Aloud)
- *Loving* (Around the World Series) (Ann Morris and Ken Heyman)
- *On the Go* (Around the World Series) (Ann Morris and Ken Heyman)
- *Shoes, Shoes, Shoes* (Around the World Series) (Ann Morris)

## ART, MUSIC, AND MEDIA

### Art

- Edgar Degas, *The Dancing Class* (1870)
- Edgar Degas, *The Little Fourteen-Year-Old Dancer* (1879–1880)
- Giovanni Domenico Tiepolo, A *Dance in the Country* (1755)

### Music

- Sergei Prokofiev, "Peter and the Wolf" (1936)

### Film

- Suzie Templeton, dir., "Peter and the Wolf" (2006)

### Dance

- *The Firebird*, Stravinsky, Fokine, (Bolshoi Ballet, 1997)
- *A Folk Tale (Et Folkesagn)*, Bournonville (Royal Danish Ballet, 2011)
- *Peter and the Wolf*, Prokofiev (Royal Ballet School, 1995)

## SAMPLE ACTIVITIES AND ASSESSMENTS

## 1. READING POETRY, SPEAKING AND LISTENING

Introduce the unit by asking students about using their imaginations to go places. Introduce a poet who lived over one hundred years ago and also loved to go places in his imagination: Robert Louis Stevenson. As a child, he was sometimes sick. While confined to his bed, he created imaginary lands in his head, such as the Land of Counterpane. He also loved the sea. As students read (recite) his poems, have them think about his imagination and how he loved to wonder about the world. You may want to revisit his poetry throughout this unit, encouraging the students to look for poetic elements. Most of all, direct children to enjoy the idea of going places in their minds as you read folktales from around the world. Having a large world map to mark the place from which the story comes will give this unit a stronger geography focus. (RL.2.4)

## 2. READING POETRY, SPEAKING AND LISTENING

Introduce the poem "The Pied Piper of Hamelin" by Robert Browning. This poem is a narrative based on a legend that takes place in Hamelin, Germany. Remind students that a legend is a story in which some things really happened and other things have been exaggerated over time as the story has passed down through generations. Ask the students which parts of the legend are probably true and which events have been exaggerated over time. Read the poem to the children. Give the students an opportunity to retell the story, confirming that they understand the main events of the story. Using a program such as Comic Life, allow students to create a comic strip of the Pied Piper story told in the narrative poem. (The language in this poem is quite sophisticated. Reading the Kellogg book first will scaffold student comprehension of the poem. It will also provide another opportunity to compare versions.) Ask such questions as: "How many of you think this story could have really happened?" "What was the story teaching?" (RL.2.2, SL.2.4. L.2.4)

## 3. LANGUAGE USAGE, SPEAKING AND LISTENING

After reading "The Pied Piper of Hamelin," do a word activity based on the poem. Collect some plural nouns from the poem. Talk about the singular for each word and how it is made plural (e.g., *rats, babies, vats, children, tongues, shoes,* and *mice*). Extend this activity by collecting the plurals of irregular nouns in particular. (L.2.1b)

## 4. READING LITERATURE, SPEAKING AND LISTENING

Introduce the characteristics of folktales by reading one or two and asking students what the tales have in common. Then invite speakers to read folktales from their home country. For example, invite someone from Cuba or the Caribbean to read *Martina the Beautiful Cockroach: A Cuban Folktale* by Carmen Agra Deedy and Michael Austin. As the visitor reads the story, have students consider what message the folktale might teach. When the story is over, the speaker could share some information about the country from which the folktale comes. Give an opportunity for students to ask questions about the folktale and the country. (SL.2.3, RL.2.2)

## 5. READING LITERATURE, SPEAKING AND LISTENING

Read the book *Stone Soup* by Marcia Brown aloud to the students. Introduce other versions of the book (e.g., by Muth, Seeger, and Davis). Compare and contrast the versions of the story, using a graphic organizer you have created that addresses *who, what, where, why, when,* and *how* questions or a graphic organizer that addresses *character, setting, plot,* and *conclusion* categories. Encourage student participation by handing each child three sticky notes to use to post information on the graphic organizer. (RL.2.2, RL.2.9)

## 6. READING LITERATURE, READING COMPREHENSION

Have students select a folktale to read. Provide each student with a piece of plain white paper. Then give these instructions:

Read a folktale with a partner [a stronger reader can read to a weaker reader, or they can take turns or read chorally]. When you are finished reading the folktale, follow these directions:

- Fold your paper into fourths.
- Draw a picture of the main characters in one square.
- Draw the setting in another square.
- Draw your favorite part of the plot in another square.
- In the last part, write a few sentences describing what you think the folktale is teaching.

Each time the students do this activity, substitute one more square with writing instead of drawing. As students read the last book independently, have them use the four-square outline to write a retelling of the folktale. Ask them to describe why they know it is a folktale (i.e., elicit common characteristics of folktales). (RL.2.2, RL.2.5, RL.2.7, RL.2.10, W.2.7, SL.2.2)

## 7. READING INFORMATIONAL TEXT, SPEAKING AND LISTENING

The informational books in this unit are based on themes like shoes or bread. For example, the author of most of these books, Ann Morris, studied interesting shoes from all around the world, had photographs taken of them, and then published them in a book, *Shoes, Shoes, Shoes.* As students read the books, ask them to look at the way the book is organized and locate the information about each photograph by using the index. As they study the book, challenge them to find on a world map the location from where those shoes came. To link to geography, give each pair of students a world map to mark as the text moves from one place to another. (After the students have had an opportunity to study multiple books in this series, ask them why they think the author wrote these books for children.) (RI.2.5, RI.2.6, RI.2.10)

## 8. READING INFORMATIONAL TEXT, RESEARCH

*If the World Were a Village: A Book About the World's People* by David Smith and Shelagh Armstrong is an informational book packed with rich facts about the world. One of the interesting things about this book is that it shows the world as if it were a village of just one hundred people. Although you may have time for just a few pages, focus on how much information can be learned from the illustrations and text. Keep a list of the information that the students glean from the pages as you read. (RI.2.3, RI.2.6, RI.2.7)

## 9. READING LITERATURE, NARRATIVE WRITING, LANGUAGE MECHANICS

Give the students this prompt: "Write an imaginary narrative telling about a time you passed through a mysterious door and ended up in a different country. The country may be from the folktale unit, from a book you have read, or just a place you want to visit. Be sure to say where you find the door, the country where the door leads, and how you arrive back where you began. Include details to describe action, thoughts, and feelings. Be sure to end your story well, thinking about how authors wrap up stories." Remind the students that their sentences should have subjects, verbs, and proper end punctuation. (W.2.3, L.2.2a)

## 10. MUSIC, ART, SPEAKING AND LISTENING

Explain to the students that Sergei Prokofiev was a Russian music composer who wrote a musical rendition of the folktale called "Peter and the Wolf." Explain that he used different musical instruments to represent the characters in the story. Compare and contrast different productions of this piece (e.g., animated version, music-only CD, video of the ballet). (RL.2.2, RL.2.6, RL.2.9, SL.2.2)

## 11. ART, SPEAKING AND LISTENING

How can we view folktales in an artistic way? Have students view clips of the ballets provided. After viewing clips of each folktale ballet, discuss with students: "Can you see the storytelling clearly in these works? If so, how? If not, how would you, as a dancer or choreographer, make this clearer for the viewer? Does viewing a folktale, rather than reading it, change the meaning for the viewer? How so?" For background on ballet, see the essay titled "The Ballet" at the Metropolitan Museum of Art. It may be helpful to introduce concepts of ballet through the artworks listed previously. (SL.2.5)

## 12. READING POETRY, PERFORMANCE

Revisit the Robert Louis Stevenson poems, reminding students how they have used their imaginations to visualize the folktale being read and the places being read about (see Reading Poetry, Speaking and Listening, Activity 1). Discuss how repeated readings may deepen a poem's meaning, and challenge the students to memorize one of the poems to share in front of the class. Record the students' poetry performances with a video camera. (RL.2.4, SL.2.5)

## 13. NARRATIVE WRITING, LANGUAGE USAGE, LANGUAGE MECHANICS

Give the students this prompt: "All of the stories we read in this unit were folktales of some kind. Why do you think stories are handed down from one group of people to another? Be sure to support your opinion with strong reasons." Remind the students that their sentences should have subjects, verbs, and proper end punctuation. (W.2.1)

## READING FOUNDATIONS: A PACING GUIDE FOR READING INSTRUCTION

See Grade Two, Level Five, in the Reading Foundations section at the beginning of this book for a complete pacing guide for this unit.

## ADDITIONAL ONLINE RESOURCES

- PBS musical version of *The Pied Piper* (Part One and Part Two)
- North American and Central American folklore
- "The Ballet" (The Metropolitan Museum of Art)

## TERMINOLOGY

| | | |
|---|---|---|
| Character | Legend | Plural |
| Conclusion | Narrative poem | Setting |
| Folktale | Noun | |
| Index | Plot | |

## INTERDISCIPLINARY CONNECTIONS

This unit teaches:
- **Music/dance:** Sergei Prokofiev, ballet
- **History/geography:** World geography (e.g., places of origin for folktales: Nigeria, Thailand, Mexico, Peru; cultural comparisons)

This unit could be extended to teach:
- **History/geography:** Immigration in the United States (e.g., *e pluribus unum*, Ellis Island)

# Grade Two, Unit Five Sample Lesson Plan

*"How the Camel Got His Hump" by Rudyard Kipling*

In this series of two lessons, students listen to you read "How the Camel Got His Hump" by Rudyard Kipling, and they:

Consider the moral of "How the Camel Got His Hump" by Rudyard Kipling (RL.2.1, RL.2.2, SL.2.1)

Provide and evaluate an artistic interpretation of the tale (SL.2.1)

## Summary

| Lesson I: "How the Camel Got His Hump"–A Story and Its Moral | Lesson II: Illustrating "How the Camel Got His Hump" by Rudyard Kipling |
| --- | --- |
| Explore the plot of "How the Camel Got His Hump" (RL.2.1, RL.2.3, RL.2.5, SL.2.1) | Reread "How the Camel Got His Hump" by Rudyard Kipling (RL.2.1, RL.2.5) |
| Identify the characters of the story (RL.2.1) | Identify sections in the story (RL.2.1, RL.2.5) |
| Note the setting and the time that the story takes place (RL.2.1) | Draw illustrations interpreting the story |
| Examine Camel and his actions (RL.2.1, RL.2.3, SL.2.1) | Display and evaluate the illustrated stories (SL.2.1) |
| Consider the moral of the story (RL.2.1, RL.2.2, SL.2.1) | Revisit the moral of the story (RL.2.1, RL.2.2, SL.2.1) |

Lesson I: "How the Camel Got His Hump"–A Story and Its Moral

*Objectives*

Explore the plot of "How the Camel Got His Hump" (RL.2.1, RL.2.3, RL.2.5, SL.2.1)

Identify the characters of the story (RL.2.1)

Note the setting and the time that the story takes place (RL.2.1)

Examine Camel and his actions (RL.2.1, RL.2.3, SL.2.1)

Consider the moral of the story (RL.2.1, RL.2.2, SL.2.1)

### Required Materials

☐ Copies of "How the Camel Got His Hump" by Rudyard Kipling (The copies contain only the text, no illustrations.)

### Procedures

1. **Lead-In:**

   Read "How the Camel Got His Hump" aloud.

2. **Step by Step:**

   a. Lead a brief discussion of the plot of the story.

   b. Discuss the characters next. Students will identify:

      ○ Man

      ○ Camel

      ○ Horse

      ○ Dog

      ○ Ox

      ○ *Djinn* (genie)

   c. Students explore the setting of the story ("a Howling Desert" and "the beginning of years").

   d. Students continue their discussion, evaluating Camel's behavior and the consequences of his acts.

3. **Closure:**

   Prompt the students to consider the moral of the story.

### Differentiation

#### Advanced

- Students will read (or listen to) more "Just So Stories" by Kipling that focus on the "How the . . ." theme. Each student chooses one of the other stories to illustrate. Use the illustrations and recorded narration to create a multimedia presentation of "Just So Stories" for the other students.

*Struggling*

- Following the reading of the story and brief discussion of plot, assign the students a character. As you read the story again, students will act out the parts of each of the characters. Students watching should echo the repeated word "HUMPH" on cue. Continue the lesson as described with step c.

## Homework/Assessment

N/A

# Taking Care of Ourselves

In this sixth six-week unit of second grade, students will enjoy a wide range of reading and practice informative/explanatory writing while studying human body systems.

## ESSENTIAL QUESTION

Why should we support our opinions with reasons?

## OVERVIEW

Examining still-life paintings of food for detail, students describe what they see, and arrange and paint or draw a still life of healthy snacks. Building on the painting experience in this unit and the bridge writing in Unit Three, students write informative/explanatory pieces. They read informational texts on body systems in the grade 2 to grade 3 reading range with fluency. As they discover a range of food-related titles, students independently read fiction and poetry, looking for an underlying message.

## FOCUS STANDARDS

These Focus Standards have been selected for the unit from the Common Core State Standards.

**RL.2.4:** Describe how words and phrases (e.g., regular beats, alliteration, rhymes, repeated lines) supply rhythm and meaning in a story, poem, or song.

**RL.2.10:** By the end of the year, read and comprehend literature, including stories and poetry, in the grades 2–3 text complexity band proficiently, with scaffolding as needed at the high end of the range.

**SL.2.5:** Create audio recordings of stories or poems; add drawings or other visual displays to stories or recounts of experiences when appropriate to clarify ideas, thoughts, and feelings.

**RI.2.8:** Describe how reasons support specific points the author makes in a text.

**RI.2.10:** By the end of year, read and comprehend informational texts, including history/social studies, science, and technical texts, in the grades 2–3 text complexity band proficiently, with scaffolding as needed at the high end of the range.

**W.2.1:** Write opinion pieces in which they introduce the topic of the book they are writing about, state an opinion, supply reasons that support the opinion, use linking words (e.g., *because, also*) to connect opinion and reasons, and provide a concluding statement or section.

## SUGGESTED OBJECTIVES

- Write an informative/explanatory piece describing the experience of creating art.
- Use descriptive words (adjectives) to describe food they taste.
- Consult a dictionary on the spelling of descriptive words.
- Read to understand more on a specific topic (e.g., the systems of the body in a narrative informational text, *The Magic School Bus Inside the Human Body*).
- Read texts independently and fluently in both literary and informative genres, on grade level and into the stretch 2 through 3 level of text.
- Read books with a common theme (e.g., food) to explore the treatment of themes in literature.
- Sing songs about a given topic, noting how the rhythm and rhyme of the music and lyrics might help understanding of the topic.
- Use reference books to research a scientific topic (e.g., names of bones in the human body).
- Write a paragraph with an introductory sentence, at least one supporting sentence, and a conclusion.
- Write an opinion piece about a given topic (e.g., an important thing to do to stay healthy).
- Use reflexive pronouns (e.g., *myself, yourself*, and *ourselves*) correctly.

## SUGGESTED WORKS

(E) indicates a CCSS exemplar text; (EA) indicates a text from a writer with other works identified as exemplars.

### LITERARY TEXTS

*Stories*

- *Cloudy with a Chance of Meatballs* (Judi and Ron Barrett)
- *Dim Sum for Everyone* (Grace Lin)
- *Everybody Brings Noodles* (Norah Dooley and Peter J. Thornton)
- *Everybody Serves Soup* (Norah Dooley and Peter J. Thornton)
- *Gregory the Terrible Eater* (Mitchell Sharmat, Jose Aruego, and Ariane Dewey)
- *How My Parents Learned to Eat* (Ina R. Friedman and Allen Say)
- *In the Night Kitchen* (Maurice Sendak) (EA)
- *Tar Beach* (Faith Ringgold)

- *Thunder Cake* (Patricia Polacco)
- *Yoko* (Rosemary Wells)

## Stories (Read Aloud)
- *Chato's Kitchen* (Gary Soto and Susan Guevara)
- *Everybody Bakes Bread* (Norah Dooley and Peter J. Thornton)
- *Everybody Cooks Rice* (Norah Dooley and Peter J. Thornton)
- *The Magic School Bus Inside the Human Body* (Joanna Cole and Bruce Degan)
- *My Mom Loves Me More Than Sushi* (Filomena Gomes and Ashley Spires)
- *Something's Happening on Calabash Street* (Judith Ross)
- *Strega Nona* (Tomie dePaola)
- *The Sweetest Fig* (Chris Van Allsburg)
- *Too Many Tamales* (Gary Soto and Ed Martinez)

## Poems
- "Bananas and Cream" (David McCord)
- "Boa Constrictor" (Shel Silverstein) (Read Aloud)
- *Chicken Soup with Rice: A Book of Months* (Maurice Sendak) (EA)
- *Eats: Poems* (Arnold Adoff and Susan Russo) (Read Aloud)
- "The Pizza" (Ogden Nash)
- "Sick" (Shel Silverstein)
- "Turtle Soup" (Lewis Carroll) (EA) (Read Aloud)

# INFORMATIONAL TEXTS
## Nonfiction Books
- *The Digestive System* (Rebecca L. Johnson)
- *Good Enough to Eat: A Kid's Guide to Food and Nutrition* (Lizzy Rockwell)
- *The Nervous System* (Joelle Riley)
- *The Skeleton Inside You* (Philip Balestrino and True Kelley)
- *What Happens to a Hamburger?* (Paul Showers and Edward Miller)

## Nonfiction Books (Read Aloud)
- *The Astounding Nervous System: How Does My Brain Work?* (John Burstein)
- "Bones" (*Kids Discover*)
- *Bones: Our Skeletal System* (Seymour Simon) (EA)
- "Brain" (*Kids Discover*)
- *Break It Down: The Digestive System* (Steve Parker)
- *Digestive System* (Cheryl Jakab)
- *The Digestive System* (Kristin Petrie)
- *The Digestive System* (Christine Taylor-Butler)

- *Eat Your Vegetables! Drink Your Milk!* (Alvin Silverstein, Virginia B. Silverstein, and Laura Silverstein Nunn)
- *Guts: Our Digestive System* (Seymour Simon) (EA)
- *Healthy Eating Series* (Susan Martineau and Hel James)
- *The Mighty Muscular and Skeletal Systems: How Do My Muscles and Bones Work?* (John Burstein)
- "Muscles" (*Kids Discover*)
- *Muscles: Our Muscular System* (Seymour Simon) (EA)
- *The Nervous System* (Christine Taylor-Butler)
- "Nutrition" (*Kids Discover*)
- *Showdown at the Food Pyramid* (Rex Barron)

## ART, MUSIC, AND MEDIA

### Art

- Annibale Carracci, *The Beaneater* (1584–1585)
- Claes Oldenburg, *Two Cheeseburgers, with Everything* (1962)
- Guiseppe Arcimboldo, *Vertumnus* (1590–1591)
- Michelangelo Merisi da Caravaggio, *Basket of Fruit* (ca. 1597)
- Pieter Claesz, *Still Life with Two Lemons* (1629)
- Wayne Thiebaud, *Cakes* (1963)
- Willem Claeszoon Heda, *Still Life on a Table* (1638)
- William Bailey, *Still Life with Rose Wall and Compote* (1973)

### Music

- Lionel Bart, "Food, Glorious Food" (from *Oliver*)
- Traditional, "Dry Bones"
- Traditional, "I'm Being Swallowed by a Boa Constrictor"

## SAMPLE ACTIVITIES AND ASSESSMENTS

### 1. SPEAKING AND LISTENING

Why do our brains need good food? To begin this unit, students will need to think about the relationship between good food and brain function—how to nurture a healthy body. Encourage the students to look at the figurative meaning of the term *good food*. (SL.2.1)

### 2. ART, SPEAKING AND LISTENING

Introduce the genre of still life to the students. As students view the paintings, talk about the details, objects, and positions of objects that they notice. Closely examine the works by Heda and Claesz. Explain that these artists did "high-definition" work almost two hundred years before photography was invented. They called it *trompe l'oeil*, which is French for "deceive the eye." Students should notice how these paintings are "realer than real." Put cut fruit, a basket, or metalware on the table and have students try to paint or draw one of the objects precisely. (SL.2.1, SL.2.2)

## 3. ART, CLASS DISCUSSION

Look at the Thiebaud versus the Bailey. How are the colors different? Are we looking at the objects from above, below, or straight on? Did the artists place the objects close together or far apart? Why do you think Bailey chose to space the objects in his painting asymmetrically, versus the symmetry of the Thiebaud? Introduce the Arcimboldo painting into the discussion. Continue to talk about color, perspective, symmetry, and detail and the many different ways in which artists choose to paint, even when they are all painting a still life. (SL.2.1, SL.2.2)

## 4. ART, INFORMATIVE WRITING

After students have painted or drawn the still life (see Art, Speaking and Listening, Activity 2), extend the activity by writing. Give the students this prompt: "Write an explanatory how-to piece focused on how you created your piece of art. Include a description of your still life, the steps of setting up the display through to creating your art, and a strong conclusion." (W.2.2)

## 5. VOCABULARY

Have the students taste-test healthy snacks, fruits, and vegetables. Encourage them to use adjectives by challenging them to come up with at least three descriptive words between each new taste. For example, "This apple is tangy, sweet, and crunchy!" Encourage students to use a dictionary to check the spelling of the words as needed. (L.2.2e, L.2.5a)

## 6. READING LITERATURE, SPEAKING AND LISTENING, RESEARCH

Introduce the book *The Magic School Bus Inside the Human Body* by Joanna Cole and Bruce Degan. Remind the students that this book is a fantasy but contains information that is true. Use this book to introduce the body systems for the informational side of this unit: skeletal, muscular, digestive, and nervous systems. Begin a chart for each of the body systems to add content learning from other read-aloud and student-read books. Students can post information from their own reading on a chart by using index cards or sticky notes. (RI.2.4)

## 7. READING INFORMATIONAL TEXT, RESEARCH

Have students independently read informational books to learn about each body system. Students should record new learning about each of the body systems in a notebook. They should look for the ways the author supports the main idea. For example, when reading a book about nutrition, ask students to find reasons in the text for why a person should eat healthy foods. (RI.2.8, RI.2.10)

## 8. READING LITERATURE, SPEAKING AND LISTENING

Introduce the book *Everybody Cooks Rice* by Norah Dooley and Peter J. Thornton, which is about a girl who lives in an ethnically diverse neighborhood. She makes a very interesting discovery about her neighbors when she sees what each one is cooking. Read the book aloud. When you are finished, ask the children such questions as: "What do you think the author wanted you to learn in this book?" "What are the clues from the text that helped you come to that conclusion?" (RL.2.2)

## 9. READING LITERATURE, READING FLUENCY, READING COMPREHENSION

In order to stretch students' reading skills and test for comprehension and fluency, have students read a variety of fictional texts independently. Although the books share the common theme of food, they have very different messages. For example, *Tar Beach* by Faith Ringgold, which includes a picnic scene, is literally about rising above prejudice. *Gregory the Terrible Eater*, by Mitchell Sharmat, Jose Aruego, and Ariane Dewey, is a funny book about a goat, but carries a message about healthy eating. These books offer a range of reading in the 2–3 band of grade level and stretch texts. (RL.2.2, RL.2.10)

## 10. LANGUAGE USAGE, VOCABULARY

The title of this unit is Taking Care of Ourselves. Ask students what other words they know that end with -self or -selves. (Possible answers: *myself, himself, herself, themselves, yourself,* and *yourselves.*) Practice using these special kinds of pronouns in sentences: "I can do it _____." "She climbed the monkey bars by _____." "They went to the playground by _____." (L.2.1c, SL.2.6)

## 11. MUSIC, VOCABULARY

Explore text, rhythm, and rhyme in the song "Dry Bones." Discuss how bones are connected in the song. It's fun, though not necessarily accurate (e.g., the "toe bone" is not connected directly to the "heel bone"). Then have the students research the scientific names of the bones. Assign each pair of students one of the bones in the song to research online or in an encyclopedia. They should be sure to find out how the bones are actually attached and note the real names for each of the bones mentioned. (For example, there are twenty-six bones in the foot, and the toes are actually called "phalanges.") Extend this activity to the stretch level by having the students sing the song with the scientific names. (RL.2.4, RI.2.7)

## 12. OPINION WRITING, LANGUAGE USAGE

Ask the students to choose one thing that they think is most important to do in order to stay healthy. Tell them to support their opinions with facts that they learned from one of the books they read. Remind them to stay on topic, include details, use appropriate linking words between ideas, and provide a strong conclusion. (W.2.1)

## READING FOUNDATIONS: A PACING GUIDE FOR READING INSTRUCTION

See Grade Two, Level Six, in the Reading Foundations section at the beginning of the book for a complete pacing guide for this unit.

## ADDITIONAL ONLINE RESOURCE

- Harvard School of Public Health

# TERMINOLOGY

| | | |
|---|---|---|
| Adjectives | Explanatory writing | Opinion writing |
| Dictionary | Fantasy | Reflexive pronouns |

# INTERDISCIPLINARY CONNECTIONS

This unit teaches:

- **Art:** Seventeenth-century Dutch still-life painting, William Bailey, Wayne Thiebaud
- **Science:** Body systems (e.g., digestive, nervous, muscular, and skeletal)
- **Nutrition:** (e.g., foods to eat and healthy living)

This unit could be extended to teach:

- **Science:** Healthy living (e.g., teeth, safety, and environmental hazards)

# Grade Two, Unit Six Sample Lesson Plan

## In the Night Kitchen *by Maurice Sendak*

In this series of two lessons, students read *In the Night Kitchen* by Maurice Sendak, and they:

- Explore Mickey and his night adventures in the kitchen (RL.2.1, RL.2.3, SL.2.1, SL.2.4)
- Explore the significance of rereading texts (RL.2.1, RL.2.3, SL.2.1, SL.2.4)

## Summary

| Lesson I: Mickey's Adventures in the Night Kitchen | Lesson II: Rereading *In the Night Kitchen* |
| --- | --- |
| Closely study Sendak's illustrations (RL.2.7) | Revisit Mickey's adventures (RL.2.1, RL.2.3, SL.2.1, SL.2.4) |
| Note the minimal use of words | Reassess (Lesson I) assumptions about Mickey's character (RL.2.1, RL.2.3, SL.2.1, SL.2.4) |
| Chronicle Mickey's adventures (RL.2.1, RL.2.3, SL.2.1, SL.2.4) | Explore the significance of rereading *In the Night Kitchen* (SL.2.1, SL.2.4, RL.2.10) |
| Examine Mickey's character (RL.2.1, RL.3, SL.2.1) | Examine Mickey's night (W.2.1, RL.2.3, RL.2.5) |

## Lesson II: Rereading *In the Night Kitchen*

### *Objectives*

Revisit Mickey's adventures (RL.2.1, RL.2.3, SL.2.1, SL.2.4)

Reassess (Lesson I) assumptions about Mickey's character (RL.2.1, RL.2.3, SL.2.1, SL.2.4)

Explore the significance of rereading *In the Night Kitchen* (SL.2.1, SL.2.4, RL.2.10)

Examine Mickey's night (W.2.1, RL.2.3, RL.2.5)

### *Required Materials*

☐ Class set of *In the Night Kitchen* by Maurice Sendak

*Procedures*

1. Lead-In:

   Students (quietly) reread *In the Night Kitchen* by Maurice Sendak.

2. Step by Step:

   a. In a class discussion, students revisit Mickey's adventures.

   b. Students reassess their understanding of Mickey and his actions.

   c. Student volunteer rereads the final page of the book, "And that's why, thanks to Mickey, we have cake every morning."

3. Closer:

   Students discuss how this passage changes the way that they reread the book.

## Differentiation

*Advanced*

- Ask students to give an opinion about Mickey's character *and* his adventure, supporting each with evidence from the text.

*Struggling*

- Students prepare for the homework by writing the first sentence together in a small group. Students orally review their opinions about Mickey's character or adventures and find support in the text. Students discuss the conclusion of the paper.

## Homework/Assessment

Students write a paragraph in which they express their view of Mickey's night. The paragraph should have

- A sentence introducing the topic, the text, and the author
- A sentence expressing an opinion about Mickey (his character or his adventures)
- Evidence from the text to support their view
- A concluding sentence

# Grade 3

When students enter third grade, they should be confident readers, able to sound out words, read with expression, and make meaning of what they read. They should be familiar with a repertoire of poems, stories, fables, folktales, myths, biographies, artistic and musical works, and historical and scientific texts. During this year, students continue to make connections between literature and other subjects. They read stories inspired by the sea while learning about oceans. They study myths from ancient Greece; learn about the branches of government in the United States; read about artists, musicians, and inventors; find common themes in trickster tales across many cultures; come to recognize the beauty of poetic language; and more. Throughout the units, they write reports, letters, stories, poems, and descriptions; they continue to work on grammar and punctuation. They participate in structured class discussions and learn how to take notes and conduct basic research. By the end of third grade, students should be ready to start writing simple essays and speeches. They are able to write on a range of topics and have background knowledge that will help them with the challenges of upper elementary school and beyond.

# Standards Checklist for Grade Three

| Standard | Unit 1 | Unit 2 | Unit 3 | Unit 4 | Unit 5 | Unit 6 |
|---|---|---|---|---|---|---|
| **Reading–Literature** | | | | | | |
| 1 | A | FA | FA | A | A | A |
| 2 | FA | A | A | | A | FA |
| 3 | FA | A | A | A | | |
| 4 | | | | A | A | FA |
| 5 | | A | A | A | FA | A |
| 6 | A | A | | | | FA |
| 7 | A | | A | A | | |
| 8 n/a | | | | | | |
| 9 | A | A | | A | | |
| 10 | | | | A | | FA |
| **Reading–Informational Text** | | | | | | |
| 1 | A | | | A | A | |
| 2 | | FA | A | | A | A |
| 3 | | A | FA | | | |
| 4 | | | | FA | | |
| 5 | A | A | A | | A | A |
| 6 | | A | | A | | |
| 7 | A | | A | | FA | |
| 8 | | | | FA | | |
| 9 | | FA | | A | | |
| 10 | | | A | | | FA |
| **Writing** | | | | | | |
| 1 | | | A | | FA | A |
| 1a | | A | | | | |
| 1b | | A | | | A | A |
| 1c | | A | | | A | A |
| 1d | | A | | | A | A |
| 2 | | A | FA | A | A | |
| 2a | | | | | | |
| 2b | | | | | A | |
| 2c | | | | | | |
| 2d | | | | | | |
| 3 | FA | F | A | | A | A |
| 3a | A | | | | | |
| 3b | | F | | | | |
| 3c | | | | | | |
| 3d | | | | | | |
| 4 | A | A | | A | | |
| 5 | A | A | A | A | A | |
| 6 | A | | | A | | A |
| 7 | A | | A | FA | A | A |
| 8 | A | | A | | A | |
| 9 n/a | | | | | | |
| 10 | | A | A | A | A | A |
| **Speaking and Listening** | | | | | | |
| 1 | FA | FA | FA | A | A | A |
| 1a | | FA | FA | | A | A |
| 1b | A | A | | | A | A |
| 1c | FA | A | | | A | A |

| Standard | Unit 1 | Unit 2 | Unit 3 | Unit 4 | Unit 5 | Unit 6 |
|---|---|---|---|---|---|---|
| 1d | A | A | | | A | A |
| 2 | A | A | | A | A | A |
| 3 | A | A | A | FA | A | A |
| 4 | A | A | A | A | | A |
| 5 | | A | A | | | FA |
| 6 | A | A | | | A | |
| **Language** | | | | | | |
| 1 | FA | FA | FA | A | A | A |
| 1a | FA | FA | A | | A | A |
| 1b | A | | | A | A | |
| 1c | A | | | A | A | |
| 1d | A | A | | | A | |
| 1e | A | A | | | | |
| 1f | A | A | | | | |
| 1g | | A | | | | |
| 1h | | A | FA | | | |
| 1i | | A | FA | | A | |
| 2 | A | A | A | A | A | A |
| 2a | | A | | | | |
| 2b | | | | | | |
| 2c | | | A | A | A | A |
| 2d | | | A | A | A | A |
| 2e | | | | | A | |
| 2f | A | | | | | |
| 2g | | | | A | | |
| 3 | A | A | A | A | A | A |
| 3a | | A | | | | |
| 3b | | | | | | |
| 4 | A | | | F | | |
| 4a | | | | | A | |
| 4b | | | A | A | FA | |
| 4c | | | A | | | |
| 4d | | | | FA | | |
| 5 | | | | | A | |
| 5a | | | | | A | |
| 5b | | A | A | A | | |
| 5c | | | A | | A | |
| 6 | A | A | | A | | |
| **Reading Foundations** | | | | | | |
| 1 n/a | | | | | | |
| 2 n/a | | | | | | |
| 3 | | | A | | F | |
| 3a | | | | A | | |
| 3b | | | | | FA | |
| 3c | | | A | A | | |
| 3d | | | | | | |
| 4 | | | A | FA | | F |
| 4a | | | | | | |
| 4b | A | | A | FA | A | |
| 4c | | | | | A | FA |

F = Focus Standards; A = Activity/Assessment

# Stories Worth Telling Again and Again

In this first six-week unit of third grade, students read stories that are worth telling and retelling.

## ESSENTIAL QUESTION

Why do we hand stories down to the next generation?

## OVERVIEW

Students read the tales of grandparents, and they become familiar with the tradition of "trickster stories" across multiple cultures. They read a Langston Hughes poem, and review the parts of speech through Ruth Heller's World of Language books. The students engage the texts in multiple ways: they write stories they want to preserve; they also build on their knowledge of geographical settings of folktales from previous grades as they research the cultural backgrounds of the trickster tales. They dramatically interpret a poem by Langston Hughes.

## FOCUS STANDARDS

These Focus Standards have been selected for the unit from the Common Core State Standards.

**RL.3.2:** Recount stories, including fables, folktales, and myths from diverse cultures; determine the central message, lesson, or moral, and explain how it is conveyed through key details in the text.

**RL.3.3:** Describe characters in a story (e.g., their traits, motivations, or feelings) and explain how their actions contribute to the sequence of events.

**SL.3.1:** Engage effectively in a range or collaborative discussions (one-on-one, in groups, and teacher-led) with diverse partners on grade 3 topics and texts, building on others' ideas and expressing their own clearly.

**SL.3.1(c):** Ask questions to check understanding of information presented, stay on topic, and link their comments to the remarks of others.

**W.3.3:** Write narratives to develop real or imagined experiences or events using effective technique, descriptive details, and clear event sequences.

**L.3.1:** Demonstrate command of the conventions of standard English grammar and usage when writing or speaking.

**L.3.1(a):** Explain the function of nouns, pronouns, verbs, adjectives, and adverbs in general and their functions in particular sentences.

## SUGGESTED OBJECTIVES

- Tell stories from personal experiences and write narratives telling those stories.
- Revise and edit narratives with the help of peers and adults.
- Determine and analyze characters' traits and motivations in realistic fiction such as *The Stories Julian Tells*.
- Distinguish nouns, pronouns, and verbs from each other, understanding the role of each in a sentence.
- Perform a poem dramatically (e.g., a Langston Hughes poem), with expression and appropriate phrasing for meaning.
- Compare and contrast the message and characters in two books with the same theme (e.g., "grandparent" books).
- Determine the trickster, the fool, the problem, and the solution in various cultures' trickster tales.
- Research one of the trickster tale's cultures, as part of responding to class-generated questions.
- Create a class book or a multimedia presentation based on the culture research.
- Discuss artists' contributions to the preservation of Native American culture through art.

## SUGGESTED WORKS

(E) indicates a CCSS exemplar text; (EA) indicates a text from a writer with other works identified as exemplars.

### LITERARY TEXTS

*Stories*
- *The Apple and the Arrow* (Mary Buff and Conrad Buff) (Read Aloud)
- *Gloria's Way* (Ann Cameron and Lis Toft) (EA)
- *More Stories Julian Tells* (Ann Cameron and Ann Strugnell) (EA)
- *Sign of the Beaver* (Elizabeth George Speare) (Read Aloud)

- *The Stories Huey Tells* (Ann Cameron and Roberta Smith) (EA)
- *The Stories Julian Tells* (Ann Cameron and Ann Strugnell) (E)

*Grandparents' Stories*

- *Annie and the Old One* (Miska Miles and Peter Parnall)
- *Grandfather's Journey* (Allen Say) (EA)
- *Knots on a Counting Rope* (Bill Martin Jr., John Archambault, and Ted Rand)
- *The Memory String* (Eve Bunting and Ted Rand)
- *Snowed In with Grandmother Silk* (Carol Fenner and Amanda Harvey)
- *Song and Dance Man* (Karen Ackerman and Stephen Gammell)
- *Tea with Milk* (Allen Say) (EA)
- *Through Grandpa's Eyes* (Patricia MacLachlan and Deborah Kogan Ray) (EA)

*Cultural Trickster Stories*

- *Bruh Rabbit and the Tar Baby Girl* (Virginia Hamilton and James Ransome)
- *Iktomi and the Berries* (Paul Goble)
- *Iktomi and the Boulder* (Paul Goble)
- *Iktomi and the Buzzard* (Paul Goble)
- *Iktomi and the Coyote* (Paul Goble)
- *Iktomi Loses His Eyes* (Paul Goble)
- *Love and Roast Chicken: A Trickster Tale from the Andes Mountains* (Barbara Knutson)
- *Tops & Bottoms* (Janet Stevens) (E)

*Poems*

- "Aunt Sue's Stories" (Langston Hughes) (EA)
- "By Myself" (Eloise Greenfield)
- "Grandpa's Stories" (Langston Hughes) (E)
- "Mother to Son" (Langston Hughes) (EA)

*Poems (Read Aloud)*

- "For want of a nail, the shoe was lost . . ." (Traditional)
- "Nani" (Alberto Rios)
- "The Telephone" (Robert Frost) (EA)
- "You Are Old, Father William" (Lewis Carroll) (EA)
- "Your World" (Georgia Douglas Johnson) (E)

## INFORMATIONAL TEXTS

Students will do Internet research on a culture related to a favorite trickster tale:

- African American slave culture
- Andes Mountain culture

- European culture (choose a specific country)
- Native American (Plains) culture

## Nonfiction Books (Read Aloud)

- A *Cache of Jewels and Other Collective Nouns* (World of Language) (Ruth Heller)
- *Kites Sail High: A Book About Verbs* (World of Language) (Ruth Heller)
- *Merry-Go-Round: A Book About Nouns* (World of Language) (Ruth Heller)
- *Mine, All Mine: A Book About Pronouns* (World of Language) (Ruth Heller)
- *Throw Your Tooth on the Roof: Tooth Traditions Around the World* (Selby Beeler and G. Brian Karas) (E)

## ART, MUSIC, AND MEDIA

### Art

- Jacopo Pontormo, *Descent from the Cross* (1528)
- Jan van Eyck, *Arnolfini Portrait* (1434)
- Pablo Picasso, *Guernica* (1937)
- Trajan's Column, in Rome, Italy (completed 113 CE) (detail)

## SAMPLE ACTIVITIES AND ASSESSMENTS

Note: This unit is a natural fit for inviting grandparents or older family friends into the classroom to tell their own stories or to read the stories listed in the Grandparents' Stories section. At the beginning of the school year, you may see some unique opportunities to engage the grandparents with their own grandchildren's learning or to volunteer in the classroom. A Grandparents' Day would be a perfect celebration to include in this unit.

## 1. READING LITERATURE, SPEAKING AND LISTENING

Introduce the unit by asking students if they have family stories they love to tell. Allow students to share favorite family stories for a few minutes. Introduce that day's new chapter book: *The Stories Julian Tells* by Ann Cameron and Ann Strugnell. As students read the first chapter of the book, "The Pudding Like a Night on the Sea," ask them to examine Julian as a character. You might post these leading questions to spark discussion:

- How would you describe Julian?
- What are his character traits?
- Why does he do what he does?

Tell students to cite evidence from the text as they answer the questions. Read the chapter aloud to the students as they follow along. Continue reading the subsequent chapters in the days that follow, encouraging as much independent reading as possible. Continue to focus on character traits and motivation. As students finish this book, allow them to choose to move to other character stories in this series or to continue with Julian. This provides the opportunity to compare and contrast books and/or characters by the same author. (RL.3.3, RL.3.9, SL.3.1b, SL.3.4, SL.3.6)

## 2. NARRATIVE WRITING, LANGUAGE USAGE, VOCABULARY

Students have been sharing favorite family stories, so shift the discussion to how stories are passed down from grandparents specifically. Then assign the following: "Interview one of your family members (e.g., a parent, grandparent, aunt, or uncle) to learn a family story. Save the story by taking notes or by recording it digitally. Use the story you record to write a narrative." This writing project should be worked on over an extended period of time, focusing on elaboration, revision, and editing, using the standards as guidance. Create a word wall to gather word families and words used most often in writing. (W.3.3, W.3.4, W.3.5, L.3.1, L.3.2, L.3.2f, L.3.3)

## 3. READING INFORMATIONAL TEXT, LANGUAGE MECHANICS

Ruth Heller has written a series of informational books that teach parts of speech. Remind students that they learned about nouns in second grade. As you read the book *Merry-Go-Round: A Book About Nouns* by Ruth Heller, have the students listen for more information about nouns. Pause as you read to allow the students to share what they are learning or to ask questions. Review nouns, pronouns, and verbs using the Ruth Heller series. Create word banks for each part of speech and add vocabulary from class work to reinforce the application. (RI.3.1, L.3.1a, L.3.1b, L.3.1c, L.3.1d, L.3.1e, L.3.1f)

## 4. READING POETRY, PERFORMANCE

Give the students this prompt: "Choose one of Langston Hughes's poems to memorize or read interpretively. Be sure to communicate the meaning of the poem in the way you recite or read it." Demonstrate fluent reading to the children, being sure to show how meaningful phrasing and expression guide the dramatic interpretation of a poem. (RF.3.4b)

## 5. READING LITERATURE, SPEAKING AND LISTENING

After reading *Knots on a Counting Rope* by Bill Martin Jr., John Archambault, and Ted Rand, review the character traits of the boy and his grandfather. Have the students partner and list three characteristics for each. Introduce another story that honors grandparents: *Through Grandpa's Eyes* by Patricia MacLachlan and Deborah Kogan Ray. As students finish reading the new book, have them work with the same partner to list at least three characteristics of each character in the new story.

- How are the grandparents similar and different?
- How are the grandchildren similar and different?
- What is the message of each book?
- What do you think the author might have wanted you to learn? (RL.3.3)

## 6. READING LITERATURE, SPEAKING AND LISTENING

Lead a discussion with the students to introduce the genre of trickster tales, using questions such as these:

One of the types of folk stories handed down in cultures is the "trickster tale."

- What root word do you hear in *trickster*?
- Have you ever played a trick on someone?
- Have you ever had a trick played on you?

Tell students that trickster tales are stories that involve playing tricks to solve problems, and—to make these stories even more interesting—that they are from different cultures. As students read, encourage them to think about characters and their traits. Remind them that the story is not just in the text, but also in the illustrations. The illustrations help to tell the story and to give hints about the culture or origin. Use the following questions to guide discussions after they (or you) read the trickster stories. Eventually require students to answer these questions independently.

- Who is the trickster?
- Who is the fool who gets tricked?
- What was the problem in the story?
- How did the trick solve the problem?

Think about what the message of the story might be and why these stories have been told for hundreds of years. (RL.3.2, RL.3.3, RL.3.7)

## 7. READING INFORMATIONAL TEXT, RESEARCH, INFORMATIVE WRITING

Students have read a variety of trickster tales from various cultures. Now it is time to focus on one of the cultures. You could, for example, choose to focus on the Plains Native American culture by first reading the Iktomi tales by Paul Goble and then assigning a short class research project on it. In small groups, have students generate open-ended questions that can be answered about the culture. Assign each small group a question to answer. To answer the questions, help students create a list of resources, such as the Internet, encyclopedias, and informational books. As students read and research, circulate to help them select the most relevant and useful information. When the small groups have finished their information gathering and organization, they should create a class book or multimedia presentation to show what they have learned about the culture. When they are finished, ask: "Why did the Plains Indians create trickster stories to tell to their children?" This activity can be repeated and extended with any of the cultures from which trickster stories came by giving small groups of students the following prompt: "Research a culture that tells trickster tales. Generate questions related to the culture and assign a person to research each question. Create a book or multimedia presentation to communicate your findings." (RI.3.1, RI.3.5, W.3.4, W.3.5, W.3.6, W.3.7, W.3.8, SL.3.1, SL.3.4)

## 8. ART, SPEAKING AND LISTENING

In each of the images you choose to study, see if you can identify a story or event that has been passed down through generations. These might be stories for a civilization to remember, or perhaps just a family. Discuss how these images also serve as records. What does the artist do to document the importance of an event (e.g., include unique elements or details)? How might these stories be retold because of these images? (SL.3.1c, SL.3.1d, SL.3.2, SL.3.3)

## 9. ART, SPEAKING AND LISTENING

Closely examine the van Eyck image, noticing the work's many unique and peculiar details. Why is there only one candle in the chandelier? Is that the artist's signature in the center of the painting? Can you see other figures reflected in the mirror at center? Discuss how close examination of a painting, like a literary work, often reveals hidden or deeper meaning. (SL.3.1c, SL.3.1d, SL.3.2, SL.3.3)

# ADDITIONAL ONLINE RESOURCES

- *Dylan Pritchett: Storyteller* (cuesheet) (The Kennedy Center) (SL.3.4, W.3.3)
- "Fables and Trickster Tales Around the World" (National Endowment for the Humanities) (RL.3.2)
- *Dynamite Diamante Poetry* (ReadWriteThink) (L.3.1a) Note: This is an activity on nouns.
- *Composing Cinquain Poems with Basic Parts of Speech* (ReadWriteThink) (L.3.1a)
- *Using Picture Books to Teach Characterization in Writing Workshop* (ReadWriteThink) (RL.3.3)
- "Maps of United States Indians by State" (Native Languages of the Americas) (RI.3.7)
- *Native American Informational Chart* (Mountain City Elementary School, Mountain City, TN) (RI.3.5)
- *A Collection of Trickster Tales* (AmericanFolklore.net) (RL.3.2)

# TERMINOLOGY

| | | |
|---|---|---|
| Author | Illustrator | Shared research |
| Character motivation | Internet search | Solution |
| Character traits | Narrative writing | The trickster |
| Collective noun | Noun | Trickster tales |
| Editing | Problem | Verb |
| The fool | Pronoun | Verb tenses |
| Generational stories | Revising | |

# INTERDISCIPLINARY CONNECTIONS

This unit teaches:

- **Art:** Artists as historians and documentarians (e.g., Jan van Eyck)
- **Geography:** Cultures (e.g., Plains Native Americans and Andes Mountain tribes)

This unit could be extended to teach:

- **Music:** Music of featured cultures (e.g., spirituals and Quechua songs)
- **Geography:** U.S. geography (as related to Native Americans)
- **History:** Native American Nations (e.g., the Bering land bridge theory, Southwest, Eastern "Woodland")

# Grade Three, Unit One Sample Lesson Plan

## The Stories Julian Tells *by Ann Cameron*

In this series of four lessons, students read *The Stories Julian Tells* by Ann Cameron, and they:

> Explore the tales of *The Stories Julian Tells* (RL.3.3.1, RL.3.3.2, RL.3.3.3, RL.3.3, RL.3.9, SL.3.1, SL.3.2)
>
> Identify memoir as a genre
>
> Compose memoirs (W.3.3a, W.3.4, W.3.5)

## Summary

### Lesson I: Reading Julian's Stories

Revisit Julian's stories (RL.3.1, RL.3.2, RL.3.3, RL.3.9)

Select one of Julian's stories for close analysis

Identify the use of first-person narrative (RL.3.6)

Identify the elements of the short story (plot, characters, setting, conflict, and theme) in the selected story (RL.3.1, RL.3.2, RL.3.3, RL.3.9)

(In groups, begin to) identify personal stories to retell (SL.3.4)

### Lesson III: Revising Memoirs

Read memoirs critically

Identify areas that need revisions (W.3.3a, W.3.4, W.3.5)

Who are the characters?

Is the plot clear?

Is the setting described in detail?

Does the lead character in the story have a conflict?

Does the story have a theme?

Revise memoirs (W.3.5)

### Lesson II: Memoirs—Writing Personal Narratives (Memoirs)

Identify memoir as a literary genre

Note the similarities between Julian's stories and memoirs (SL.3.1, SL.3.2)

Recall details of personal stories (SL.3.4)

Compose the first draft of a memoir, incorporating elements of the short story (W.3.3)

### Lesson IV: Telling Stories

Record strengths of peers' memoirs (SL.3.1, SL.3.2)

Reflect on the similarities between the fictional tales of Julian and the memoirs (SL.3.4)

## Lesson III: Revising Memoirs

### Objectives

Read memoirs critically

Identify areas that need revisions (W.3.3a, W.3.4, W.3.5)

- Who are the characters?
- Is the plot clear?
- Is the setting described in detail?
- Does the lead character in the story have a conflict?
- Does the story have a theme?

Revise memoirs (W.3.5)

### Required Materials

☐ Class set of *The Stories Julian Tells* by Ann Cameron

☐ First drafts of memoirs

### Procedures

1. Lead-In:

   Students read their own memoirs quietly.

2. Step by Step:

   a. Students' revision process focuses on the elements of the short story that were identified earlier. Your prompts may include questions like:

   - What are the details that describe the setting?
   - If the setting is the bedroom, is it large, small, or perhaps messy with candy wrappers on the floor?
   - Who is the leading character of the memoir–perhaps a grandmother?
   - Does she speak with an accent? Does she love cooking?
   - What is the story about? Is it about a missing baseball card? Or is it really about friendship and the missing card is part of the story?

You may choose to select passages from Julian's stories to explain the type of revisions expected. On page two of *The Stories Julian Tells*, for example, Ann Cameron dedicates a paragraph to describe Julian's father: "My father is a big man . . ."

b. Students revise their work.

3. Closure:

   At the end of the lesson, remind the students to complete their revisions at home.

## Differentiation

### Advanced

- Supplied with a list of the revision prompting questions, students work with a partner to do revisions.

### Struggling

- Pre-teaching: as you read the Julian story, use the same list of prompting questions to analyze the setting, characters, plot, and theme.
- Students read their story drafts to an adult. As the adult prompts the child for revision, the adult takes dictation from the child.
- Students write their newly revised story on a computer, making use of spell check.

## Homework/Assessment

Conclude revisions.

# Inspired by the Sea

In this second six-week unit of third grade, students read stories, poetry, and informational texts that are inspired by a love of or curiosity about the sea.

## ESSENTIAL QUESTION

Why does the sea inspire writers?

## OVERVIEW

Students read about characters who long for or live near the sea. They become familiar with the wide range of informational texts on the topic of oceans and water. They continue to review the parts of speech by comparing two poems written about oysters. The students engage the texts in several ways. For example, they write stories modeled after the haystack scene in *Sarah, Plain and Tall*, showing action, thoughts, and feelings. They also build their knowledge of ocean animals as they research their favorite sea creature.

## FOCUS STANDARDS

These Focus Standards have been selected for the unit from the Common Core State Standards.

**RI.3.2:** Determine the main idea of a text; recount the key details and explain how they support the main idea.

**RI.3.9:** Compare and contrast the most important points and key details presented in two texts on the same topic.

**RL.3.1:** Ask and answer questions to demonstrate understanding of a text, referring explicitly to the text as the basis for the answers.

**L.3.1:** Demonstrate command of the conventions of standard English grammar and usage when writing or speaking.

**L.3.1(a):** Explain the function of nouns, pronouns, verbs, adjectives, and adverbs in general and their functions in particular sentences.

**W.3.3:** Write narratives to develop real or imagined experiences or events using effective technique, descriptive details, and clear event sequences.

**W.3.3(b):** Use dialogue and descriptions of actions, thoughts, and feelings to develop experiences and events or show the response of characters to situations.

**SL.3.1:** Engage effectively in a range of collaborative discussions (one-on-one, in groups, and teacher-led) with diverse partners on grade 3 topics and texts, building on others' ideas and expressing their own clearly.

**SL.3.1(a):** Come to discussions prepared, having read or studied required material; explicitly draw on that preparation and other information known about the topic to explore ideas under discussion.

## SUGGESTED OBJECTIVES

- Cite textual evidence to support an interpretation of characters' motivations.
- Write imaginary narratives using dialogue and descriptions of actions, thoughts, and feelings.
- Explain the function of adverbs and adjectives in speech, literature, and writing.
- Compare and contrast two poems written about oysters.
- Compare and contrast two informational books about the same topic (e.g., a drop of water).
- Determine the main idea and supporting details of informational text.
- Research a favorite sea animal.
- Write a short informative piece about a favorite thing (e.g., a sea animal); apply growing understanding of what makes a strong, focused paragraph.

## SUGGESTED WORKS

(E) indicates a CCSS exemplar text; (EA) indicates a text from a writer with other works identified as exemplars.

### LITERARY TEXTS

*Stories*

- *Amos & Boris* (William Steig) (E)
- *Canoe Days* (Gary and Ruth Wright Paulsen)
- *Minn of the Mississippi* (Holling Clancy Holling) (Read Aloud)
- *Paddle-to-the-Sea* (Holling Clancy Holling) (Read Aloud)
- *The Raft* (Jim LaMarche) (E)
- "The River Bank" in *The Wind in the Willows* (Kenneth Grahame) (Read Aloud)

- *Sarah, Plain and Tall* (Patricia MacLachlan) (E)
- *The Storm* (The Lighthouse Family series) (Cynthia Rylant and Preston McDaniels) (E)
- *Three Days on a River in a Red Canoe* (Vera B. Williams)
- *The Whale* (The Lighthouse Family series) (Cynthia Rylant and Preston McDaniels) (EA)

## Poems

- "At the Seaside" (Robert Louis Stevenson)
- "The Barracuda" (John Gardner) (Read Aloud)
- "Beach Stones" (Lilian Moore)
- "Do Oysters Sneeze?" (Jack Prelutsky)
- "From the Shore" (Carl Sandburg) (EA) (Read Aloud)
- "The Jumblies" (Edward Lear) (E) (Read Aloud)
- "A Sand Witch for a Sandwich" (Emily Sweeney)
- "Seal Lullaby" (Rudyard Kipling) (EA) (Read Aloud)
- "Sleepy Pearl" (Frances Gorman Risser)
- "Song of a Shell" (Violet L. Cuslidge) (Read Aloud)
- "Undersea" (Marchette Chute)
- "A Wave" (Gussie Osborne)
- "The Waves" (Gertrude M. Jones)

## INFORMATIONAL TEXTS

### Nonfiction Books

- *Disasters at Sea* (DK Readers) (Andrew Donkin)
- *Journey of a Humpback Whale* (DK Readers) (Caryn Jenner)
- *Life in a Kelp Forest* (Mary Jo Rhodes and David Hall)
- *Octopuses and Squids* (Mary Jo Rhodes and David Hall)
- *Partners in the Sea* (Mary Jo Rhodes and David Hall)
- *Seahorses and Sea Dragons* (Mary Jo Rhodes and David Hall)
- *Sea Turtles* (Mary Jo Rhodes and David Hall)
- *Shark Attack!* (DK Readers) (Cathy East Dubowski)
- *Titanic: Disaster That Rocked the World* (DK Readers) (Mark Dubowski)
- *Whales* (Smithsonian) (Seymour Simon) (EA)

### Nonfiction Books (Read Aloud)

- *The Cod's Tale* (Mark Kurlansky and S. D. Schindler) excerpts (e.g., informative illustrations/ text features)
- *Crabs* (Mary Jo Rhodes and David Hall)
- *Dolphins, Seals, and Other Sea Mammals* (Mary Jo Rhodes and David Hall)
- *A Drop Around the World* (Barbara Shaw McKinney and Michael S. Maydak)

- *A Drop of Water: A Book of Science and Wonder* (Walter Wick) (E)
- *John Muir: America's Naturalist* (Images of Conservationists) (Thomas Locker)
- *The Lamp, the Ice, and the Boat Called Fish: Based on a True Story* (Jacqueline Briggs Martin and Beth Krommes)
- *Life on a Coral Reef* (Mary Jo Rhodes and David Hall)
- *Many Luscious Lollipops: A Book About Adjectives* (World of Language) (Ruth Heller)
- *Predators of the Sea* (Mary Jo Rhodes and David Hall)
- *Rachel Carson: Preserving a Sense of Wonder* (Thomas Locker and Joseph Bruchac)
- *Survival Secrets of Sea Animals* (Mary Jo Rhodes and David Hall)
- *Swimming with Hammerhead Sharks* (Kenneth Mallory)
- *Up, Up and Away: A Book About Adverbs* (World of Language) (Ruth Heller)

## ART, MUSIC, AND MEDIA

*Art*

- Edward Hopper, *Ground Swell* (1939)
- Joseph Turner, *Margate, from the Sea* (1835–1840)
- Katsushika Hokusai, *Mount Fuji Seen Below a Wave at Kanagawa* (1826–1833)
- Richard Diebenkorn, *Horizon: Ocean View* (1959)
- Claude Monet, *Garden at Sainte-Adresse* (1867)

## SAMPLE ACTIVITIES AND ASSESSMENTS

Note: This unit can be tailored to meet science or social studies standards. By filling your class library with books about food chains, ecosystems, and/or nature preservation, you have a rich science unit. By focusing on the geography of and the people who live near lakes, rivers, and oceans, you have a strong social studies unit.

## 1. READING LITERATURE, SPEAKING AND LISTENING

Review characters and character motivation from the first unit. Introduce the book *Sarah, Plain and Tall* by Patricia MacLachlan as historical fiction: a fictional story from the days of settling the prairies. Introduce also the name of the unit: Inspired by the Sea. As you read the first chapter of this book, challenge students to look for specific places in the text where they can prove that a character in the story is "inspired by the sea." Ask students to give you a thumbs-up when they hear/see a line in the text that talks about a character "inspired by the sea." Students should easily detect Sarah as the character motivated by her love of the sea. One of her letters reads, "I have always loved to live by the sea." Create a chart and write down any evidence of Sarah's motivation. Discuss what motivates the other characters. Each day, as students come together to discuss the reading, instruct them to be prepared to give textual evidence of Sarah's motivation and the motivation of at least one other character. (RL.3.1, RL.3.3, SL.3.1a, SL.3.4)

## 2. READING LITERATURE, NARRATIVE WRITING

Chapter 5 of *Sarah, Plain and Tall* contains a narrative about haystacks. Prepare students to write well-developed narratives and guide a discussion of the way Patricia MacLachlan wrote the haystack section by asking them the following questions about the narrative in the chapter:

- How many of you wanted to try sliding down a haystack after reading that scene?

- What was it in her writing that made you feel as though you were there?

- How did you know what the characters were feeling?

- How did the dialogue help you to "be there"?

- How did she communicate action? thoughts? feelings?

- How did she order the events?

- How did she close the scene?

Then give the students this task: "Write a personal narrative about something similar to the haystack slide, such as riding a roller coaster, sledding down a snowy hill, or rolling down a hill. Be sure to show your actions, your thoughts, and your feelings through dialogue and description." (RL.3.1, W.3.3, W.3.4, W.3.5, W.3.10, L.3.1, L.3.2, L.3.2c, L.3.3, L.3.3a, L.3.6)

## 3. LANGUAGE USAGE, SPEAKING AND LISTENING

*Many Luscious Lollipops* by Ruth Heller teaches about adjectives through several language lessons. Read this book to the class, covering a few pages a day so that students may incorporate what they learn each day into conversation and writing. Use the adjectives and adverbs (which are covered in another Heller book, *Up, Up and Away*) to build interesting sentences about the sea and in students' own narratives. Be sure that students can explain the function of each part of speech (adjectives and adverbs) and its use in literature, speech, and writing. (L.3.1a, L.3.1g, L.3.2d, L.3.5b)

## 4. READING POETRY, SPEAKING AND LISTENING

Encourage the dramatic interpretation and recitation of poetry in this unit. Read two poems aloud that have similar topics, such as "Sleepy Pearl" by Frances Gorman Risser and "Do Oysters Sneeze?" by Jack Prelutsky. Ask the students the following questions:

- What do you think is the message of each poem? Cite evidence from the poem, by stanza and line, that hints at the meaning.

- How are these poems similar? How are they different?

- Which of the poems do you think is better? Why? (RL.3.5, RL.3.9, SL.3.1a, SL.3.1d)

## 5. READING INFORMATIONAL TEXT, SPEAKING AND LISTENING

Read aloud two books with similar topics, such as *A Drop of Water: A Book of Science and Wonder* by Walter Wick and *A Drop Around the World* by Barbara Shaw McKinney and Michael S. Maydak. As you read the books, discuss the following questions:

- What is the main idea of the book? of each section?

- What are the key points used to create the main idea?

- How are the two books similar?

- How are they different?

- What are the text features used by the authors/illustrators to teach more about a drop of water?

- Do these books have the same purpose?
- Does one of the books teach more than the other?
- How could one of the books be improved? (SL.3.1d, SL.3.2, RI.3.2, RI.3.9, RI.3.6)

## 6. READING INFORMATIONAL TEXT, SPEAKING AND LISTENING

Choose a book that has good examples of text features (e.g., cross-section diagram, table), such as *The Cod's Tale* by Mark Kurlansky and S. D. Schindler. Create a list of all the text features the students will see in the book. Display the text as you read, instructing students to look for text features as you turn each page. Give each student one sticky note. As they spot a text feature, have them write the page number on the sticky note and put it by the name of the text feature on the list. Discuss the purpose of each text feature in general and in the text you are reading. (RI.3.5)

## 7. READING INFORMATIONAL TEXT, INFORMATIVE WRITING, RESEARCH

Give the students this prompt: "You have read books about animals that live in the sea. Think about which animal has been most interesting to you. Write a paragraph about what you have learned about a specific sea animal: its habitat, its adaptations, and its diet. You may want to do more research on the Internet, in encyclopedias, or in a library book to add to your learning." Some students will need guidance in generating open-ended questions about their specific animal or creating a plan for locating the most relevant and useful information, and organizing their information into focused paragraphs. (SL.3.1a, W.3.2, W.3.10, RI.3.2)

## 8. LANGUAGE USAGE, SPEAKING AND LISTENING

Choose an interesting sea animal from the books you have read together as a class. Ask the students to come up with five adjectives each to describe the animal. Generate a list of adjectives from the list of student ideas. Then have students come up with movements the animal makes and five adverbs to go with the movements. Create short sentences using the adjectives and adverbs (e.g., "*Huge* whales glide *gracefully*."). After students write several of the sentences on a chart, have them practice making new sentences with comparative or superlative adjectives and adverbs (e.g., "This huge whale glides *more gracefully* than that one.") To extend this activity in a different form, ask pairs of students to choose a sea animal. Gather strong adjectives, verbs, and adverbs to describe the animal and its movements. Use the words to create a "wordle" (from www.wordle.net) with the name of the animal as the center. (L.3.1g, SL.3.6)

## 9. ART, SPEAKING AND LISTENING

Continue with class discussion about the title of the unit, Inspired by the Sea. What do you see in each artwork–can you see the sea? Cover the part of the work that is not part of the sea. What changes about the sea? What do you notice in the water? Why did the artist choose those colors? Is it obvious that this detail is a picture of the sea? What else could it be? Closely compare the Diebenkorn image with the Hopper. Discuss the differences in color, line, texture, and shape of each seascape. Discuss the ideas of abstraction and realism by contrasting these works. (SL.3.1, SL.3.3)

## 10. ART, SPEAKING AND LISTENING

Review all of the artworks. Ask students to describe differences among the works. You might pose such questions as:

- Which one depicts the sea most accurately?
- Is it realistic or abstract?

- What would you create if you painted or drew your own image of the sea?
- Describe your "ideal" sea image in words. (W.3.3, SL.3.4, SL.3.5)

## ADDITIONAL ONLINE RESOURCES

- "Ocean Poems" (Kaunakakai Multiage Primary School, Kaunakakai, HI) (RL.3.5)
- Patricia MacLachlan (1938–), *Biography* (JRank Encyclopedia) (RI.3.3)
- *Reading and Writing About Pollution to Understand Cause and Effect* (ReadWriteThink) (RI.3.3)
- *History of America "On the Water"* (Smithsonian, National Museum of American History) (RI.3.3)
- *Blue Planet: Seas of Life* (five-disc box set, BBC, 2008)

## TERMINOLOGY

| | | |
|---|---|---|
| Adjectives | Illustrator | Stanza |
| Adverbs | Line | Text evidence |
| Author | Poem | Text features |
| Comma | Poet | |
| Dialogue | Quotation marks | |

## INTERDISCIPLINARY CONNECTIONS

This unit teaches:

- **Art:** Edward Hopper
- **Geography:** Rivers of North America (e.g., the Mississippi River and the St. Lawrence River)
- **Science:** Aquatic life (e.g., animals, habitats, and environmental conservation)

This unit could be extended to teach:

- **Geography:** Exploration (e.g., search for the Northwest Passage)
- **History:** Life on the prairie (e.g., related to *Sarah, Plain and Tall*)
- **Science:** Animal classifications (e.g., amphibians, reptiles, birds, and mammals) and ecology (e.g., interdependence, ecosystems, and environmental conservation)

# Grade Three, Unit Two Sample Lesson Plan

## Sarah, Plain and Tall *by Patricia MacLachlan*

In this series of four lessons, students read *Sarah, Plain and Tall* by Patricia MacLachlan, and they:

> Explore Sarah and her love for the sea (RL.3.2)
> Examine Sarah's ability to share her love (RL.3.1, RL.3.2)

## Summary

### Lesson I: Caleb, Anna, Papa, and Sarah (Chs. 1–3)

Identify the main characters in *Sarah, Plain and Tall* (RL.3.1, RL.3.3)

Explore the narrator's point of view (RL.3.6)

Examine the cause of sadness in the family (RL.3.1)

Explore the content of the letters (RL.3.1, RL.3.5, SL.3.1)

(Begin to) note Sarah's feeling for the sea (RL.3.1, RL.3.3, SL.3.1)

### Lesson III: Sarah's Ways (Ch. 7–end)

Explore Sarah's ways (RL.3.1)

Examine Papa's attitude toward Sarah (RL.3.1, RL.3.3)

Analyze Caleb's words: "Papa, come quickly! Sarah has brought the sea!" (RL.3.1)

Revisit Sarah's story and give titles to the chapters of the book (SL.3.1)

### Lesson II: Life on the Farm (Chs. 4–6)

(Begin to) explore Sarah's personality (RL.3.3, SL.3.1)

Explore Sarah's new life (RL.3.1, RL.3.3, SL.3.1)

Examine Sarah's relationship with Caleb and Anna (RL.3.1, RL.3.3)

(Continue to) note Sarah's life by the sea (RL.3.1, RL.3.3)

### Lesson IV: Sarah's Sea

Identify Maine on a map

Explore the ways that Sarah manages to keep the sea close to her (RL.3.1, RL.3.3, W.3.1a,b,c,d, SL.3.1)

Select passages that depict Sarah's feelings for the sea (RL.3.1, RL.3.3)

Analyze the means by which Sarah shares the sea with others (RL.3.1, RL.3.3, W.3.1a,b,c,d)

## Lesson IV: Sarah's Sea

### Objectives

Identify Maine on a map

Explore the ways that Sarah manages to keep the sea close to her (RL.3.1, RL.3.3, W.3.1a, W.3.1b, W.3.1c, W.3.1d, SL.3.1)

Select passages that depict Sarah's feelings for the sea (RL.3.1, RL.3.3)

Analyze the means by which Sarah shares the sea with others (RL.3.1, RL.3.3, W.3.1a, W.3.1b, W.3.1c, W.3.1d)

### Required Materials

☐ Class set of *Sarah, Plain and Tall* by Patricia MacLachlan

☐ Map of the United States

☐ Sticky notes

### Procedures

1. Lead-In:

   Students identify Sarah's home state, Maine, on a map of the United States. They note that Maine is in the northeast of the United States, along the Atlantic Ocean.

2. Step by Step:

   a. In groups, students discuss what they know so far about Sarah and the sea.

   b. Students independently go back to the text and, using sticky notes as markers, select passages that depict Sarah's feeling for the sea.

   c. Lead a class discussion. Students, referring to specific passages from the book (marked by the sticky notes), analyze Sarah's ways of keeping the sea close to her and her new family.

3. Closure:

   Introduce the students to the homework assignment.

## Differentiation

### Advanced

- Following the completion of the opinion paragraph to be given as homework, students will build on their knowledge of the Maine coastline. Students will choose a feature (geographic or biological) of the Maine coastline to research. Students will create informational posters about the feature they study.

### Struggling

- Before leaving school, students will meet in a small group with you to draft their first sentence.
- Students will create a list of evidence from the text and from the sticky notes to support an opinion related to Sarah and the sea.
- Students will complete the assignment at home.
- Students will work with you the following morning to review (and revise) the work completed.

## Homework/Assessment

In paragraph form, students discuss Sarah and the sea. The paragraph will have:

- A sentence introducing the topic, the text, and the author
- A sentence introducing an opinion
- Several sentences that support the point of view and provide evidence from the text
- A concluding sentence

# Creative, Inventive, and Notable People

In this third six-week unit of third grade, students read biographies about musicians, artists, and inventors of the early twentieth century.

---

## ESSENTIAL QUESTION

How are the words *creative* and *inventive* similar? How are they different?

---

## OVERVIEW

Students read fiction that shows the passion of an artist, poetry that shows a different way of thinking, and biographies of creative people living and working in the same time period. They also read about conjunctions and use them while composing sentences that describe what they learned about the inventors. They create a slide presentation and build on the word work on conjunctions by writing an opinion piece about a favorite person in the unit. Finally, they record themselves fluently reading a poem, illustrate the poem, and post the work on the Internet for parents to enjoy.

## FOCUS STANDARDS

These Focus Standards have been selected for the unit from the Common Core State Standards.

**RI.3.3:** Describe the relationship between a series of historical events, scientific ideas or concepts, or steps in technical procedures in a text, using language that pertains to time, sequence, and cause/effect.

**RL.3.1:** Ask and answer questions to demonstrate understanding of a text, referring explicitly to the text as the basis for the answers.

**SL.3.1:** Engage effectively in a range of collaborative discussions (one-on-one, in groups, and teacher-led) with diverse partners on grade 3 topics and texts, building on others' ideas and expressing their own clearly.

**SL.3.1(a):** Come to discussions prepared, having read or studied required material; explicitly draw on that preparation and other information known about the topic to explore ideas under discussion.

**W.3.2:** Write informative/explanatory texts to examine a topic and convey ideas and information clearly.

**L.3.1:** Demonstrate command of the conventions of standard English grammar and usage when writing or speaking.

**L.3.1(h):** Use coordinating and subordinating conjunctions.

**L.3.1(i):** Produce simple, compound, and complex sentences.

## SUGGESTED OBJECTIVES

- Define and apply words such as *creative* and *inventive* to describe artists, musicians, and inventors.
- Work with base words to create new words by adding prefixes and suffixes.
- Read biographies (e.g., of artists, musicians, and inventors) and explain the characteristics of a biography.
- Take simple research notes while reading biographies.
- Design and create five slides for a presentation on a notable person (e.g., an inventor).
- Learn about conjunctions and use them to create simple, compound, and complex sentences.
- Write an opinion piece based on the three key words in this unit (*creative*, *inventive*, and *notable*).
- Record themselves reading a poem.
- Create an accompanying illustration that captures a poem's meaning and display it on a class Internet page.

## SUGGESTED WORKS

(E) indicates a CCSS exemplar text; (EA) indicates a text from a writer with other works identified as exemplars.

### LITERARY TEXTS

*Stories*

- *Emma's Rug* (Allen Say) (EA)
- *Rocks in His Head* (Carol Otis Hurst and James Stevenson)
- *The Sign Painter* (Allen Say) (E) (Read Aloud)

*Poems*

- "The Folk Who Live in Backward Town" (Mary Ann Hoberman)
- "Jimmy Jet and His TV Set" (Shel Silverstein)

- *No One Saw: Ordinary Things Through the Eyes of an Artist* (Bob Raczka) (Read Aloud)
- "Paper I" (Carl Sandburg) (EA)
- "Paper II" (Carl Sandburg) (EA)
- *The Pot That Juan Built* (Nancy Andrews-Goebel and David Diaz) (Read Aloud)

## INFORMATIONAL TEXTS

### Nonfiction Books

- *Alexander Graham Bell: Inventor of the Telephone* (TIME for Kids Biographies) (Editors of TIME for Kids with John Micklos Jr.)
- *Amelia and Eleanor Go for a Ride* (Pam Muñoz Ryan and Brian Selznick)
- *Ella Fitzgerald: The Tale of a Vocal Virtuosa* (Andrea Davis Pinkney and Brian Pinkney)
- *Fabulous: A Portrait of Andy Warhol* (Bonnie Christensen)
- *Henry Ford: Putting the World on Wheels* (TIME for Kids Biographies) (Editors of TIME for Kids with Dina El Nabli)
- *Hooray for Inventors!* (Marcia Williams)
- *My Name Is Georgia: A Portrait* (Jeanette Winter)
- *Picasso and the Girl with a Ponytail* (Laurence Anholt)
- *Thomas Edison: A Brilliant Inventor* (TIME for Kids Biographies) (Editors of TIME for Kids with Lisa DeMauro)
- *Timeless Thomas: How Thomas Edison Changed Our Lives* (Marfe Ferguson Delano)
- *Vincent van Gogh: Sunflowers and Swirly Stars* (Brad Bucks and Joan Holub)
- *When Marian Sang: The True Recital of Marian Anderson* (Pam Muñoz Ryan and Brian Selznick)
- *The Yellow House: Vincent van Gogh and Paul Gauguin Side by Side* (Susan Goldman Rubin)

### Nonfiction Books (Read Aloud)

- *Ah, Music!* (Aliki) (E)
- *Fantastic! Wow! and Unreal! A Book About Interjections and Conjunctions* (World of Language) (Ruth Heller)
- *Here's Looking at Me: How Artists See Themselves* (Bob Raczka)
- *Hidden Worlds: Looking Through a Scientist's Microscope* (Stephen Kramer and Dennis Kunkel)
- *Inventing the Future: A Photobiography of Thomas Alva Edison* (Marfe Ferguson Delano and Jennifer Emmett)
- *The Museum Book: A Guide to Strange and Wonderful Collections* (Jan Mark and Richard Holland) (E)
- *Paul Gauguin* (Getting to Know the World's Greatest Artists) (Mike Venezia)
- *To Fly: The Story of the Wright Brothers* (Wendie Old and Robert Andrew Parker)
- *Van Gogh* (Getting to Know the World's Greatest Artists) (Mike Venezia)

## ART, MUSIC, AND MEDIA

### Visual Artists

- Alice Neel, *Faith Ringgold* (1976)
- Andy Warhol, *Self-Portrait* (1967)

- Pablo Picasso, *Gertrude Stein* (1906)
- Paul Gauguin, *Self-Portrait* (1889)
- Vincent van Gogh, *Self-Portrait* (1887–1888)

## Musicians

- Arnold Newman, *Igor Stravinsky* (1946)
- Richard Avedon, *Marian Anderson, Contralto, New York* (1955)
- World-Telegram staff photographer, *Louis Armstrong* (1953)

## Writers

- Artist unknown, *Helen Keller with Anne Sullivan* (1888)
- Edoardo Gelli, *The Last Portrait of Mark Twain* (1904)
- Winold Reiss, *Portrait of Langston Hughes* (no date)

# SAMPLE ACTIVITIES AND ASSESSMENTS

Note: Although the fiction titles are more contemporary, the artists, musicians, and inventors are all from the twentieth century. You may want to study the artists and musicians in the first half of the unit and then spend the last three weeks on the inventors.

## 1. SPEAKING AND LISTENING

Begin this new unit with a discussion of its title: Creative, Inventive, and Notable People. Use some of the following questions to guide the conversation, and ask students first to write answers in complete sentences in their journals before the class discussion begins:

- What does it mean to be *creative*? (base word: *create*)
- Whom do you know who is creative?
- What other words can we make from the base word *create*? (Possible answers: *creation, created, creating, re-create, uncreative,* and *recreation*)
- What does it mean to be *inventive*? (base word: *invent*)
- Whom do you know who is inventive?
- What does it mean to be *notable*? (base word: *note*)
- Whom do you know who is notable?
- How are the words *creative* and *inventive* similar?
- How are they different? (RF.3.3c, L3.2e, L.3.4b, L.3.4c, L.3.5b, L.3.5c)

## 2. READING LITERATURE, SPEAKING AND LISTENING

Introduce *The Sign Painter*, written and illustrated by Allen Say (who also wrote *Grandfather's Journey*, from Unit Two). In this book about a man and a boy who paint billboards, the illustrations play an important role in telling the story. While you read it aloud, challenge the students to question and think, and ask them to jot down questions. Read at a leisurely pace so that students have the opportunity to ask questions about specific illustrations, words, or pages of the book where they might lose focus or struggle with understanding the story. (RL.3.1)

## 3. READING INFORMATIONAL TEXT, RESEARCH

Reading biographies of artists and musicians provides an opportunity for students to focus on noting important information in the text. Teach students about the title of a biography and how it is sometimes the name of the person and how it is sometimes a description of the person's main contribution. Tell students that while they are reading or listening to someone else read a biography, they should note the key events that occur in the subject's life. Have students recall and generate a list of the key question words to consider: *who, what, where, when, why,* and *how.* Divide students into small groups and assign each group a question stem. Have students create a chart with the questions down the left-hand column of the chart. Then create a similar chart on the board or a notepad in the front of the room. Using the key question words to guide comprehension, read aloud a biography of a famous person, such as the singer Marian Anderson. As students hear answers to their questions, have them raise their hands. Write answers on a class chart and have the students write the information on their own charts. As you repeat this activity with other biographies, ask students to generate additional open-ended research questions. (RI.3.1, RI.3.3, RI.3.7, W.3.8, L.3.2a)

## 4. READING INFORMATIONAL TEXT, RESEARCH, INFORMATIVE WRITING

Have students choose an age-appropriate biography to read from a series, such as the TIME *for Kids* series of biographies. Instruct the students to take notes based on the key questions (as described in the previous activity) while reading the biographies. If there is time, students should generate one open-ended question to research after finishing the biography. After students have located a few additional sources and answered their last question, partner the students to share information and create a short series of slides to answer each of the questions (*who, what, where, when, why,* and *how*), as well as to highlight three to five key events in the person's life. Have students combine multiple questions on one slide such as *where* and *when.* Limit each pair to a total of five slides, with the last slide showing the key events in the inventor's life. Combine the slides into one presentation and present it to an audience, such as the students' parents or another class. You might also choose to give students this writing prompt: "Choose a famous person's biography to read. Write about the person. Be sure to answer the questions *who, what, where, when, why,* and *how* and highlight three to five key events in the person's life." Make sure that students cite their main source properly. Following this research, a class could present a "Wax Museum," where students dress as their assigned person and tell about her or his life. (SL.3.1a, SL.3.4, RI.3.3, W.3.2, W.3.5, W.3.8, W.3.10, L.3.1, L.3.2, L.3.3)

## 5. RESEARCH, ORAL PRESENTATION

Have each student choose an invention that they love (e.g., a bicycle, an MP3 player). Or students can choose a painting or song listed in the Art, Music, and Media section. Students will then formulate open-ended questions using the question stems (*who, what, where, when, why,* and *how*) to guide the research about who invented or created the item they selected. Have students create a presentation of the information they discover about the inventor of their favorite object. Require students to use the guiding question stems as an organizational tool in their presentations. Allow students to photograph the object so that they can display an image of it while they tell about the history of their invention. If a student picked an artwork or a song, display the work or play a recording as the student shares his or her research. You may choose to give the students the assignment in the form of a research prompt: "Choose an invention, an artwork, or song that you love. Research to find out who invented it, created it, or wrote it. Photograph the object or artwork, or record the song to use for an oral presentation of your research results." Make sure that students cite their source properly. (RI.3.5, W.3.7, W.3.8, SL.3.4)

## 6. LANGUAGE USAGE

Using Ruth Heller's book *Fantastic! Wow! and Unreal! A Book About Interjections and Conjunctions*, teach the coordinating conjunctions (*and, but, or, nor, for, yet, so*) and subordinating conjunctions (*after, before, when, while, since, until*). Apply conjunctions by creating simple, compound, and complex sentences from a cause-and-effect graphic organizer. For example, consider the invention of the assembly line by Henry Ford. What caused him to invent it? What were the effects of the invention?

Have students create cause-and-effect-related sentences orally, and then have them write the sentences down. Teach about the use of coordinating and subordinating conjunctions in their work. (L.3.1h, L.3.1i, RI.3.3)

## 7. READING POETRY, READING FLUENCY

The poems in this unit show how poets look at the world in a different way. Students should choose one of the poems and then practice reciting it in the way that best exemplifies the meaning of the poem. With a video camera, record the students reading (reciting) poems. Then have students create an accompanying illustration to display while you play the recording of their poetry reading. Alternatively, both the recording and the illustration can be posted on the Internet for parents to listen to and see. (SL.3.5, RF.3.4b)

## 8. OPINION WRITING

Give the students this prompt: "You began this unit with a discussion about three words: *creative, inventive,* and *notable*. Choose the person from this unit who you believe to be the most creative, inventive, and notable. Write about the person you choose, and give reasons why you believe he or she is creative, inventive, and notable." (W.3.1, L.3.2)

## 9. ART, SPEAKING AND LISTENING

Select two works to compare in a large-group discussion—for instance, the Warhol self-portrait and the photograph of Louis Armstrong. Discussion should focus on choices that the artist made to communicate the importance of the subject, including the subject's unique creative sensibility in art, music, or writing. In this example, students might explore why the trumpet is the focal point of the photograph—does the photographer want the viewer to focus mainly on the music or on the man? How is the self-portrait of Warhol different? What details does he give us, and what remains ambiguous? How did the painter or photographer choose to depict the artist (or musician or writer) and portray his or her talents? (SL.3.1, SL.3.3)

## 10. ART, SPEAKING AND LISTENING

Encourage students to examine one of the portraits that they admire most. Pose the following question(s): "If you were to create either a self-portrait or a portrait of someone you respect, what features would you include?" "What aspects of these artists' works would you use in your own interpretations?" After a discussion, ask students to write a brief narrative describing your imagined portrait. (W.3.3)

# ADDITIONAL ONLINE RESOURCES

- "When Marian Sings" (RF.3.4)
- Bio Cube Planning Sheet (ReadWriteThink) (RI.3.2)
- *Spark Lab Inventor Profiles* (Smithsonian, the Lemelson Center for the Study of Invention & Innovation) (RI.3.10)
- *Rooting Out Meaning: Morpheme Match-Ups in the Primary Grades* (ReadWriteThink) (RF.3.3)

# TERMINOLOGY

| | | |
|---|---|---|
| Biographies | Coordinating conjunction | Research questions |
| Complex sentence | Note taking | Simple sentence |
| Compound sentence | Presentation | Subordinating conjunction |

# INTERDISCIPLINARY CONNECTIONS

This unit teaches:

- **Art:** Andy Warhol, Pablo Picasso, Alice Neel
- **Music:** Jazz (e.g., Louis Armstrong, Ella Fitzgerald) and opera (e.g., Marian Anderson)
- **History:** Inventors (e.g., Thomas Edison and Alexander Graham Bell)
- **Science:** Inventions (e.g., the assembly line, light bulb, and telephone) and flight (e.g., the Wright Brothers and Amelia Earhart)

This unit could be extended to teach:

- **History:** Inventors (e.g., before and after the twentieth century)
- **Science:** Light/optics (e.g., light, reflection, and lenses), sound (e.g., sound waves, the human voice, and the human ear), and vision/hearing (i.e., how they work in the human body)

## Grade Three, Unit Three Sample Lesson Plan

### Emma's Rug *by Allen Say*

In this series of four lessons, students read *Emma's Rug* by Allen Say, and they:

- Explore the power of artists' inspiration (RL.3.2)
- Examine an individual's ability to overcome a crisis (RL.3.1, RL.3.2)
- Consider the role that illustrations play in telling Emma's story (RL.3.7, SL.3.1)

### Summary

#### Lesson I: Emma's World

- Explore the story line of *Emma's Rug* (RL.3.1, RL.3.2)
- Identify the characters in the story (RL.3.3)
- List key events in the story (RL.3.5)

#### Lesson II: Emma's Rug

- Reread Emma's story (through p. 19) (RF.3.4)
- Describe the rug (RL.3.1, SL.3.1)
- List Emma's activities (RL.3.1, RL.3.3, W.3.2)
- Identify the source of Emma's inspiration (RL.3.1, SL.3.1)
- Analyze Emma's response to the attention that she receives (RL.3.1, SL.3.1)
- Note the use of illustrations in the story (RL.3.7)

#### Lesson III: A Crisis

- Reread the rest of the story (p. 20–end of story) (RF.3.4)
- Explore the reasons for Emma's scream (RL.3.1, RL.3.3)
- Consider the act of Emma's mother (RL.3.1, RL.3.3)
- Examine Emma's response to the crisis (RL.3.1, RL.3.3)

#### Lesson IV: Inspiration

- Revisit the ending of the story
- Analyze the meaning of the narrator's words: "She saw eyes watching her and then the faces of creatures all around." (RL.3.1, RL.3.4)
- Consider the importance of the illustration at the end of the story (RL.3.7)
- Discuss the following question: Where does inspiration come from? (SL.3.1)

## Lesson II: Emma's Rug

### Objectives

Reread Emma's story (through p. 19) (RF.3.4)

Describe the rug (RL.3.1, SL.3.1)

List Emma's activities (RL.3.1, RL.3.3, W.3.2)

Identify the source of Emma's inspiration (RL.3.1, SL.3.1)

Analyze Emma's response to the attention that she receives (RL.3.1, SL.3.1)

Note the use of illustrations in the story (RL.3.7)

### Required Materials

☐ Class set of *Emma's Rug* by Allen Say

### Procedures

1. Lead-In:

   Reread *Emma's Rug* through page 19.

2. Step by Step:

   a. Students discuss the description of the rug. They use specific examples from the text: It is "shaggy" and "plain," and it "keeps the feet warm."

   b. Students look at the illustrations of the rug and note that it is indeed "plain" (i.e., there are no pictures on it).

   c. Students, citing the text, note Emma's relationship to the rug (p. 6).

   d. Students note the way that Emma stares into the rug as if she sees something in it (illustration on p. 7).

   e. Students analyze Emma's response to the attention she receives.

3. Closure:

   Student volunteers summarize the details of the discussion.

## Differentiation

### Advanced

- Students will write a paragraph about the illustration on page 7 of the book, discussing the way Emma stares into the rug and what she might see in it.

### Struggling

- Read the story aloud to the students, as they "whisper-read" along with you. Each time the rug is described in the text, ask the students to chorally read aloud the sentences. Using a real rug, show the students the meaning of "shaggy," "plain," and "keeps the feet warm."

## Homework/Assessment

Students reread the ending of the story.

# The People, the Preamble, and the Presidents

In this fourth six-week unit of third grade, students read about the people, the Preamble (to the Constitution), and the presidents of the United States.

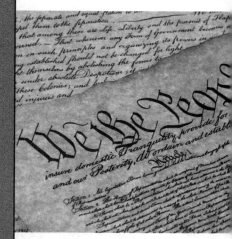

---

## ESSENTIAL QUESTION

Why is it important to choose words carefully?

---

## OVERVIEW

Building on knowledge of the notable people in the last unit, students read informational texts about the people who came to America and established a new government in the eighteenth century. They read about the lives of presidents, research a president of interest, and write a "bio-poem" (a biography in poem form). Finally, students create and perform a cumulative choral reading of the Preamble to the U.S. Constitution and memorize it for an oral recitation.

## FOCUS STANDARDS

These Focus Standards have been selected for the unit from the Common Core State Standards.

**RI.3.4:** Determine the meaning of general academic and domain-specific words and phrases in a text relevant to a grade 3 topic or subject area.

**RI.3.8:** Describe the logical connection between particular sentences and paragraphs in a text (e.g., comparison, cause/effect, first/second/third in a sequence).

**SL.3.3:** Ask and answer questions about information from a speaker, offering appropriate elaboration and detail.

**RF.3.4:** Read with sufficient accuracy and fluency to support comprehension.

**RF.3.4(b):** Read on-level prose and poetry orally with accuracy, appropriate rate, and expression on successive readings.

**W.3.7:** Conduct short research projects that build knowledge about a topic.

**L.3.4:** Determine or clarify the meaning of unknown and multiple-meaning words and phrases based on grade 3 reading and content, choosing flexibly from a range of strategies.

**L.3.4(d):** Use glossaries or beginning dictionaries, both print and digital, to determine or clarify the precise meaning of key words and phrases.

## SUGGESTED OBJECTIVES

- Ask and answer questions of a speaker (e.g., a visitor invited to discuss immigration).
- Sequence the events in an informational text (e.g., *Coming to America: The Story of Immigration* by Betsy Maestro and Susannah Ryan).
- Define key words in the Preamble to the U.S. Constitution.
- Create an acrostic poem for a key word in the Preamble, demonstrating study of the definition.
- Dramatically read the Preamble in collaboration with classmates through a cumulative choral reading.
- Orally recite the Preamble.
- Study the illustrations in *We the Kids: The Preamble to the Constitution* by David Catrow and explain the role of the illustrator in illuminating the meaning of a text.
- Compare and contrast two similar books on the same topic (e.g., the presidents).

## SUGGESTED WORKS

(E) indicates a CCSS exemplar text; (EA) indicates a text from a writer with other works identified as exemplars.

### LITERARY TEXTS

*Stories*

- *Annushka's Voyage* (Edith Tarbescu and Lydia Dabcovich)
- *Arthur Meets the President: An Arthur Adventure* (Marc Brown)
- *At Ellis Island: A History in Many Voices* (Louise Peacock)
- *Bravest Woman in America* (Marissa Moss)
- *The Dream Jar* (Bonnie Pryor and Mark Graham)
- *The Garden on Green Street* (Meish Goldish)
- *Grace for President* (Kelly S. DiPucchio)
- *Hannah's Journal: The Story of an Immigrant Girl* (Marissa Moss)
- *Hope in My Heart: Sofia's Immigrant Diary, Book 1* (Kathryn Lasky)
- *In America* (Marissa Moss)
- *In the Year of the Boar and Jackie Robinson* (Bette Bao Lord and Marc Simont)

- *Lily and Miss Liberty* (Carla Stevens and Deborah Kogan Ray)
- *The Long Way to a New Land* (Joan Sandin)
- *Make a Wish, Molly* (Barbara Cohen and Jan Naimo Jones)
- *The Memory Coat* (Elvira Woodruff and Michael Dooling)
- *Molly's Pilgrim* (Barbara Cohen and Daniel Mark Duffy)
- *Oranges on Golden Mountain* (Elizabeth Partridge)
- *The Orphan of Ellis Island* (Elvira Woodruff)
- *Otto Runs for President* (Rosemary Wells)
- *Together in Pinecone Patch* (Thomas F. Yezerski)
- *Vote!* (Eileen Christelow)
- *When Jesse Came Across the Sea* (Amy Hest and P. J. Lynch)
- *Woodrow for President: A Tail of Voting, Campaigns, and Elections* (Peter J. and Cheryl Shaw Barnes)

## Poems (Read Aloud)

- "The Flag Goes By" (H. H. Bennett)
- "George Washington" (Rosemary and Stephen Vincent Benet)
- "A Nation's Strength" (Ralph Waldo Emerson)
- "The Star-Spangled Banner" (Francis Scott Key)
- *The Star-Spangled Banner* (Francis Scott Key, illustrated by Peter Spier)
- "Washington Monument by Night" (Carl Sandburg) (EA)

## INFORMATIONAL TEXTS

### Nonfiction Books

- *14 Cows for America* (Carmen Agra Deedy, Thomas Gonzalez, and Wilson Kimeli Naiyomah) (E)
- *Ellis Island* (Elaine Landau)
- *Smart About the Presidents* (Smart About History) (Jon Buller, Susan Schade, Maryann Cocca-Leffler, Dana Regan, and Jill Weber)
- *So You Want to Be President?* (Judith St. George and David Small) (E)

### Nonfiction Books (Read Aloud)

- *Coming to America: The Story of Immigration* (Betsy Maestro and Susannah Ryan)
- *If You Were There When They Signed the Constitution* (Elizabeth Levy and Joan Holub)
- *James Madison: Fourth President 1809–1817* (Mike Venezia)
- *Lives of the Presidents: Fame, Shame (and What the Neighbors Thought)* (Kathleen Krull and Kathryn Hewitt)
- *The Presidency* (True Books) (Patricia Ryon Quiri)
- *The Presidency* (True Books) (Christine Taylor-Butler)
- *Remember the Ladies: 100 Great American Women* (Cheryl Harness)

- *Shh! We're Writing the Constitution* (Jean Fritz and Tomie dePaola)
- *We the Kids: The Preamble to the Constitution* (David Catrow)

## ART, MUSIC, AND MEDIA

*Art*

- Aaron Shikler, *Oil Portrait of John F. Kennedy* (official portrait) (1970)
- Artist unknown, *Reagan Inaugural Parade* (1981)
- Chuck Close, *Portrait of Bill Clinton* (2005)
- Daniel Chester French, *Lincoln Memorial* (1922)
- Emanuel Leutze, *Washington Crossing the Delaware* (1851)
- Gilbert Stuart, *George Washington* (1796)
- Jean-Antoine Houdon, *Bust of Thomas Jefferson* (1789)
- John Trumbull, *John Adams* (1792–1793)
- Robert Rauschenberg, *Retroactive 1* (1964)

## SAMPLE ACTIVITIES AND ASSESSMENTS

Note: For the people part of this unit, bring in as many immigration stories, through texts and speakers (especially parents and grandparents), as you can, to represent the students in your class. (SL.3.3)

### 1. LANGUAGE USAGE, SPEAKING AND LISTENING

Introduce the unit by writing the three key words on the board: *people, preamble,* and *presidency*. As you work through each word (possibly over a few days/class periods), give students a copy of a semantic map and display yours (e.g., on an overhead projector, document camera, or an interactive whiteboard). Using dictionaries for reference, begin with the word *people*. To ensure full participation, require each student to turn to a partner and talk about each part of the map before filling in the spaces. Maps such as these create a richer understanding of a word students already know (e.g., *people*) by looking at parts of speech and the word's synonyms. (L.3.1b, L.3.1c, L.3.4b, L.3.4d, L.3.6, RF.3.3a)

### 2. LANGUAGE USAGE, VOCABULARY

Divide students into groups of three or four and give them one of the key words (*people, preamble,* or *presidency*). Ask them to write the word on a poster in large bold print. Then have them use their semantic maps to create symbols, pictures, and words (synonyms) that illustrate the rich meaning of each word. Hang the posters around the room to refer to throughout the unit. (L.3.1b, L.3.1c, L.3.4b, L.3.6, RF.3.3a)

### 3. READING FLUENCY, PERFORMANCE, SPEAKING AND LISTENING

Divide the class into eight groups to perform a cumulative choral reading of the Preamble to the U.S. Constitution. Have the first group read to the first comma, the second group read to the next comma, and so on. Continue adding voices/phrases until the whole class is reading the

Preamble. Students will quickly and naturally memorize the Preamble and can perform it independently as an oral recitation. (RF.3.3c, RF.3.4, RF.3.4b)

## 4. LANGUAGE USAGE, WRITING POETRY

Using the formatted Preamble text below, give students the following writing prompt: "Choose a key word (in bold) from the Preamble. Use defining phrases, simple similes, or synonyms to show that you understand the key word." You may want to do one as a class example and then have the students work independently or with partners to complete the task. (RI.3.4, W.3.2b, W.3.10, L.3.2 g, L.3.4d, SL.3.1)

We the People of the United States, in Order to form a more perfect **Union**, establish **Justice**, insure domestic **Tranquility**, provide for the common **defense**, promote the general **Welfare**, and secure the Blessings of **Liberty** to ourselves and our **Posterity**, do ordain and establish this **Constitution** for the United States of America.

## 5. LANGUAGE USAGE, WRITING POETRY

Using the book *We the Kids: The Preamble to the Constitution* by David Catrow, discuss the role of an illustrator in telling a story. Showing only the illustrations (e.g., by covering the text with sticky notes), have the students concoct a story aloud and together. After the students have created a story, show them that the text for the book is actually the Preamble to the U.S. Constitution. Together, read the book again to see how each illustration illustrates the meaning of a phrase. (RL.3.7, SL.3.1)

## 6. READING INFORMATIONAL TEXT, SPEAKING AND LISTENING

Choose two books about presidents for the students to compare and contrast, such as *So You Want to Be President?* by Judith St. George and David Small and *Lives of the Presidents* by Kathleen Krull and Kathryn Hewitt. Ask students the following questions:

- In what ways are the two books similar?
- How are they different?
- Did you feel that any of the humorous comments made about the presidents were inappropriate?

(Note: Be sure they quote from the text to back up their opinion.) ( RI.3.1, RI.3.6, RI.3.9, SL.3.1)

## 7. RESEARCH, INFORMATIVE WRITING

Give the students this research prompt: "From the books we've read about the presidents, choose the president who interests you most. Research that president using the Internet, an encyclopedia, and a biography of him." You will want to remind the students to generate research questions before they begin locating sources. When they have completed the research, challenge them with this writing prompt: "Write an informative bio-poem based on the American president you chose to research." Students may use the format described next to organize the poem. Students should use the process of revising and editing before publishing their work. (Note: The example about George Washington that follows is for you, though you may decide to share it with the class to explain the activity.) To help struggling students, you may want to create a graphic organizer to aid with gathering the necessary information for the bio-poem. (W.3.2, W.3.5, W.3.6, W.3.7, W.3.10, L.3.1, L.3.2, L.3.3)

## Formatting Guidelines

Line 1: First, middle, and last name

Line 2: Four jobs held by the man during his life (other than presidency)

Line 3: Birthplace, child of

Line 4: Lover of

Line 5: Educated

Line 6: Resident of

Line 7: Three contributions

Line 8: Number order of president (ordinal number)

Line 9: Nickname

### Sample Poem

George Washington
Surveyor, planter, soldier, commander
Born in Virginia, son of Mary
Lover of Martha, math, and farming
Educated in elementary school
Resident of Mount Vernon
Revolutionary commander, government creator, humble leader
First president
Father of our country

## 8. ART, SPEAKING AND LISTENING

Select one of the following comparisons: *Washington Crossing the Delaware* (Leutze) versus *Reagan Inaugural Parade* (photographer unknown) or *George Washington* (Stuart) versus *Oil Portrait of John F. Kennedy* (Shikler). Discuss how the style of depicting presidents has changed over time—and how it has remained the same. What elements that have remained can you identify in each painting? Subjects, details, themes? (SL.3.1, SL.3.3)

## 9. ART, SPEAKING AND LISTENING

What have modern artists chosen to omit or add in more recent portraits—such as the portrait of Bill Clinton by Chuck Close or Rauschenberg's portrait of John F. Kennedy? How do these images differ from previous presidential portraits? (SL.3.1, SL.3.3)

## 10. READING LITERATURE, SPEAKING AND LISTENING

Introduce the book *Coming to America: The Story of Immigration* by Betsy Maestro and Susannah Ryan as telling the story of immigration. Tell students that America is unique because its people have come from so many different backgrounds. To understand how all of these people came to the same place, challenge students to think about the sequence of events in America's history. Define *chronological order* and relate it to something like your daily schedule or school calendar. As you read the book aloud, have students jot down important events on sticky notes, keeping them in chronological order. Ask them also to be thinking about why we might need to have rules to guide our government. (You can extend this lesson to discuss those government rules by pausing on page 14, where students will notice how many people were living together in the growing cities of New York, Boston, Philadelphia, Charleston, Baltimore, and New Orleans. As the page turns, students will see how people started moving west and the growing need for different laws. Use this to launch a discussion of the need for a central government.) (RI.3.4, RI.3.8, SL.3.1, L.3.5b)

## 11. READING LITERATURE, SPEAKING AND LISTENING

Introduce a collection of historical fiction books based on the topic of immigration. Allow students to choose a book that interests them. As students read, ask them to use sticky notes to respond to questions and prompts such as:

- Who came to America?

- When did they come?

- Why did they come?

- From where did they come?

- Where did they settle in America?

- Note examples of the adjustments they made in America.

- Note a passage in the book that shows challenges faced by the main character in a strange new country.

Use these guiding questions and prompts to conduct whole-group discussions about the people who came previously and continue to come to America. Require students to show evidence of their findings from their books. Extend these discussions by assigning students to craft a well-developed paragraph about the book's main character and that character's greatest challenge. (RL.3.1, RL.3.3, RL.3.5, RL.3.9, RL.3.10, RF.3.4b, W.3.10)

## ADDITIONAL ONLINE RESOURCES

- *The Preamble to the Constitution: How Do You Make a More Perfect Union?* (National Endowment for the Humanities) (RI.3.4)

- *Voting! What's It All About?* (ReadWriteThink) (RI.3.9)

- *Hands-On Presidential Activity: Children Write to the President* (Smithsonian, National Museum of American History) (W.3.4)

- *What Happens in the White House?* (National Endowment for the Humanities)

- *A President's Home and the President's House* (National Endowment for the Humanities)

- *How Was the White House Designed?* (National Endowment for the Humanities)

- "Preamble," *Schoolhouse Rock* (1976)

## TERMINOLOGY

| | | |
|---|---|---|
| Bio-poem | Cumulative choral reading | Sequence |
| Chronological order | Dictionary | Synonyms |

## INTERDISCIPLINARY CONNECTIONS

This unit teaches:

- **Art:** Portraiture, Gilbert Stuart, Emanuel Leutze, Chuck Close, Robert Rauschenberg
- **Geography:** U.S. geography (e.g., as related to immigration and migration)
- **History:** U.S. Constitution (e.g., James Madison and the Preamble), immigration, and the presidency

This unit could be extended to teach:

- **Geography:** Early American settlements
- **History:** Colonial times (e.g., focus on life before the first presidency)

## Grade Three, Unit Four Sample Lesson Plan

*"The Flag Goes By" by H. H. Bennett*

In this series of three lessons, students read "The Flag Goes By" by H. H. Bennett, and they:

Examine the imagery in "The Flag Goes By" (RL.3.1, RL.3.4, RL.3.5, RL.3.10, SL.3.2)

Probe the patriotic message of "The Flag Goes By" (RL.3.5, RL.3.9, SL.3.2)

Explore the history of "Old Glory" (RI.3.5, W.3.7)

### Summary

**Lesson I: "The Flag Goes By" by H. H. Bennett**

Examine the visual description of the flag and the people in the poem (RL.3.1, RL.3.4, RL.3.5, RL.3.10, SL.3.2)

Explore the repeated use of the words *Hats off!* (RL.3.4, SL.3.1)

Probe the patriotic theme of "The Flag Goes By" (RL.3.5, RL.3.9, SL.3.2)

**Lesson II: Researching the History of "Old Glory"**

Investigate the story of "Old Glory" (RI.3.5, W.3.7)

History of the flag

Origins of the name "Old Glory"

Gradual transformation of the flag

Record findings (W.3.2, W.3.8)

**Lesson III: Reporting the History of "Old Glory"**

Recall findings (W.3.8)

Lay out findings (SL.3.2)

Share results (SL.3.4)

## Lesson II: Researching the History of "Old Glory"

### Objectives

Investigate the story of "Old Glory" (RI.3.5, W.3.7)

- History of the flag
- Origins of the name "Old Glory"
- Gradual transformation of the flag

Record findings (W.3.2, W.3.8)

### Required Materials

- [ ] Class set of "The Flag Goes By" by H. H. Bennett
- [ ] Computers with Internet access
- [ ] Printers
- [ ] Paper
- [ ] Poster boards

### Procedures

1. Lead-In:

   Explain the research project to the students. Introduce the students to the "Step by Step" process.

2. Step by Step:

   a. In small groups, students will conduct online research. (A resource is www.usflag.org.) They will investigate the

      - History of the flag
      - Origins of the name "Old Glory"
      - Gradual transformation of the flag

   b. Students record their findings. The format may be decided by you or by the groups themselves.

3. Closure:

   Students will tour their class exhibits.

## Differentiation

### Advanced

- Students in each group may want to use a shared spreadsheet as they research, so that they can compile their information into one document.
- In subsequent class times, students could pull the organized information from the document to create a multimedia presentation on the flag, set to patriotic music and introduced by a dramatic reading of the poem.

### Struggling

- In advance of this lesson, students will work together to perform the poem "The Flag Goes By," focusing on reading fluency and on internalizing the ideas in the poem.
- Work with students to create a graphic organizer on which to record their research findings.

## Homework/Assessment

Reread the findings in preparation for communicating them to the class.

# A Feast of Words on a Planet Called Earth—and Beyond

In this fifth six-week unit of third grade, students read stories, poems, and informational text full of rich language, a "feast of words."

---

## ESSENTIAL QUESTION

What makes a word or phrase the "right" word or phrase?

---

## OVERVIEW

Students read fiction that demonstrates the use of idioms and exhibits carefully chosen diction. They read poems that focus on a simple topic such as corn or grass to see how the topics are developed line by line and stanza by stanza. They write to express their own opinions about the idea of having laws that legislate what people can and cannot eat. Working with Latin suffixes, they will see the way that suffixes transform one part of speech into another. Students illustrate an idiom to express their own interpretation of its meaning and then write a note to Amelia Bedelia about the idiom. Finally, the students will stretch beyond this world to read about and research other planets.

## FOCUS STANDARDS

These Focus Standards have been selected for the unit from the Common Core State Standards.

**RI.3.7:** Use information gained from illustrations (e.g., maps, photographs) and the words in a text to demonstrate understanding of the text (e.g., where, when, why, and how key events occur).

**RF.3.3:** Know and apply grade-level phonics and word analysis skills in decoding words.

**RF.3.3(b):** Decode words with common Latin suffixes.

**L.3.4:** Determine the meaning of the new word formed when a known affix is added to a known word.

**RL.3.4:** Determine the meaning of words and phrases as they are used in a text, distinguishing literal from nonliteral language.

**RL.3.5:** Refer to parts of stories, dramas, and poems when writing or speaking about a text, using terms such as chapter, scene, and stanza; describe how each successive part builds on earlier sections.

**W.3.1:** Write opinion pieces on topics or texts, supporting a point of view with reasons.

## SUGGESTED OBJECTIVES

- Independently read stories, poems, and informational text.
- Use dictionaries and thesauruses, both in print and online, to look up words and to consider varied shades of meaning.
- Decode and analyze words with Latin suffixes.
- Collect words from poems, both from read-aloud selections and from independent reading.
- Comprehend poems by seeing how each stanza or line builds on its predecessor for meaning (e.g., "Eating While Reading" by Gary Soto).
- Listening to a read-aloud novel such as *The Search for Delicious* by Natalie Babbitt, note how each chapter builds on earlier sections, requiring careful reading/listening for comprehension.
- Write an opinion piece based on one's own thinking (e.g., about food legislation); apply growing understanding of strong, focused paragraphs.
- Dramatically read a poem (or recite it from memory).
- Learn the meaning of idioms both within stories and in books about idioms.
- Research and write a report about a planet, using the key questions (*who, what, where, when, why*, and *how*) to guide research.

## SUGGESTED WORKS

(E) indicates a CCSS exemplar text; (EA) indicates a text from a writer with other works identified as exemplars.

## LITERARY TEXTS

### Stories

- *Amelia Bedelia* (Peggy Parish and Fritz Siebel)
- *Amelia Bedelia, Rocket Scientist* (Herman Parish and Lynn Sweat)
- *Dog Breath! The Horrible Trouble with Hally Tosis* (Dav Pilkey)
- *Even More Parts: Idioms from Head to Toe* (Tedd Arnold)
- *Frindle* (Andrew Clements and Brian Selznick) (Read Aloud)

- *My Momma Likes to Say* (Denise Brennan-Nelson and Jane Monroe Donavan)
- *The Search for Delicious* (Natalie Babbitt) (E) (Read Aloud)
- *Thank You, Amelia Bedelia* (Peggy Parish and Barbara Siebel Thomas)

## Picture Books

- *Birds of a Feather: A Book of Idioms* (Vanita Oelschlager and Robin Hegan)
- *In a Pickle and Other Funny Idioms* (Marvin Terban and Giulio Maestro)
- *Mad as a Wet Hen! And Other Funny Idioms* (Marvin Terban and Giulio Maestro)
- *Punching the Clock: Funny Action Idioms* (Marvin Terban and Thomas Huffman)
- *Raining Cats and Dogs: A Collection of Irresistible Idioms and Illustrations to Tickle the Funny Bones of Young People* (Will Moses)
- *There's a Frog in My Throat: 440 Animal Sayings a Little Bird Told Me* (Loreen Leedy and Pat Street)
- *Ve Lo Que Dices/See What You Say: Modismos en Español e Ingles/ Spanish and English Idioms* (Nancy Maria Grande Tabor)
- *Why the Banana Split: Adventures in Idioms* (Rick Walton and Jimmy Holder)

## Poems

- "Barefoot Days" (Rachel Field)
- *Candy Corn: Poems* (James Stevenson)
- "Catch a Little Rhyme" (Eve Merriam) (EA)
- "The City" (Langston Hughes) (EA)
- "Eating While Reading" (Gary Soto) (E)
- "The Grass" (Emily Dickinson) (Read Aloud)
- "The Grass on the Mountain" (Paiute American Indian) transcribed by Mary Austin (Read Aloud)
- "I Wandered Lonely as a Cloud" (William Wordsworth) (Read Aloud)
- *Popcorn: Poems* (James Stevenson)
- "Skyscrapers" (Rachel Field)
- "Spring Grass" (Carl Sandburg) (EA) (Read Aloud)
- *Sweet Corn: Poems* (James Stevenson)

# INFORMATIONAL TEXTS

## Nonfiction Books

- *Boy, Were We Wrong About the Solar System* (Kathleen V. Kudlinski)
- *Discover the Planets* (Kids Can Read) (Cynthia Pratt Nicolson and Bill Slavin)
- *Earth* (A True Book: Space) (Larry Dane Brimner)
- *Faraway Worlds* (Paul Halpern)
- *Jupiter* (A True Book: Space) (Larry Dane Brimner)

- *Jupiter* (Scholastic News Nonfiction Readers) (Christine Taylor-Butler)
- *Mars* (A True Book: Space) (Larry Dane Brimner)
- *Mars* (Scholastic News Nonfiction Readers) (Melanie Chrismer)
- *Mars: The Red Planet* (All Aboard Science Reader) (Patricia Brennan Demuth)
- *A Medieval Feast* (Aliki) (E)
- *Meet the Planets* (John McGranaghan)
- *Mercury* (A True Book: Space) (Larry Dane Brimner)
- *Mercury* (Scholastic News Nonfiction Readers) (Christine Taylor-Butler)
- *Moonshot: The Flight of Apollo 11* (Brian Floca) (E)
- *Neptune* (A True Book: Space) (Larry Dane Brimner)
- *Neptune* (Scholastic News Nonfiction Readers) (Melanie Chrismer)
- *Our Solar System* (Revised Edition) (Seymour Simon)
- *The Planets* (Gail Gibbons) (EA)
- *Planets!* (TIME for Kids Science Scoops) (Editors of TIME *for Kids* with Lisa Jo Rudy)
- *Pluto: From Planet to Dwarf* (True Books) (Elaine Landau)
- *Saturn* (A True Book: Space) (Larry Dane Brimner)
- *Saturn* (True Books) (Elaine Landau)
- *The Solar System* (Gregory Vogt)
- *Uranus* (A True Book: Space) (Larry Dane Brimner)
- *Uranus* (Scholastic News Nonfiction Readers) (Christine Taylor-Butler)
- *Uranus* (True Books) (Elaine Landau)
- *Venus* (A True Book: Space) (Larry Dane Brimner)
- *Venus* (Scholastic News Nonfiction Readers) (Melanie Chrismer)

## Nonfiction Books (Read Aloud)

- *11 Planets: A New View of the Solar System* (David A. Aguilar)
- *It's Disgusting and We Ate It! True Food Facts from Around the World and Throughout History* (James Solheim and Eric Brace)
- *Next Stop Neptune: Experiencing the Solar System* (Alvin Jenkins and Steve Jenkins)
- *What the World Eats* (Faith D'Aluisio and Peter Menzel) (E)
- *When Is a Planet Not a Planet? The Story of Pluto* (Elaine Scott)

## References

- Dictionaries
- Online dictionaries
- Online thesauruses
- *Scholastic Dictionary of Idioms* (Revised) (Marvin Terban)
- Thesauruses

## ART, MUSIC, AND MEDIA

*Art*

- Helen Frankenthaler, *Canyon* (1965)
- Helen Frankenthaler, *Wales* (1966)
- Jackson Pollock, *One: Number 31, 1950* (1950)
- Jackson Pollock, *Number 1, 1950 (Lavender Mist)* (1950)
- Morris Louis, *Number 182* (1961)
- Sam Gilliam, *Red Petals* (1967)

# SAMPLE ACTIVITIES AND ASSESSMENTS

*Note:* You may want to do the planets in science at the same time that you are doing fiction/poetry in language arts. The two parts of the unit will come together in the research project at the end of the unit.

## 1. LANGUAGE USAGE, SPEAKING AND LISTENING

Display this list of words with a common Latin suffix (e.g., *-able, -ible, -ation, -fy, -ify, -ment, -ty, -ity*): *likeable, readable, drivable, laughable,* and *teachable.* Ask students, "What does each word have in common with the rest?" (*Answer:* the same Latin suffix, *-able*). Then explain that this is an example of a Latin suffix. Have students use whiteboards to write the root word for each (i.e., *like, read, drive, laugh,* and *teach*). Then ask students, "What part of speech is *read?*" (*Answer:* verb).

Explain that when we add the suffix *-able,* it becomes a different part of speech (i.e., an adjective). Then use the new word in a sentence so that students see the part of speech change. For example, "I was surprised to find that this thick book was very readable." Then explain that *readable* describes the book, which means it's an adjective. Extend this lesson by continuing to collect words that end in *-able* or *-ible.* (RF.3.3b, L.3.2e, L.3.4b)

## 2. LANGUAGE USAGE, VOCABULARY

Have students look up the word *know* in an online thesaurus. Create a horizontal line on the board with *wonder* at one end and *know* at the other. To show shades of meaning, discuss the placement of other state-of-mind words (i.e., the synonyms and antonyms of *know*) on the scale. Repeat this activity with verbs and/or adjectives (such as *warm*) that come up in student reading. (L.3.5c)

## 3. READING POETRY, LANGUAGE USAGE

As you and the students read (recite) poems throughout this unit, ask them to use their journals to collect words that they like. Read aloud a poem such as "I Wandered Lonely as a Cloud" by William Wordsworth several times, modeling fluent reading. Choose an evocative word from the poem because, for example, of the way it sounds, or what it means. Every time the class reads a poem, either together or individually, give the students a few minutes to choose one or two words that they like and then use them in a sentence. (RF.3.4c)

## 4. READING POETRY, READING COMPREHENSION

Use a poem such as "Eating While Reading" by Gary Soto to illustrate how each new line builds meaning on the preceding lines. Have students read multiple poems aloud to each other, explaining their understanding of the poem, line by line and stanza by stanza. (RL.3.5)

## 5. READING LITERATURE, INFORMATIVE WRITING, LANGUAGE USAGE

Read several books that use idioms in the story (e.g., the *Amelia Bedelia* series) or a book that uses idioms as the text (e.g., Terban's work). Then assign the students this prompt: "Choose an idiomatic saying. Draw a picture of the literal and figurative meaning of the saying. Write a short paragraph to explain to someone like Amelia Bedelia why it is important to know what the saying really means." Find examples of more idioms on the Internet. (RL.3.4, RI.3.5, L.3.4a, L.3.5a)

## 6. READING POETRY, READING FLUENCY, PERFORMANCE

Give the students this prompt: "Choose one of the poems in this unit's collection. Memorize it (or read it) and perform it for the class. Be sure to use your best expression as you read." To add a twist to the poetry performance, pair up the students and have them choose a poem with personification, such as "Skyscrapers" by Rachel Field. As one student reads, have the other student play the role of the skyscraper (or the personified object in the poem of choice). (RF.3.4b)

## 7. READING LITERATURE, SPEAKING AND LISTENING

Before this lesson, gather some cubes or building blocks to use as a visual representation. Using a chapter book such as *The Search for Delicious* by Natalie Babbitt or *Frindle* by Andrew Clements and Brian Selznick, use the building blocks to show how the author of a book builds meaning. At the end of each chapter, have students write on sticky notes what they believe is the main idea of the chapter. Place the sticky notes on the board and look to see how well the students comprehended the text, discussing as you read them aloud. After the class comes to consensus, write down the main idea of the chapter on another sticky note and place it on the block. Do this with each chapter (or in each reading session if time prevents you from completing a chapter) to show how events build on each other. If, later in the book, the class realizes (with your guidance) that they have forgotten something important in a previous chapter, go back and revise the building blocks. This will teach the students that good readers tailor their thinking– rethinking the importance of events and ideas–as they read. (RL.3.5, SL.3.2)

## 8. READING INFORMATIONAL TEXT, OPINION WRITING, SPEAKING AND LISTENING

Using a book such as *What the World Eats* by Faith D'Aluisio and Peter Menzel, discuss the differences in the ways people eat around the world. Challenge the students to think critically about nutrition, their eating habits, and the ways other cultures look at food. Use the following questions to guide the discussion:

- What do you think the authors were trying to say in this text?
- Can you support your opinion with evidence from the text?
- How did the illustrations support the ideas in the print part of the text?
- Do you think the authors fairly described the way people in the United States eat?

Finally, assign an opinion writing piece: "In your opinion, do you think there should be laws passed to tell people what they can and cannot eat? Support your answer with strong reasons." (RI.3.2, RI.3.7, SL.3.1a, SL.3.1b, SL.3.1c, SL.3.1d, SL.3.2, W.3.1, L.3.1i, L.3.2)

## 9. INFORMATIVE WRITING, RESEARCH

Give students the following writing task: "Generate questions to answer about a planet other than Earth. Write a report based on the research." Assign each student to complete a research project on a planet other than Earth. Create a display of many books on the planets and have students choose a book with which to start their research. Using the key words *where, when, why,* and *how,* students should begin by creating a list of open-ended questions they want to answer through their research. The generating of questions could happen as a class if students need modeling of the process. To help students with organizing information, give students large index cards with each question on one side and have them write the answers on the other side. When they are finished finding the answers, have them use these cards to help them write a report on the planet. As students revise, they should focus on word choice to make their reports as literary and interesting as possible. Students should create one prop to help explain their most interesting finding about the planet. (L.3.1, L.3.2, L.3.3, L.3.5, W.3.2, W.3.7, W.3.8, W.3.10)

## 10. ART, LANGUAGE USAGE, SPEAKING AND LISTENING

Building on the use of verbs, idioms, and dramatic reading, show the students *One: Number 31, 1950* (Pollock) and *Canyon* (Frankenthaler). Ask students: "What words come to mind when you see these paintings? What words might you use to describe the colors? the texture? What forms do you see? Is there action in the paintings? How so?" Define any of the words used (e.g., *texture, shape, form*). Review the difference between realism and abstraction. (L.3.1, L.3.3, L.3.5, SL.3.1, SL.3.3)

## 11. ART, OPINION WRITING

Compare Gilliam with Louis. Both artists were concerned with and interested in truly combining paint with canvas. Ask students: "Why do you think each artist chose these colors? Do you think he or she meant to make it look like this, or is it random? How do these paintings make you feel? Write a brief paragraph answering these questions." (W.3.1)

## ADDITIONAL ONLINE RESOURCES

- *Figurative Language: Teaching Idioms* (ReadWriteThink) (L.3.5a)
- *Dancing Minds and Shouting Smiles: Teaching Personification Through Poetry* (ReadWriteThink) (RL.3.5)
- *Delicious, Tasty, Yummy: Enriching Writing with Adjectives and Synonyms* (ReadWriteThink) (W.3.5)
- *Martian Real Estate: A Good Investment?* (National Geographic) (W.3.7)
- *The Idiom Dictionary*

## TERMINOLOGY

Idiom

Latin suffixes

Thesaurus

Word roots

## INTERDISCIPLINARY CONNECTIONS

This unit teaches:

- **Art:** Abstract painting (e.g., Jackson Pollock, Helen Frankenthaler, Sam Gilliam, Morris Louis)
- **Geography:** World geography (e.g., continents and countries)
- **Science:** The solar system (i.e., the planets)

This unit could be extended to teach:

- **Science:** Astronomy (e.g., the universe, galaxies, orienteering, and exploration of space)

## Grade Three, Unit Five Sample Lesson Plan

### *"Eating While Reading"* by Gary Soto

In this series of three lessons, students read "Eating While Reading" by Gary Soto, and they:

Examine the form of the poem (RL.3.5)

Explore the content of the poem (RL.3.1, RL.3.2)

Write poems triggered by Soto's "Eating While Reading" (W.3.3)

Explore the use of a poem as an inspiration to write another poem (SL.3.6)

## Summary

### Lesson I: "Eating While Reading"

Explore the form of the poem (RL.3.5)

Note the use of punctuation (RL.3.5)

Examine the purpose of the repetitions (RL.3.5)

Examine the change between the first and the second question (RL.3.1, SL.3.2, SL.3.3)

Consider the title of the poem (SL.3.2)

Discuss the message of the speaker (RL.3.3)

### Lesson II: Writing Triggered Poems

Revisit "Eating While Reading" (RL.3.1)

Initiate ideas for personal poems using Soto's opening lines as a trigger: ("What is better/than this song/And a walk in the park...") (SL.3.6)

Compose a poem (W.3.3)

Rewrite the poem (W.3.5)

### Lesson III: Sharing Poems

Revisit personal poems

Share results (SL.3.6)

Explore the use of a poem as an inspiration to write another poem (SL.3.6)

## Lesson I: "Eating While Reading"

### Objectives

Explore the form of the poem (RL.3.5)

Note the use of punctuation (L.3.2)

Examine the purpose of the repetitions (RL.3.5)

Examine the change between the first and the second question (RL.3.1, SL.3.2, SL.3.3)

Consider the title of the poem (SL.3.2)

Discuss the message of the speaker (RL.3.3)

### Required Materials

☐ Copies of the poem "Eating While Reading" by Gary Soto

☐ Large copy of "Eating While Reading" by Gary Soto

☐ (*Recommended*: Add numbers to the lines of the poem.)

### Procedures

1. Lead-In:

   After the students receive copies of the poem "Eating While Reading" by Gary Soto, student volunteers read the poem aloud.

   The poem should be read at least twice.

2. Step by Step:

   a. Prompt the students as they explore the form of the poem:

      ○ There is only one stanza; when you read the poem, what is the impact of a single stanza?

      ○ Are there different parts of the poem, even though there are no stanzas?

      ○ The line "What is better" repeats. Why?

      ○ The list that follows "Or the . . ." occurs five times. What is its purpose?

      ○ Why are there two question marks?

      During the class discussion, students refer to the text. The numbered lines and the large copy on the board facilitate the reading.

b. The final prompt offers a transition to the next step, which is a close examination of the beginning of the two questions:

"What is better

Than this book . . . ?"

and the second:

"What is better than this sweet dance

On the tongue . . . ?"

Students discuss the difference between the two questions ("book"/"sweet dance").

c. The final two lines of the poem present a transition to a discussion about the content of the poem. Students then consider the title of the poem and ask, "What is the poem about?"

3. Closure:

Students volunteer to reread the poem aloud.

## Differentiation

### Advanced

- Using a thesaurus, students think of new and challenging words that would fit in Gary Soto's poem (i.e., words to be substituted for "churn," "crack," "swig," "twist," "slither," and "sticky"). Students create a "revised" poem using their newly discovered words. Students share the poem with the rest of the class.

### Struggling

(Following the Lead-In for this lesson, do this activity with a small group or the whole class.)

- Focus on the vivid words in this poem by allowing different students to experience them (i.e., the "churn" of a chewy candy, the "balloon" of bubble gum, the "crack" of sunflower seeds).
- Display favorite class books. Students discuss the feelings they had when it was time to read the next chapter.

## Homework/Assessment

N/A

# Fantastic Adventures with Dragons, Gods, and Giants

In this sixth six-week unit of third grade, students read fantasies, adventure poetry, mythology, and informational texts about ancient Greece and ancient Rome.

## ESSENTIAL QUESTION

Why is it important to know mythology?

## OVERVIEW

Beginning with fantasy stories and poems about dragons, students learn to summarize and illustrate chapters, seeing how they are building blocks to the ending. They record themselves reading fluently an assigned chapter (i.e., with a video camera or tape recorder). They combine the recording with their illustrated chapter summaries to create a multimedia presentation. They will also hear a variety of myths, both Greek and Roman, and read a book based on Homer's *The Odyssey*. Finally, students will research an Olympic sport and compare it to an Olympic sport in the days of ancient Greece.

## FOCUS STANDARDS

These Focus Standards have been selected for the unit from the Common Core State Standards.

**RI.3.10:** By the end of year, read and comprehend informational texts, including history/social studies, science, and technical texts, at the high end of the grades 2–3 text complexity band independently and proficiently.

**RF.3.4:** Read with sufficient accuracy and fluency to support comprehension.

**RF.3.4(c):** Use context to confirm or self-correct word recognition and understanding, rereading as necessary.

**RL.3.2:** Recount stories, including fables, folktales, and myths from diverse cultures; determine the central message, lesson, or moral and explain how it is conveyed through key details in the text.

**RL.3.6:** Distinguish their own point of view from that of the narrator or those of the characters.

**RL.3.10:** By the end of the year, read and comprehend literature, including stories, dramas, and poetry, at the high end of the grades 2–3 text complexity band independently and proficiently.

**SL.3.5:** Create engaging audio recordings of stories or poems that demonstrate fluid reading at an understandable pace; add visual displays when appropriate to emphasize or enhance certain facts or details.

## SUGGESTED OBJECTIVES

- Independently read books in the grade 2–3 stretch text range with fluency and comprehension.
- Summarize and illustrate the chapters of a book (e.g., *My Father's Dragon* by Ruth Stiles Gannett and Ruth Chrisman Gannett).
- Create an audio recording of a dramatic reading of a chapter in a challenging chapter book.
- Create a multimedia presentation (e.g., a set of slides) of the recording and the illustrations of the book summaries.
- Write an opinion piece describing the "most interesting" mythical character.
- Retell myths with key details, noting the message of each.
- Quote from the text to support the main idea of a nonfiction book.
- Read a variety of informational books on ancient Greece and ancient Rome.
- Research a current Olympic sport, comparing and contrasting it to a sport in the days of ancient Greece.
- Write a short fantasy narrative.

## SUGGESTED WORKS

(E) indicates a CCSS exemplar text; (EA) indicates a text from a writer with other works identified as exemplars.

## LITERARY TEXTS

*Stories (Read Aloud)*

- *Classic Myths to Read Aloud: The Great Stories of Greek and Roman Mythology* (William F. Russell)
- *Could Be Worse!* (James Stevenson)
- *D'Aulaires' Book of Greek Myths* (Ingri d'Aulaire and Edgar Parin d'Aulaire)
- *Favorite Greek Myths* (Mary Pope Osborne and Troy Howell)
- *The Gods and Goddesses of Olympus* (Aliki)
- *Greek Myths for Young Children* (Heather Amery and Linda Edwards)
- *My Father's Dragon* (Ruth Stiles Gannett and Ruth Chrisman Gannett)

- *The One-Eyed Giant* (Mary Pope Osborne and Troy Howell)
- *The Orchard Book of Roman Myths* (Geraldine McCaughrean and Emma Chichester)

## Poems

- "Adventures of Isabel" (Ogden Nash)
- "A Dragon's Lament" (Jack Prelutsky)
- *The Dragons Are Singing Tonight* (Jack Prelutsky)
- "Life Doesn't Frighten Me" (Maya Angelou)
- "The Tale of Custard the Dragon" (Ogden Nash) (Read Aloud)

# INFORMATIONAL TEXTS

## Nonfiction Books

- *Ancient Greece and the Olympics: A Nonfiction Companion to Magic Treehouse #16: Hour of the Olympics* (Magic Tree House Research Guide #10) (Mary Pope Osborne, Natalie Pope Boyce, and Sal Murdocca) (EA)
- *Ancient Rome and Pompeii: A Nonfiction Companion to Magic Treehouse #13: Vacation Under the Volcano* (Magic Tree House Research Guide #14) (Mary Pope Osborne, Natalie Pope Boyce, and Sal Murdocca) (EA)
- *Boy, Were We Wrong About Dinosaurs!* (Kathleen V. Kudlinski and S. D. Schindler) (E)
- *If I Were a Kid in Ancient Greece* (ed. Ken Sheldon)
- *Rome: In Spectacular Cross Section* (Andrew Solway and Stephen Biesty)

## Nonfiction Books (Read Aloud)

### Greece

- *Ancient Greece* (DK Eyewitness Books) (Anne Pearson)
- *I Wonder Why Greeks Built Temples: and Other Questions About Ancient Greece* (Fiona MacDonald)
- *If I Were a Kid in Ancient Greece: Children of the Ancient World* (ed. Ken Sheldon)

### Rome

- *Ancient Rome* (DK Eyewitness Books) (Simon James)
- *If I Were a Kid in Ancient Rome: Children of the Ancient World* (ed. Ken Sheldon)
- *Science in Ancient Rome* (Jacqueline L. Harris)
- *Tools of the Ancient Romans: A Kid's Guide to the History & Science of Life in Ancient Rome* (Rachel Dickinson)

# ART, MUSIC, AND MEDIA

## Art

- The Colosseum, Rome, Italy (80 CE)
- Greek and Roman art collection (The Metropolitan Museum of Art)
- The Parthenon, Athenian Acropolis, Greece (438 BCE)

## SAMPLE ACTIVITIES AND ASSESSMENTS

Note: If you choose to begin with *My Father's Dragon* by Ruth Stiles Gannett and Ruth Chrisman Gannett, it will create a transition to the adventures in *The One-Eyed Giant* by Mary Pope Osborne and Troy Howell. Because there is so much literature in the mythology of ancient Greece, you may want to spend a week or two on the Gannetts' book and then move on to the mythology for the remainder of the unit. Because this may be the first time that students are introduced to myths, it is helpful to keep a list of the mythological gods, creatures, and characters as you read. By focusing on the outstanding characteristic (e.g., strength as represented by Heracles/Hercules) or domain (e.g., the sea, ruled by Poseidon) of each, students will begin to see the foundational role played by these names and places in word derivations.

### 1. READING LITERATURE, READING INFORMATIONAL TEXT, INFORMATIVE WRITING

Give students this writing task: "While reading a chapter book such as *My Father's Dragon*, write a summary of each chapter and illustrate it. Compile the chapter summaries for an abridged version of the book." As students read the book *My Father's Dragon* by Ruth Stiles Gannett and Ruth Chrisman Gannett, focus on how each chapter builds on the last to tell the story. As students finish each chapter, have them write down a short summary of what happened and illustrate it with a drawing. Have the students turn this into a mini-book of the larger book. As students write their summaries in this activity, you could teach a strategy for writing succinct summaries, such as "Somebody-Wanted-But-So." (RL.3.10, RF.3.4c, L.3.1, L.3.2, L.3.3)

### 2. READING FLUENCY, PERFORMANCE

As a class, create a set of audio recordings of the book *My Father's Dragon* by Ruth Stiles Gannett and Ruth Chrisman Gannett. Using the illustrations from the chapter summaries (see Activity 1), assign to each student a chapter to rehearse reading aloud. With a video camera or tape recorder, have students record themselves reading a chapter in their best reading voice, interpreting the parts of each character. To extend this fluency activity, choose poems to read (recite) interpretively and record. (SL.3.5, RL.3.10, RF.3.4c)

### 3. OPINION WRITING, LANGUAGE USAGE

Give the students this prompt: "Choose the most interesting mythical character. Support your opinion with strong evidence from the texts you have read and connect your writing to specific parts of the myth. Be sure also to use linking words and phrases (e.g., *because, therefore, since,* and *for example*) to connect your opinion and reasons. Provide a concluding statement." (RL.3.2, W.3.1, W.3.1c, L.3.1)

### 4. READING LITERATURE, READING COMPREHENSION, SPEAKING AND LISTENING

After reading each of the myths, have students retell the story with as many key details as they can. Have them partner to retell, helping the partner when he or she forgets what came next. Discuss the following prompts/questions as a class, or have them write down their thoughts for more independent thinking and accountability before discussing as a group.

- As we read the myth and as we retell the stories, let's think about the message in the myth.

- Why was the myth told during the time of the ancient Greeks?

- Why is it still told today? (RL.3.2, SL.3.2, L.3.1, L.3.2, L.3.3)

## 5. READING INFORMATIONAL TEXT, SPEAKING AND LISTENING

Introduce the book *Boy, Were We Wrong About Dinosaurs!* by Kathleen V. Kudlinski and S. D. Schindler by explaining that this book will teach them how scientists sometimes change their thinking after new evidence is collected. Tell students that in the discussion after reading, they should be prepared to share two different specific places in the book where this happened. Have them write down their thoughts on a whiteboard or a sticky note. (RI.3.2, RI.3.10, RF.3.4c, SL.3.1a)

## 6. READING INFORMATIONAL TEXT, RESEARCH, MULTIMEDIA PRESENTATION

Read a variety of nonfiction texts on the first Olympic games in ancient Greece. Then give the students this prompt: "Using online resources, research one sport from the most recent summer Olympics. Tell how it is similar and how it is different from the first games. Create a teaching poster or multimedia slide and report orally on your learning." (RI.3.5, W.3.6, W.3.7, SL.3.4, L.3.2, L.3.3)

## 7. READING LITERATURE, NARRATIVE WRITING, SPEAKING AND LISTENING

Lead a class discussion based on *Could Be Worse!* by James Stevenson using the following prompts/questions:

- How do you think the children felt when they tried to tell the grandfather of an adventure and he always topped it with a fantastic tale?
- If you were the grandfather, what story would you have told?
- Write a fantastic grandfather response to this: "I fell off the monkey bars on the playground and scraped my knee." (RL.3.6, W.3.3, W.3.10, L.3.1, L.3.2, L.3.3)

## 8. ART, SPEAKING AND LISTENING

Introduce some of the art held in the Greek and Roman collections at the Metropolitan Museum of Art. Then lead a discussion about how the students see the mythology influencing ancient Greek and Roman art. In particular, discuss the relationship between the stories of the people (myths) and the inspiration for artistic pieces. (RL.3.2)

## 9. ART, SPEAKING AND LISTENING

Compare images of the Colosseum and the Parthenon. Explain that one of these buildings was used for contests, battles, and dramas based on mythology. The other was used as a place of worship as well as a treasury, dedicated to a special goddess known as Athena. Can you tell which building was which, just by looking at them? What would you need to know in order to tell the difference? (SL.3.1, SL.3.3)

## 10. ART, SPEAKING AND LISTENING

Ask students what they notice first about the architecture of each building. What features do the buildings have in common? The Parthenon was built many years before the Colosseum—what traditions were carried into Roman society in terms of architectural style? What didn't the Romans do that the Greeks did on their colossal building? (SL.3.1, SL.3.3)

## ADDITIONAL ONLINE RESOURCES

- *Powerful Writing: Description in Creating Monster Trading Cards* (ReadWriteThink) (L.3.1a, RL.3.2)
- *It Came from Greek Mythology* (National Endowment for the Humanities) (RL.3.2)
- Folklore and mythology electronic texts

## TERMINOLOGY

Fantasy

Mythology

Narrative poem

Summary

## INTERDISCIPLINARY CONNECTIONS

This unit teaches:

- **Art:** Ancient Greek and Roman art (e.g., the Parthenon, the Colosseum)
- **History:** Ancient Greece (e.g., the Olympics and life in ancient Greece) and ancient Rome (e.g., Roman mythology, government, and life)

This unit could be extended to teach:

- **History:** Vikings (e.g., Norse mythology, Norsemen, and Leif Ericson)

## Grade Three, Unit Six Sample Lesson Plan

*"Adventures of Isabel" by Ogden Nash*

In this series of three lessons, students read "Adventures of Isabel" by Ogden Nash, and they:

- Identify the stanzas of the poem (RL.3.5, SL.1.1)
- Explore the story in each stanza (RL.3.1, RL.3.5, SL.3.1)
- Visualize the adventures of Isabel (SL.3.5)
- Illustrate the adventures of Isabel (SL.3.5)

## Summary

### Lesson I: "Adventures of Isabel"

Consider the content of the four stanzas (RL.3.1, RL.3.5, SL.3.1)

(In groups) select one of the four stanzas

(In groups) examine the progression of the stanza (RL.3.1, RL.3.5, SL.3.1)

### Lesson III: "Adventures of Isabel" Illustrated

Display the illustrations (from Lesson II)

Examine the illustrations (RL. 3.7)

Reflect on the process (SL.3.4)

### Lesson II: Illustrating the Poem

(In groups) recall the details of the assigned stanza (RL.3.1, RL.3.5, SL.3.1)

(In groups) note specific scenes in the stanza (RL.3.5)

Illustrate a select scene (SL.3.5)

### Lesson II: Illustrating the Poem
*Objectives*

(In groups) recall the details of the assigned stanza (RL.3.1, RL.3.5, SL.3.1)

(In groups) note specific scenes in the stanza (RL.3.5)

Illustrate a select scene (SL.3.5)

*Required Materials*

☐ Copies of "Adventures of Isabel" by Ogden Nash (not illustrated)

☐ Colored pencils and markers

☐ Drawing paper

*Procedures*

1. Lead-In:

    Reread "Adventures of Isabel."

2. Step by Step:

    a. In groups from the previous lesson, students revisit the stanza that they were assigned. They explore the specific details that they will illustrate. For example: The first stanza depicts the bear as "enormous" and says that it has a "cavernous" mouth. Isabel "wash[es] her hands" and she "straighten[s] her hair up."

    b. Students draw select scenes from their assigned stanza.

3. Closure:

    Student volunteers read "Adventures of Isabel" aloud.

Differentiation

*Advanced*

• In a small group, students explore the use of the thesaurus by choosing five new vocabulary words from the poem.

• Each student looks up one word, finding five new similar words for each of the original five words.

• If time allows, students could take one of those new words and create a scale showing the words in order of intensity. For example, a scale for *scurry* might look like this: – *scamper – bustle – hasten – tear – zip*

*Struggling*

- Students will focus on vocabulary by comparing/contrasting vocabulary words. For example, the description of the bear's hunger in stanza one uses *hungry* and then *ravenous*.
- Write both words on a whiteboard.
- Students discuss how the words are the same and how they are different.
- Words and/or phrases to compare could include *cruel/cavernous, scream/scurry, rage/rancor, hairy/horrid, punched/poked, coughs/chills.*

Homework/Assessment

N/A

# Grade 4

Fourth grade is an important time of transition in elementary school. At this point, students have learned the fundamentals of reading and writing, have read and listened to many stories and poems from a range of cultures, and have learned about a variety of historical and scientific topics, as well as myths. They now begin to consider the nature of literature—its forms, themes, and relation to nonfiction—as they write essays, speeches, reports, and stories. In the unit Tales of the Heart, students consider how stories reveal what we have in common. Next, students look at geography as it relates to seasons and weather, and how these settings are represented in literature. Later in the year, students compare fictional and nonfictional portrayals of animals; investigate the scientific aspects of science fiction; read literature from America's past, in particular the American Revolution; compare narratives and informational texts about earth and sky; and consider what heroes have in common. The units draw connections among literature and other subjects, including history, science, geography, and art. Conducting research in libraries and online, students prepare and deliver persuasive speeches and compare differing accounts of historical events. Throughout the year, they study vocabulary from different subject areas and begin to learn about word roots. By the end of fourth grade, students can explain how fictional and nonfictional accounts reveal different aspects of reality. They have learned to draw connections between literary form and meaning, identify common themes in stories from many cultures, and write short essays on a variety of topics.

# Standards Checklist for Grade Four

| Standard | Unit 1 | Unit 2 | Unit 3 | Unit 4 | Unit 5 | Unit 6 |
|---|---|---|---|---|---|---|
| **Reading–Literature** | | | | | | |
| 1 | A | FA | A | A | A | |
| 2 | FA | A | A | A | A | A |
| 3 | A | FA | A | A | A | A |
| 4 | A | A | A | A | A | FA |
| 5 | A | A | FA | A | A | A |
| 6 | A | | A | FA | | A |
| 7 | | A | | A | | |
| 8 n/a | | | | | | |
| 9 | | | A | A | FA | A |
| 10 | A | | | | | A |
| **Reading–Informational Text** | | | | | | |
| 1 | FA | A | A | A | A | A |
| 2 | A | A | FA | A | | |
| 3 | A | FA | | | A | |
| 4 | | A | A | | | A |
| 5 | | A | A | FA | | |
| 6 | A | A | | FA | | |
| 7 | | A | A | A | FA | |
| 8 | A | | | | A | FA |
| 9 | A | A | A | A | A | A |
| 10 | | | | | | A |
| **Writing** | | | | | | |
| 1 | | | A | FA | A | FA |
| 1a | | | A | A | | |
| 1b | | | A | | | |
| 1c | | | A | A | | |
| 1d | | | A | A | | |
| 2 | FA | A | | A | A | A |
| 2a | FA | | A | | | |
| 2b | FA | | A | | | |
| 2c | | | A | | | |
| 2d | A | | | | | |
| 3 | | A | F | | FA | |
| 3a | A | | | | | |
| 3b | A | A | | | | |
| 3c | | | | | | |
| 3d | | | | | | |
| 3e | | | | | | |
| 4 | A | A | A | A | A | A |
| 5 | A | | A | A | A | A |
| 6 | | | A | A | A | |
| 7 | A | FA | A | A | A | A |
| 8 | | | A | A | A | A |
| 9 | A | A | A | | | |
| 9a | A | A | A | A | A | A |
| 9b | A | A | A | A | A | A |
| 10 | | | | | | A |

| Standard | Unit 1 | Unit 2 | Unit 3 | Unit 4 | Unit 5 | Unit 6 |
|---|---|---|---|---|---|---|
| **Speaking and Listening** | | | | | | |
| 1 | FA | FA | A | A | A | A |
| 1a | FA | A | | A | | A |
| 1b | FA | | | A | | |
| 1c | | FA | | | | |
| 1d | | FA | | | | |
| 2 | | | | | A | FA |
| 3 | | A | | FA | A | A |
| 4 | A | A | | A | FA | A |
| 5 | A | A | FA | A | A | A |
| 6 | | | | | | A |
| **Language** | | | | | | |
| 1 | A | | A | A | A | A |
| 1a | A | A | A | A | A | |
| 1b | | | A | A | | |
| 1c | | A | A | A | | |
| 1d | | A | A | A | | |
| 1e | | | | A | | |
| 1f | | | | | | |
| 1g | A | A | A | A | | |
| 2 | A | | A | A | A | A |
| 2a | A | A | A | | A | |
| 2b | | A | A | | | |
| 2c | | | A | | | |
| 2d | | | | | | |
| 3 | | | A | A | FA | A |
| 3a | A | | | | | |
| 3b | | | | A | A | |
| 3c | | | A | | | |
| 4 | F | | | FA | A | A |
| 4a | FA | A | A | A | A | A |
| 4b | | | A | A | A | |
| 4c | | | | | A | A |
| 5 | | F | FA | A | A | A |
| 5a | A | FA | A | | | |
| 5b | | | FA | A | | |
| 5c | | | FA | | | |
| 6 | | | | | | FA |
| **Reading Foundations** | | | | | | |
| 1 n/a | | | | | | |
| 2 n/a | | | | | | |
| 3 | FA | | | | | |
| 3a | FA | | | | | |
| 4 | A | F | F | | | |
| 4a | | FA | | | | |
| 4b | | FA | | | | |
| 4c | | | FA | | | |

F = Focus Standards; A = Activity/Assessment

# Tales of the Heart

This four-week unit invites students to explore the mixture of emotions that accompany the transition to fourth grade, as well as to learn from informational text about the body.

---

## ESSENTIAL QUESTION

How do stories reveal what we have in common?

---

## OVERVIEW

Students examine emotions, beginning with a traditional favorite, Judy Blume's *Tales of a Fourth Grade Nothing* and continuing with Sharon Creech's *Love That Dog*, Grace Nichols's poem "They Were My People," and the traditional "Monday's Child Is Fair of Face." *Harriet the Spy* by Louise Fitzhugh is the suggested read aloud for this unit because, just as Harriet writes everything down in her journal, students keep a journal of what they learn throughout the year. Nonfiction text about body systems is supplemented with nonfiction biographies of doctors. Students summarize fiction and nonfiction texts, write informative/explanatory pieces, and engage in collaborative discussions—all skills that will be used throughout the fourth-grade year. Finally, this unit ends with a class discussion and paragraph response to the essential question.

## FOCUS STANDARDS

These Focus Standards have been selected for the unit from the Common Core State Standards.

**RL.4.2:** Determine a theme of a story, drama, or poem from details in the text; summarize the text.

**RI.4.1:** Refer to details and examples in a text when explaining what the text says explicitly and when drawing inferences from the text.

**RF.4.3:** Know and apply grade-level phonics and word analysis skills in decoding words.

**RF.4.3(a):** Use combined knowledge of all letter-sound correspondences, syllabication patterns, and morphology (e.g., roots and affixes) to read accurately unfamiliar multisyllabic words in context and out of context.

**W.4.2:** Write informative/explanatory texts to examine a topic and convey ideas and information clearly.

**W.4.2(a):** Introduce a topic clearly and group related information in paragraphs and sections; include formatting (e.g., headings), illustrations, and multimedia when useful to aid comprehension.

**W.4.2(b):** Develop the topic with facts, definitions, concrete details, quotations, or other information and examples related to the topic.

**SL.4.1:** Engage effectively in a range of collaborative discussions (one-on-one, in groups, and teacher-led) with diverse partners on grade 4 topics and texts, building on others' ideas and expressing their own clearly.

**SL.4.1(a):** Come to discussions prepared, having read or studied required material; explicitly draw on that preparation and other information known about the topic to explore ideas under discussion.

**SL.4.1(b):** Follow agreed-upon rules for discussions and carry out assigned roles.

**L.4.4:** Determine or clarify the meaning of unknown and multiple-meaning words and phrases based on grade 4 reading and content, choosing flexibly from a range of strategies.

**L.4.4(a):** Use context (e.g., definitions, examples, or restatements in text) as a clue to the meaning of a word or phrase.

## SUGGESTED OBJECTIVES

- Find similarities and differences in story characters, and how they change over the course of a story.
- Write a variety of responses to stories and poems using coherent paragraphs.
- Research a famous doctor or scientist and write a bio-poem (i.e., a biography in poem form) about him or her.
- Recite poetry for classmates.
- Become more fluent in the use of terminology related to poetry.
- Begin to make connections between poetic/literary devices and the theme of a story, drama, or poem.

## SUGGESTED WORKS

(E) indicates a CCSS exemplar text; (EA) indicates a text from a writer with other works identified as exemplars.

### LITERARY TEXTS

*Stories*

- *Clarice Bean Spells Trouble* (Lauren Child)
- *Fourth Grade Rats* (Jerry Spinelli)
- *Harriet the Spy* (Louise Fitzhugh) (Read Aloud)

- *Just Juice* (Karen Hesse and Robert Andre Parker)
- *Love That Dog* (Joanna Cotler Books) (Sharon Creech) (EA)
- *Porch Lies: Tales of Slicksters, Tricksters, and Other Wily Characters* (Patricia McKissack and Andre Carrilho)
- *Red Ridin' in the Hood: and Other Cuentos* (Patricia Santos Marcantonio and Renato Alarcáo)
- *Tales of a Fourth Grade Nothing* (Judy Blume)

## Poems

- "Dreams" (Langston Hughes) (EA)
- "The Drum" (Nikki Giovanni)
- *Honey, I Love: And Other Love Poems* (Eloise Greenfield and Leo and Diane Dillon)
- "Humanity" (Elma Stuckey)
- "Monday's Child Is Fair of Face" (Mother Goose)
- "On the Way to School" (Charles Ghigna)
- "They Were My People" (Grace Nichols) (E)

# INFORMATIONAL TEXTS

## Nonfiction Books

- *The ABCs of Asthma: An Asthma Alphabet Book for Kids of All Ages* (Kim Gosselin and Terry Ravanelli)
- *The Amazing Circulatory System: How Does My Heart Work?* (John Burstein)
- *The Circulatory System* (A True Book) (Darlene R. Stille)
- *The Circulatory System* (Kristin Petrie)
- *The Endocrine System* (Rebecca Olien)
- *The Exciting Endocrine System: How Do My Glands Work?* (John Burstein)
- *Grossology and You: Really Gross Things About Your Body* (Sylvia Branzei and Jack Keely)
- *The Heart and Circulation* (Exploring the Human Body) (Carol Ballard)
- *The Heart: Our Circulatory System* (Seymour Simon)
- *I Wonder Why I Blink: And Other Questions About My Body* (Brigid Avison)
- *Lungs: Your Respiratory System* (Seymour Simon)
- *The Remarkable Respiratory System: How Do My Lungs Work?* (John Burstein)
- *The Respiratory System* (A True Book) (Darlene R. Stille)
- *The Respiratory System* (Susan Glass)
- *The Respiratory System* (Kristin Petrie)
- *Skin Like Milk, Hair of Silk: What Are Similes and Metaphors?* (Words Are Categorical) (Brian P. Cleary)
- *What Makes You Cough, Sneeze, Burp, Hiccup, Blink, Yawn, Sweat, and Shiver?* (My Health) (Jean Stangl)

## Biographies

- *100 African Americans Who Shaped History* (chapter on Daniel Hale Williams) (Chrisanne Beckner)
- *Charles Drew: Doctor Who Got the World Pumped Up to Donate Blood* (Getting to Know the World's Greatest Inventors and Scientists) (Mike Venezia) (Read Aloud)
- *Clara Barton* (History Maker Bios) (Candice F. Ransom)
- *Elizabeth Blackwell: Girl Doctor* (Childhood of Famous Americans) (Joanne Landers Henry)
- *The Mayo Brothers: Doctors to the World* (Community Builders) (Lucile Davis) (Read Aloud)

## ART, MUSIC, AND MEDIA

### Art

- Alexander Calder, *Untitled* (1976)
- *Dying Gaul* in Rome, Italy (230 BCE–220 BCE)
- Giotto di Bondone, *Lamentation* (1305–1306)
- Jean-Honoré Fragonard, *The Swing* (1766)
- Pablo Picasso, *Guernica* (1937)
- Vincent van Gogh, *Portrait of Dr. Gachet* (1890)

## SAMPLE ACTIVITIES AND ASSESSMENTS

### 1. READING LITERATURE, SPEAKING AND LISTENING

As a class, when we read stories and poems, we will keep a chart with information organized by the categories listed below. As the chart is filled in, we will use the information to talk about what we learned from literature.

- Title and author
- Type of literature (story or poem)
- Main character(s)
- Problem
- Solution
- Summary (using the "Somebody-Wanted-But-So" strategy)

Write your own response on a sticky note, on a whiteboard, or in your journal and share it with a partner before each section of the class chart is filled in. (RF.4.3a, RL.4.1, RL.4.2, RL.4.5, L.4.4a)

### 2. READING LITERATURE, SPEAKING AND LISTENING

Compare and contrast what is the same and what is different about characters, problems, and solutions in literature. Does any of this remind you of experiences you've had? Turn and talk about your ideas with a partner. Then look back for specific lines or paragraphs from the stories and poems we have read that describe what you mean. (RL.4.2, SL.4.1a, SL.4.1b)

## 3. READING INFORMATIONAL TEXT, RESEARCH, VOCABULARY

As a class, keep a chart of information about the respiratory, circulatory, and endocrine systems. As the chart is filled in, use open-ended research questions to select the most useful and relevant information to include in a discussion about related information in nonfiction books.

- The body system
- What does it do?
- What are its parts?
- What are some interesting facts?
- What are the words we should know? (e.g., *cardiology, pulmonology*)

Write your own response on a sticky note, on a whiteboard, or in your journal and share it with a partner before each section of the class chart is filled in. (RI.4.1, RI.4.2, RI.4.4, RI.4.9, L.4.4a, RF.4.3a)

## 4. INFORMATIVE WRITING, LANGUAGE USAGE

As a follow-up to completing the chart on the respiratory, circulatory, and endocrine systems (found in the previous Reading Informational Text, Research, and Vocabulary activity), choose a system about which to write a well-developed essay that includes at least two supporting details and a summary of how these systems are interrelated. Before turning in your essay, edit your work for correct capitalization, use of relative pronouns and adverbs, and homophones (see Standards for more details). (W.4.9a, W.4.9b, W.4.4, L.4.1a, L.4.1g, L.4.2a)

## 5. INFORMATIVE WRITING

Following a class discussion of each body system and the similarities and differences between them, be ready to write in your journal about each system and how they work together, citing evidence from what you have read. (SL.4.1a, SL.4.1b, W.4.2a, W.4.2b, W.4.4, W.4.7, L.4.1a, L.4.1g, L.4.2a)

## 6. READING LITERATURE

Jack changes from the beginning to the end of *Love That Dog* by Sharon Creech. Create a two-column chart in your journal with two headings: "Beginning of School Year" and "End of School Year." Under each heading, list examples of the things Jack does, thinks, and says at the beginning of the year compared to the end of the year. What do you think Jack can teach you about yourself? (RL.4.1, RL.4.3)

## 7. READING POETRY, WRITING POETRY

Not only do poets use a variety of verses, rhyme schemes, and meters, but they use specific techniques to make their poems unique. Find examples of rhyme schemes, alliteration, similes, and metaphors in *Love That Dog* by Sharon Creech and other poems read in this unit. As a class, create a T-chart that includes the name of the technique and examples of each. Mark your poems with sticky notes so you can easily reference the examples you found when it's time for class discussion. Finally, try to write your own poem that imitates a poet of choice. (RL.4.4, L.4.5a, W.4.4)

## 8. NARRATIVE WRITING, SPEAKING AND LISTENING

How do Peter's experiences in *Tales of a Fourth Grade Nothing* by Judy Blume remind you of your family? Talk with a partner and share your ideas. Then write a short story about a family member and share it with the same partner. Ask your partner to tell you what they like and what could be improved (for example, if a specific section needs more details to be clear). Your teacher may ask you to type your story and possibly draw and scan an illustration for publication on the class web page. (W.4.3a, W.4.3b, W.4.4, W.4.5)

## 9. READING INFORMATIONAL TEXT, RESEARCH, WRITING POETRY, MULTIMEDIA PRESENTATION

Read a biography and other informational text about famous doctors and scientists. Generate several open-ended research questions to guide your research. Write a bio-poem about the person that includes important facts you think your classmates should know. Include audio or visual displays in your presentation, as appropriate. Share your poem with your class. Before turning in your poem, edit your work for correct capitalization, use of relative pronouns and adverbs, and homophones (see Standards for more details). Your teacher may ask you to type your poem and insert a picture of the person from the Internet for publication on the class web page. (RI.4.1, RI.4.6, RI.4.8, RI.4.9, W.4.2d, W.4.7, SL.4.4, SL.4.5, L.4.1a, L.4.1g, L.4.2a)

## 10. READING POETRY, READING FLUENCY, PERFORMANCE

Choose one of the poems from this unit, such as "They Were My People" by Grace Nichols, to read and discuss with a partner. Perform the poem as a duet with a classmate. Record the readings using a video camera for future reference and to see how your fluency improves during the course of the year. (RF.4.3a)

## 11. VOCABULARY, LANGUAGE USAGE

Words that share roots are related in their meanings. As an individual and as a class, keep an index card file of new words learned in this unit (e.g., *cardiovascular, cardiac, cardiology; pulmonology, pulmonologist*). Keeping the words on index cards will allow you to use and sort the words by meaning and spelling features. (Note: This will be an ongoing activity all year long.) You may also be asked to work in groups to create semantic maps of the body systems in order to explore your understanding of the interconnectedness of the body systems. (RI.4.6, L.4.4a)

## 12. ART, SPEAKING AND LISTENING

View each of the images and try to identify the emotion that the artist wanted to impart to the viewer. Compare the *Dying Gaul* with the *Lamentation*. What did the artists want you to feel? Next, look at *The Swing*. How is this different? What elements of the artists' painting styles, color palettes, or details did they include that help to convey these emotions? Is it the subject matter that mostly conveys the emotions, or is it the artists' way of presenting it? (SL.4.1)

## 13. ART, SPEAKING AND LISTENING

Review the elements of art (e.g., line, color, texture, shape, form). Identify and describe these in Picasso's *Guernica* and van Gogh's *Portrait of Dr. Gachet*. How did these artists use formal elements to convey emotion in these works? (SL.4.1)

## 14. SPEAKING AND LISTENING, INFORMATIVE WRITING

As a class, summarize what was learned in this unit as it relates to the essential question "How do stories reveal what we have in common?" Following the class discussion, write your response in your journal. Edit your work for correct capitalization, use of relative pronouns and adverbs, and homophones (see Standards for more details) before sharing it with your teacher.

Your teacher may ask you to type your essay and respond to a poll about the unit on the classroom blog. (W.4.4, W.4.9a, W.4.9b, L.4.1a, L.4.1g, L.4.2a)

## 15. LANGUAGE USAGE

Your teacher will teach mini-lessons on the individual language standards. For example, he or she will explain relative pronouns to the class, and then you will practice some cloze activities as a class—for example, "The story was about a girl _____ [who, what, which] wanted a dog of her own." Select a piece of your own writing, circle the relative pronouns, and ensure that you used the correct ones. (L.4.1a)

## 16. LANGUAGE MECHANICS

As a class, create a Mechanics/Grammar bulletin board where, throughout the year, you will add to a checklist of editing topics as they are taught through targeted mini-lessons (e.g., proper use of punctuation and capitalization). Once skills are taught in a mini-lesson and listed on the bulletin board, you are expected to edit your work for the elements before publication. (L.4.1, L.4.2, L.4.3)

## 17. LANGUAGE MECHANICS

Your teacher will teach mini-lessons on the individual language standards. For example, as a class you will make a list of times when capitalization is used (e.g., first word of a sentence, proper nouns, important words in a title of a book or article, and abbreviations). Then you will choose a piece of your own writing and underline words that should be capitalized (using appropriate editing marks). Check your work with a partner. (L.4.2a)

## 18. VOCABULARY, LANGUAGE USAGE

As a class, create a Vocabulary Word Wall bulletin board where, throughout the year, you will add and sort words as you learn them in each unit of study. (L.4.4)

## ADDITIONAL ONLINE RESOURCES

- *Today Is Native American Writer Leslie Marmon Silko's Birthday* (ReadWriteThink) (RL.4.6)
- *Judy Blume Author Study* (Scholastic) (RI.4.9)
- *Dr. Christian Barnard Performed the First Human Heart Transplant* (ReadWriteThink) (W.4.7)
- *Question and Answer Books—from Genre Study to Report Writing* (ReadWriteThink) (W.4.2)
- *Poems About Family and Childhood* (Inquiry Unlimited)
- *Circulatory System Lesson* (Instructor Web)
- *Lessons for Grade 4* (Texas Heart Institute)
- *The Human Heart* (The Franklin Institute)
- *Guide to Cardiovascular Health* (The Nemours Foundation) (PDF)
- "Somebody-Wanted-But-So" strategy (West Virginia Department of Education)

## TERMINOLOGY

Bio-poem

Characters

Dramatization

Fluency

Graphic organizer

Metaphor

Poetic devices: rhyme scheme, meter, alliteration

Poetic terms: stanza, line, verse

Problem and solution

Semantic map

Simile

## INTERDISCIPLINARY CONNECTIONS

This unit teaches:

- **Science:**
  - Body systems: circulatory (e.g., chambers of the heart, four blood types), respiratory (e.g., parts of the lungs, carbon dioxide/oxygen exchange, dangers of smoking, asthma), endocrine (e.g., pituitary, adrenal, thyroid glands)
  - Doctors (e.g., Elizabeth Blackwell, Benjamin Banneker, Charles Drew) and their contributions to science
- **Art:** Form in art, Vincent van Gogh, Giotto di Bondone, Jean-Honoré Fragonard, Pablo Picasso

This unit could be extended to teach:

- **Music:** Elements of music (e.g., steady beat, rhythmic patterns, accents, downbeats)
- **Mathematics:**
  - Graphing (e.g., heartbeats per minute at rest vs. during exercise)
  - Measurement (e.g., liters [blood], pounds [weight], inches/centimeters [height], peak flow meter [lung capacity])
- **Physical education/health:** Ways to keep the heart and lungs healthy (e.g., cardiovascular exercise, healthy diet)

## Grade Four, Unit One Sample Lesson Plan

*Love That Dog by Sharon Creech*

*"The Red Wheelbarrow" by William Carlos Williams*

*"Stopping by Woods on a Snowy Evening" by Robert Frost*

*"The Tyger" by William Blake*

*"dog" by Valerie Worth*

*"The Pasture" by Robert Frost*

*"Street Music" by Arnold Adoff*

*"The Apple" by S. C. Rigg*

*"Love That Boy" by Walter Dean Myers*

In this series of ten lessons, students read *Love That Dog* by Sharon Creech, and they:

Identify the speaker of the novel/poem (RL.4.2, RL.4.6)

Infer missing details (RL.4.1, RL.4.3)

Explore poetry along with the speaker (RL.4.2, RL.4.5, RL.4.6, RL.4.10, RF.4.4)

Note the speaker's evolving view of poetry (RL.4.3, RL.4.6)

Examine the function of the subplot in the novel (RL.4.1, RL.4.3)

Record responses to poems (RL.4.1, RL.4.2, RL.4.5, RL.4.6, L.4.4)

Challenge their views of poetry (RL.4.2, W.4.9)

Summary

## Lesson I: Meet Jack, Room 105, Miss Stretchberry, and "The Red Wheelbarrow"

Identify key components of the unit *Love That Dog* (RL.4.5, SL.4.1)

Record thoughts while reading "The Red Wheelbarrow" (RL.4.2, RL.4.10, RF.4.4, W.4.9)

Explore responses to "The Red Wheelbarrow" (SL.4.1, RL.4.5)

Examine Jack's reflections when he reads "The Red Wheelbarrow" (RL.4.1, RL.4.2, RL.4.5, RL.4.6, L.4.4)

(Begin to) probe the missing details between Jack's entries (RL.4.1, RL.4.3)

## Lesson II: The Woods and a Blue Car

(Continue to) probe the missing details between Jack's entries (RL.4.1, RL.4.3, SL.4.1)

Record responses to "Stopping by Woods on a Snowy Evening" (RL.4.2, RL.4.5, RL.4.10, RF.4.4, W.4.9)

Explore Jack's responses to "Stopping by Woods on a Snowy Evening" (RL.4.1, RL.4.2, RL.4.3)

Note Jack's reference to the blue car (RL.4.3)

## Lesson III: "The Tyger" and a Blue Car

(Continue to) probe the missing details between Jack's entries (RL.4.1, RL.4.3)

Record responses to "The Tyger" (RL.4.2, RL.4.5, RL.4.10, RF.4.3, RF.4.4, W.4.9)

Probe why Jack says that "The Tyger" "sounded good" (RL.4.2)

Trace Jack's evolving description of the blue car

## Lesson IV: "dog"

Consider the details in "dog" (RL.4.2)

(Along with Jack) describe a pet (even a pretend one) (SL.4.1)

Explore why Jack likes "dog" (RL.4.1, RL.4.3)

(Continue to) probe the missing details between Jack's entries (RL.4.1, RL.4.3)

Note the emergence of a subplot (RL.4.1, RL.4.3)

## Lesson V: "The Pasture"

Consider Jack's views of poetry following his reading of "The Pasture" (RL.4.2, RL.4.6)

Explore and record personal views of poetry (RL.4.5, RL.4.10, RF.4.4, W.4.9)

Note the significance of Jack's January 24 entry (RL.4.1, RL.4.3)

Continue to trace the novel's subplot (RL.4.1)

## Lesson VI: "Street Music," "The Apple," and "My Yellow Dog"

Consider the form of "Street Music" and "My Yellow Dog" (RL.4.2, RL.4.5)

Explore Jack's response to "Street Music" (RL.4.2, RL.4.5, RL.4.6, RL.4.10, RF.4.4)

Note the return of a car to Jack's reflections (RL.4.1, RL.4.3)

Reflect on Jack's decision to identify himself as the poet of "My Yellow Dog" (RL.4.3)

Revisit personal reflections

(Begin to) identify topics for writing own poems (W.4.9)

## Lesson VII: "Love That Boy" and Sky

Explore Jack's March 14 entry and the revelation of a new name, Sky (RL.4.1)

Record personal reflection in response to Jack's excitement (RL.4.10, RF.4.4, W.4.9)

(Following the reading of March 22 entry, return to folders and begin to) compose drafts of personal poems (W.4.9, W.4.10, L.4.1, L.4.2, L.4.3, L.4.5)

## Lesson VIII: Walter Dean Myers

Examine Jack's letter to Walter Dean Myers (RL.4.3)

Conduct research and record facts about the life and writing of Myers (RI.4.1, W.4.7)

Explore the life of Myers (based on findings) (RI.4.1)

(Continue to) work on personal poems (W.4.9, W.4.10, L.4.1, L.4.2, L.4.3, L.4.5)

## Lesson IX: Miss Stretchberry and "My Sky"

Explore Miss Stretchberry's contribution to Jack's evolving understanding of poetry (RL.4.3, RL.4.5, RL.4.6)

Examine "My Sky" and note how Jack integrates what he has learned into his own composition (RL.4.2, RL.4.3, RL.4.5, RL.4.10, RF.4.4)

Revise personal poems (W.4.4, W.4.5, W.4.10, L.4.1, L.4.2, L.4.3, L.4.5)

## Lesson X: Love That Dog

Revisit Jack's story (RL.4.1, RL.4.3)

Explore and share select entries from folder (W.4.10)

Share personal poem (RL.4.5, SL.4.4)

Reflect on the idea of inspiration (L.4.4, SL.4.1)

## Lesson I: Meet Jack, Room 105, Miss Stretchberry, and "The Red Wheelbarrow"

### Objectives

Identify key components of the unit Love That Dog (RL.4.5, SL.4.1)

Record thoughts while reading "The Red Wheelbarrow" (RL.4.2, RL.4.10, RF.4.4, W.4.4, W.4.9)

Explore responses to "The Red Wheelbarrow" (SL.4.1, RL.4.5)

Examine Jack's reflections when he reads "The Red Wheelbarrow" (RL.4.1, RL.4.2, RL.4.5, RL.4.6, L.4.4)

(Begin to) probe the missing details between Jack's entries (RL.4.1, RL.4.3)

### Required Materials

☐ Class set of Love That Dog by Sharon Creech

☐ Pocket folders with fasteners (contents below)

*Procedures*

1. Lead-In:

   Distribute folders and instruct students to study their contents. They will find:

   ○ "The Red Wheelbarrow" by William Carlos Williams

   ○ "Stopping by Woods on a Snowy Evening" by Robert Frost

   ○ "The Tyger" by William Blake

   ○ "dog" by Valerie Worth

   ○ "The Pasture" by Robert Frost

   ○ "Street Music" by Arnold Adoff

   ○ "The Apple" by S. C. Rigg

   ○ "Love That Boy" by Walter Dean Myers

   ○ Loose-leaf paper

2. Step by Step:

   a. Introduce the structure of the unit on *Love That Dog* by Sharon Creech. Tell them that

      ○ The folders they just looked through will be used *only* for this unit

      ○ All the poems that they will read are in the folder

      ○ The loose-leaf will be used to record their responses to the poems and to the novel *Love That Dog* by Sharon Creech

   b. Ask a student to volunteer to read "The Red Wheelbarrow" aloud.

   c. Instruct the students to reread "The Red Wheelbarrow" in the folder. Tell them to record their initial responses to the poem in the space around the poem.

   d. Lead a discussion exploring the students' responses.

   e. Introduce *Love That Dog* by Sharon Creech. Tell the students to read Jack's first three entries.

3. Closure:

   Using prompts, guide a discussion in which the students compare Jack's response to the "The Red Wheelbarrow" to their own.

## Differentiation

### Advanced

- Students will conduct research on a poet of choice from this unit and study three more of his or her poems.
- At the close of the unit (or as each poet is featured), students will share their research with the rest of the class through a multimedia or creative video presentation. Students should include commentary on the style of the poet's work.

### Struggling

- Make recordings of poems available to students in a listening center, freeing them to focus on meaning instead of the actual decoding of the poems.
- Encourage students to draw pictures to go with stanzas of poetry as a first step in responding to the poems. As they try to visualize the poet's ideas, it may lead to a deeper understanding of the poem.

## Homework/Assessment

Students will write (in the unit folder) a brief poem, emulating "The Red Wheelbarrow."

# Literature Settings: Weather or Not

This six-week unit invites students to explore geography as it relates to seasons and weather. Students discover how these settings are represented in–and affect events in–literature.

---

## ESSENTIAL QUESTION

How does the author's use of setting affect the plot of a story?

---

## OVERVIEW

Students read contrasting styles of poems about weather, including Carl Sandburg's "Fog" and Robert Frost's "Dust of Snow," and discuss how poetic techniques affect the interpretation of poems. Then students read informational texts, such as "Kenya's Long Dry Season" by Nellie Gonzalez Cutler, and apply the information learned to their appreciation of the setting of *Safari Journal* by Hudson Talbott. Students learn about geography and weather through a variety of informational texts. Class discussions will focus on the back-and-forth relationship between information gleaned from the informational texts and the insights students develop from literature.

## FOCUS STANDARDS

These Focus Standards have been selected for the unit from the Common Core State Standards.

**RL.4.1:** Refer to details and examples in a text when explaining what the text says explicitly and when drawing inferences from the text.

**RL.4.3:** Describe in depth a character, setting, or event in a story or drama, drawing on specific details in the text (e.g., a character's thoughts, words, or actions).

**RI.4.3:** Explain events, procedures, ideas, or concepts in a historical, scientific, or technical text, including what happened and why, based on specific information in the text.

**RF.4.4:** Read with sufficient accuracy and fluency to support comprehension.

**RF.4.4(a):** Read on-level text with purpose and understanding.

**RF.4.4(b):** Read on-level text orally with accuracy, appropriate rate, and expression on successive readings.

**W.4.7:** Conduct short research projects that build knowledge through investigation of different aspects of a topic.

**SL.4.1:** Engage effectively in a range of collaborative discussions (one-on-one, in groups, and teacher-led) with diverse partners on grade 4 topics and texts, building on others' ideas and expressing their own clearly.

**SL.4.1(c):** Pose and respond to specific questions to clarify or follow up on information, and make comments that contribute to the discussion and link to the remarks of others.

**SL.4.1(d):** Review the key ideas expressed and explain their own ideas and understanding in light of the discussion.

**L.4.5:** Demonstrate understanding of figurative language, word relationships, and nuances in word meaning.

**L.4.5(a):** Explain the meaning of simple similes and metaphors (e.g., *as pretty as a picture*) in context.

## SUGGESTED OBJECTIVES

- Find similarities and differences in story settings, and note how the author's use of setting affects a story.
- Explain how having factual knowledge of a topic (e.g., weather) can increase your appreciation of literature about the topic.
- Track information and take notes on a topic studied over time (e.g., weather).
- Write a question-and-answer report that includes audio and/or visual aids to communicate research findings about different aspects of a topic (e.g., a particular weather phenomenon).
- Identify similes and metaphors in texts read.
- Recite poetry written in different styles about the same topic.

## SUGGESTED WORKS

(E) indicates a CCSS exemplar text; (EA) indicates a text from a writer with other works identified as exemplars.

### LITERARY TEXTS

*Stories*

- *Hurricane* (Jonathan London and Henri Sorensen)
- *Hurricane Book and CD* (Read Along) (David Wiesner)
- *The Long Winter* (Little House series) (Laura Ingalls Wilder) (EA)
- *One Day in the Prairie* (Trophy Chapter Book) (Jean Craighead George)
- *Owen and Mzee: The True Story of a Remarkable Friendship* (Isabella Hatkoff, Craig Hatkoff, Paula Kahumbu, and Peter Greste)

- *A Prairie Alphabet (ABC Our Country)* (Jo Bannatyne-Cugnet)
- *Rainbow Crow* (Nancy Van Laan)
- *Safari Journal* (ASPCA Henry Bergh Children's Book Awards) (Hudson Talbott)
- *Strawberry Girl* (Lois Lenski)
- *Time of Wonder* (Robert McCloskey)

## Poems

- "Clouds" (Christina Rossetti)
- "Dust of Snow" (Robert Frost) (E)
- "Fog" (Carl Sandburg) (E)
- *The Storm Book* (Charlotte Zolotow)
- *A Visit to William Blake's Inn: Poems for Innocent and Experienced Travelers* (Nancy Willard)

## INFORMATIONAL TEXTS

### Nonfiction Books

- *Can It Rain Cats and Dogs? Questions and Answers About Weather* (Scholastic Question and Answer Series) (Melvin and Gilda Berger) (EA)
- *The Cloud Book: Words and Pictures* (Tomie dePaola) (EA)
- *Cloud Dance* (Thomas Locker)
- *Do Tornadoes Really Twist? Questions and Answers About Tornadoes and Hurricanes* (Scholastic Question and Answer Series) (Melvin and Gilda Berger) (EA)
- *The Everything Kids' Weather Book* (Joseph Snedeker)
- *Hurricanes* (Seymour Simon) (EA)
- *Hurricanes: Earth's Mightiest Storms* (Patricia Lauber) (E)
- *If You're Not from the Prairie* (David Bouchard)
- *It Figures! Fun Figures of Speech* (Marvin Terban and Giulio Maestro)
- "Kenya's Long Dry Season" (Nellie Gonzalez Cutler) (E)
- *Let's Investigate Marvelously Meaningful Maps* (Madelyn Wood Carlisle and Yvette Santiago Banek) (E)
- *The Snowflake: A Water Cycle Story* (Neil Waldman)
- *Storms* (Seymour Simon) (EA)
- *Weather Whys: Questions, Facts and Riddles About Weather* (Mike Artell)
- *The Weather Wizard's Cloud Book: A Unique Way to Predict the Weather Accurately and Easily by Reading the Clouds* (Louis D. Rubin Sr., Jim Duncan, and Hiram J. Herbert) (Read Aloud)
- *W Is for Wind: A Weather Alphabet* (Pat Michaels and Melanie Rose)

### References

- *National Geographic Kids Everything Weather: Facts, Photos, and Fun that Will Blow You Away* (Kathy Furgang)
- *National Geographic World Atlas for Young Explorers*

## ART, MUSIC, AND MEDIA

*Art*

- Claude Monet, *Bridge over a Pond of Water Lilies* (1899)
- Claude Monet, *Rouen Cathedral: The Portal (Sunlight)* (1893)
- Édouard Manet, *Boating* (1874)
- Gustave Caillebotte, *Paris Street, Rainy Day* (1877)
- John Constable, *Seascape Study with Rain Cloud* (1827)
- Kazimir Malevich, *Morning in the Village After Snowstorm* (1912)
- Thomas Hart Benton, *July Hay* (1943)
- Wassily Kandinsky, *Cemetery and Vicarage in Kochel* (1909)

## SAMPLE ACTIVITIES AND ASSESSMENTS

### 1. READING LITERATURE, SPEAKING AND LISTENING

As a class, we will keep a chart (with the categories listed here) of the stories and poems we read. As the chart is filled in, we will use the information to talk about what we learned from literature.

- Title and author
- Type of literature (story or poem)
- Main character(s)
- Setting (geography, season, and/or weather)
- Summary (using the "Somebody-Wanted-But-So" strategy)

Write your own response on a sticky note, on a whiteboard, or in your journal and share it with a partner before each section of the class chart is filled in. (RL.4.1, RL.4.2, RL.4.3, RL.4.5, RF.4.4a, RF.4.4b)

### 2. READING LITERATURE, SPEAKING AND LISTENING

Compare and contrast the effect that the poem or story's setting has on its events. How are similar settings portrayed similarly and differently? Look back for specific lines or paragraphs in order to find explicit details from the stories and poems we've read. What would happen if the setting of the story or poem were changed? (RL.4.2, SL.4.1)

### 3. READING INFORMATIONAL TEXT, SPEAKING AND LISTENING

As a class, keep a chart of information with the categories listed below learned about seasons and weather, at home and far away. As the chart is filled in, use the information to talk about related information in nonfiction books and/or online either explicitly read or inferred.

- Type of weather
- How is it caused?
- What positive effects does this weather have?
- What negative effects can this weather have?

- What do we need to do to prepare for this kind of weather?
- What parts of the world experience this weather?
- What are the weather words we should know? (e.g., *meteorology, prediction, forecast*)

Write your own response on a sticky note, on a whiteboard, or in your journal and share it with a partner before each section of the class chart is filled in. (RF.4.4a, RF.4.4b, RI.4.1, RI.4.2, RI.4.4, RI.4.9, L.4.4a)

## 4. INFORMATIVE WRITING, LANGUAGE USAGE, LANGUAGE MECHANICS

Following a class discussion of weather and climate, be prepared to write in your journal about the positive and negative effects of weather on real life and life in literature. Your response should be a well-developed essay that includes at least two supporting details. Before turning in your essay, edit your work for modal auxiliaries, order of adjectives, and commas and quotation marks (see Standards for more details). (W.4.2, L.4.1a, L.4.1c, L.4.1d, L.4.1g, L.4.2a, L.4.2b)

## 5. READING FLUENCY, READING COMPREHENSION, SPEAKING AND LISTENING

Here is a page from *W Is for Wind* by Pat Michaels and Melanie Rose. Find the highlighted line on your page—this is your cue line. When you hear that line read by a classmate, it is your cue to read the next passage aloud. Take two minutes to practice your passage to yourself, and then we will read the text as a class and discuss the information learned from it. (RI.4.3, RI.4.9, RF.4.4a, RF.4.4b)

## 6. SPEAKING AND LISTENING

How is reading a book similar to and different from predicting the weather? Write your own response on a sticky note, on a whiteboard, or in your journal and share it with a partner. Cite specific examples from the text and from the experience of reading stories. (RL.4.3, SL.4.1)

## 7. READING LITERATURE, SPEAKING AND LISTENING, NARRATIVE WRITING

What impact does weather have on stories such as *The Long Winter* by Laura Ingalls Wilder, *Time of Wonder* by Robert McCloskey, or *Hurricane Book and CD* by David Wiesner? What if the setting were changed (i.e., from winter to summer, from the sea to the desert, or from a hurricane to a snowy day)? How would that change the story? Turn and talk about your ideas with a partner, then write a first draft of a scene for a modified story of choice. (RL.4.3, W.4.3, SL.4.1)

## 8. READING POETRY, LANGUAGE USAGE, SPEAKING AND LISTENING

Read *It Figures! Fun Figures of Speech* by Marvin Terban and Giulio Maestro as a class, and talk about the sections on similes and metaphors. Then use sticky notes to mark where you find examples of similes and metaphors about weather in poems and stories from this unit. Continue the T-chart started in Unit One (name of the technique and examples of each). (RL.4.4, RL.4.5, L.4.5a)

## 9. READING POETRY, SPEAKING AND LISTENING

After studying meteorology and weather (specifically clouds) in informational texts, read the poems "Clouds" by Christina Rossetti and "Fog" by Carl Sandburg. How does your understanding of cloud formation increase your appreciation for these poems (or not)? Write your own response on a sticky note, on a whiteboard, or in your journal and share it with a partner before discussing as a class. ( RL.4.1, RL.4.3, SL.4.1)

## 10. READING POETRY, READING FLUENCY, PERFORMANCE

Choose one of the poems from this unit, such as "Dust of Snow" by Robert Frost, to read and discuss with a partner. Memorize and/or recite the poem for your classmates. Record the readings using a video camera for future reference and to see how your fluency improves during the course of the year. (RL.4.5, RF.4.4a, RF.4.4b)

## 11. RESEARCH, READING INFORMATIONAL TEXT, LANGUAGE USAGE, LANGUAGE MECHANICS

Read at least two informational texts, in print or online, about a specific season in a geographical region of choice. Watch a meteorologist presenting a weather forecast online or on TV, and outline what makes that style of presenting unique. Then write a weather forecast that describes at least two aspects of weather. Be sure to edit your work for modal auxiliaries, order of adjectives, and commas and quotation marks (see Standards for more details). Your teacher may ask you to type your forecast, and possibly even record it as a podcast or using a video camera, for publication on the class web page. (RI.4.1, RI.4.3, RI.4.4, RI.4.7, RI.4.9, W.4.2, W.4.7, SL.4.4, SL.4.5, L.4.1a, L.4.1c, L.4.1d, L.4.1g, L.4.2a, L.4.2b)

## 12. RESEARCH, READING INFORMATIONAL TEXT, LANGUAGE USAGE, LANGUAGE MECHANICS

Read at least two informational texts, in print or online, about a season or weather phenomenon of choice. Write a report in question-and-answer format that includes at least four logically ordered open-ended questions and the answers. Be sure to edit your work for modal auxiliaries, order of adjectives, and commas and quotation marks (see Standards for more details) before sharing with the class. Your teacher may ask you to type your forecast and insert a relevant picture from the Internet, or one taken with a digital camera, for publication on the class web page. (RI.4.1, RI.4.3, RI.4.4, RI.4.7, RI.4.9, W.4.2, W.4.7, SL.4.4, SL.4.5, L.4.1a, L.4.1c, L.4.1d, L.4.1g, L.4.2a, L.4.2b)

## 13. SPEAKING AND LISTENING, READING INFORMATIONAL TEXT

Look at the variety of maps available in books such as *Let's Investigate Marvelously Meaningful Maps* by Madelyn Wood Carlisle and Yvette Santiago Banek. Why is it helpful to use different types of weather maps? How is reading a map similar to and different from reading a book? Write your own response on a sticky note, on a whiteboard, or in your journal and share it with a partner before discussing as a class. (RI.4.7, W.4.9, SL.4.1)

## 14. VOCABULARY, LANGUAGE USAGE

As an individual and as a class, keep an index card file of new words learned in this unit (e.g., *meteorology, prediction, forecast, catastrophic, catastrophe*). How does the context of the word help you understand its meaning? Keeping the words on index cards will allow you to use and sort the words by meaning and spelling features. (Note: This will be an ongoing activity all year long.) In addition, you may be asked to create an individual semantic map of related words in order to help you explore the interconnectedness of weather and story events. (RI.4.6, L.4.4a)

## 15. ART, LANGUAGE USAGE, NARRATIVE WRITING

Look at how weather is portrayed in the various art selections. What adjectives would you use to describe the weather? Are there any similes, metaphors, or figurative language that you think work best? Write down your own response and compare your answer with others in the class. Choose your favorite artwork and find a partner who chose the same piece. Together, write an opening scene from a story that would have that weather as its setting, using at least one metaphor or simile. (RL.4.7, W.4.3b, L.4.5a)

## 16. READING INFORMATIONAL TEXT, SPEAKING AND LISTENING, INFORMATIVE/EXPLANATORY WRITING

As a class, summarize what was learned in this unit as it relates to the essential question "How does the author's use of setting affect the plot of a story?" Write your own response on a sticky note, on a whiteboard, or in your journal and share it with a partner before discussing as a class. Following the class discussion, write your response in your journal. Be sure to edit your work for modal auxiliaries, order of adjectives, and commas and quotation marks (see Standards for more details) before sharing it with your teacher. Your teacher may ask you to type your essay and respond to a poll about the unit on the classroom blog. (W.4.4, W.4.9a, W.4.9b, L.4.1a, L.4.1c, L.4.1d, L.4.1g, L.4.2a, L.4.2b)

## 17. ART, SPEAKING AND LISTENING

Examine the Constable, Benton, and Malevich pieces and discuss how the formal elements (e.g., color, line, texture, and shapes) in these works relate to the weather being shown. Ask questions such as: How do the color and texture of the sky help to convey the weather? What lines lead you to understand that this is a specific type of weather? How do the shapes that define the figures and landscape signal particular weather conditions? (SL.4.1, SL.4.3)

## 18. LANGUAGE USAGE

Your teacher will teach mini-lessons on the individual language standards. For example, he or she will explain modal auxiliaries to the class, and then you will practice some cloze activities as a class—for example, "The clouds seem to be getting lighter, so I think the rain _____ [can, may, must] stop soon." Select a piece of your own writing, circle *can, may,* and *must,* and ensure that you used the correct one. (L.4.1c)

## 19. LANGUAGE MECHANICS

As a class, continue adding to the Mechanics/Grammar bulletin board started in Unit One. Remember—once skills are taught in a mini-lesson and listed on the bulletin board, you are expected to edit your work for these elements before publication. (L.4.1, L.4.2, L.4.3)

## 20. VOCABULARY

As a class, continue adding to the Vocabulary Word Wall bulletin board where, throughout the year, you will add and sort words as you learn them in each unit of study. (L.4.4)

## ADDITIONAL ONLINE RESOURCES

- *Weather Detectives: Questioning the Fact and Folklore of Weather Sayings* (ReadWriteThink) (W.4.7)

- *Literature as a Jumping Off Point for Nonfiction Inquiry* (ReadWriteThink) (RL.4.2)

- *The Tropical Storm That Became Katrina Formed over the Bahamas in 2005* (ReadWriteThink) (RI.4.3)

- *Exploring Cause and Effect Using Expository Texts About Natural Disasters* (ReadWriteThink) (RI.4.5)
- *Using* Snowflake Bentley *as a Framing Text for Multigenre Writing* (ReadWriteThink) (RI.4.9)
- Using Picture Books to Teach Setting Development in Writing Workshop (ReadWriteThink) (W4.3)
- *How to Read Weather Maps* (Discovery Channel, Discovery Education)
- *Strawberry Girl Lesson Plan* (Lesson plan for *Strawberry Girl* by Lois Lenski) (Scholastic)
- Weather metaphors (Knowgramming.com)
- "Idiom Category: Weather" (UsingEnglish.com)
- "Musical Meteorology" (Weather Dude)
- Photographs of storms
- Animated interpretation of Robert Frost's "Dust of Snow"
- "Somebody-Wanted-But-So" strategy (West Virginia Department of Education)

# TERMINOLOGY

Context

Explicit information

Inference

Poetic devices: rhyme scheme, meter, simile, metaphor

Poetic terms: stanza, line, verse

Prediction

Setting

# INTERDISCIPLINARY CONNECTIONS

This unit teaches:

- **Art:** Texture, form in art, John Constable, Thomas Hart Benton, Kazimir Malevich
- **Geography:**
  - United States/local geography (e.g., coastal areas, plains, mountains)
  - African geography (e.g., Sahara Desert, tropical rain forests, coastal plains, grassy flatlands)
- **Science:**
  - Weather (e.g., snow, fog, wind, cold and warm fronts, air movement and air pressure, effects of altitude on weather, hurricanes, tornadoes)
  - Meteorology and weather prediction (e.g., cloud formation, weather maps, weather stations, satellite maps)

This unit could be extended to teach:

- **Geography:** Map reading (e.g., climate, physical, political, topographical)
- **Science:** Weather prediction tools and how to read them (e.g., barometer, anemometer, psychrometer, thermometer, rain gauge, Doppler radar)

# Grade Four, Unit Two Sample Lesson Plan

*"Dust of Snow" by Robert Frost*

*"Fog" by Carl Sandburg*

In this series of four lessons, students read "Dust of Snow" by Robert Frost and "Fog" by Carl Sandburg, and they:

Note the use of poetic devices in their analysis of poetry (RL.4.1, RL.4.5)

Analyze the role that nature plays as a source of inspiration for poets (RL.4.1, RL.4.2, RL.4.3, RL.4.6)

Reflect upon the power of poems to capture special moments (SL.4.1)

## Summary

### Lesson I: "Dust of Snow"

Identify the rhyme scheme of the poem "Dust of Snow" (RL.4.1, RL.4.5)

Examine the impact that the rhyme scheme has on the meaning of the poem (RL.4.1, RL.4.5)

Analyze the relationship between the form of the poem and its content (RL.4.1, RL.4.3)

Note the shift in content from the first to the second stanza

Reflect on the speaker's perspective (RL.4.2, RL.4.6)

Explore the theme of the poem (RL.4.2)

### Lesson II: "Fog"

Identify the metaphor in the poem

Annotate the poem for words that relate to the metaphor (RL.4.1, RL.4.5)

Explicate the use of the metaphor (RL.4.1)

Explore the mood of the poem (RL.4.2, RL.4.3)

Consider the speaker's perspective (RL.4.6)

Note the differences in form between "Dust of Snow" and "Fog" (RL.4.5)

Analyze the differences in the speakers' point of view (in "Dust of Snow" and "Fog") (RL.4.6)

## Lesson IV: Critiquing Personal Poems

Note the use of nature in classmates' poems

Identify metaphors

Explore the poems' forms (RL.4.5)

Identify the setting of the poems (RL.4.3)

Note the emergence of mood in the poems (SL.4.1)

Reflect upon the use of poetry to depict special moments (SL.4.1)

## Lesson III: Writing Poetry

Reread the poems "Dust of Snow" and "Fog"

Analyze the role that nature plays in both poems (RL.4.1)

Select a special moment (similar to the moments depicted in "Dust of Snow" and "Fog") to write about (W.4.3)

Identify the use of nature to depict the moment (RL.4.4)

Create a web of words that captures the moment (W.4.4, W.4.5)

Group select words in poetic form (W.4.4, W.4.5)

Refine the poems (W.4.4, W.4.5)

## Lesson III: Writing Poetry

### Objectives

Reread the poems "Dust of Snow" and "Fog"

Analyze the role that nature plays in both poems (RL.4.1)

Select a special moment (similar to the moments depicted in "Dust of Snow" and "Fog") to write about (RL.4.4)

Identify the use of nature to depict the moment (RL.4.4)

Create a web of words that captures the moment (W.4.4, W.4.5)

Group select words in poetic form (W.4.4, W.4.5)

Refine the poems (W.4.4, W.4.5)

### Required Materials

☐ Copies of "Dust of Snow" by Robert Frost, and "Fog" by Carl Sandburg

### Procedures

1. Lead-In:

   Student volunteers reread "Dust of Snow" and "Fog."

2. Step by Step:

a. A class discussion notes the different ways that the poets use nature to capture a moment. In "Dust of Snow," it is a crow that "shook down" a "dust of snow" that affects the speaker's mood. In "Fog," the speaker uses a metaphor, "little cat feet," to depict the movement of the fog. The speaker seems not to be involved in that moment.

b. Collectively, the students work on a sample; shown below is one for "Wave."

crawl

tickling     surprisingly

purrs     **wave**     beneath

bubbles     dreams

gray

c. With the students' help, highlight groupings of words, such as *surprising purr, tickling crawl, bubbling wave,* or *gray dream.*

d. Included is a possible grouping of words into a poem:

### Wave

*The wave that crawled*

*Beneath my feet*

*Surprised my morning*

*Dreams.*

e. Students individually select a moment that they wish to capture.

f. Students, either individually or in pairs, create a web of verbs, adjectives, and adverbs around the word that represents their chosen moment.

g. Students group select words in poetic form.

h. Students refine their poems.

3. Closure:

Student volunteers read their poems aloud.

## Differentiation

### Advanced

- Encourage students to create a digital slide presentation or screenshot that documents the process the class used to write the poem.

Alternately, students can record the process using a video camera.

- Allow students to set up a class web page to post all poems and record them as podcasts.

- Encourage students to create poems using richer language and more poetic devices (i.e., repetition, alliteration, simile, and metaphor) than their peers.

### Struggling

- Before beginning, orally and/or visually remind students the purpose of verbs (action words) and adjectives (describing words).

- Provide students with photos of nature moments from which to generate their list of adjectives and verbs (e.g., the sun setting or the downpour of a rainstorm). Or provide students with digital cameras to take photos in preparation for this lesson. Students write groups of words on sentence strips, read their phrases to their group members, and, as a group, assemble them in order. Students copy the poem they created together, practice reading together, and recite chorally for the class. With a video camera, you may record the students reading so they can see and hear themselves in order to improve their fluency.

## Homework/Assessment

N/A

# Animals Are Characters, Too: Characters Who Gallop, Bark, and Squeak

This eight-week unit invites students to compare how horses, dogs, and mice are portrayed in fiction and nonfiction.

---

## ESSENTIAL QUESTION

How do we portray animals in writing?

---

## OVERVIEW

Students study how animals and their traits are personified in literature and film. You may choose to have students read varied texts about the same animals to facilitate a whole-group discussion, or may choose to encourage students to read in small groups about different animals and share what they learn with each other. Students choose an animal to research and compare the research with how animals are portrayed in literature. After reading selections from *Scranimals* by Jack Prelutsky or from *The Book of Nonsense* by Edward Lear, students also try their hand at writing a poem or limerick about an unusual animal. Students also begin writing their own narratives that incorporate the techniques and vocabulary learned with animal characters. If time permits, students may have the opportunity to compare how film and print versions of texts are similar and different from each other. This unit ends with a class discussion and informative/explanatory essay response to the essential question.

## FOCUS STANDARDS

These Focus Standards have been selected for the unit from the Common Core State Standards.

**RL.4.5:** Explain major differences between poems, drama, and prose, and refer to the structural elements of poems (e.g., verse, rhythm, meter) and drama (e.g., casts of characters, settings, descriptions, dialogue, stage directions) when writing or speaking about a text.

**RI.4.2:** Determine the main idea of a text and explain how it is supported by key details; summarize the text.

**RF.4.4:** Read with sufficient accuracy and fluency to support comprehension.

**RF.4.4(c):** Use context to confirm or self-correct word recognition and understanding, rereading as necessary.

**W.4.3:** Write narratives to develop real or imagined experiences or events using effective technique, descriptive details, and clear event sequences.

**SL.4.5:** Add audio recordings and visual displays to presentations when appropriate to enhance the development of main ideas or themes.

**L.4.5:** Demonstrate understanding of figurative language, word relationships, and nuances in word meanings.

**L.4.5(b):** Recognize and explain the meaning of common idioms, adages, and proverbs.

**L.4.5(c):** Demonstrate understanding of words by relating them to their opposites (antonyms) and to words with similar but not identical meanings (synonyms).

## SUGGESTED OBJECTIVES

- Discuss and interpret poetic techniques and forms, such as rhyme scheme and limericks.
- Compare the structures of poems and their use of poetic devices.
- Find similarities and differences in how animal characters are personified in fiction.
- Collaborate with classmates in order to publish a story.
- Read informational texts about a topic (e.g., animals) and compare the factual information with fictional portrayals.
- Compare print and film versions of stories (e.g., *The Black Stallion*).
- Explain major differences among poetry, drama, and prose.
- Shape a journal response into an informative/explanatory essay; use several well-constructed paragraphs.

## SUGGESTED WORKS

(E) indicates a CCSS exemplar text; (EA) indicates a text from a writer with other works identified as exemplars.

## LITERARY TEXTS

*Stories*

*General*

- *Every Living Thing* (Cynthia Rylant and S. D. Schindler)
- *It's Raining Cats and Dogs: Making Sense of Animal Phrases* (Jackie Franza and Steve Gray)

- *James Herriot's Treasury for Children: Warm and Joyful Tales by the Author of* All Creatures Great and Small *(James Herriot)*
- *The Mayor of Central Park* (Avi and Brian Floca)
- *Nacho and Lolita* (Pam Muñoz Ryan and Claudia Rueda)
- *Tacky the Penguin* (Helen Lester and Lynn Munsinger) (easier)

Horses

- *Black Beauty: The Greatest Horse Story Ever Told* (DK Readers Level 4) (Anna Sewell and Victor Ambrus)
- *The Black Stallion* (Walter Farley) (E)
- *Gift Horse: A Lakota Story* (S. D. Nelson)
- *The Girl Who Loved Wild Horses* (Paul Goble)
- *Misty of Chincoteague* (Marguerite Henry and Wesley Dennis) (advanced)
- *Paint the Wind* (Pam Muñoz Ryan)
- *San Domingo: The Medicine Hat Stallion* (Marguerite Henry and Robert Lougheed)

Dogs

- *Because of Winn-Dixie* (Kate DiCamillo)
- *A Dog's Life: Autobiography of a Stray* (Ann M. Martin)
- *Lassie Come-Home: Eric Knight's Original 1938 Classic* (Rosemary Wells and Susan Jeffers)
- *Lewis and Clark and Me: A Dog's Tale* (Laurie Myers and Michael Dooling)
- *Marley: A Dog Like No Other—A Special Adaptation for Young Readers* (John Grogan)
- *Shelter Dogs: Amazing Stories of Adopted Strays* (Peg Kehret and Greg Farrar)
- *Shiloh* (Phyllis Reynolds Naylor and Barry Moser) (advanced)
- *Three Names* (Patricia MacLachlan and Alexander Pertzoff)
- *The Trouble with Tuck: The Inspiring Story of a Dog Who Triumphs Against All Odds* (Theodore Taylor)

Mice

- *Ben and Me: An Astonishing Life of Benjamin Franklin by His Good Mouse Amos* (Robert Lawson)
- *The Bookstore Mouse* (Peggy Christian and Gary A. Lippincott)
- *The Mouse and the Motorcycle* (Beverly Cleary)
- *Mrs. Frisby and the Rats of NIMH* (Robert C. O'Brien)
- *Poppy* (The Poppy Stories) (Avi and Brian Floca)
- *Poppy and Rye* (The Poppy Stories) (Avi and Brian Floca)
- *Poppy's Return* (The Poppy Stories) (Avi and Brian Floca)
- *The Race Across America No. 37* (Geronimo Stilton) (or any of the Geronimo Stilton series)
- *Ragweed* (The Poppy Stories) (Avi and Brian Floca)
- *Ralph S. Mouse* (Beverly Cleary and Tracy Dockray)

- *The Story of Jumping Mouse: A Native American Legend* (John Steptoe)
- *Tale of Despereaux: Being the Story of a Mouse, a Princess, Some Soup, and a Spool of Thread* (Kate DiCamillo and Timothy Basil Ering)

## Poems
- *The Beauty of the Beast: Poems from the Animal Kingdom* (Jack Prelutsky)
- "A Bird Came Down the Walk" (Emily Dickinson) (E)
- *The Complete Nonsense of Edward Lear* (Edward Lear)
- "The Erratic Rat" (traditional limerick)
- *Poetry for Young People: Animal Poems* (John Hollander and Simona Mulazzani)
- "The Rhinoceros" (Ogden Nash)
- *Scranimals* (Jack Prelutsky and Peter Sis)

# INFORMATIONAL TEXTS

## Nonfiction Books

### General
- "Good Pet, Bad Pet" (*Ranger Rick*, June 2002) (Elizabeth Schleichert) (E)
- *I Want to Be a Veterinarian* (Stephanie Maze)
- *National Geographic Encyclopedia of Animals* (Karen McGhee and George McKay)
- "Seeing Eye to Eye" (*National Geographic Explorer*) (Leslie Hall) (E)
- *Veterinarian* (Cool Careers) (William David Thomas)

### Horses
- *H Is for Horse: An Equestrian Alphabet* (Michael Ulmer and Gijsbert van Frankenhuyzen)
- *Horse Heroes: True Stories of Amazing Horses* (DK Readers Proficient Readers, Level 4) (Kate Petty)
- *Horses* (Seymour Simon) (E)
- *The Kids' Horse Book* (Sylvia Funston)
- *Panda: A Guide Horse for Ann* (Rosanna Hansen and Neil Soderstrom)
- *Your Pet Pony* (A True Book) (Elaine Landau)

### Dogs
- *A Dog's Gotta Do What a Dog's Gotta Do: Dogs at Work* (Marilyn Singer)
- *Dogs* (Seymour Simon) (EA)
- *Everything Dog: What Kids Really Want to Know About Dogs* (Kids' FAQs) (Marty Crisp)
- *W Is for Woof: A Dog Alphabet* (Ruth Strother and Gijsbert van Frankenhuyzen)
- *Why Are Dogs' Noses Wet? And Other True Facts* (Howie Dewin)
- *Your Pet Dog* (A True Book) (Elaine Landau)

### Mice
- *The Mouse* (Animal Life Stories) (Angela Royston and Maurice Pledger)
- *Outside and Inside Rats and Mice* (Sandra Markle)

## ART, MUSIC, AND MEDIA

*Media*

- Brad Bird and Jan Pinkava, dirs., *Ratatouille* (2007)
- Caroline Thompson, dir., *Black Beauty* (1994)
- Carroll Ballard, dir., *Black Stallion* (1979)
- Chris Noonan, dir., *Babe* (1995)
- Max Nosseck, dir., *Black Beauty* (1946)
- Sam Fell and Robert Stevenhagen, dirs., *Tale of Despereaux* (2008)
- Wayne Wang, dir., *Because of Winn-Dixie* (2005)

# SAMPLE ACTIVITIES AND ASSESSMENTS

## 1. READING POETRY, LANGUAGE USAGE, SPEAKING AND LISTENING, NARRATIVE WRITING

Read selections from *The Book of Nonsense* by Edward Lear aloud with a partner. You should not only discuss what the poems mean but also talk about how the poetic devices, structures, and vocabulary used are similar and different. As a class, we will define a limerick and its elements and then talk about how Lear's poems exemplify these characteristics. We will continue the T-chart started in the first unit (name of the technique and examples). At a later time, you will read selections from *Scranimals* by Jack Prelutsky aloud with the same partner. Partners will again find examples of poetic techniques and mark them with a sticky note. Last, but not least, you will work with a partner to write your own animal limerick of a single animal (e.g., a lion) or an imaginary animal (e.g., broccoli + lion = broccolion). (RL.4.4, RL.4.5, W.4.4, L.4.5a, L.4.5c)

## 2. READING LITERATURE, VOCABULARY, RESEARCH

As a class, when we read about horses, dogs, mice or other animals of interest, we will keep a chart with information organized by the categories listed below. Use the chart to generate research questions to help select the most useful and relevant information (for a research project later).

- Title and author
- Type of narration (first person, third person)
- Animal character(s)
- Character traits, and how they developed over time in the story
- Examples of personification (e.g., thoughts, words, and actions)
- Synonyms for the character
- Antonyms for the character
- Summary (using the "Somebody-Wanted-But-So" strategy)

Write your response on a sticky note, on a whiteboard, or in your journal and share it with a partner before each section of the class chart is complete. (RL.4.1, RL.4.2, RL.4.3, RL.4.4, RL.4.5, RL.4.6, L.4.5c, RF.4.4c)

## 3. READING LITERATURE, SPEAKING AND LISTENING

Compare and contrast how animals are personified. How is this personification portrayed in literature? If animals *could* talk and act like humans, which of the actions are most similar to generalizations about the animal (e.g., the "sly" fox, the "lazy" pig)? Look back for specific lines or paragraphs in order to find explicit details from the stories and poems read. (RL.4.3, SL.4.1)

## 4. NARRATIVE WRITING

Write a journal entry from an animal's perspective, being sure to give the animal human characteristics. Trade your journal entry with a partner to see if they can figure out your animal from your effort to "personify" it while still maintaining its unique animal characteristics. (RL.4.3, W.4.4, W.4.9a, W.4.9b)

## 5. READING INFORMATIONAL TEXT, SPEAKING AND LISTENING, RESEARCH

As a class, keep a chart of information using the categories here about horses, dogs, mice, or other animals of interest. Use the chart to generate open-ended research questions and to select the most useful and relevant information later for independent research.

- Name of animal
- Habitat
- Diet
- Protection/body facts
- Enemies
- Life expectancy
- Interesting facts

Write your response on a sticky note, on a whiteboard, or in your journal and share it with a partner before each section of the class chart is completed. (RI.4.1, RI.4.2, RI.4.4, RI.4.5, RI.4.7, RI.4.9, RF.4.4c)

## 6. INFORMATIVE WRITING

Following a class discussion of animals studied, write a journal response (or make a graphic representation such as a Venn diagram) that compares facts learned with how the animal is portrayed in literature. (W.4.2a, W.4.2b, W.4.2c, W.4.4, W.4.7, L.4.1a, L.4.1b, L.4.1c, L.4.1d, L.4.1g, L.4.2a, L.4.2b, L.4.2c)

## 7. RESEARCH, INFORMATIVE WRITING, LANGUAGE USAGE, LANGUAGE MECHANICS

Choose an animal or two that you would be interested in researching (see Activity 5; students may refer to their notes and research questions from that activity). Generate and make notes of (further) research questions. Find a classmate who is interested in the same animal. Together, research an animal of choice following the same categories as the chart listed in Activity 5. Create a plan for researching your animal, using both online and print sources. Write a report—either in question-and-answer format where you write four questions and provide the answers—or in a well-developed informative/explanatory essay with at least two sources of information cited. Be sure to edit your work for the use of the progressive and commas before coordinating conjunctions in compound sentences (see Standards for more details). Your teacher may ask you to type your report and possibly draw and scan an illustration or insert a relevant photo from the Internet for publication on the class web page. (W.4.4, W.4.7, L.4.1a, L.4.1b, L.4.1c, L.4.1d, L.4.1g, L.4.2a, L.4.2b, L.4.2c)

## 8. NARRATIVE WRITING, LANGUAGE USAGE, LANGUAGE MECHANICS

As your class discusses animal stories and poems, begin outlining your own narrative about an original animal character by starting with filling in the categories listed in the chart from Activity 5. Before you begin writing, reexamine the characters in stories and poems we've read in this unit, recalling how characters developed over the course of the story, examples of personification, and lists of synonyms and/or figurative language you want to use. Make sure to plan a sequence of events that makes sense, and think about key details to include, using five new vocabulary words. You will have the opportunity to work with a partner to revise, edit, and improve your story (for the use of the progressive and commas before coordinating conjunctions in compound sentences—see Standards for more details), so that it can be published on a class web page for others to see. Once the story is written, you will be asked to type it and add audio recordings and visual displays to enhance it. (W.4.1, W.4.4, W.4.5, W.4.6, W.4.8, SL.4.5, L.4.1a, L.4.1b, L.4.1c, L.4.1d, L.4.1g, L.4.2a, L.4.2b, L.4.2c, L.4.5)

## 9. SPEAKING AND LISTENING, LANGUAGE USAGE, INFORMATIVE WRITING

As a class, read and discuss It's Raining Cats and Dogs: Making Sense of Animal Phrases by Jackie Franza and Steve Gray. Illustrate the literal and figurative meaning of an animal idiom. Compile these illustrations into a class book to share with younger students, and try to incorporate phrases learned into your daily writing and speaking. An alternate class book idea is to make an ABC book of animal characters in a style similar to W Is for Woof by Ruth Strother and Gijsbert Van Frankenhuyzen. Your teacher may ask you to create a slide of your section, including a scanned illustration or relevant photo from the Internet, before assembling into a class book (either electronic or in print). (RL.4.1, SL.4.1, L.4.5b)

## 10. FILM, READING LITERATURE, SPEAKING AND LISTENING

Compare the film and print versions of a book such as Black Beauty or The Black Stallion. You can also download and compare any animal film, such as Babe, to a script of the film. (Your teacher needs to check and approve the parts of the script you want to use.) Decide what you want to compare before viewing (e.g., characters, settings, descriptions, dialogue, and/or stage directions), and keep notes in your journal about similarities and differences as well as the major differences between drama and prose. (RL.4.5, SL.4.1)

## 11. PERFORMANCE, SPEAKING AND LISTENING

After discussing the structural elements (e.g., casts of characters, settings, descriptions, dialogue, stage directions) that are unique to drama versus prose, add one or more of these elements to a Reader's Theater script of a fun animal story, such as Tacky the Penguin by Helen Lester and Lynn Munsinger. With at least two other classmates, add at least two scenes—one before the script begins and one after the script ends—to make it a one-act, three-scene play, and present it as a class. Record the presentations and edit them to create a movie to post on the class web page. (RL.4.5, W.4.4)

## 12. READING POETRY, READING FLUENCY, SPEAKING AND LISTENING

Choose one of the poems from this unit, such as "A Bird Came Down the Walk" by Emily Dickinson or "The Rhinoceros" by Ogden Nash, to read and discuss with a partner. Recite the poem for your classmates. (SL.4.5, RF.4.4c)

## 13. VOCABULARY, LANGUAGE USAGE

As an individual and as a class, keep an index card file of new words learned in this unit. You may also have a nonsense word section where you make up words for animals (based on *Scranimals*) using new prefixes and suffixes learned until this point in the year. Each index card should include the word, a definition, the word in a sentence, and, for the nonsense words, an illustration. Keeping the words on index cards will allow you to use and sort the words by meaning and spelling features. (Note: This will be an ongoing activity all year long.) (L.4.4a, L.4.4b)

## 14. SPEAKING AND LISTENING, INFORMATIVE WRITING, LANGUAGE USAGE, LANGUAGE MECHANICS

As a class, summarize what you learned in this unit as it relates to the essential question "How do we portray animals in writing?" Following the class discussion, write a response in your journal. Work with a partner to revise and shape your response into an essay. Edit the essay for the use of the progressive and commas before coordinating conjunctions in compound sentences (see Standards for more details) before sharing with your teacher. Your teacher may ask you to post your essay and respond to a poll about the unit on the classroom blog. (W.4.4, W.4.5, W.4.9a, W4.9b, L.4.1a, L.4.1b, L.4.1c, L.4.1d, L.4.1g, L.4.2a, L.4.2b, L.4.2c)

## 15. LANGUAGE USAGE, LANGUAGE MECHANICS

Your teacher will teach mini-lessons on the individual language standards. For example, he or she will teach the class about the form and use of the progressive tense, and then you will practice some cloze activities as a class—for example, "I _____ walking my dog down the street when my dad came home from work." Next, your teacher will give you the start of a sentence ("I was . . .," "I am . . .," "I will be . . ."), and you will have the opportunity to finish the sentence with a partner. Select a piece of your own writing, find examples of the progressive tense, and ensure that you used the correct forms. (L.4.1c)

## 16. LANGUAGE MECHANICS

As a class, continue adding to the Mechanics/Grammar bulletin board started in Unit One. Remember, once skills are taught in a mini-lesson and listed on the bulletin board, you are expected to edit your work for these elements before publication. (L.4.1, L.4.2, L.4.3)

## 17. READING LITERATURE, LANGUAGE MECHANICS

Select passages in your guided reading book where animals are talking. Highlight how commas and quotation marks are used to separate speaking parts from regular text. Then choose a piece of your own writing and underline the dialogue between the different characters. If two characters are talking, two different colors should be used. Edit your own writing, checking that you used a comma before a character speaks, and then quotation marks around each character's words. (L.4.2b)

## 18. VOCABULARY

As a class, continue adding to the Vocabulary Word Wall bulletin board where, throughout the year, you will add and sort words as you learn them in each unit of study. (L.4.4)

## ADDITIONAL RESOURCES

- *On Stage: Theater Games and Activities for Kids* (Lisa Bany-Winters) (RL.4.5)
- *Webcams in the Classroom: Animal Inquiry and Observation* (ReadWriteThink) (SL.4.1)
- *Black Beauty Author Anna Sewell Was Born in 1820* (ReadWriteThink) (W.4.7)
- *Animal Inquiry* (ReadWriteThink) (W.4.7)
- *Celebrate Kate DiCamillo's Birthday Today* (ReadWriteThink) (RL.4.3)
- *Alaska Native Stories: Using Narrative to Introduce Expository Text* (ReadWriteThink) (RI.4.9)
- *Multimedia Responses to Content Area Topics Using Fact-"Faction"-Fiction* (ReadWriteThink) (RL.4.9)
- *How the Fourth Grade and I Wrote a Play* (Matt Buchanan) (W.4.6)
- *Author of the Month: Jack Prelutsky* (McGraw-Hill, Child Lit)
- *Writing with Writers: Poetry Writing with Jack Prelutsky* (Scholastic)
- *Limericks* (Old-Fashioned-American-Humor.com)
- *Creative Drama Lesson Plans* (Creative Drama Classroom)
- *Reader's Theater K–3 Scripts* (Grandview Library, East Ramapo School District, NJ)
- *Horses in Art* (The Incredible Art Department)
- Movie scripts (Drew's Script-O-Rama)
- "Somebody-Wants-But-So" strategy (West Virginia Department of Education)

## TERMINOLOGY

Character traits

First person

Limerick

Narration

Personification

Poetic devices: rhyme scheme, meter, simile, metaphor

Third person

## INTERDISCIPLINARY CONNECTIONS

This unit teaches:

- **History/Geography:**
  - Importance of animals in Native American cultures (e.g., Lakota Indians)
  - Role of animals in historical events, such as exploration (e.g., Lewis and Clark)
- **Science:** Animals (e.g., horses, mice, and dogs) and their traits (e.g., classification, habitat, diet, source of protection, enemies, length of life, domesticated vs. wild); veterinarians

This unit could be extended to teach:

- **Science:**
  - Senses of animals and people
  - Optics (e.g., examining ways that animals have adapted to interpret sensory information); parts of the eye in people and animals (e.g., optic nerve, cornea, lens, iris, pupil, retina) and the function of each part
  - Ears of animals and people; parts of the ear (e.g., outer ear, ear canal, ear drum, auditory nerve) and the function of each part
- **Music:** How animals are portrayed in music (e.g., *Carnival of the Animals* by Camille Saint-Saëns)

## Grade Four, Unit Three Sample Lesson Plan

### The Black Stallion *by Walter Farley*

In this series of seven lessons, students read *The Black Stallion* by Walter Farley, and they:

Conduct a close reading of the novel *The Black Stallion* by Walter Farley (RL.4.1, RL.4.2, RL.4.3)

Perform preparatory tasks leading to a written discussion of the novel (RL.4.1, RL.4.2, RL.4.3)

Write analytical essays (W.4.1a, W.4.1b, W.4.1c, W.4.1d, W.4.4)

### Summary

**Lesson I: Meet Alec and the Black (Chs. 1–3)**

Identify the path of the *Drake* (RL.4.1)

Trace Alec's survival (RL.4.1, RL.4.3)

Investigate Alec's efforts to survive (RL.4.1, RL.4.3)

Explore Alec's personality (RL.4.1, RL.4.3, SL.4.1)

Probe the Black's character (RL.4.1, RL.4.3)

**Lesson II: Survival and Rescue (Chs. 4–6)**

(Continue to) investigate Alec's acts of survival (RL.4.1, RL.4.3)

(Continue to) explore Alec's personality (RL.4.1, RL.4.3)

(Continue to) probe the Black's character (RL.4.1, RL.4.3)

Examine the evolving relationship between the boy and the horse (RL.4.1, RL.4.2, RL.4.3, SL.4.1)

Trace Alec's rescue (RL.4.1, RL.4.3)

**Lesson III: Home (Chs. 7–9)**

Investigate Alec's and the Black's early days at home (RL.4.1, RL.4.3)

(Continue to) examine the relationship between Alec and the Black (RL.4.1, RL.4.2, RL.4.3, SL.4.1)

Note Napoleon's influence on the Black (RL.4.1, RL.4.3)

**Lesson IV: Challenges (Chs. 10–12)**

Explore the Black's evolution (RL.4.1, RL.4.2, RL.4.3, SL.4.1)

Investigate Alec's role in the Black's evolution (RL.4.1, RL.4.2, RL.4.3)

Examine Henry's contribution to Alec's relationship with the Black (RL.4.1, RL.4.2, RL.4.3, SL.4.1)

## Lesson V: Progress (Chs. 13–15)

Probe the purpose of racing the Black (RL.4.3, SL.4.1)

Explore the author's intent in shrouding the Black's identity in a cloud of mystery (RL.4.3, SL.4.1)

Revisit earlier understanding of Alec's and the Black's personalities (RL.4.1, RL.4.2, RL.4.3, SL.4.1)

## Lesson VII: Preparing to Write Essays

Revisit the development of Alec's character (RL.4.1, RL.4.2, RL.4.3)

Interpret the power of friendship as it is portrayed in the novel (RL.4.1, RL.4.2, RL.4.3)

Analyze the complexity of the Black's victory in the race (RL.4.1, RL.4.2, RL.4.3)

Provide a written analysis of a select objective (from above) (W.4.1a, W.4.1b, W.4.1c, W.4.1d, W.4.4)

## Lesson VI: A Winner (Chs. 16–18)

Examine Henry's statement that "Alec isn't the same boy that you sent to India last summer" (p. 166) (RL.4.2, SL.4.1)

Closely review the race (RL.4.1, RL.4.2, RL.4.3)

Explore the meaning of the Black's victory (RL.4.2, SL.4.1)

## Lesson VII: Preparing to Write Essays

### Objectives

Revisit the development of Alec's character (RL.4.1, RL.4.2, RL.4.3)

Interpret the power of friendship as it is portrayed in the novel (RL.4.1, RL.4.2, RL.4.3)

Analyze the complexity of the Black's victory in the race (RL.4.1, RL.4.2, RL.4.3)

Provide a written analysis of a select objective (from above) (W.4.1a, W.4.1b, W.4.1c, W.4.1d, W.4.4)

### Required Materials

☐ Class set of *The Black Stallion* by Walter Farley

☐ Sticky notes

*Procedures*

1. **Lead-In:**

    Students read the three objectives that are written on the board.

2. **Step by Step:**

    a. In preparation for students' written analysis (homework), lead a discussion about the type of textual work that the three objectives involve.

    ○ *The first objective*, "revisit the development of Alec's character," calls for a step-by-step tracing of Alec's responses to his adventures and his evolution from a young boy to a mature young man.

    ○ *The second objective*, "interpret the power of friendship as it is portrayed in the novel," calls for a discussion of the developing friendship and trust between the boy and the horse.

    ○ *The third objective*, "analyze the complexity of the Black's victory in the race" is the most advanced. Alec tries to stop the Black once he sees his injury, but the horse races on despite the pain. How is this climax described? What message is conveyed by the author?

    b. Students select one of the objectives for further study.

    c. Using sticky notes, students skim through the novel and select passages that relate to the objective that they selected.

3. **Closure:**

    Students who chose the same objective for written analysis discuss their findings in small groups.

## Differentiation

*Advanced*

- Assign students the third objective, or allow them to create their own writing prompt.
- Give students an opportunity to talk through the meaning of the assignment with a partner to ensure understanding (before beginning the sticky note activity).

*Struggling*

- Group students who have chosen the same objective together, and allow them to choose either the first or second objective from step b.
- If the suggested objectives seem too difficult, create a simpler one, such as: "Describe how Alec changed from the beginning of the novel to the end."

- Work closely with the students to skim the book, placing sticky notes throughout the text.
- Students will work together, individually or with assistance, on writing clear statements of opinion to begin their essays. Number the sticky notes to show how the passages support the opinion statements.
- As time allows, students will sketch out the rest of their essays while at school.

## Homework/Assessment

Students write an essay (you determine the number of paragraphs) on the objective of their choice. Their essays must include an introduction, state a clear opinion, be soundly developed, provide textual support, and have a conclusion.

# Revolutionaries from the Past

This eight-week unit invites students to read historical fiction and poetry from America's past—including works from the time of the American Revolution.

## ESSENTIAL QUESTION

What life lessons can we learn from revolutionaries in fiction and nonfiction?

## OVERVIEW

While reading about America's past, students not only highlight key information and supporting details about people and events in order to get a sense of chronology, but also spend time comparing and contrasting first- and third-person narratives. Students will read and discuss poetry, such as "Concord Hymn" by Ralph Waldo Emerson, and read speeches by revolutionaries including Patrick Henry and Sojourner Truth. Students read informational texts and study author Jean Fritz, who wrote books about the American Revolution, such as *Can't You Make Them Behave, King George?* After learning about revolutionary people of the past, students write their own speeches outlining their opinion on a current event, possibly taking a "revolutionary" position. This unit ends with a class discussion and essay response to the essential question.

## FOCUS STANDARDS

These Focus Standards have been selected for the unit from the Common Core State Standards.

**RL.4.6:** Compare and contrast the point of view from which different stories are narrated, including the difference between first- and third-person narrations.

**RI.4.5:** Describe the overall structure (e.g., chronology, comparison, cause/effect, problem/solution) of events, ideas, concepts, or information in a text or part of a text.

**RI.4.6:** Compare and contrast a firsthand and secondhand account of the same event or topic; describe the differences in focus and the information provided.

**W.4.1:** Write opinion pieces on topics or texts, supporting a point of view with reasons and information.

**SL.4.3:** Identify the reasons and evidence a speaker provides to support particular points.

**L.4.4:** Determine or clarify the meaning of unknown and multiple-meaning words and phrases based on grade 4 reading and content, choosing flexibly from a range of strategies.

## SUGGESTED OBJECTIVES

- Describe the differences between firsthand accounts (primary sources) and secondhand accounts (secondary sources) in informational text.
- Order events in informational and literary text chronologically.
- Compare and contrast first- and third-person narrations.
- Discuss and interpret the literal and figurative meaning of idioms.
- Identify the reasons that speakers provide to support their positions (e.g., Patrick Henry and Sojourner Truth).
- Write opinion pieces about people and events explored in reading (e.g., American revolutionaries), supporting your point of view with at least two reasons.

## SUGGESTED WORKS

(E) indicates a CCSS exemplar text; (EA) indicates a text from a writer with other works identified as exemplars.

## LITERARY TEXTS

### Stories

- *Heroes of the Revolution* (David A. Adler and Donald A. Smith)
- *John Henry: An American Legend* (Ezra Jack Keats)
- *The Madcap Mystery of the Missing Liberty Bell* (Real Kids, Real Places) (Carole Marsh) (advanced)
- *The Mystery on the Freedom Trail* (Real Kids, Real Places) (Carole Marsh)
- *Navajo Long Walk* (The Council for Indian Education) (Nancy M. Armstrong and Paulette Livers Lambert)
- *Poor Richard's Almanack* (Benjamin Franklin) (Read Aloud)
- *A Ride into Morning: The Story of Tempe Wick* (Ann Rinaldi)
- *The Secret of Sarah Revere* (Ann Rinaldi)
- *Sleds on Boston Common: A Story from the American Revolution* (Louise Borden and Robert Andrew Parker)
- *Trail of Tears* (Step-Into-Reading, Step 5) (Joseph Bruchac)
- *War Comes to Willy Freeman* (Arabus Family Saga) (James and Christopher Collier)
- *Yankee Doodle* (Gary Chalk)

*Poems*

- "Concord Hymn" (Ralph Waldo Emerson)
- "The Flag" (unknown)
- "George Washington" (Rosemary and Stephen Vincent Benet)
- "A Nation's Strength" (Ralph Waldo Emerson)
- "A Tragic Story" (William Makepeace Thackeray)

## INFORMATIONAL TEXTS

*Nonfiction Books*

- *A Is for America* (Devin Scillian and Pam Carroll)
- *The American Revolutionaries: A History in Their Own Words 1750–1800* (Milton Meltzer)
- *And Then What Happened, Paul Revere?* (Jean Fritz and Margot Tomes)
- *Can't You Make Them Behave, King George?* (Jean Fritz and Margot Tomes)
- *Crispus Attucks: Black Leader of Colonial Patriots* (Childhood of Famous Americans) (Dharathula H. Millender and Gary Morrow)
- *A History of US: From Colonies to Country* (Joy Hakim)
- *If You Lived at the Time of the American Revolution* (Kay Moore and Daniel O'Leary)
- *Molly Pitcher: Young Patriot* (Childhood of Famous Americans) (Augusta Stevenson)
- *O, Say Can You See? America's Symbols, Landmarks, and Important Words* (Sheila Keenan and Ann Boyajian)
- *The Revolutionary War* (True Books: American History) (Brendan January)
- *Where Was Patrick Henry on the 29th of May?* (Jean Fritz and Margot Tomes)
- *Why Don't You Get a Horse, Sam Adams?* (Jean Fritz and Trina Schart Hyman)
- *Will You Sign Here, John Hancock?* (Jean Fritz and Trina Schart Hyman)

*Biographies*

- *Abigail Adams: Girl of Colonial Days* (Childhood of Famous Americans) (Jean Brown Wagoner)
- *How Ben Franklin Stole the Lightning* (Rosalyn Schanzer)
- *In Their Own Words: Paul Revere* (George Sullivan)
- *In Their Own Words: Sojourner Truth* (Peter and Connie Roop)
- *Now & Ben: The Modern Inventions of Benjamin Franklin* (Gene Barretta)
- *The Secret Soldier: The Story of Deborah Sampson* (Scholastic Biography) (Ann McGovern, Harold Goodwin, and Katherine Thompson)
- *Sojourner Truth: Ain't I a Woman?* (Scholastic Biography) (Patricia C. McKissack and Frederick McKissack)
- *Susan B. Anthony: Champion of Women's Rights* (Childhood of Famous Americans) (Helen Albee Monsell)
- *Victory or Death! Stories of the American Revolution* (Doreen Rappaport, Joan Verniero, and Greg Call)

*Speeches*

- Patrick Henry, "Give Me Liberty or Give Me Death," March 23, 1775
- Sojourner Truth, "Ain't I a Woman?" May 29, 1851
- Susan B. Anthony, "On a Woman's Right to Vote," 1873

## ART, MUSIC, AND MEDIA

*Art*

- Grant Wood, *The Midnight Ride of Paul Revere* (1931)
- John Singleton Copley, *Paul Revere* (1768)

*Media*

- Rock and Revolution, "Too Late to Apologize" (2010)

# SAMPLE ACTIVITIES AND ASSESSMENTS

## 1. READING LITERATURE

As a class, when we read historical fiction stories and poems, we will keep a chart with information organized by the categories listed below. Use the information to talk about related information learned from literature.

- Title and author
- Text structure(s) used
- Type of narration (first person, third person)
- Character(s) (major and minor)
- Does this character remind you of other characters? Who/why?
- What information was changed that shows you this is historical fiction?
- What did you learn from the major characters?
- Summary

Write your response on a sticky note, on a whiteboard, or in your journal and share it with a partner before each section of the class chart is filled in. (RL.4.1, RL.4.2, RL.4.3, RL.4.5, RL.4.6, RL.4.9)

## 2. READING LITERATURE, SPEAKING AND LISTENING

Compare and contrast the points of view from which these stories and poems are narrated. Which clues/key words provide information about the point of view? How are the narratives different? Look back for specific lines or paragraphs in order to find explicit details from the stories and poems read. (RL.4.6, SL.4.1)

## 3. READING POETRY, WRITING POETRY, LANGUAGE USAGE

Choose a poem or story and change the point of view from which it is written. In other words, if the story is in first person, rewrite it in third, or if the story is in third person, rewrite it in first. Alternatively, choose a story to write in poetic form, or a poem to rewrite in story form. Discuss with a partner which style of writing you prefer and why. (RL.4.6, W.4.4, L.4.1a, L.4.1b, L.4.1c, L.4.1d, L.4.1e, L.4.1g, L.4.2)

## 4. RESEARCH, INFORMATIVE WRITING, LANGUAGE MECHANICS

As a class, when we read about historical events from the American Revolution, we will keep a chart with information organized by the categories listed below. Read informational texts about people and events that are both firsthand (primary sources) and secondhand (secondary sources), and talk about how the differences in point of view affect understanding. Does the overall structure of the text (chronology, cause/effect, etc.) affect your understanding of events as they are presented? As the chart is filled in, use the information to talk about what we learned from nonfiction books.

- Person or event
- Where this took place
- When this took place
- What is the historical significance of this event?
- From whose point of view is this account written?
- What other significant information do you want to remember about this person or event?
- Notes about text structure (chronology, cause/effect, etc.)

Write your response on a sticky note, on a whiteboard, or in your journal and share it with a partner before each section of the class chart is filled in. (RI.4.1, RI.4.2, RI.4.5, RI.4.6, RI.4.7, RI.4.9, SL.4.3)

## 5. RESEARCH, SPEAKING AND LISTENING

Following a class discussion of historical events, create a time line of events that shows the chronology and cause/effect relationships among them. You may use a free online time line generator or make your own. (W.4.2, W.4.4, W.4.7, L.4.1a, L.4.1b, L.4.1c, L.4.1d, L.4.1e, L.4.1g, L.4.2)

## 6. RESEARCH, ORAL PRESENTATION

Select an author who writes nonfiction in the style of a story, such as Jean Fritz. Conduct research about him or her and why he or she chooses to write about historical topics; take notes in your journal. As you use online sources for your research, be sure to evaluate them for credibility. Share findings as a class. (SL.4.1, W.4.7)

## 7. SPEAKING AND LISTENING, LANGUAGE USAGE, MULTIMEDIA PRESENTATION

Benjamin Franklin coined a number of phrases still used today, and they are found in *Poor Richard's Almanack*. Illustrate the literal and figurative meaning of two idioms that enhance understanding of the foundations of our country. What did Ben Franklin hope people would learn from these phrases? Compile these illustrations into a class book to share (e.g., with younger students), and try to incorporate the phrases you learned into your daily writing and speaking. Your teacher may ask you to create a slide of your page, including scanned illustrations or relevant photos from the Internet, before assembling them into a class book (either electronic or in print). (RL.4.1, SL.4.1, L.4.5b)

## 8. READING INFORMATIONAL TEXT, SPEAKING AND LISTENING

Listen to your teacher read Sojourner Truth's "Ain't I a Woman?" and discuss the message. Then look online to find Frances D. Gage's memories of listening to Sojourner Truth's speech. Compare the text of the speech with what Gage remembers. What are the similarities and differences? Do the points of view differ? How do Gage's memories enhance your understanding of the speech? Share your answers to these questions with a partner before participating in class discussion. (RI.4.6, SL.4.3)

## 9. INFORMATIVE WRITING, OPINION WRITING, SPEAKING AND LISTENING, LANGUAGE USAGE

With a partner, discuss the message of Patrick Henry's speech "Give Me Liberty or Give Me Death." Then discuss the message of his speech as a class within the context of learning about the American Revolution. Does knowing historical information change your understanding of the message? Why or why not? Then, individually, write a letter to Patrick Henry, explaining your reactions to the message of his speech. Be sure to support your opinion by referring back to a specific line or quotation from his speech. Edit your work for the use of prepositional phrases and spelling (see Standards for more details) before turning it in. (W.4.1, SL.4.1, SL.4.3, SL.4.4, L.4.1a, L.4.1b, L.4.1c, L.4.1d, L.4.1e, L.4.1g, L.4.2)

## 10. OPINION WRITING, LANGUAGE USAGE, ORAL PRESENTATION

Applying what you have learned from the speeches discussed in this unit, write your own speech expressing an opinion from the point of view of a revolutionary character. Think about the audience as well as the message when writing your speech. Be sure your opinion is supported by two pieces of evidence. Edit your work for the use of prepositional phrases and spelling (see Standards for more details) before turning it in. You may also record your presentation using a video camera to compare the difference in impact between "seeing" and "hearing" the words. (W.4.1, W.4.7, SL.4.3, L.4.1a, L.4.1b, L.4.1c, L.4.1d, L.4.1e, L.4.1g, L.4.2)

## 11. NARRATIVE WRITING, PERFORMANCE

After reviewing the structural elements (e.g., casts of characters, settings, descriptions, dialogue, stage directions) that are unique to drama (i.e., compared to prose), add these elements to a Reader's Theater script of a historical story. With at least two other classmates, add at least two scenes—one before the script begins and one after the script ends—to make it a one-act, three-scene play; present it as a class. You may record and create a movie from the presentations. (RL.4.5, W.4.4)

## 12. READING POETRY, PERFORMANCE

Read and discuss the meaning of "The Flag" by an unknown author. How does the first-person point of view influence your appreciation of the poem? Perform the poem with a classmate. (RL.4.6, SL.4.5)

## 13. INFORMATIVE WRITING, LANGUAGE USAGE

Design and create a flag that symbolically represents your family, your classroom, or your school. Explain the symbolism of the flag in your journal in a first-person narrative, similar to the presentation of "The Flag" (in Activity 12), and share it with a classmate. Be sure to edit your work for the use of prepositional phrases and spelling (see Standards for more details). (RL4.4, SL.4.4, W.4.1a, W.4.1c, W.4.1d, L.4.1a, L.4.1b, L.4.1c, L.4.1d, L.4.1e, L.4.1g, L.4.2)

## 14. OPINION WRITING, LANGUAGE USAGE, ORAL PRESENTATION

Revolutionaries aren't always popular during the time that they live, but they believe in something so passionately that they are willing to go out on a limb to express their beliefs. Think about a current event that you believe everyone should understand. Write a speech, supported by two pieces of evidence, about your thoughts and ideas, and present it to the class. Edit your work for the use of prepositional phrases and spelling (see Standards for more details) before turning it in. You may record your presentation using a video camera. (W.4.1, W.4.4, W.4.5, W.4.6, W.4.7, W.4.8, SL.4.5, L.4.1a, L.4.1b, L.4.1c, L.4.1d, L.4.1e, L.4.1g, L.4.2, L.4.5)

## 15. MEDIA, SPEAKING AND LISTENING

Independently or as a class, view the video "Too Late to Apologize." After watching the video, talk about the meaning and historical significance of the words. Then view the video a second time, stopping to discuss the images used and how they represent America's past in a contemporary manner. *Optional extension:* Create or remix your own music video to accompany your speech (from Activity 14). (RL.4.7, RL.4.9, RI.4.7, RI.4.9, SL.4.1)

## 16. VOCABULARY, LANGUAGE USAGE

As an individual and as a class, keep an index card file of new words learned in this unit (e.g., *revolution, revolutionary, revolt*). Keeping the words on index cards will allow you to use and sort the words by spelling features, root words, prefixes, and suffixes. Find root words, and discuss how the prefixes and suffixes add clues to the meaning of the words. Consult reference materials to confirm pronunciations and clarify the meaning of the words and phrases. (Note: This will be an ongoing activity all year long.) (L.4.4a, L.4.4b)

## 17. SPEAKING AND LISTENING, OPINION WRITING, LANGUAGE USAGE

As a class, summarize what was learned in this unit as it relates to the essential question "What life lessons can we learn from revolutionaries in fiction and nonfiction?" Following the class discussion, individually write a response in your journal. Work with a partner to edit your work for the use of prepositional phrases and spelling (see Standards for more details), and strengthen the content before turning it in to your teacher. Your teacher may ask you to type your essay and respond to a poll about the unit on the classroom blog. (W.4.9a, W.4.9b, W.4.4, W.4.5, L.4.1a, L.4.1b, L.4.1c, L.4.1d, L.4.1e, L.4.1g, L.4.2)

## 18. LANGUAGE USAGE

As a class, generate a list of the most common prepositions. Your teacher will give you a worksheet of sentences that contain prepositional phrases (e.g., *The girl with the blue scarf sang first*). First, circle the preposition and underline the entire phrase. On the next day, your teacher will give you simple sentences (e.g., *The girl sang first*), and you will work with partners to create prepositional phrases to expand them. Finally, find simple sentences in your own writing and add prepositional phrases to add more details. (L.4.1e)

## 19. LANGUAGE MECHANICS

As a class, continue adding to the Mechanics/Grammar bulletin board started in Unit One. Remember, once skills are taught in a mini-lesson and listed on the bulletin board, you are expected to edit your work for these elements before publication. (L.4.1, L.4.2, L.4.3)

## 20. VOCABULARY

As a class, continue adding to the Vocabulary Word Wall bulletin board where, throughout the year, you will add and sort words as you learn them in each unit of study. (L.4.4)

## 21. ART, SPEAKING AND LISTENING

Compare Copley's and Wood's portrayals of Paul Revere. How are they different? Do they have anything common—aside from both showing Revere? Think about what you know about Revere and his famous ride as you consider the works. What do you see first in each image? Is it Revere or something else? Each artist meant to tell a story through his painting—can you describe this story? (SL.4.1, SL.4.3, L.4.3)

## 22. ART, SPEAKING AND LISTENING

View the Copley and Wood paintings again. One work is a portrait painted while the person was living; the second, the artist's interpretation a hundred years later. Notice the differences in perspective (e.g., eye-level view vs. bird's-eye view). Why do you think the earlier image focuses more on the man and the later one on the event that made him famous? (SL.4.1, SL.4.3, L.4.3)

## ADDITIONAL ONLINE RESOURCES

- *Slave Narratives: Constructing U.S. History Through Analyzing Primary Sources* (National Endowment for the Humanities) (RI.4.6)
- *American Colonial Life in the Late 1700s: Distant Cousins* (National Endowment for the Humanities) (RI.4.7)
- *Learning About Research and Writing Using the American Revolution* (ReadWriteThink) (W.4.7)
- *Looking for the History in Historical Fiction: An Epidemic for Reading* (ReadWriteThink) (RI.4.9)
- *History Comes Alive: Developing Fluency and Comprehension Using Social Studies* (ReadWriteThink) (RL.4.5)
- *The American Revolution: Lighting Freedom's Flame* (National Parks Service)
- *African Americans in the American Revolution* (Buzzle.com)
- *Indians in the American Revolution* (Wilcomb E. Washburn, speech) (AmericanRevolution.org)
- *Featured Author: Jean Fritz* (Carol Hurst's Children's Literature Site)
- *Meet the Author: Jean Fritz* (Houghton Mifflin Reading)

## TERMINOLOGY

Audience

Autobiography

Biography

First-person point of view

Informational text structure

Major character

Minor character

Point of view

Primary source

Secondary source

Third-person point of view

Writing style

Speech

## INTERDISCIPLINARY CONNECTIONS

This unit teaches:

- **History/Geography:**
  - Causes and provocations of the American Revolution (e.g., the Boston Massacre, Boston Tea Party, Intolerable Acts, Thomas Paine's *Common Sense*)
  - Biographies of revolutionaries (e.g., Crispus Attucks, Molly Pitcher, Paul Revere, Deborah Sampson, John Hancock, John Henry)

- Introduction to the Trail of Tears (e.g., involuntary relocation, Cherokee Nation, Indian Removal Act, passive resistance)
- Women's rights advocates and legislation through history (e.g., Susan B. Anthony, Sojourner Truth, Fourteenth Amendment)

- **Art:** John Singleton Copley, Grant Wood

This unit could be extended to teach:

- **History/Geography:**
  - The making of a constitutional government (e.g., the ideas behind the Declaration of Independence, the Constitution, levels and functions of government)
  - Biographies (e.g., Elizabeth Freeman, Phillis Wheatley)
  - Equal rights advocates through history (e.g., Eleanor Roosevelt, Mary McLeod Bethune, Rosa Parks, Martin Luther King Jr., Suraya Pakzad)

# Grade Four, Unit Four Sample Lesson Plan

*"Concord Hymn" by Ralph Waldo Emerson*

*A History of US: From Colonies to Country by Joy Hakim*

In this series of five lessons, students read "Concord Hymn" by Ralph Waldo Emerson and passages from *A History of US: From Colonies to Country by Joy Hakim*, and they:

Explore the historical background of the battles of Lexington and Concord (RI.4.6)

Investigate the life and ideas of Ralph Waldo Emerson (RL.4.6, W.4.7)

Reflect upon the power of a poem to depict historical events (RL.4.2, RL.4.3, RL.4.5, RL.4.6, RL.4.9)

Probe the significance of events in the history of a people (RI.4.3)

## Summary

| Lesson I: Battles of Lexington and Concord | Lesson II: Ralph Waldo Emerson |
|---|---|
| Identify key events leading to the battles of Lexington and Concord (RI.4.1, RI.4.6) | Explore the life of Ralph Waldo Emerson (RI.4.9, W.4.7, SL.4.2) |
| Explore the battle of Lexington (RI.4.5) | Note important works by Emerson (RI.4.2, RI.4.6) |
| Explore the battle of Concord (RI.4.5) | Identify key ideas of Emerson (RI.4.6, RI.4.9) |
| Examine the significance of the two battles (SL.4.1, SL.4.4) | |
| **Lesson III: "Concord Hymn" by Ralph Waldo Emerson** | **Lesson IV: History in Art–Paintings of the Concord Bridge** |
| Read and reread "Concord Hymn" (RL.4.2, RL.4.10, RF.4.4, L.4.4) | Identify the location of the Concord Bridge |
| Annotate "Concord Hymn" for its historical details (RL.4.6) | Explore the artistic renditions of the battle of Concord (RI.4.6, RI.4.7, SL.4.5) |
| Note the event (completion of Concord Monument, April 19, 1836) that prompted the writing of the hymn (RI.4.1, RL.4.2) | Explore the artistic renditions of the Concord Bridge (RI.4.6, RI.4.7, SL.4.5) |

## Lesson V: Significance of Events in the History of a People

Recall the details of the battle of Concord (RI.4.1, RI.4.9)

Note the contribution of Emerson to immortalizing the event (RL.4.2, RL.4.6)

Reflect upon the power of a poem to depict historical events (RL.4.2, RL.4.6, RI.4.9)

Revisit the artistic works that depict the event (RI.4.6, RI.4.7, SL.4.5)

Explore the importance of the lingering memory of the battle of Concord (SL.4.1)

## Lesson V: Significance of Events in the History of a People

### Objectives

Recall the details of the battle of Concord (RI.4.1, RI.4.9)

Note the contribution of Emerson to immortalizing the event (RL.4.2, RL.4.6)

Reflect on the power of a poem to depict historical events (RL.4.2, RL.4.6, RI.4.9)

Revisit the artistic works that depict the event (RI.4.6, RI.4.7, SL.4.5)

Explore the importance of the lingering memory of the battle of Concord (SL.4.1)

### Required Materials

☐ "Concord Hymn" by Ralph Waldo Emerson

☐ Artwork and photos of the Concord Bridge

☐ Artwork depicting the Battle of Concord

☐ A History of US: From Colonies to Country by Joy Hakim

☐ Poster boards

☐ Markers

## Procedures

1. Lead-In:

   Students will prepare the material of the previous four lessons.

2. Step by Step:

   a. Divide the class into several groups and assign each group one of the lessons' objectives. (Depending on the number of students in the class and the size of the groups, more than one group may be assigned to the same objective.) Using the information that the students gathered in the Lead-In, the groups will record their findings on a poster board.

   b. Each group will report their recalled findings to the rest of the class.

3. Closure:

   Lead a class discussion that probes the significance of events in the history of a people.

## Differentiation

### Advanced

- Extend this lesson by challenging students to explore the poet Henry Wadsworth Longfellow's role in Paul Revere's fame by reading the poem "Paul Revere's Ride."

- Challenge students to write an essay taking a position on the poet's role in communicating history. Students should argue whether the poet did more to preserve history or whether the poet did more to distort history. This could also take the form of a debate.

### Struggling

- Creative groupings of students provide the support needed for this lesson. Students might be paired with a supportive partner who is strong in research and skilled at determining the importance of the collected information. You may choose to work with a small group of students, taking on one of the objectives.

- Provide an outline or graphic organizer related to the information needed on the poster board, giving students the support they need to work in either a heterogeneous group or a homogeneous group.

## Homework/Assessment

Students will write a one-page reflection about the significance of events in the history of a people.

# Stories of the Earth and Sky

This four-week unit pairs Native American stories with informational text about the earth and sky.

---

## ESSENTIAL QUESTION

How are the earth and sky portrayed in fiction and nonfiction?

---

## OVERVIEW

The unit begins with a discussion about stories that explain nature's mysteries, and how these stories are often passed down orally from generation to generation. Students are asked to share any personal stories about the earth and sky that they have been told. After a brief introduction to Native Americans' reverence and respect for the earth and sky, students read Native American stories and compare and contrast them as a genre. Students alternate reading stories, such as *The Earth Under Sky Bear's Feet* by Joseph Bruchac, and related informational texts, such as *Zoo in the Sky: A Book of Animal Constellations* by Jacqueline Mitton. Class discussions focus on how the informational text helps us to appreciate literature and how authors use artistic license to make a good story. Students also conduct and present research on constellations. After discussing Vincent van Gogh's *Starry Night* and El Greco's *View of Toledo*, students write their own story and publish it on a class web page. This unit ends with a class discussion and informative/explanatory essay in response to the essential question.

## FOCUS STANDARDS

These Focus Standards have been selected for the unit from the Common Core State Standards.

**RL.4.9:** Compare and contrast the treatment of similar themes and topics (e.g., opposition of good and evil) and patterns of events (e.g., the quest) in stories, myths, and traditional literature from different cultures.

**RI.4.7:** Interpret information presented visually, orally, or quantitatively (e.g., in charts, graphs, diagrams, time lines, animations, or interactive elements on web pages) and explain how the information contributes to an understanding of the text in which it appears.

**W.4.3:** Write narratives to develop real or imagined experiences or events using effective technique, descriptive details, and clear event sequences.

**SL.4.4:** Report on a topic or text, tell a story, or recount an experience in an organized manner, using appropriate facts and relevant, descriptive details to support main ideas or themes; speak clearly at an understandable pace.

**L.4.3:** Use knowledge of language and its conventions when writing, speaking, reading, or listening.

## SUGGESTED OBJECTIVES

- Explain how knowledge of a topic (e.g., Native American mound builders, the earth, the sun, the moon, and the stars) increases understanding of literature that addresses the topics (e.g., Native American stories).

- Summarize information presented visually, orally, or quantitatively (e.g., in charts, graphs, diagrams, time lines, animations, or interactive elements on web pages) using appropriate facts and descriptive details.

- Write a story based on a painting (e.g., Vincent van Gogh's *Starry Night*; El Greco's *View of Toledo*), incorporating factual information and stylistic techniques used by authors.

## SUGGESTED WORKS

(E) indicates a CCSS exemplar text; (EA) indicates a text from a writer with other works identified as exemplars.

## LITERARY TEXTS

### Stories

- *Butterfly Eyes and Other Secrets of the Meadow* (Joyce Sidman and Beth Krommes)
- *Common Ground: The Water, Earth, and Air We Share* (Molly Bang)
- *Follow the Moon* (Sarah Weeks and Suzanne Duranceau)
- *Midnight on the Moon* (Magic Tree House Book #8) (Mary Pope Osborne and Sal Murdocca)
- *The Mission Possible Mystery at Space Center Houston* (Real Kids, Real Places) (Carole Marsh) (Read Aloud)
- *My Light* (Molly Bang)
- *Space Explorers* (The Magic School Bus Chapter Book, No. 4) (Eva Moore and Ted Enik)
- *They Dance in the Sky: Native American Star Myths* (Ray A. Williamson, Jean Guard Monroe, and Edgar Stewart) (Read Aloud)

*Myths and Legends*

- *And Still the Turtle Watched* (Sheila MacGill-Callahan)
- *Children of the Earth and Sky: Five Stories About Native American Children* (Stephen Krensky and James Watling)
- *Coyote Places the Stars* (Harriet Peck Taylor)
- *The Earth Under Sky Bear's Feet* (Joseph Bruchac)
- *The Girl Who Loved Wild Horses* (Paul Goble)
- *How the Stars Fell into the Sky: A Navajo Legend* (Jerrie Oughton and Lisa Desimini)
- *Keepers of the Earth: Native American Stories and Environmental Activities for Children* (Michael J. Caduto and Joseph Bruchac)
- *Keepers of the Night: Native American Stories and Nocturnal Activities for Children* (Michael J. Caduto and Joseph Bruchac)
- *Ming Lo Moves the Mountain* (Arnold Lobel)
- *Moon Rope/Un lazo a la luna: A Peruvian Folktale* (Lois Ehlert and Amy Prince)
- *Moonstick: The Seasons of the Sioux* (Eve Bunting and John Sandford)
- *A Pride of African Tales* (Donna L. Washington and James Ransome)
- *Star Boy* (Paul Goble)
- *Thirteen Moons on Turtle's Back* (Joseph Bruchac)
- *The Woman Who Outshone the Sun/La mujer que brillaba aún más que el sol* (Alejandro Cruz Martinez and Fernando Olivera)

## Poems

- "Indian Names" (Lydia Howard Huntley Sigourney)
- *A Pizza the Size of the Sun* (Jack Prelutsky)

## INFORMATIONAL TEXTS

*Nonfiction Books*

Native Americans

- *The Mound Builders of Ancient North America* (E. Barrie Kavasch) (E)
- *Mounds of Earth and Shell* (Native Dwellings) (Bonnie Shemie)

*Space*

- *Can You Hear a Shout in Space? Questions and Answers About Space Exploration* (Scholastic Question and Answer) (Melvin Berger, Gilda Berger, and Vincent Di Fate) (EA)
- *Discovering Mars: The Amazing Story of the Red Planet* (Melvin Berger and Joan Holub) (E)
- *Space: A Nonfiction Companion to Midnight on the Moon* (Magic Tree House Research Guide #6) (Mary Pope, Wil Osborne, and Sal Murdocca)
- *A Walk Through the Heavens: A Guide to Stars and Constellations and Their Legends* (Milton D. Heifetz and Wil Tirion) (Read Aloud)

*Earth, Sun, Moon, and Stars*

- *A Child's Introduction to the Night Sky: The Story of the Stars, Planets, and Constellations—and How You Can Find Them in the Sky* (Michael Driscoll and Meredith Hamilton)
- *Constellations* (True Books) (Flora S. Kim)
- *Constellations* (True Books: Space) (Diane M. Sipiera and Paul P. Sipiera)
- *Destined for Space: Our Story of Exploration* (Don Nardo)
- *Do Stars Have Points?* (Scholastic Question and Answer) (Melvin Berger) (EA)
- *Earth* (Picture Reference) (World Book) (Christine Butler-Taylor)
- *Earth* (True Books) (Elaine Landau)
- *Earth: Our Planet in Space* (Seymour Simon)
- *Find the Constellations* (H. A. Rey)
- *G Is for Galaxy* (Janis Campbell, Cathy Collison, and Alan Stacy)
- *I Wonder Why Stars Twinkle: And Other Questions About Space* (Carole Stott)
- *See the Stars: Your First Guide to the Night Stars* (Ken Croswell)
- *The Moon* (Seymour Simon)
- *The Moon* (Starting with Space) (Paulette Bourgeois, Cynthia Pratt Nicolson, and Bill Slavin)
- *The Stars* (Starting with Space) (Cynthia Pratt Nicolson and Bill Slavin)
- *Stars* (True Books: Space) (Paul P. Sipiera)
- *The Sun* (Seymour Simon)
- *The Sun* (Starting with Space) (Paulette Bourgeois and Bill Slavin)
- *The Sun* (True Books) (Elaine Landau)
- *Zoo in the Sky: A Book of Animal Constellations* (Jacqueline Mitton and Christina Balit)

*Reference*

- *Eats, Shoots & Leaves* (Lynne Truss) (Read Aloud)

## ART, MUSIC, AND MEDIA

### Art

*Earth Images*

- Albert Pinkham Ryder, *Seacoast in Moonlight* (1890)
- Jean-Francois Millet, *Landscape with a Peasant Woman* (early 1870s)
- Louisa Matthíasdóttir, *Gul* (1990)
- Piet Mondrian, *View from the Dunes with Beach and Piers* (1909)

*Sky Images*

- Alfred Stieglitz, *Equivalents* (1923)
- El Greco, *View of Toledo* (c. 1595)
- John Constable, *Hampstead Heath, Looking Towards Harrow at Sunset* (1823)
- John Constable, *Study of Clouds* (1822)
- Vija Celmins, *Untitled #3 (Comet)* (1996)
- Vincent van Gogh, *The Starry Night* (1889)

# SAMPLE ACTIVITIES AND ASSESSMENTS

## 1. READING LITERATURE, SPEAKING AND LISTENING

*Children of the Earth and Sky* by Stephen Krensky and James Watling is a book about Native American traditions and cultures. While reading this book, notice instances in which the Native Americans' respect for the earth and sky is described or inferred. Your teacher will ask you to write, on sticky notes or in your journal, how the earth and sky are described in Native American literature and to compare the portrayals with what you already know about these topics. Do you have any stories about the earth or sky that you were told by your family when you were young? (RL.4.3, RL.4.9, SL.4.1, SL.4.2, L.4.3)

## 2. READING LITERATURE

As a class, keep a chart with the categories listed here of the Native American and other stories the class read about the earth and sky. As the chart is completed, use the information to talk about what the class learned from literature.

* Title and author
* Which culture is this story from?
* What role does the earth or sky play in this story? (e.g., personified character, setting)
* What is important about the character's interaction with the earth or sky?
* Summary
* Theme of the story
* What is unique about this story's portrayal of the earth and/or sky?

Code your book with sticky notes, or write your response on a whiteboard or in your journal, before each section of the class chart is filled in. (RL.4.1, RL.4.2, RL.4.3, RL.4.5, RL.4.9)

## 3. OPINION WRITING, LANGUAGE MECHANICS

Of the stories read in this unit, which was your favorite, and why? Choose a story about which to write a well-developed essay. Support your opinion by citing details from the favorite text. Edit your work for complete sentences, punctuation, and use of language and conventions (see Standards for more details) before turning it in to your teacher. Your teacher may ask you to type your opinion paper for publication on a class blog about the books read in this unit. (W.4.1, L.4.1, L.4.2, L.4.3, L.4.5)

## 4. READING LITERATURE, SPEAKING AND LISTENING

Compare and contrast how the earth and sky are treated in Native American stories and other texts. Look back in the stories and poems we've read for specific lines or paragraphs in order to find specific details. (RL.4.9, SL.4.1, L.4.3)

## 5. READING LITERATURE, READING INFORMATIONAL TEXT, SPEAKING AND LISTENING

First, read and discuss a story about rock carving, such as *And Still the Turtle Watched* by Sheila MacGill-Callahan. Then, read informational books, such as *The Mound Builders of Ancient North America* by E. Barrie Kavasch or *Mounds of Earth and Shell* by Bonnie Shemie, which tell why the Native Americans created structures and dwellings from the earth. Your teacher may ask you to write, on a sticky note, on a whiteboard, or in your journal, what you learned about the purposeful nature of Native American artifacts and structures. Finally, review the story and see if any additional information or insights are apparent that you didn't notice the first time. (RL.4.1, RL.4.3, RI.4.1, RI.4.3, RI.4.9, SL.4.1, SL.4.2, L.4.1a, L.4.3)

## 6. READING POETRY, READING FLUENCY, PERFORMANCE

Read and discuss the meaning of the poem "Indian Names" by Lydia Howard Huntley Sigourney. What is the message of the poem? Locate the rivers from the poem on a map of the United States. Discuss additional names of places whose names may have Native American origins, especially local places, and keep an ongoing list in your journal. Divide the poem into stanzas and, with a group of three other classmates, perform the poem as a quartet. Record the readings using a video camera to compare the similarities and differences in expression used by different groups. (RL.4.4, SL.4.1, SL.4.1c, L.4.3)

## 7. READING INFORMATIONAL TEXT, RESEARCH, ORAL PRESENTATION

As a class, keep a chart of information learned about constellations using the categories below. With a partner, research a constellation on the Internet. Be sure to evaluate your sources for credibility, citing only the sources that gave you the most relevant and useful information.

- Constellation name
- Where does the name come from?
- What is the definition of a constellation?
- What is unique about this constellation?
- What does it look like? (Draw a picture.)

In your journal, write what you learn, as well as where you found the information, in case you need to go back to find a reference. Present your findings to the class. As a class, complete the class chart of all the constellations. (RI.4.1, RI.4.3, RI.4.7, RI.4.8, RI.4.9, SL.4.2, SL.4.3, SL.4.4, W.4.7)

## 8. INFORMATIVE WRITING

Following partner presentations about constellations (in Activity 7), write a summary of what you learned, using appropriate facts and descriptive details. (W.4.2, W.4.4, W.4.7, L.4.1, L.4.2, L.4.3)

## 9. READING LITERATURE, OPINION WRITING

Choose one of the stories about the earth or sky, such as *Butterfly Eyes and Other Secrets of the Meadow* by Joyce Sidman and Beth Krommes or *A Pride of African Tales* by Donna L. Washington and James Ransome. Compare how the facts we know about the earth and sky are modified in order to make a good story. This is called taking "artistic license." Keep an ongoing T-chart in your journal with two columns—Fact and Fiction—to track the amount of artistic license taken in each book we read. Write a response to this question in your journal: "Why do you think the author changed some facts and kept others?" (RL.4.1, RL.4.9, W.4.4)

## 10. ART, NARRATIVE WRITING

After looking at and discussing as a class van Gogh's *The Starry Night* and El Greco's *View of Toledo*, select one of the two works and write a story that could take place at the time of day and in the location depicted in the painting. Look closely at the painting before beginning to write, and refer back to it repeatedly. Begin by outlining your story using the "Somebody-Wanted-But-So" strategy. Then make a list of the main events for your story. Next, add details by incorporating some facts you learned from your research, as well as some imaginary information, because we have learned that taking artistic license is an effective technique that authors use to build a story. Write a draft of your story and work with a partner to choose words and phrases that have the effect you want and that fit the painting you selected. Once you and your partner believe that your story is of the highest quality, record yourself reading it. Upload this as a podcast to the class web page, which will have van Gogh's and El Greco's paintings displayed nearby. (W.4.3, W.4.4, W.4.5, W.4.6, W.4.7, W.4.8, SL.4.5, L.4.1, L.4.2, L.4.3, L.4.5)

## 11. VOCABULARY

Examine words that describe the earth and sky. As an individual and as a class, keep an index card file of new words learned in this unit (e.g., *astronaut, astronomer, constellation, eclipse*). Keeping the words on index cards will allow you to use and sort the words by spelling feature, root words, prefixes, and suffixes. Find prefixes (*astro-*) and suffixes (*–ologist, -ology*) and discuss how the prefixes and suffixes add clues to the part of speech and meaning of the words. Consult reference materials to confirm pronunciations and clarify the meaning of the words and phrases. (*Note:* This will be an ongoing activity all year long.) In addition, you may be asked to create an individual semantic map of related words in order to help you explore understanding of the inter-connectedness of words related to the earth and sky. (L.4.4a, L.4.4b, L.4.4c)

## 12. READING LITERATURE, READING INFORMATIONAL TEXT, INFORMATIVE WRITING

As a class, summarize what was learned in this unit as it relates to the essential question "How are the earth and sky portrayed in fiction and nonfiction?" Following the class discussion, write your response in your journal. Work with a partner to edit and strengthen your writing. Shape your response into an informative/explanatory essay before sharing with your teacher. Your teacher may ask you to type your essay and respond to a poll about the unit on the class-room blog. (W.4.4, W.4.5, W.4.9a, W.4.9b, L.4.1, L.4.2, L.4.3)

## 13. ART, INFORMATIVE WRITING, ORAL PRESENTATION

Study Millet's and Constable's works closely. Note that they both include earth and sky and an individual figure. Compare and contrast the two works, answering questions such as: What different choices did each painter make to distinguish between the earth and sky, land and air–colors, textures, light? What role does the figure play in the work? Next, write a short essay outlining your responses. Present the works, along with your essay, to the class. (W. 4.1, SL.4.1, SL.4.3, L.4.3)

## 14. ART, SPEAKING AND LISTENING

View Stieglitz's and Celmins's works closely. Guess which work is a photograph and which one a drawing. What is happening in each image of the sky? How has the artist depicted the sky? What types of artistic techniques has he or she employed? Is one depiction more mysterious than the other? (SL.4.1, SL.4.3)

## 15. LANGUAGE MECHANICS

As a class, continue adding to the Mechanics/Grammar bulletin board started in Unit One. Remember, once skills are taught in a mini-lesson and listed on the bulletin board, you are expected to edit your work for these elements before publication. (L.4.1, L.4.2, L.4.3)

## 16. LANGUAGE MECHANICS

Read *Eats, Shoots & Leaves* by Lynne Truss as a class and discuss how the placement of the comma changes the meaning of the sentences. Make a list of times when commas are used for effect (e.g., after an introductory phrase: "After she went to the movie, she wanted to read the book"). Choose a piece of your own writing and circle punctuation used (reviewing periods, exclamation points, and question marks in addition to commas). Read your writing aloud to a partner and decide if the punctuation used gives the desired effect. Revise as necessary. (L.4.3b)

## 17. VOCABULARY

As a class, continue adding to the Vocabulary Word Wall bulletin board where, throughout the year, you will add and sort words as you learn them in each unit of study. (L.4.4)

## ADDITIONAL RESOURCES

- *Integrating Literacy into the Study of the Earth's Surface* (ReadWriteThink) (W.4.7)
- *Earth Verse: Using Science in Poetry* (ReadWriteThink) (RL.4.5)
- *Science Writer Seymour Simon Was Born in 1931* (ReadWriteThink) (W.4.7)
- *Constellation Myth Project* (MiddleSchoolScience.Com) (W4.3)
- *Native American Lore*
- NASA
- "Star Bright, Starry Night" (artLibrary)
- *Our Earth as Art Gallery* (NASA, Goddard Space Flight Center)
- *Educator's Guide to Eats, Shoots & Leaves*
- "Somebody-Wanted-But-So" strategy (West Virginia Department of Education)

## TERMINOLOGY

| | | |
|---|---|---|
| Artistic license | Lore | Theme |
| Details | Myth | Word choice |
| Facts | Narrative writing | |
| Legend | Research | |

## INTERDISCIPLINARY CONNECTIONS

This unit teaches:

- **Art:** Vincent van Gogh, El Greco, Jean-Francois Millet, John Constable, Alfred Stieglitz, Vija Celmins

- **Science:**
  - Space (a review of planets from grade 3)
  - Astronomy (e.g., the sun as a star and as a source of light and heat; how an eclipse happens; the Milky Way and Andromeda galaxies; constellations such as the Big Dipper; the moon and its phases)
- **History/Geography:** Introduction to culture and life of Native Americans (e.g., mound builders)

This unit could be extended to teach:

- **Science:**
  - The earth and its layers and formations (e.g., crust, mantle, core, volcanoes, hot springs and geysers, how mountains are formed)
  - The atmosphere (e.g., troposphere, stratosphere, mesosphere, thermosphere, exosphere; how the sun and the earth heat the atmosphere)
- **History/Geography:** Introduction to culture and life of other native cultures, such as:
  - Mayas (e.g., knowledge of astronomy and mathematics, located in Central America)
  - Aztecs (e.g., warrior culture, Tenochtitlan, located in Mexico)
  - Incas (e.g., empire along the coast of South America, Machu Picchu, Cuzco)

# Grade Four, Unit Five Sample Lesson Plan

## Can You Hear a Shout in Space? Questions and Answers About Space Exploration by Melvin and Gilda Berger, and Vincent Di Fate

In this series of four lessons, students read Can You Hear a Shout in Space? Questions and Answers About Space Exploration by Melvin and Gilda Berger, and Vincent Di Fate, and they:

Identify questions to explore (RI.4.1, RI.4.3)

Conduct exploration (RI.4.3, RI.4.7, RI.4.10, RF.4.4, W.4.8)

Document explorations (W.4.2, W.4.4, W.4.9b, W.4.10, L.4.1, L.4.2, L.4.6)

Share results (SL4.1, SL.4.4, L.4.3)

## Summary

| Lesson I: Questions and Answers About Space Exploration | Lesson II: Researching Space Exploration |
|---|---|
| Explore the questions in Can You Hear a Shout in Space? Questions and Answers About Space Exploration by Melvin and Gilda Berger, and Vincent Di Fate (RI.4.1, RI.4.3, RI.4.7, SL.4.1)<br><br>Select a question to investigate (RI.4.3) | Explore NASA's website for more answers (RI.4.3, RI.4.7, RI.4.10, RF.4.4, W.4.8)<br><br>Expand research (RI.4.7)<br><br>Record results (in the form of notes) (W.4.8) |
| Lesson III: Documenting Result of Exploration | Lesson IV: Sharing Results |
| Review notes (W.4.7, W.4.8)<br><br>(In paragraph form), document exploration results (W.4.2, W.4.4, W.4.9b, W.4.10, L.4.1, L.4.2, L.4.6)<br><br>Revise paragraph (W.4.5)<br><br>Rewrite paragraph (W.4.4, W.4.10, L.4.1, L.4.2, L.4.6) | Share answers to their explorations (SL.4.1, SL.4.4, L.4.3)<br><br>Probe results (RI.4.7)<br><br>Point to lingering questions (RI.4.7) |

## Lesson III: Documenting Result of Exploration

### Objectives

Review notes (W.4.7, W.4.8)

(In paragraph form) document exploration results (W.4.2, W.4.4, W.4.9b, W.4.10, L.4.1, L.4.2, L.4.6)

Revise paragraph (W.4.5)

Rewrite paragraph (W.4.4, W.4.10, L.4.1, L.4.2, L.4.6)

### Required Materials

☐ Notes taken in Lessons I and II

☐ Paper and pencils or pens

### Procedures

1. Lead-In:

    Review notes from Lessons I and II.

2. Step by Step:

    a. Students, in paragraph form, document results of their exploration (the answer to the question that they selected in Lesson I and the research they conducted in Lesson II). The paragraph must consist of

    ○ The original question

    ○ A topic sentence that uses that question as a starting point

    ○ An answer to the question that is composed of at least four sentences

    ○ A concluding observation

    b. Students revise their paragraphs.

3. Closure:

    Instruct students that for homework they will rewrite their paragraphs based on the in-class revisions. Also remind them that the original paragraph must be attached to the final draft.

## Differentiation

### Advanced

- If applicable to the research, students will go deeper into their question by creating a three-dimensional model showing an even richer understanding of the question. Students will present these displays to another class, sharing new learning.

- Students will find relevant websites and work with the teacher to create a WebQuest, pulling ideas for extended exploration from the questions and research.

- Students will use the final products of individual research to create a digital version of *Jeopardy*.

### Struggling

- Work closely with students to outline their paragraphs, revise and edit. Provide students with a graphic organizer for paragraph construction, if necessary.

- Choose websites to aid students in conducting research (and provide links to those websites through Internet-based bookmarking tools).

- Give students the option of using a word processing program at school (or home) to help with spell-check and grammar editing. (It may be helpful to use a shared spreadsheet with a partner.)

## Homework/Assessment

Students rewrite paragraph.

# Literary Heroes

This six-week unit ends the year by looking at heroes, real and imagined.

---

## ESSENTIAL QUESTION

Can heroism be conveyed in words?

---

## OVERVIEW

Generate a definition of *hero* that will evolve over the course of this unit. Students choose a story from this unit to study using all the strategies and skills learned up to this point in the year. Through reading about overtly brave and courageous literary characters (e.g., King Arthur, Robin Hood) or real people who made an impact on the world (e.g., Shakespeare, Davy Crockett, Booker T. Washington), students continue to revise the definition of hero to accommodate what these varied people have in common. After reading about famous heroes, students turn their attention to the unsung hero, and class discussions reveal the importance of those people who often remain unnoticed and behind the scenes. The class reviews characters from other novels read this year who, upon reflection, may be heroes. In a culminating project, students design their own multimedia presentation of an unsung hero based on what they learned in this unit about heroism.

## FOCUS STANDARDS

These Focus Standards have been selected for the unit from the Common Core State Standards.

**RL.4.4:** Determine the meaning of words and phrases as they are used in a text, including those that allude to significant characters found in mythology (e.g., Herculean).

**RI.4.8:** Explain how an author uses reasons and evidence to support particular points in a text.

**W.4.1:** Write opinion pieces on topics or texts, supporting a point of view with reasons and information.

**SL.4.2:** Paraphrase portions of a text read aloud or information presented in diverse media and formats, including visually, quantitatively, and orally.

**L.4.6:** Acquire and use accurately grade-appropriate general academic and domain-specific words and phrases, including those that signal precise actions, emotions, or states of being (e.g., *quizzed, whined, stammered*) and that are basic to a particular topic (e.g., *wildlife, conservation,* and *endangered* when discussing animal preservation).

## SUGGESTED OBJECTIVES

- Collaboratively define the word *hero*.
- Read and discuss a variety of fiction and nonfiction texts about literary and real heroes, from the Middle Ages and beyond.
- Explain how knowledge of classic stories such as those about King Arthur increases understanding of others, such as *Knights of the Kitchen Table*.
- Conduct short research projects on famous and not-so-famous heroes.
- Compare print and film versions of stories about heroes, such as Robin Hood.
- Write acrostic poems.
- Design and share a multimedia presentation about unsung heroes.

## SUGGESTED WORKS

(E) indicates a CCSS exemplar text; (EA) indicates a text from a writer with other works identified as exemplars.

### LITERARY TEXTS

*Stories*
- *Merlin and the Dragons* (Jane Yolen and Li Ming) (Read Aloud)
- *Saint George and the Dragon* (Margaret Hodges and Trina Schart Hyman) (Read Aloud)

*Middle Ages*
- *The Adventures of Robin Hood* (Classic Starts) (Howard Pyle and Lucy Corvino)
- *Christmas in Camelot* (Magic Tree House Book #29) (Mary Pope Osborne and Sal Murdocca)
- *Days of the Knights: A Tale of Castles and Battles* (DK Readers Proficient Readers, Level 4) (Christopher Maynard)
- *The Door in the Wall* (Marguerite De Angeli)
- *Ella Enchanted* (Gail Carson Levine)
- *Favorite Medieval Tales* (Mary Pope Osborne and Troy Howell)

- *The Grey King* (The Dark Is Rising Sequence) (Susan Cooper) (EA)
- *King Arthur* (Scholastic Junior Classics) (Jane B. Mason and Sarah Hines Stephens)
- *King Arthur* (Troll Illustrated Classics) (Howard Pyle, Don Hinkle, and Jerry Tiritilli)
- *The Kitchen Knight: A Tale of King Arthur* (Margaret Hodges and Trina Schart Hyman)
- *The Knights of the Kitchen Table #1* (Time Warp Trio) (Jon Scieszka and Lane Smith)
- *Sir Cumference and the First Round Table: A Math Adventure* (Cindy Neuschwander and Wayne Geehan)
- *The Story of King Arthur & His Knights* (Classic Starts) (Howard Pyle and Dan Andreasen)
- *The Whipping Boy* (Sid Fleischman and Peter Sis)
- *The Young Merlin Trilogy: Passager, Hobby, and Merlin* (Jane Yolen)

### Other Time Periods

- *Adventures of the Greek Heroes* (Anne M. Wiseman, Mollie McLean, and Witold T. Mars)
- *The Children's Book of Heroes* (William J. Bennett, Michael Hague, and Amy Hill)
- *Kaya's Hero: A Story of Giving* (American Girls Collection) (Janet Beeler Shaw, Bill Farnsworth, and Susan McAliley)
- *The Library Card* (Jerry Spinelli)
- *The Mystery of the Alamo Ghost* (Real Kids, Real Places) (Carole Marsh)
- *Welcome to the Globe: The Story of Shakespeare's Theatre* (DK Readers Proficient Readers, Level 4) (Peter Chrisp)

## Poems

- "Robin Hood and Little John" (Anonymous)
- "Robin Hood and Maid Marian" (Anonymous)
- "Why Dragons?" (Jane Yolen)

## INFORMATIONAL TEXTS

### Nonfiction Books

- *Adventures in the Middle Ages* (Good Times Travel Agency) (Linda Bailey and Bill Slavin)
- *England: The Land* (Erinn Banting) (E)
- *Illuminations* (Jonathan Hunt)
- *Knights and Castles* (Magic Tree House Research Guide #2) (Mary Pope Osborne, Will Osborne, and Sal Murdocca)
- *Knights: Warriors of the Middle Ages* (High Interest Books) (Aileen Weintraub)
- *The Middle Ages: An Interactive History Adventure* (You Choose: Historical Eras) (Allison Lassieur)
- *Women and Girls in the Middle Ages* (Medieval World) (Kay Eastwood)

### Biographies

- *Booker T. Washington: A Photo-Illustrated Biography* (Margo McLoone)
- *Chief Joseph of the Nez Perce: A Photo-Illustrated Biography* (Bill McAuliffe)

- *Davy Crockett: A Photo-Illustrated Biography* (Kathy Feeney)
- *Elizabeth Cady Stanton: A Photo-Illustrated Biography* (Lucile Davis)
- *George Washington: Soldier, Hero, President* (DK Readers Reading Alone, Level 3) (Justine and Ron Fontes)
- *Henry Ford: A Photo-Illustrated Biography* (Erika L. Shores)
- *Joan of Arc: The Lily Maid* (Margaret Hodges and Robert Rayevsky)
- *William Shakespeare & the Globe* (Aliki)

## ART, MUSIC, AND MEDIA

### Art

- Donatello, *St. George* (1415–1417)
- Raphael, *St. George and the Dragon* (1504–1506)
- *The Unicorn Tapestries* (late fifteenth through early sixteenth centuries)

### Film

- Michael Curtiz and William Keighley, dirs., *The Adventures of Robin Hood* (1938)
- Richard Thorpe, dir., *Knights of the Round Table* (1953)

## SAMPLE ACTIVITIES AND ASSESSMENTS

### 1. READING LITERATURE

As a class, create a chart (using the Frayer Model) that outlines the definitions, characteristics, and examples of heroes as we know them. Continue to add to this chart as the literature and informational texts read in this unit expand and alter the definition. (RL.4.4, RI.4.4, L.4.4a, L.4.4c)

### 2. READING LITERATURE

As a class, begin by examining our understanding of *hero* through one of its common definitions: "the primary character in a literary work." Record characteristics, examples, and nonexamples of the heroes that appear in the books. You will be asked to share your notes with a partner, and together share your ideas with the class. First, focus on the Red Cross Knight in *Saint George and the Dragon* by Margaret Hodges and Trina Schart Hyman. On another day, focus on Young Arthur in *Merlin and the Dragons* by Jane Yolen and Li Ming. After summarizing and discussing insights from these books with the class, write a response about how your understanding of the word *hero* changed or remained the same after hearing each story. (RL.4.2, RL.4.3, RL.4.9, W.4.1)

### 3. READING POETRY, SPEAKING AND LISTENING, PERFORMANCE

Read and discuss the poem "Why Dragons?" by Jane Yolen. How does knowing the story of St. George from reading the book *Saint George and the Dragon* (see Activity 2) increase your understanding of, and appreciation for, this poem? What are the poetic techniques used that you recognize? Does this poem remind you of *Merlin and the Dragons* (since it's written by the same author and it's about the same time period)? Your teacher may ask you to write your own response on a whiteboard or on a sticky note before discussing as a class. After the class discussion, divide up the stanzas and recite the poem as a class. (RL.4.4, RL.4.5, RL.4.9, W.4.8)

## 4. READING LITERATURE, NARRATIVE WRITING

Choose an eventful scene or chapter from a Middle Ages story you are reading. Write a journal entry retelling the scene from another point of view (i.e., if it's in first person, rewrite it in third; if it's in third person, rewrite it in first). Trade your journal entry with a classmate who is reading the same book and ask him or her to tell you if your new version makes sense and why (or why not). Revise if needed. (RL.4.3, RL.4.6, RL.4.10, W.4.4)

## 5. RESEARCH, READING INFORMATIONAL TEXT

Work with a partner to generate some research questions about a historical event from the Middle Ages. Using the Internet, an encyclopedia, and informational texts, read as much as you can about the event. Present your findings in a short report with visuals, similar to the illuminated manuscript pages found in Jonathan Hunt's *Illuminations*, to the class. Your teacher may ask you to type your report, include visuals, and publish it on the class web page. (W.4.4, W.4.7, L.4.1, L.4.2, L.4.3, L.4.6)

## 6. OPINION WRITING

If heroism demands courage and taking risks, which legendary character, King Arthur or Robin Hood, is a better hero? Support your opinion with strong evidence from the text. (W.4.1, W.4.4, W.4.7, W.4.10, L.4.1, L.4.2, L.4.3, L.4.6)

## 7. READING LITERATURE, SPEAKING AND LISTENING

After reading the King Arthur myths, read the *Knights of the Kitchen Table* by Jon Scieszka and Lane Smith. Discuss how knowing the original story and historical information about the time period helps you appreciate the details in this humorous version. (RL.4.9, SL.4.1)

## 8. READING INFORMATIONAL TEXT

As a class, we will keep a chart of information, using the categories and research questions below, about the heroes we have learned about from a variety of times and places. Start with the nonfiction texts from this unit, but also review all historical figures studied this year. As the chart is filled in, use the information to talk about how this changes or reinforces our understanding of a *hero*.

- Person's name
- When did he or she live?
- Where did he or she live?
- Why is he or she considered a hero or heroine?
- Are there any fiction stories written about him or her? What are they?
- Other memorable/interesting facts

Write your own responses in your journal and share them with a partner before presenting your findings to the class. (RL.4.3, RL.4.4, RL.4.5, RI.4.1, RI.4.8, RI.4.9, RI.4.10, SL.4.1, SL.4.2, SL.4.4)

## 9. WRITING POETRY

Following a class discussion of heroes, write an acrostic poem about your favorite hero/heroine. Recall from grade 3 that an acrostic poem is one that uses each letter of a word to provide the first letter of each line. Use descriptive words to exemplify the hero's traits, and include words that describe historical ideas or actions of the period (e.g., *chivalrous* and *medieval*). Your teacher may ask you to type your poem and insert a relevant picture of the person from the Internet, for publication in a class book. (RL.4.4, RI.4.4, W.4.4, W.4.7, L.4.1, L.4.2, L.4.3, L.4.6)

## 10. READING LITERATURE, SPEAKING AND LISTENING

What is the role of point of view when describing heroes? Review an old favorite where the perspective of the story is turned around, such as *The True Story of the Three Little Pigs* by Jon Scieszka. Discuss how the "villain" portrays himself or herself as a hero. Can this strategy—taking a different point of view in order to change the story—always work? Write your ideas in your journal and share them with a partner before discussing as a class. How does point of view change our class definition of a hero or not? (RL.4.5, SL.4.1)

## 11. FILM, READING LITERATURE, SPEAKING AND LISTENING

Compare film and print versions of a book such as *The Adventures Robin Hood* or *Knights of the Round Table*. (Note: You may need to ask your teacher which scenes would be appropriate to watch.) While viewing select scenes, discuss major differences between drama and prose, and structural elements (e.g., casts of characters, settings, descriptions, dialogue, and stage directions). (RL.4.5, SL.4.1)

## 12. READING INFORMATIONAL TEXT, OPINION WRITING

Does heroism require overt acts of courage and bravery? Who are some everyday people who are also heroes? Read the article titled "Foster Parents Are the Unsung Heroes of Kids" and then read descriptions of heroes from *The Cullman Times*. After reading these articles, write a journal entry in which you nominate someone you know who you feel is an unsung hero. Be sure to explain with strong reasons why you chose that person. (RI.4.8, W.4.4, W.4.9a, W.4.9b)

## 13. VOCABULARY, LANGUAGE USAGE, MULTIMEDIA PRESENTATION

As a class, summarize what was learned in this unit as it relates to the essential question "Can heroism be conveyed in words?" Then work with a classmate to revise and edit your unsung hero nomination (see Activity 12) to include as many new vocabulary words, phrases, and figurative language descriptions as make sense. Add audio recordings and visual displays to enhance the impact of the nomination. Add your presentation to a class web page. As a culmination, host a ceremony where class members share their presentations with each other about unsung heroes. (W.4.2, W.4.5, W.4.6, W.4.7, W.4.8, SL.4.5, SL.4.6, L.4.1, L.4.2, L.4.3, L.4.5, L.4.6)

## 14. LANGUAGE MECHANICS

As a class, continue adding to the Mechanics/Grammar bulletin board started in Unit One. Remember, once skills are taught in a mini-lesson and listed on the bulletin board, you are expected to edit your work for these elements before publication. (L.4.1, L.4.2, L.4.3)

## 15. VOCABULARY

As a class, continue adding to the Vocabulary Word Wall bulletin board where, throughout the year, you will add and sort words as you learn them in each unit of study. (L.4.4)

## 16. ART, SPEAKING AND LISTENING

Explore the imagery in the *Unicorn Tapestries*. What do you see? Continuing with what you have learned about the medieval European world, who are the characters featured in the tapestries? What is the meaning of the medieval hunt? Why does the unicorn seem symbolic—is it treated specifically in the tapestries? What about other animal imagery? (SL.4.1, SL.4.3)

## 17. ART, SPEAKING AND LISTENING

Examine Raphael's painting of St. George. What imagery do you see? How has Raphael depicted St. George? How does he look? Now look at the Donatello sculpture of St. George. What are the differences? How did each artist choose to render his character? Can you see any of the same elements in the St. George characterizations as you did in the *Unicorn Tapestries*? (SL.4.1, SL.4.3)

## ADDITIONAL ONLINE RESOURCES

- *Is Superman Really All That Super? Critically Exploring Superheroes* (ReadWriteThink) (RL.4.6)
- *Question and Answer Books—From Genre Study to Report Writing* (ReadWriteThink) (RL.4.5)
- *Heroes Around Us* (ReadWriteThink) (W.4.7)
- *Jane Yolen for Kids* (JaneYolen.com)
- *Black History Month: Unsung Heroes Project* (*National Association for the Advancement of Colored People, NAACP*)
- *Contributions of Americans of Hispanic Heritage* (America USA)
- "The Cullman Times 2010 Unsung Heroes Named," *The Cullman Times*, March 28, 2010
- The Frayer Model (West Virginia Department of Education)
- "Foster Parents Are the Unsung Heroes of Kids," *The Wichita Eagle*, May 16, 2010

## TERMINOLOGY

Acrostic poem

Character development

Hero/heroine

Literary terms: novel, plot, setting

Perspective

Point of view

Unsung hero

Villain

## INTERDISCIPLINARY CONNECTIONS

This unit teaches:

- **History:**
  - Middle Ages (e.g., feudalism, life in a castle, chivalry, knights, castles, Joan of Arc)
  - Biographies (e.g., William Shakespeare, George Washington, Davy Crockett, Booker T. Washington, Henry Ford, Chief Joseph)
- **Art:** Medieval tapestry, Raphael, Donatello

This unit could be extended to teach:

- **Geography:** Geographic features of England and Western Europe (e.g., rivers, mountain ranges)
- **Mathematics:** Geometry (e.g., the circumference, diameter, and radius of circles; perimeter of quadrilaterals)

# Grade Four, Unit Six Sample Lesson Plan

## King Arthur *by Howard Pyle*

In this series of three lessons, students read *King Arthur* by Howard Pyle, Don Hinkle, and Jerry Tiritilli, and they:

Explore the story of King Arthur according to Howard Pyle et al. (RL.4.4, RL.4.10, RF.4.4)

Conduct online exploration of King Arthur's life (RI.4.3, RI.4.8, W.4.7, W.4.8)

Examine facts vs. fiction (RI.4.3, RI.4.8, RI.4.9)

## Summary

### Lesson I: King Arthur

Explore the life of King Arthur, as told by Howard Pyle et al. (RL.4.4, RL.4.10, RF.4.4)

Examine King Arthur's role as a leader (RL.4.2, RL.4.3)

Investigate King Arthur's legacy (RL.4.9)

### Lesson II: Looking for Facts

Recall details of Howard Pyle's book *King Arthur* (RL.4.1, RL.4.3, SL.4.1)

Conduct research into the life of King Arthur (RI.4.3, RI.4.8)

Explore a variety of sources (RI.4.3, W.4.7)

Record findings (W.4.8)

Note the emerging uncertainty about the facts surrounding King Arthur's life (RI.4.9, W.4.9b)

### Lesson III: Facts and Fiction

Present findings from Lesson II (SL.4.2, SL.4.4, L.4.6)

Note differences concerning King Arthur's life that the sources reveal (RI.4.3, RI.4.8, RI.4.9)

Consider Pyle's presentation of events (RL.4.3, RL.4.9)

Point to the author's point of view (RL.4.6)

Revisit King Arthur's role as a leader (RL.4.2, RL.4.3)

## Lesson II: Looking for Facts

### Objectives

Recall details of Howard Pyle's book *King Arthur* (RL.4.1, RL.4.3, SL.4.1)

Conduct research into the life of King Arthur (RI.4.3, RI.4.8)

Explore a variety of sources (RI.4.3, W.4.7)

Record findings (W.4.8)

Note the emerging uncertainty about the facts surrounding King Arthur's life (RI.4.9, W.4.9b)

### Required Materials

☐ *King Arthur* by Howard Pyle, Don Hinkle, and Jerry Tiritilli

☐ Computers with Internet access

### Procedures

1. Lead-In:

   Recall details of *King Arthur* by Howard Pyle, Don Hinkle, and Jerry Tiritilli.

2. Step by Step:

   a. Students, in several small groups (or individually), conduct online research about King Arthur. Steer the students toward multiple sites.

   b. Students record their findings.

3. Closure:

   Class discussion reveals what emerges during research.

### Differentiation

#### Advanced

- Using the results of the class research, students will create a multimedia presentation titled "Facts and Fiction: The Making of a Legend." Tell students to alternate slides with factual information and slides with evolved fictional detail to reinforce the idea of how a legend evolves over time. Students take other legends or tall tales and do additional study on "facts and fiction."

- Students explore why legendary characters evolve and their role in culture.

*Struggling*

- Students will have five to ten minutes at the beginning of the class to review the Howard Pyle book and place sticky notes on pages with details they want to remember. Following the review time, they will turn and talk to a neighbor about the details they remember.

- Provide the students with a two-column graphic organizer showing the Howard Pyle detail on one side of the paper and the research finding on the opposite side.

- Choose websites to aid students in conducting research (and provide access to these websites through web-based bookmarking tools).

## Homework/Assessment

In preparation for Lesson III, instruct the students to review their class notes. Then instruct them to be prepared to share with the rest of the class at least two conflicting facts about the life of King Arthur.

# Grade 5

Having built an elementary foundation in reading, writing, literature, history, and science, fifth-grade students are ready to start tackling complex literature and ideas. The fifth-grade units present a series of ideas related to the life of the mind: play, invention, clues, conflict, exploration, and coming of age. In the unit on playing with words, students explore the delight of literary language, exemplified in works such as Richard Wilbur's *The Disappearing Alphabet* and William Blake's "The Echoing Green." This leads into a unit on inventive thinking, where students learn about scientific, artistic, musical, and literary inventors. As the year progresses, students learn how literature can provide insight into culture and history. The units provide many connections with history, science, and the arts; students listen to Renaissance music, examine art from the Civil War, and consider how illustrations contribute to a text. While building vocabulary and learning multiple meanings of words, students begin to study etymology, thus gaining insight into the relationships among languages. Students develop their writing within many genres: reflective essays, reports, journals, stories, responses to literary and artistic works, and more. In their essays, they are able to articulate a central idea and illustrate it with examples, integrate information from several texts, and discuss literary themes. As they continue to learn grammatical concepts and refine their style, students at this level should demonstrate some command of standard English grammar and usage. By the end of fifth grade, students are ready for deeper study of literature and the origins of words.

# Standards Checklist for Grade Five

| Standard | Unit 1 | Unit 2 | Unit 3 | Unit 4 | Unit 5 | Unit 6 |
|---|---|---|---|---|---|---|
| **Reading–Literature** | | | | | | |
| 1 | | A | FA | A | A | A |
| 2 | FA | A | | A | A | A |
| 3 | | A | A | | A | FA |
| 4 | A | A | | A | A | A |
| 5 | | | | | FA | A |
| 6 | A | | A | FA | | A |
| 7 | A | | | | FA | A |
| 8 n/a | | | | | | |
| 9 | | FA | A | A | | A |
| 10 | | | A | A | A | A |
| **Reading–Informational Text** | | | | | | |
| 1 | FA | A | FA | A | | |
| 2 | A | FA | A | | | A |
| 3 | A | A | A | FA | | A |
| 4 | F | A | A | | | |
| 5 | A | A | A | FA | | |
| 6 | A | | A | A | | FA |
| 7 | A | A | FA | A | | A |
| 8 | | | A | | FA | |
| 9 | A | FA | A | A | | |
| 10 | | | A | | | A |
| **Writing** | | | | | | |
| 1 | | A | FA | | A | A |
| 1a | | A | A | | | |
| 1b | | A | A | | | |
| 1c | | A | A | | | |
| 1d | | A | A | | | |
| 2 | A | FA | A | A | | A |
| 2a | | A | A | | | |
| 2b | | A | A | | | |
| 2c | | A | A | | | |
| 2d | | A | A | | | |
| 2e | | A | | | | |
| 3 | A | | | FA | FA | A |
| 3a | | | | | | |
| 3b | | | | | | |
| 3c | | | | | | |
| 3d | | | | | | |
| 3e | | | | | | |
| 4 | A | A | A | A | A | A |
| 5 | A | A | | | FA | |
| 6 | A | | A | | | FA |
| 7 | FA | A | A | A | A | A |
| 8 | A | A | A | A | A | FA |
| 9 | | A | A | | A | A |
| 9a | A | A | A | | A | A |

| Standard | Unit 1 | Unit 2 | Unit 3 | Unit 4 | Unit 5 | Unit 6 |
|---|---|---|---|---|---|---|
| 9b | A | A | A | | A | A |
| 10 | | A | | | A | |
| **Speaking and Listening** | | | | | | |
| 1 | FA | FA | | | A | A |
| 1a | FA | A | | | A | A |
| 1b | FA | A | | | | |
| 1c | | FA | | | | |
| 1d | | FA | | | | |
| 2 | | A | A | A | FA | A |
| 3 | | | FA | A | A | |
| 4 | | A | A | FA | | A |
| 5 | | A | A | A | A | FA |
| 6 | | | | | | A |
| **Language** | | | | | | |
| 1 | A | FA | FA | A | A | A |
| 1a | A | FA | A | A | | A |
| 1b | A | FA | A | A | | A |
| 1c | | A | FA | A | | A |
| 1d | | | FA | A | | |
| 1e | | | | | A | |
| 2 | A | A | | A | A | A |
| 2a | | | A | A | A | A |
| 2b | | | A | A | A | A |
| 2c | | | | A | A | |
| 2d | | | | | A | |
| 2e | | | | | | |
| 3 | A | A | A | A | A | FA |
| 3a | | | | | A | FA |
| 3b | | | | | | FA |
| 4 | A | A | FA | FA | A | A |
| 4a | A | A | A | | A | A |
| 4b | A | | A | FA | A | |
| 4c | A | | FA | A | A | |
| 5 | FA | | | A | FA | |
| 5a | | | | | A | |
| 5b | A | | | | A | |
| 5c | | | | | A | |
| 6 | | | | | | A |
| **Reading Foundations** | | | | | | |
| 1 n/a | | | | | | |
| 2 n/a | | | | | | |
| 3 | FA | | | | | |
| 3a | FA | | A | | | |
| 4 | | F | F | FA | FA | FA |
| 4a | | | | FA | | |
| 4b | | | | A | A | |
| 4c | | | | FA | A | |

F = Focus Standards; A = Activity/Assessment

# Playing with Words

This four-week unit encourages students to experiment with language and to explore their personal writing style.

---

## ESSENTIAL QUESTION

Why (and how) do we play with language?

---

## OVERVIEW

Reading both spoonerisms and classic poetry provides students a chance to explore and appreciate language. Students bring in a book about an important figure, such as an artist or an inventor, as a springboard for writing about their own interests and for researching famous scientists. Students explore word origins, compare literal and figurative language, and present a poem they have written. Students write an opinion essay in response to the essential question.

## FOCUS STANDARDS

These Focus Standards have been selected for the unit from the Common Core State Standards.

**RL.5.2:** Determine a theme of a story, drama, or poem from details in the text, including how characters in a story or drama respond to challenges or how the speaker in a poem reflects upon a topic; summarize the text.

**RI.5.1:** Quote accurately from a text when explaining what the text says explicitly and when drawing inferences from the text.

**RI.5.4:** Determine the meaning of general academic and domain-specific words and phrases in a text relevant to a grade 5 topic or subject area.

**RF.5.3:** Know and apply grade-level phonics and word analysis skills in decoding words.

**RF.5.3(a):** Use combined knowledge of all letter-sound correspondences, syllabication patterns, and morphology (e.g., roots and affixes) to read accurately unfamiliar multisyllabic words in context and out of context.

**W.5.7:** Conduct short research projects that use several sources to build knowledge through investigation of different aspects of a topic.

**SL.5.1:** Engage effectively in a range of collaborative discussions (one-on-one, in groups, and teacher-led) with diverse partners on grade 5 topics and texts, building on others' ideas and expressing their own clearly.

**SL.5.1(a):** Come to discussions prepared, having read or studied required material; explicitly draw on that preparation and other information known about the topic to explore ideas under discussion.

**SL.5.1(b):** Follow agreed-upon rules for discussions and carry out assigned roles.

**L.5.5:** Demonstrate understanding of figurative language, word relationships, and nuances in word meanings.

## SUGGESTED OBJECTIVES

- Conduct research on people of interest (e.g., notable scientists), select and cite the most relevant and useful information gathered, and make a plan for presenting the findings.
- Devise ways to present research using available digital resources (i.e., multimedia presentations); present findings to the class or to a wider audience.
- Apply understanding of poetic devices (e.g., figurative language), word relationships, and nuances in word meanings to the composition of original poems.
- Develop an opinion about authors' use of figurative language and present it in an opinion essay.

## SUGGESTED WORKS

(E) indicates a CCSS exemplar text; (EA) indicates a text from a writer with other works identified as exemplars.

## LITERARY TEXTS

*Stories*

- *Baseball Saved Us* (Ken Mochizuki)
- *The Cat's Pajamas* (Wallace Edwards) (Read Aloud)
- *The Disappearing Alphabet* (Richard Wilbur and David Diaz)
- *In a Pickle and Other Funny Idioms* or *Mad as a Wet Hen! and Other Funny Idioms* (Marvin Terban)
- *The King Who Rained* (Fred Gwynne)
- *My Teacher Likes to Say* (Denise Brennan-Nelson)
- *The Phantom Tollbooth* (Norton Juster and Jules Feiffer) (Read Aloud)
- A *Picture Book of George Washington Carver* (Picture Book Biography) (David A. Adler and Dan Brown)

- *What Are You Figuring Now? A Story About Benjamin Banneker* (Creative Minds Biography) (Jeri Ferris)
- *What's the Big Idea, Ben Franklin?* (Jean Fritz)

## Poems
- *Carver: A Life in Poems* (Marilyn Nelson)
- "Casey at the Bat" (Ernest Lawrence Thayer) (E)
- "The Echoing Green" (William Blake) (E)
- "Eletelephony" (Laura Richards)
- *Joyful Noise: Poems for Two Voices* (Paul Fleischman and Eric Beddows)
- "Little Red Riding Hood and the Wolf" (Roald Dahl) (E)
- "My Shadow" (Robert Louis Stevenson)
- *Runny Babbit: A Billy Sook* (Shel Silverstein)
- *The Tree Is Older Than You Are: A Bilingual Gathering of Poems & Stories from Mexico with Paintings by Mexican Artists* (Naomi Shihab Nye) (Read Aloud)

# INFORMATIONAL TEXTS
## Biographies
- *Alexander Graham Bell: An Inventive Life* (Snapshots: Images of People and Places in History) (Elizabeth MacLeod)
- *Always Inventing: A Photobiography of Alexander Graham Bell* (Tom Matthews)
- *Amelia to Zora: Twenty-Six Women Who Changed the World* (Cynthia Chin-Lee, Megan Halsey, and Sean Addy)
- *A Strong Right Arm* (Michelle Green)
- *In Their Own Words: Thomas Edison* (George Sullivan)
- *John Muir: Young Naturalist* (Childhood of Famous Americans) (Montrew Dunham)
- *Meet the Authors and Illustrators Volume 1: 60 Creators of Favorite Children's Books Talk About Their Work* (Grades K–6) (Deborah Kovacs and James Preller)
- *Musicians* (Women in Profile) (Leslie Strudwick)
- *Rachel Carson: Pioneer of Ecology* (Women of Our Time) (Kathleen V. Kudlinski)
- *Tales of Famous Americans* (Peter and Connie Roop)
- *Visual and Performing Artists* (Women in Profile) (Shaun Hunter)
- *We Are the Ship: The Story of Negro League Baseball* (Kadir Nelson) (E)
- *Who Was Albert Einstein?* (Jess M. Brallier and Robert Andrew Parker)
- *Who Was Dr. Seuss?* (Janet Pascal and Nancy Harrison)
- *Who Was Jackie Robinson?* (Gail Herman, Nancy Harrison, and John O'Brien)
- *Who Was Louis Armstrong?* (Yona Zeblis McDonough, John O'Brien, and Nancy Harrison)
- *Who Was Pablo Picasso?* (True Kelley)
- *Who Was Thomas Alva Edison?* (Margaret Frith, John O'Brien, and Nancy Harrison)
- *Who Was William Shakespeare?* (Celeste Mannis)
- *The World at His Fingertips: A Story About Louis Braille* (Creative Minds Biographies) (Barbara O'Connor and Rochelle Draper)

*Reference*

- *Scholastic Dictionary of Idioms* (Revised) (Marvin Terban)

## ART, MUSIC, AND MEDIA

*Art*

- Joseph Cornell, *Cassiopeia 1* (1960)
- Joseph Cornell, *L'Egypte de Mlle Cleo de Merode, cours élémentaire d'histoire naturelle* (1940)
- Joseph Cornell, *Object (Roses des Vents)* (1942–1953)
- Joseph Cornell, *Untitled (Solar Set)* (1956–1958)

*Music*

- Benjamin Britten, *The Young Person's Guide to the Orchestra*, op. 34 (1946)
- Jack Norworth, "Take Me Out to the Ballgame" (1908)

*Media*

- Bud Abbott and Lou Costello, "Who's on First?" (ca. 1936)

## SAMPLE ACTIVITIES AND ASSESSMENTS

### 1. RESEARCH, WRITING POETRY

Read all you can about an inventor, scientist, author, poet, illustrator, artist, sports figure, or musician who made a historic contribution to his or her field. To select the most relevant and useful information, make a chart in your journal that includes the following open-ended research inquiries:

- Name of your person
- Where he or she lived
- When he or she lived
- What did he or she do that made him or her famous?
- What are some additional facts you found interesting?

Design a plan for your informational search. After finishing this research, create a bio-poem based on the person you chose. Make sure you can explain why you chose the words you put into the bio-poem, and create a digital presentation of both. (RI.5.1, W.5.6, W.5.7, L.5.1a)

### 2. VOCABULARY, LANGUAGE USAGE

As you and your classmates read and research different scientists and inventors, keep track of information in categories similar to those in your journal (listed in Activity 1). After taking notes in your journal, select the most relevant and useful information gathered and make a plan for presenting your findings in a short report that is logically ordered and cites at least two sources of information. Edit your writing for correct use of conjunctions, prepositions, and interjections. Your teacher may ask you to publish your report and insert a picture of the person from the web. (RI.5.1, RI.5.2, RI.5.3, W.5.7, L.5.1a)

### 3. READING INFORMATIONAL TEXT, SPEAKING AND LISTENING

How are the scientists and inventors you have read about similar? How are they different? How and why do scientists and inventors "play"? (SL.5.1a, SL.5.1b, RI.5.9)

### 4. READING LITERATURE, READING INFORMATIONAL TEXT, INFORMATIVE WRITING, SPEAKING AND LISTENING

Compare and contrast the presentation of a topic in two different formats, such as baseball in "Casey at the Bat" by Ernest Lawrence Thayer and *We Are the Ship: The Story of Negro League Baseball* by Kadir Nelson, drawing on specific details from the text. Your teacher may ask you to write your own response in your journal and share it with a partner before or during the class discussion. (RL.5.2, SL.5.1a, SL.5.1b)

### 5. READING POETRY, WRITING POETRY, LANGUAGE USAGE

Poets use not only a variety of forms, rhyme schemes, and meters, but also specific devices to enliven their poems and reveal their themes. Find examples of similes, metaphors, alliteration, and onomatopoeia in poems from this unit, and mark them with coded sticky notes. Create a T-chart in your journal that lists the poetic devices and includes examples of each. Try to write your own poem that uses at least two of the devices found. If you write a poem with a partner, use a shared spreadsheet so you can work collaboratively on it. (RL.5.4, L.5.5, W.5.4)

### 6. NARRATIVE WRITING, LANGUAGE USAGE

Explore your own style of writing. Write your own humorous story or poem in which you incorporate figurative language or idioms learned. Share it with a classmate. Ask your classmate what he or she thinks would improve your writing. (L.5.5, W.5.4, W.5.5)

### 7. READING POETRY, READING FLUENCY, PERFORMANCE

Choose a poem, such as one from the anthology *Joyful Noise* (Paul Fleischman and Eric Beddows), to memorize and recite with a classmate. After the performance, discuss specific passages and poetic devices that made the poem come alive. Record the readings using a video camera for future reference and to see how your fluency improves during the course of the year. (RF.5.3a)

### 8. LANGUAGE USAGE

Illustrate the literal and figurative meaning of an idiom from a text such as *The King Who Rained* by Fred Gwynne. We will compile these illustrations into a class book to share with younger students. Try to use phrases learned in your daily writing and speaking as well. Your teacher may ask you to create a slide of your idiom, including scanned illustrations or relevant photos from the Internet, before assembling them into a class book (either electronic or in print). (L.5.5b)

### 9. VOCABULARY

As an individual and as a class, keep an index card file of words and phrases learned from the stories and poems in this unit, especially homonyms (e.g., *saw*, noun/*saw*, past participle of the verb "to see"; *bat*, the rodent/*bat*, the baseball implement) and homophones (e.g., *sea/see*; *weather/whether*). Keeping the words on index cards will help you when you sort words by prefix, suffix, root words, meaning, spelling feature, etc. (*Note*: This will be an ongoing activity all year long.) (L.5.4a, RI.5.6)

## 10. MUSIC, SPEAKING AND LISTENING

Listen to Benjamin Britten's *The Young Person's Guide to the Orchestra* as a class. Discuss how the ideas of "theme and variations" are expressed through music. As a class, choose a common topic about which to write, and then a student who is interested may share his or her draft with the class. Discuss the similarities and differences in writing, just as "themes and variations" exist in music. (SL.5.1a, SL.5.1b)

## 11. OPINION WRITING

Write an opinion essay response to the essential question "Why (and how) do we play with language?" Your teacher may give you the opportunity to "give one, get one" before writing your response. Discuss at least three examples of figurative language or other word play (e.g., the inclusion in a poem of words with multiple meanings). Edit your writing for correct use of conjunctions, prepositions, and interjections before sharing with your teacher. Your teacher may ask you to type your essay and respond to a poll about the unit on the classroom blog. (W.5.5, W.5.7, W.5.9a, W.5.9b, L.5.1a)

## 12. LANGUAGE USAGE

Your teacher will teach mini-lessons on the individual language standards. For example, he or she will explain what conjunctions are. Then he or she will give you a set of three sentences to combine into one thought—for example, "(1) The girl walked to school. (2) The girl is named Jesse. (3) The girl wore a yellow skirt." Using conjunctions, work with a partner to combine the three sentences. Select a piece of your own writing, circle shorter sentences, and try to use conjunctions to make longer, more interesting sentences. (L.5.1a)

## 13. LANGUAGE MECHANICS

As a class, create a Mechanics/Grammar bulletin board where, throughout the year, you will add to a checklist of editing topics as they are taught through targeted mini-lessons (e.g., proper use of punctuation, capitalization). Once skills are taught in a mini-lesson and listed on the bulletin board, you are expected to edit your work for the elements before publication. (L.5.1, L.5.2, L.5.3)

## 14. VOCABULARY

As a class, create a Vocabulary Word Wall bulletin board where, throughout the year, you will add and sort words as you learn them in each unit of study. (L.5.4)

## 15. ART, SPEAKING AND LISTENING

Do visual artists "play" with materials the way other artists do? Examine the works of Joseph Cornell. This early-twentieth-century American artist spent his life collecting and arranging objects into imaginative and whimsical works. What do you notice about his assemblages? What types of objects did he use? Are Cornell's boxes like visual poems? What questions are you left with once you look at each box? (SL.5.1)

## 16. ART, NARRATIVE WRITING

The Joseph Cornell boxes are carefully arranged to let your eye wander and find hidden objects. Cornell has created an assemblage, or a three-dimensional artistic composition made out of found objects. If you could create an assemblage box in the manner of Cornell, what would you put inside? Would you hide objects in drawers and small spaces, or let your viewer see everything? Write a short narrative describing your process for creating an assemblage. (W.5.3, W.5.4)

## ADDITIONAL ONLINE RESOURCES

- *David Weisner's Book June 29, 1999, Showcases This Day* (ReadWriteThink) (RL.5.7)
- *Alliteration All Around* (ReadWriteThink) (RL.5.4)
- *Noah Webster Published His American Dictionary of the English Language in 1828* (ReadWriteThink) (L.5.4a, L.5.4b, L.5.4c)
- *Spelling Patterns "Go Fish" Card Game* (ReadWriteThink) (L.5.4a,b,c)
- *Elizabeth Blackwell Became the First Woman to Earn a MD Degree in 1849* (ReadWriteThink) (RI.5.9)
- *Biographies for Children* (Pitara Kids Network)
- *All About Adolescent Literacy* (AdLit.org)
- *Great People of the 20th Century* (Oracle ThinkQuest, Projects by Students for Students)
- *"Give One Get One"* (RRISD Math Team)

## TERMINOLOGY

Biography

Dialogue

Homonym

Homophone

Idiom/cliché

Literal and figurative language

Poetic devices: rhyme scheme, meter, stanza, metaphors, similes, alliteration, onomatopoeia

Spoonerism

Theme (and variation)

## INTERDISCIPLINARY CONNECTIONS

This unit teaches:

- **Art:** Assemblage, Joseph Cornell
- **Science:** Biographies (e.g., Albert Einstein, Alexander Graham Bell) and their (respective) related field of study (e.g., physics)

This unit could be extended to teach:

- **Science:** Scientists and the type of science to which they contributed (e.g., ecology, biology, chemistry, astronomy, geology, meteorology, electricity)
- **History/Geography:** Famous people throughout history (e.g., How have these people changed our world? What makes them famous?)
- **Physical Education:** Baseball (e.g., rules and history)

## Grade Five, Unit One Sample Lesson Plan

### We Are the Ship: The Story of Negro League Baseball *by Kadir Nelson*

In this series of six lessons, students read *We Are the Ship: The Story of Negro League Baseball* by Kadir Nelson, and they:

Explore the story of the Negro League along with Kadir Nelson (RI.5.2, RI.5.5)

Conduct research that expands their appreciation of the league and its players (RI.5.9, W.5.7, SL.5.1)

Publish their findings (W.5.2, W.5.4, W.5.5, W.5.7)

### Summary

#### Lessons I–II: *We Are the Ship*

Identify and contextualize the term *Negro* (L.5.4)

Note the "nine-inning" format of the book (RI.5.5)

Examine the use of first-person narration (RL.5.6)

Explore Kadir Nelson's depiction of the Negro League (RI.5.2, RI.5.5)

#### Lessons III–IV: Investigating the Negro League

Expand the study of the Negro League (RI.5.7, RI.5.9)

Use online and library resources (RI.5.7, RI.5.9)

Extract necessary information (RI.5.7, RI.5.9)

Establish categories for investigation (RI.5.7, RI.5.9)

Record findings (W.5.8)

Identify areas for further research (SL.5.1)

Generate discussion of findings (SL.5.1)

Probe tensions (SL.5.1)

Note emerging themes (SL.5.1)

#### Lessons V–VI: Reporting the Story of the Negro League

Record the findings of the research (RI.5.9, W.5.7, SL.5.1)

Map out the presentation of the research (RI.5.9, W.5.7)

Coherently articulate findings (RI.5.9, SL.5.1)

Challenge conventions (W.5.6)

Produce a work for publication (W.5.2, W.5.4, W.5.5, W.5.7)

Publish research (W.5.7)

## Lessons V–VI: Reporting the Story of the Negro League

### Objectives

Record the findings of the research (RI.5.9, W.5.7, SL.5.1)

Map out the presentation of the research (RI.5.9, W.5.7)

Coherently articulate findings (RI.5.9, SL.5.1)

Challenge conventions (W.5.6)

Produce a work for publication (W.5.2, W.5.4, W.5.5, W.5.7)

Publish research (W.5.7)

(The class selects a format for publication: a newspaper, a magazine, a yearbook, a scrapbook, or a series of posters. Each of these works well for this type of collective effort.)

### Required Materials

☐ Research material

☐ Computers

☐ Markers, glue, and paper

### Procedures

1. Lead-In:

   Introduce the collective class project.

2. Step by Step:

   a. Students form groups based on the categories that were established in earlier lessons. They review the material they already have and begin to consider the type of presentation that is most suitable for their work (e.g., an article, a set of illustrations, letters, or photographs).

   b. Group work continues. Students write and edit articles, draw illustrations, and select photographs.

   c. Students put together the various components of the project. Student editors begin the process of assembling the material.

3. Closure:

The students will share projects with each other, which gives them a chance to appreciate their collective efforts. Part of the class conversation should include reflection upon the experience and what they have learned about the Negro League.

## Differentiation

### Advanced

- If the students are good editors, have them peer-edit the articles written by classmates.
- Students can choose a more challenging form of presentation (e.g., setting up a web page, electronic slides, or wiki where student presentations can be collected).
- Students should find additional modern-day resources to discuss how the current game of baseball is similar to or different from earlier years of baseball (e.g., *Baseball Saved Us* by Ken Mochizuki or *A Strong Right Arm* by Michelle Green).

### Struggling

- Work with a small group in order to provide more intensive support. Students divide the categories for research tasks among the group members. Partners record their findings on index cards to facilitate sharing and sorting of information.
- Students may select a set of illustrations to record on a podcast to demonstrate understanding of the topic, discussing the illustrations prior to writing their article.
- Using a shared online document or a document camera, students collaboratively write their article. Print out the first draft for students to edit individually before editing as a group.

## Homework/Assessment

N/A

# Renaissance Thinking

This six-week unit focuses on the research process, as well as the creative and critical thinking used by writers, inventors, and famous people from the Renaissance and beyond.

---

## ESSENTIAL QUESTION

How does creativity change the world?

---

## OVERVIEW

Through the pairing of fiction and nonfiction books on related topics, this unit builds on students' understanding of the Renaissance as a period of new learning and discovery. This unit is particularly effective for teaching the research process, as the people involved or the historical context of particular inventions are most likely new to students. Students publish and present their research papers to the class. Students then find commonalities among inventors and innovators, share these insights in group discussions, and use this information as a springboard for their own innovative and creative writing. This unit sets in motion the reading, writing, researching, and word analysis processes that will be a hallmark of their fifth-grade year. This unit ends with an informative/explanatory essay in response to the essential question.

## FOCUS STANDARDS

These Focus Standards have been selected for the unit from the Common Core State Standards.

**RL.5.9:** Compare and contrast stories in the same genre (e.g., mysteries and adventure stories) on their approaches to similar themes and topics.

**RI.5.2:** Determine two or more main ideas of a text and explain how they are supported by key details; summarize the text.

**RI.5.9:** Integrate information from several texts on the same topic in order to write or speak about the subject knowledgably.

**RF.5.4:** Read with sufficient accuracy and fluency to support comprehension.

**W.5.2:** Write informative/explanatory texts to examine a topic and convey ideas and information clearly.

**SL.5.1:** Engage effectively in a range of collaborative discussions (one-on-one, in groups, and teacher-led) with diverse partners on grade 5 topics and texts, building on others' ideas and expressing their own ideas clearly.

**SL.5.1(c):** Pose and respond to specific questions by making comments that contribute to the discussion and elaborate on the remarks of others.

**SL.5.1(d):** Review the key ideas expressed and draw conclusions in light of information and knowledge gained from the discussions.

**L.5.1:** Demonstrate command of the conventions of standard English grammar and usage when writing or speaking.

**L.5.1(a):** Explain the function of conjunctions, prepositions, and interjections in general and their function in particular sentences.

**L.5.1(b):** Form and use the perfect (e.g., *I had walked; I have walked; I will have walked*) verb tenses.

## SUGGESTED OBJECTIVES

- Read and compare information learned from fiction and nonfiction books about an inventor of choice (e.g., *Leonardo: Beautiful Dreamer* by Robert Byrd and *The Usborne Book of Inventors from da Vinci to Biro* by Struan Reid, Patricia Fara, and Ross Watton).

- Explain the characteristics of historical fiction.

- Compare and contrast historical fiction stories using those characteristics as a guide.

- Describe the value of primary source documents (e.g., Leonardo's notebook) when studying a historical period, such as the Renaissance.

- Conduct research and develop/present a multimedia presentation that integrates information from more than one source (e.g., on an inventor of choice); anticipate and respond to questions from classmates.

- Explain the historical context surrounding an invention of choice, based on information gathered from multiple print or digital sources.

- Define related words and identify their parts of speech (e.g., *inventor, invention, venue, innovator, innovative, innovate, new*).

## SUGGESTED WORKS

(E) indicates a CCSS exemplar text; (EA) indicates a text from a writer with other works identified as exemplars.

### LITERARY TEXTS

*Stories*

- *The Apprentice* (Pilar Molina Llorente and Juan Ramon Alonso)
- *The Children's Shakespeare* (Edith Nesbit and Rolf Klep)

- *Fine Print: A Story About Johann Gutenberg* (Creative Minds) (Joann Johansen Burch and Kent Alan Aldrich)
- *The Invention of Hugo Cabret* (Brian Selznick) (Note: This book illustrates the creative process beautifully, but is not set in the Renaissance.)
- *Leonardo: Beautiful Dreamer* (Robert Byrd)
- *Leonardo da Vinci* (Diane Stanley)
- *Midnight Magic* (Avi)
- *Starry Messenger: Galileo Galilei* (Peter Sis)

## Poems
- Riddles from chapter 5, "Riddles in the Dark," *The Hobbit* (J.R.R. Tolkien)
- "Time" (Valerie Bloom)

# INFORMATIONAL TEXTS

## Nonfiction Books
- *About Time: A First Look at Time and Clocks* (Bruce Koscielniak) (E)
- *Amazing Leonardo da Vinci Inventions You Can Build Yourself* (Build It Yourself Series) (Maxine Anderson)
- *Leonardo da Vinci: A Nonfiction Companion to Magic Treehouse #38: Monday with a Mad Genius* (Magic Tree House Research Guide #19) (Mary Pope Osborne, Natalie Pope Boyce, and Sal Murdocca)
- *Michelangelo* (Getting to Know the World's Greatest Artists) (Mike Venezia)
- *The New How Things Work* (David Macaulay and Neil Ardley)
- *Outrageous Women of the Renaissance* (Vicki Leon)
- *Renaissance Artists Who Inspired the World* (Explore the Ages) (Gregory Blanch and Roberta Stathis)
- *The Renaissance* (History Opens Windows) (Jane Shuter)
- *The Renaissance* (Understanding People in the Past) (Mary Quigley)
- *Science in the Renaissance* (Brendan January)
- *Science in the Renaissance* (Renaissance World) (Lisa Mullins)
- *So You Want to Be an Inventor?* (Judith St. George and David Small)
- *Telescopes: The New Book of Knowledge* (Scholastic) (Colin A. Ronan) (E)
- *Toys! Amazing Stories Behind Some Great Inventions* (Don L. Wulffson and Laurie Keller) (E)
- *The Usborne Book of Inventors from da Vinci to Biro* (Struan Reid, Patricia Fara, and Ross Watton)
- *Where Do You Get Your Ideas? Favorite Authors Reveal Their Writing Secrets* (Sandy Asher and Susan Hellard)
- *Women Inventors* (series) (Jean F. Blashfield)
- *You Wouldn't Want to Be Mary Queen of Scots: A Ruler Who Really Lost Her Head* (Fiona MacDonald and David Antram)

## ART, MUSIC, AND MEDIA

### Art

- Donatello, *St. George* (c. 1416)
- Leonardo da Vinci, *The Last Supper* (1495–1498)
- Leonardo da Vinci, *Mona Lisa* (c. 1503–1506)
- Michelangelo, ceiling of the Sistine Chapel (1508–1512)
- Michelangelo, dome of St. Peter's Basilica (1506–1626)
- Pieter Bruegel, *Peasant Wedding* (1567)
- Raphael, *School of Athens* (1510–1511)

### Music

- Canadian Brass, "English Renaissance Music"
- The King's Singers, "Madrigals"
- Traditional, possibly Henry VIII of England, "Greensleeves" (1580)

## SAMPLE ACTIVITIES AND ASSESSMENTS

### 1. READING LITERATURE

Works of "historical fiction" are set in the past, but have fictional characters or fictional elements as well. As a class, compare and contrast various historical fiction stories. In order to prepare for class discussions, create a T-chart in your journal where you take notes about people, places, or events that you believe are represented accurately and about people, places, or events that you believe are fictional. Be sure to include in your notes the page number and book title for each example so that you can refer back to the text. (RL.5.1, RL.5.9)

### 2. READING LITERATURE

In your journal, create a character map of the main character in the historical novel you are reading. Show how the character changes (or develops) over the course of the text. Compare your character with one chosen by a classmate. How are the characters similar? How are they different? (RL.5.2, RL.5.3)

### 3. READING INFORMATIONAL TEXT

As a class, keep a chart about the creative and inventive people you read about; the chart will include the following information/research inquiries:

- Name of your person
- Where he or she lived
- When he or she lived
- What did he or she do that made him or her famous?
- What are some additional facts you found interesting?
- What adjectives would you use to describe this person? Why?

Your teacher may ask you to write your responses in your journal and share them with a partner before each section of the class chart is filled in. Be sure to include page numbers and the title of the book so that you can refer back to the text if needed. Your teacher may also ask you to type your information into a shared spreadsheet so that you can collaboratively work on it as a class. (RI.5.4, RL.5.9)

## 4. SPEAKING AND LISTENING

How would you define creative/inventive thinkers? What are the common characteristics of the creative/inventive thinkers studied? (SL.5.1a, SL.5.1b, RI.5.9)

## 5. READING LITERATURE, READING INFORMATIONAL TEXT, SPEAKING AND LISTENING

Read and compare what you learn about Leonardo da Vinci from fiction and nonfiction text (e.g., *Leonardo: Beautiful Dreamer* by Robert Byrd and *The Usborne Book of Inventors from da Vinci to Biro* by Struan Reid, Patricia Fara, and Ross Watton). How does knowing the historical information enhance your understanding of the fictional story? (RL.5.9, SL.5.1)

## 6. RESEARCH, INFORMATIVE WRITING, MULTIMEDIA PRESENTATION

Using the Internet, biographies, and informational texts, read all you can about an inventor. As a class, create a time line of the inventors studied in order to understand when each inventor lived throughout history. Write a short, informative/explanatory essay about an inventor of choice that answers the question "How is necessity the mother of invention?" Your response should be a well-developed essay with three sources of information cited. Edit your writing for form and use of the perfect tenses (see Standards for more details). Your teacher may give you the option of adding a multimedia component to your paper—either a slide presentation to highlight key points, a film, or a podcast. Publish both the paper and the digital presentation, and present them to the class. Anticipate and respond to questions from classmates. (RI.5.2, RI.5.3, RI.5.9, W.5.2, RF.5.4a, L.5.1b)

## 7. INFORMATIVE WRITING

Inventors are creative people who turn their ideas into reality. Leonardo da Vinci is one of many famous inventors who kept notebooks of ideas. Look at one of his original notebooks online. Start a section of your writing journal for ideas. What ideas for inventions do *you* have? Create lists and draw and label pictures. Share your ideas with a classmate to strengthen your ideas. (W.5.5, W.5.9b)

## 8. VOCABULARY, LANGUAGE USAGE

As an individual and as a class, keep an index card file of words studied (e.g., *Renaissance; inventiveness, inventor, innovation; creativity, creation*). Keeping the words on index cards will help you when you sort words by prefix, suffix, root words, meaning, spelling feature, and so on. How do the root words help you understand the meaning of the words? (Note: This will be an ongoing activity all year long.) You may also be asked to work in groups to create semantic maps of the words *creativity* and *innovation* in order to explore your understanding of these words. (RI.5.4, L.5.4a)

## 9. MUSIC, SPEAKING AND LISTENING

Listen to music from the Renaissance (see the Art, Music, and Media section). How does this music reflect the time period in which it was written? How is it similar to and different from music you listen to today? Discuss as a class. (SL.5.1a, SL.5.1b)

## 10. ART, SPEAKING AND LISTENING

To help you appreciate, in some small part, the challenges that Michelangelo faced in painting the ceiling of the Sistine Chapel, tape paper under your desk and then draw a detailed picture for ten minutes without stopping. After ten minutes, switch from pencil to paint. With your classmates, discuss the experience and how it helps you to appreciate the amount of work that went into creating the Sistine Chapel ceiling. Finally, write in your journal about what it must have been like for Michelangelo to tackle a project that took years to complete under difficult conditions. (SL.5.1a, SL.5.1b, W.5.1a, W.5.1b, W.5.1c, W.5.1d)

## 11. ART, READING LITERATURE, SPEAKING AND LISTENING

Usually pictures enhance a story, but sometimes pictures are *part* of the story, such as in *The Invention of Hugo Cabret* by Brian Selznick. How do pictures tell a story? Justify your answer by citing specific pages from the text during class discussion. (SL.5.1, SL.5.5)

## 12. INFORMATIVE WRITING

Write an informative/explanatory essay in response to the essential question "How has inventive thinking, as revealed in fiction and nonfiction, changed our world?" Give at least three reasons/examples. Your teacher may give you the opportunity to "give one, get one" before writing your response. Edit your writing for form and use of the perfect tense (see Standards for more details) before sharing with your teacher. Your teacher may ask you to type your essay and respond to a poll about the unit on the classroom blog. (W.5.7, W.5.9a, W.5.9b, SL.5.4, L.5.1a, L.5.1b)

## 13. LANGUAGE USAGE

Your teacher will teach mini-lessons on the individual language standards. For example, he or she will teach the class about the form and use of the perfect tense, and then you will practice some cloze activities as a class—for example, "I _____ walking my dog down the street before you came home. I _____ walking my dog down the street in an hour." Next, your teacher will give you the start of a sentence ("I had . . .," "I have . . .," "I will have . . ."), and you will have the opportunity to finish the sentence with a partner. Select a piece of your own writing, find examples of the perfect tense, and ensure that you have used the correct forms. (L.5.1c)

## 14. LANGUAGE MECHANICS

As a class, continue adding to the Mechanics/Grammar bulletin board started in Unit One. Remember, once skills are taught in a mini-lesson and listed on the bulletin board, you are expected to edit your work for these elements before publication. (L.5.1, L.5.2, L.5.3)

## 15. VOCABULARY

As a class, continue adding to the Vocabulary Word Wall bulletin board where, throughout the year, you will add and sort words as you learn them in each unit of study. (L.5.4)

## 16. ART, SPEAKING AND LISTENING

Compare Raphael's *School of Athens* with Leonardo da Vinci's *The Last Supper*. How does each artist create a narrative? Discuss the idea of *composition*—how does the artist organize the painting and the story it tells? Discover the underlying structure of each work and compare them. Identify the central figures in each story. Examine the way each artist chose to focus viewers' attention on those figures and then move the eye around the scene. What details did the artists include that help tell their stories? *Note to the teacher*: You can photocopy both images and have students draw on the pages, grouping the characters. (SL.5.1, SL.5.5)

## 17. ART, SPEAKING AND LISTENING

Compare Leonardo da Vinci's *Mona Lisa* and Donatello's *St. George*. How has the artist captured the subject's essence in this portrait? What is different between the two? Both portraits are believed to be of real people. How did each artist seem to take this into consideration in their portrayal? (SL.5.1)

## ADDITIONAL ONLINE RESOURCES

- *Write a Gem of a Poem* (ReadWriteThink) (RL.5.4, W.5.4)
- *Great American Inventors: Using Nonfiction to Learn About Technology Inventions* (ReadWriteThink) (RI.5.9)
- *Research Building Blocks: "Organize This!"* (ReadWriteThink) (RI.5.9)
- *Research Building Blocks: Skim, Scan, and Scroll* (ReadWriteThink) (RI.5.9)
- *Famous Inventors: A to Z* (About.com)
- "Leonardo da Vinci (1452–1519): Notebook" (The British Library)
- "Give One Get One" (RRISD Math Team)

## TERMINOLOGY

| | | |
|---|---|---|
| Bibliography | Fiction | Paraphrase |
| Character development | Nonfiction | Primary source documents |

## INTERDISCIPLINARY CONNECTIONS

This unit teaches:
- **Science:**
  - Inventors through various time periods (e.g., Galileo and his contributions to astronomy; Thomas Edison and his contributions to telecommunications, electricity, and sound recording; Benjamin Banneker and his contributions to astronomy and mathematics)
  - A study of "how things work" (e.g., similar to the information in the book by David Macaulay)
- **History/Geography:**
  - The Renaissance (e.g., a "rebirth" of ideas; patrons of the arts and learning; Leonardo da Vinci and Michelangelo)
  - The Reformation (e.g., Gutenberg; Ptolemaic [earth-centered] vs. sun-centered models of the universe)

- **Art:** Renaissance painting and sculpture, Leonardo da Vinci, Raphael, Donatello

This unit could be extended to teach:

- **Science:** The scientific method; force and motion (e.g., simple machines); astronomy (e.g., constellations, moon phases)
- **Art:** Further study of Renaissance art and architecture (e.g., Botticelli, Michelangelo, Brunelleschi)

## Grade Five, Unit Two Sample Lesson Plan

### About Time: A First Look at Time and Clocks *by Bruce Koscielniak*

In this series of four lessons, students read *About Time: A First Look at Time and Clocks* by Bruce Koscielniak, and they:

Explore the concept of time and the inventors of clocks (RI.5.1, RI.5.2, RI.5.5)

Conduct research on inventors and their inventions (RI.5.1, RI.5.2, RI.5.5, RI.5.7, W.5.7, W.5.8)

Present the collected data (RI.5.9, SL.5.2, SL.5.5)

### Summary

### Lesson I: *About Time: A First Look at Time and Clocks*

Expand understanding of time (RI.5.2, RI.5.3)

Explore early ways of telling time (RI.5.3)

Develop a detailed time line for the invention of the clock (RI.5.3)

Reflect on the long process that leads inventors to their inventions (SL.5.1, SL.5.2, SL.5.4)

### Lesson III: Preparing to Present Data

Continue research (RI.5.1, RI.5.2, RI.5.5, RI.5.7, W.5.7)

Compose essays based on the data that was collected (W.5.2a, W.5.2b, W.5.2c, W.5.2d, W.5.2e, W.5.8, W.5.10)

Revise essays (W.5.5)

Draw illustrations of inventions (SL.5.5)

### Lesson II: Inventors and Inventions

Examine the list of inventors and their inventions (SL.5.1)

Select an inventor (W.5.5, W.5.8)

Conduct research (RI.5.1, RI.5.2, RI.5.5, RI.5.7, W.5.7, W.5.8)

Review research material (SL.5.1, SL.5.2, SL.5.4, W.5.8)

### Lesson IV: Inventions Fair

Mount research results onto display boards (SL.5.2, SL.5.5)

Emphasize three sections: (SL.5.5)

Inventor

Invention

Significance in history

Survey peers' work (RI.5.5)

## Lesson II: Inventors and Inventions

### Objectives

Examine the list of inventors and their inventions (SL.5.1)

Select an inventor (W.5.5, W.5.8)

Conduct research (RI.5.1, RI.5.2, RI.5.5, RI.5.7, W.5.7, W.5.8)

Review research material (SL.5.1, SL.5.2, SL.5.4, W.5.8)

### Required Materials

☐ Copies of "Renaissance & Elizabethan Inventions and Inventors Timeline" (http://www.elizabethan-era.org.uk/elizabethan-inventions.htm)

☐ Computers with Internet access

☐ Printer

☐ Notebooks

☐ Pens and pencils

### Procedures

1. Lead-In:

   Students examine handouts of Renaissance and Elizabethan Inventions and Inventors Time Line.

   1450: Johannes Gutenberg invents the printing press with movable type in Germany

   1510: Leonardo da Vinci designs a horizontal water wheel

   1540: Toriano invents a mandolin-playing automaton

   1543: John Dee creates a wooden beetle that can fly for an undergraduate production—one of the first robots

   1565: Conrad Gesner of Switzerland invents the pencil

   1583: Leonard and Thomas Digges invent the telescope

   1589: William Lee invents the knitting machine

   1590: Dutchmen Hans and Zacharias Janssen invent the compound microscope

1591: Sir John Harington invents the flush toilet in England

1593: Galileo Galilei invents a water thermometer

1609: Galileo Galilei introduces the first telescope to astronomy

*Source of list (adapted):* http://www.elizabethan-era.org.uk/elizabethan-inventions.htm

2. Step by Step:

   a. In groups of three, students select an invention to research.

   b. The focus of the research is on

      ○ A biography of the inventor

      ○ A map locating the country where the inventor was born

      ○ Data discussing his inventions

      ○ A single important invention

      ○ Illustrations or photographs of his inventions

      ○ The impact of the invention on society

   c. Students print informational texts that they select online.

   d. Group members divide the research material among themselves. Individuals identify main ideas in the material and take notes.

3. Closure:

   At the conclusion of the lesson, the groups reconvene. They share their notes and determine what further research is needed.

## Differentiation

### Advanced

- Students will create a commercial for an invention studied in the research. Using a musical composition or visual art masterpiece from the era in the commercial will yield extra points. Students will be allowed to create their commercial as an electronic slide presentation, record it using a video camera, or create it as a movie.

*Struggling*

- Students will work in heterogeneous groups, using a graphic organizer to aid in the research tasks and organization. Students may collaborate on a shared online spreadsheet, if desired.
- Intervene to be sure the student can be successful with his/her assigned part.
- Students may paste selected informational text into a document formatted for "text to speech" or partner with a student willing to read aloud the information.

Homework/Assessment

N/A

# Clues to a Culture

This six-week unit focuses on aspects of
Native American nations and cultures as
revealed through pairings of literature and
informational text.

## ESSENTIAL QUESTION

How does literature provide insight into a culture?

## OVERVIEW

This unit begins with students collectively defining and discussing the word *culture*. Next, students compare nineteenth-century America from the Ojibway point of view in *The Birchbark House* to depictions in texts such as *Little House on the Prairie* and *If You Were a Pioneer on the Prairie*. In order to glean the similarities and differences across nations, students read trickster stories and informational text; they also listen to music and examine art from a variety of Native American cultures. Class discussions reinforce awareness of how someone's perspective can affect his or her view of events and people. This unit ends with an informative/explanatory essay in response to the essential question.

## FOCUS STANDARDS

These Focus Standards have been selected for the unit from the Common Core State Standards.

**RL.5.1:** Quote accurately from a text when explaining what the text says explicitly and when drawing inferences from the text.

**RI.5.1:** Quote accurately from a text when explaining what the text says explicitly and when drawing inferences from the text.

**RI.5.7:** Draw on information from multiple print or digital sources, demonstrating the ability to locate an answer to a question quickly or to solve a problem efficiently.

**RF.5.4:** Read with sufficient accuracy and fluency to support comprehension.

**RF.5.4(c):** Use context to confirm or self-correct word recognition and understanding, rereading as necessary.

**W.5.1:** Write opinion pieces on topics or texts, supporting a point of view with reasons and information.

**SL.5.3:** Summarize the points a speaker makes and explain how each claim is supported by reasons and evidence.

**L.5.1:** Demonstrate command of the conventions of standard English grammar and usage when writing or speaking.

**L.5.1(c):** Use verb tense to convey various times, sequences, states, and conditions.

**L.5.1(d):** Recognize and correct inappropriate shifts in verb tense.

**L.5.4:** Determine or clarify the meaning of unknown and multiple-meaning words and phrases based on grade 5 reading and content, choosing flexibly from a range of strategies.

**L.5.4(c):** Consult reference materials (e.g., dictionaries, glossaries, thesauruses), both print and digital, to find the pronunciation and determine or clarify the precise meaning of key words and phrases.

## SUGGESTED OBJECTIVES

- Compare fiction and nonfiction books about a specific topic (e.g., Native American nations during pioneer times in America), quoting accurately from the texts.
- Find similarities and differences in stories (e.g., trickster tales) from various cultures.
- Create a multimedia presentation based on information drawn from various types of sources (e.g., a presentation on a Native American nation of choice based on fiction, nonfiction, art, or other media).
- Summarize and evaluate the content and structure of a classmate's presentation, evaluating how well he or she supports his or her claims.
- Define related words and identify their parts of speech (e.g., *nation, national, nationality, nationwide; culture, cultural, cultivate*)

## SUGGESTED WORKS

(E) indicates a CCSS exemplar text; (EA) indicates a text from a writer with other works identified as exemplars.

### LITERARY TEXTS

*Note:* The list of Native American nations is illustrative, not comprehensive; please choose a local nation to examine in a similar manner.

*Stories*
- *The Birchbark House* (Louise Erdrich) (E)
- *A Boy Called Slow* (Joseph Bruchac and Rocco Baviera)
- *Dreamcatcher* (Audrey Osofsky and Ed Young)

- *Guests* (Michael Dorris)
- *Island of the Blue Dolphins* (Scott O'Dell)
- *Julie of the Wolves* (Jean Craighead George and John Schoenherr)
- *Knots on a Counting Rope* (Bill Martin Jr., John Archambault, and Ted Rand)
- *Little House on the Prairie* (Laura Ingalls Wilder and Garth Williams) (EA)
- *Sign of the Beaver* (Elizabeth George Speare)
- *Walk Two Moons* (Sharon Creech)

## Trickster Tales

- *Coyote: A Trickster Tale from the American Southwest* (Gerald McDermott)
- *How Rabbit Tricked Otter: And Other Cherokee Trickster Stories* (Gayle Ross and Murv Jacob)
- *Raven: A Trickster Tale from the Pacific Northwest* (Gerald McDermott)
- *A Ring of Tricksters: Animal Tales from North America, the West Indies, and Africa* (Virginia Hamilton and Barry Moser) (EA)
- *Trickster Tales: Forty Folk Stories from Around the World* (World Storytelling) (Josepha Sherman)

## Poems

- "Dream Catchers" (Ojibway, Traditional)
- "You Are Part of Me" (Cherokee, Lloyd Carl Owle)

## INFORMATIONAL TEXTS

### Nonfiction Books

- *Black Frontiers: A History of African-American Heroes in the Old West* (Lillian Schlissel)
- *A History of US: First Americans: Prehistory–1600* (Joy Hakim) (E)
- *A History of US: The New Nation: 1789–1850* (Joy Hakim) (E)
- *If You Lived with the Cherokees* (If You . . . Series) (Peter and Connie Roop and Kevin Smith)
- *If You Lived with the Sioux Indians* (If You . . . Series) (Ann McGovern and Jean Syverud Drew)
- *If You Were a Pioneer on the Prairie* (If You . . . Series) (Anne Kamma and James Watling)
- *The Nez Perce* (True Books) (Stefanie Takacs)
- *Sequoyah: The Cherokee Man Who Gave His People Writing* (James Rumford) (Read Aloud)
- *You Wouldn't Want to Be an American Pioneer! A Wilderness You'd Rather Not Tame* (You Wouldn't Want to . . . Series) (Jacqueline Morley, David Salariya, and David Antram)

### Speech

"I Will Fight No More Forever" (Chief Joseph the Younger, October 5, 1877)

## ART, MUSIC, AND MEDIA

### Art

#### Apache

- Artist unknown, *San Juan, a Mescalero Apache Chief* (no date)
- Edward S. Curtis, *Apache Still Life* (1907)

- Noah H. Rose, *View of Two Native American Apache Women Outside Their Cloth-Covered Wickiups in a Camp in Arizona* (1880)

*Hopi*

- Edward Curtis, *East Side of Walpi* (1921)
- *Hopi Girl with Jar* (no date)
- Wooden Hopi Kachina doll (1925)

*Haida*

- Bill Hupe, *Dedication Potlatch: The Honoring of Ancient Traditions* (2006)
- Haida mask (1879)
- *Indian Village, Alaska* (1897)

## Music

- Thomas Vennum, *Ojibway Music from Minnesota: A Century of Song for Voice and Drum*

## Media

- *Will Fight No More* (video of the speech of Chief Joseph)

# SAMPLE ACTIVITIES AND ASSESSMENTS

## 1. SPEAKING AND LISTENING

What is meant by the word *culture*? For which elements does one look when learning about a culture? Write your ideas down on a sticky note and "give one, get one." (*Note:* Answers may include language, social organization, customs/traditions, arts, religion, symbols, etc.) Create a class chart of elements to look for, and look to find examples in texts read during this unit. (SL.5.1)

## 2. READING LITERATURE, OPINION WRITING

*The Birchbark House* by Louise Erdrich is described as a realistic and sympathetic portrayal of a Native American culture during the period of westward expansion. Compare pioneer life as presented from Omakayas's perspective in *The Birchbark House* with Laura's perspective in *Little House on the Prairie* by Laura Ingalls Wilder and Garth Williams or *If You Were a Pioneer on the Prairie* by Anne Kamma and James Watling. Choose an event in the story and write about what surprised you the most about Omakayas's experience. (RL.5.1, RL.5.3)

## 3. READING LITERATURE, SPEAKING AND LISTENING

The title of Sharon Creech's book *Walk Two Moons* comes from the Native American phrase "Don't judge a man until you have walked two moons in his moccasins." What have you learned about the Native American nation studied? Turn and talk with a neighbor about this prompt before responding in your journal. (RL.5.1)

## 4. INFORMATIVE WRITING, MULTIMEDIA PRESENTATION, LANGUAGE MECHANICS, LANGUAGE USAGE

Read all you can about a Native American nation, drawing on information from multiple print or digital sources. Be sure that the digital and print sources are credible. Use indexes, tables of contents, digital searches, and key words as you work. Use the most relevant and useful information to write an informative/explanatory piece about your nation of choice. Your response should be a well-developed essay with three sources of information cited, including accurate quotations from the texts. Edit your writing for proper verb tenses and punctuation, especially commas (see Standards for more details). Your teacher may give you the option of adding a multimedia component to your paper—either creating an electronic slide presentation to highlight key points or sharing links to music and/or images of the Native American nation of choice. Publish both and present them to the class. Answer questions from classmates about your presentation. (RI.5.1, RI.5.7, RI.5.8, W.5.2a, W.5.2b, W.5.2c, W.5.2d, RF.5.4c, L.5.1a, L.5.1b, L.5.1c, L.5.1d, L.5.2a, L.5.2b)

## 5. READING LITERATURE, LANGUAGE USAGE

Sharon Creech uses sound imagery, often linked to personification, throughout her novel *Walk Two Moons*. Find an example of how these literary techniques were used to increase the feeling of being part of the story, mark it with a sticky note, and share it with a partner. (RF.5.4c)

## 6. OPINION WRITING, LANGUAGE USAGE, LANGUAGE MECHANICS

Consider the speech of Chief Joseph the Younger ("I Will Fight No More Forever"). In your opinion, do you think he needed to be consoled or encouraged to go on? Write your position on a sticky note, and your teacher will divide the class based on your position. Share ideas with classmates who are of the same opinion. Then, begin individually drafting an essay in your journal. Work with classmates to revise your essay, ensuring that it includes accurate quotations from the speech to support your opinion. Edit your writing for verb tense and punctuation, especially commas (see Standards for more details). Publish your essay on a classroom blog to encourage additional conversation. (SL.5.3, W.5.1a, W.5.1b, W.5.1c, W.5.1d, W.5.6, L.5.1a, L.5.1b, L.5.1c, L.5.1d, L.5.2a, L.5.2b)

## 7. LANGUAGE MECHANICS

As a class, continue adding to the Mechanics/Grammar bulletin board started in Unit One. Remember, once skills are taught in a mini-lesson and listed on the bulletin board, you are expected to edit your work for these elements before publication. (L.5.1, L.5.2, L.5.3)

## 8. VOCABULARY

As a class, continue adding to the Vocabulary Word Wall bulletin board where, throughout the year, you will add and sort words as you learn them in each unit of study. (L.5.4)

## 9. SPEAKING AND LISTENING, OPINION WRITING

As a class, discuss how trickster stories can reveal insights into a culture different from your own. What did you learn about the nation from the trickster story you've just read? What does a story/poem reveal about a culture that reading solely from an informational text does not? Write your ideas down in your journal prior to class discussion. (RL.5.9, SL.5.3)

## 10. SPEAKING AND LISTENING, OPINION WRITING

Why do tricksters ignore conventional cultural behavior? Why are these characters often personifications and not human? What impact does culture have on the tale? Talk with a classmate to share ideas and then write your favorite ideas down in your journal prior to class discussion. (RL.5.9)

## 11. VOCABULARY, LANGUAGE USAGE

As an individual and as a class, keep an index card file of words studied (e.g., *tribe, tribute; nation, nationality, nationwide; culture, cultural*). Keeping the words on index cards will help you when you sort words by prefix, suffix, root words, meaning, and so on. How do the prefixes and suffixes help you understand the meaning of the words while changing the part of speech? (*Note:* This will be an ongoing activity all year long.) (RI.5.4, L.5.4a, L.5.4b, L.5.4c, RF.5.3a)

## 12. MUSIC, SPEAKING AND LISTENING

Discuss how art and music can provide insights into a culture. From which do you prefer to learn? Why? Your teacher may ask you to write your own response and reasons on sticky notes, on a whiteboard, or in your journal before discussing as a class. (SL.5.1)

## 13. INFORMATIVE WRITING, LANGUAGE USAGE, LANGUAGE MECHANICS

Write an informative/explanatory essay in response to the essential question "How does literature provide insight into a culture?" Your teacher may give you the opportunity to "give one, get one" before writing your response. Edit your writing for verb tense and punctuation, especially commas (see Standards for more details). Your teacher may ask you to type your essay and respond to a poll about the unit on the classroom blog. (W.5.4, W.5.7, W.9a, W.9b, L.5.1a, L.5.1b, L.5.1c, L.5.1d, L.5.2a, L.5.2b)

## 14. ART, OPINION WRITING

View Rose's and Curtis's photographs, along with *Indian Village, Alaska*. What can we learn about these tribes through images of their housing? Why do you believe that each tribe has a different form of home? For instance, why might the Apache build more temporary housing and the Hopi build into the land? What about these images can lead you to make educated guesses? Write an essay describing what you have learned by viewing the photographs. (W.5.1, W.5.2, W.5.4, W.5.8)

## 15. ART, SPEAKING AND LISTENING

Compare the Haida mask with the Kachina doll. Are the colors, fabrics, and textures used similar? Why do you believe this is so? What is the purpose of each of these objects? Discuss the use of pattern in these two works. (SL.5.1)

## ADDITIONAL ONLINE RESOURCES

- *November Is National American Indian Heritage Month* (ReadWriteThink) (RL.5.9)
- *Native Americans Today* (ReadWriteThink) (RI.5.7)
- *Culture Clues Expedition* (National Geographic) (RI.5.7)

- *Teaching Point of View with Two Bad Ants* (ReadWriteThink) (RL.5.6)
- *Life of a Navajo Weaver* (ArtsEdge, The Kennedy Center)
- *Native American Chants and Movement* (ArtsEdge, The Kennedy Center)
- *Countries and Their Cultures* (EveryCulture.com)
- "Native Languages of America: Native American Indian Legends and Folklore" (Native Languages of the Americas)
- "Give One Get One" (RRISD Math Team)

## TERMINOLOGY

| | | |
|---|---|---|
| Culture | Perspective | Sound imagery |
| Personification | Point of view | Trickster tale |

## INTERDISCIPLINARY CONNECTIONS

This unit teaches:

- **History/Geography:**
  - Native American cultures (e.g., Great Basin and Plateau, Northern and Southern Plains, Pacific Northwest) and famous Native Americans (e.g., Chief Joseph the Younger)
  - Life in the American west (e.g., the transcontinental railroad, pioneers, wagon trains)
- **Art:** Photography, Native American decorative arts

This unit could be extended to teach:

- **History/Geography:**
  - Where different Native American tribes lived (e.g., Great Basin and Plateau, Northern and Southern Plains, Pacific Northwest), and how the shelters, clothing, and artwork varied based upon geography
  - Conflicts between Native Americans and European settlers (e.g., American government policies, Bureau of Indian Affairs, Sand Creek Massacre, Little Big Horn, Wounded Knee)
  - Native American nations or famous Native Americans (e.g., Tecumseh, Osceola, Sacagawea, Sequoyah)
  - Westward expansion before the Civil War (e.g., Lewis and Clark, Daniel Boone, Wilderness Trail, Erie Canal, Pony Express)

## Grade Five, Unit Three Sample Lesson Plan

### A History of US: The New Nation: 1789–1850 *by Joy Hakim*

In this series of five lessons, the students read *A History of US: The New Nation: 1789-1850* by Joy Hakim, and they:

Recall and list main events and important historical figures in *The New Nation* (RI.5.1, RI.5.3, RI.5.10, SL.5.1)

Expand their knowledge and understanding of late eighteenth- and early nineteenth-century America (RI.5.1, RI.5.2, RI.5.5, RI.5.6, RI.5.7, RI.5.10, W.5.7, W.5.8, RF.5.4)

Record their findings (RI.5.9, W.5.4, W.5.5, W.5.6, W.5.8)

Publish their findings (SL.5.2, SL.5.4, SL.5.5, L.5.3)

## Summary

### Lesson I: *The New Nation*

(In groups) explore main events and important historical figures in *The New Nation* (RI.5.1, RI.5.3, RI.5.10, SL.5.1)

(In groups) list the topics generated in the previous objective (RI.5.3, SL.5.1)

Examine results of groups' research (SL.5.1, SL.5.2, SL.5.4, W.5.8)

Select research topics (W.5.5, W.5.8)

### Lesson IV: Document Findings

Investigate options for presenting the data (poster boards, class newspaper, magazine, multimedia, etc.) (SL.5.5)

Explore sections of presentation (essays, maps, photos, etc.) (W.5.10)

Document results of research (RI.5.9, W.5.8)

Edit and revise all work (W.5.4, W.5.5, W.5.6)

### Lessons II–III: Researching *The New Nation*

(In groups) conduct research of selected topic (RI.5.1, RI.5.2, RI.5.5, RI.5.6, RI.5.7, RI.5.10, W.5.7, W.5.8, RF.5.4)

(In groups) record information (W.5.8)

(In groups) identify needs for further research (SL.5.1c)

(In groups) conclude research (SL.5.1d)

### Lesson V: *The New Nation* Revisited–Publishing Research

Display findings (SL.5.2, SL.5.4, SL.5.5, L.5.3)

Probe classmates' exploration of *The New Nation* (L.5.1, SL.5.1, SL.5.3)

Reflect upon the results (SL.5.1d)

## Lesson I: *The New Nation*

### Objectives

(In groups) explore main events and important historical figures in *The New Nation* (RI.5.1, RI.5.3, RI.5.10, SL.5.1)

(In groups) list the topics generated in the previous objective (RI.5.3, SL.5.1)

Examine results of groups' research (SL.5.1, SL.5.2, SL.5.4, W.5.8)

Select research topics (W.5.5, W.5.8)

### Required Materials

☐ Class set of *A History of US: The New Nation: 1789–1850* by Joy Hakim

☐ Computers with Internet access

☐ Chart paper

☐ Markers

### Procedures

1. Lead-In:

   Break the students into groups.

2. Step by Step:

   a. In the groups, students revisit *A History of US: The New Nation: 1789–1850* by Joy Hakim, and generate a list of important historical figures and events in *The New Nation*.

   b. Still in groups, the students record their findings on chart paper. The lists are likely to include the presidents of the period, maps of Lewis and Clark explorations, the War of 1812, the growth of industry, the Abolitionists, and more.

   c. Lead a discussion of the students' findings.

3. Closure:

   Students select research topics.

## Differentiation

### Advanced

- After the list of people and events has been generated and discussed, students choose topics made more interesting by the multiple viewpoints of the contributions of a historical figure or a historical event.

- Throughout the research, students will discuss—at the upper end of Bloom's taxonomy (i.e., analyzing, evaluating)—the effects of the figure's or event's contribution to America.

### Struggling

- Students will brainstorm a list of helpful informational text features to cue importance (chapter titles, subtitles, picture captions, bold print, table of contents, etc.).

- During the initial reading of this text, you and your students may want to keep a running list of important people and events in ongoing preparation for this research project.

## Homework/Assessment

N/A

# America in Conflict

This nine-week unit focuses on the causes and consequences of the American Civil War, as revealed through literature and informational text.

---

## ESSENTIAL QUESTION

How are fictionalized characters and real people changed through conflict?

---

## OVERVIEW

Students read historical fiction and informational texts about the Civil War in the United States and compare and contrast the ways in which each type of text describes key historical events. In order to gain a deeper understanding of the period beyond what is addressed in print, students listen to music and examine art from the Civil War period. The culminating activity is to compose a narrative that is set within a historical context, includes a fictional character with a conflict to grow from, and incorporates authentic facts, photos, or artwork.

## FOCUS STANDARDS

These Focus Standards have been selected for the unit from the Common Core State Standards.

**RL.5.6:** Describe how a narrator's or speaker's point of view influences how events are described.

**RI.5.3:** Explain the relationships or interactions between two or more individuals, events, ideas, or concepts in a historical, scientific, or technical text based on specific information in the text.

**RI.5.5:** Compare and contrast the overall structure (e.g., chronology, comparison, cause/effect, problem/solution) of events, ideas, concepts, or information in two or more texts.

**RF.5.4:** Read with sufficient accuracy and fluency to support comprehension.

**RF.5.4(a):** Read on-level text with purpose and understanding.

**W.5.3:** Write narratives to develop real or imagined experiences or events using effective technique, descriptive details, and clear event sequences.

**SL.5.4:** Report on a topic or text or present an opinion, sequencing ideas logically and using appropriate facts and relevant, descriptive details to support main ideas or themes; speak clearly at an understandable pace.

**L.5.4:** Determine or clarify the meaning of unknown and multiple-meaning words and phrases based on grade 5 reading and content, choosing flexibly from a range of strategies.

**L.5.4(b):** Use common, grade-appropriate Greek and Latin affixes and roots as clues to the meaning of a word (e.g., *photograph*, *photosynthesis*).

## SUGGESTED OBJECTIVES

- Compare and contrast the points of view in fictional and nonfictional texts about the same topic or time period.
- Compare and contrast the ways in which fictional and informational texts treat historical events (e.g., the Civil War and slavery in the United States).
- Analyze two accounts of the same event and describe important similarities and differences in the details they provide.
- Write a historical narrative, incorporating knowledge gained from fictional and informational texts about a particular period in history (e.g., the Civil War).
- Define related words and identify their parts of speech (e.g., *civil, civilization, civilian*).

## SUGGESTED WORKS

(E) indicates a CCSS exemplar text; (EA) indicates a text from a writer with other works identified as exemplars.

## LITERARY TEXTS

### Stories

- *Across Five Aprils* (Irene Hunt)
- *After the Rain: Virginia's Civil War Diary, Book Two* (Mary Pope Osborne) (EA)
- *Ballad of the Civil War* (Mary Stoltz and Sergio Martinez)
- *Bull Run* (Paul Fleischman)
- *Charley Skedaddle* (Patricia Beatty)
- *Dear Austin: Letters from the Underground Railroad* (Elvira Woodruff and Nancy Carpenter)
- *The Journal of James Edmond Pease: A Civil War Union Soldier, Virginia, 1863* (Dear America Series) (Jim Murphy) (EA)
- *Just a Few Words, Mr. Lincoln* (Jean Fritz)
- *A Light in the Storm: The Civil War Diary of Amelia Martin, Fenwick Island, Delaware, 1861* (Dear America Series) (Karen Hesse)

- *Maritcha: A Nineteenth-Century American Girl* (Tonya Bolden)
- *A Picture of Freedom: The Diary of Clotee, a Slave Girl, Belmont Plantation, Virginia, 1859* (Dear America Series) (Patricia C. McKissack)
- *Steal Away . . . to Freedom* (Jennifer Armstrong)
- *A Time to Dance: Virginia's Civil War Diary, Book Three* (Mary Pope Osborne) (EA)
- *Underground Man* (Milton Meltzer)
- *When Will This Cruel War Be Over? The Civil War Diary of Emma Simpson, Gordonsville, Virginia, 1864* (Dear America Series) (Barry Denenberg)

## Picture Books
- *Follow the Drinking Gourd* (Jeanette Winter) (for the introductory activity)
- *Sweet Clara and the Freedom Quilt* (Deborah Hopkins) (for the introductory activity)

## Poems
- "The Eagle" (Alfred, Lord Tennyson)
- "I Hear America Singing" (Walt Whitman) (EA)
- "I, Too, Sing America" (Langston Hughes) (E)
- "The New Colossus" (Emma Lazarus) (E)

## INFORMATIONAL TEXTS

### Nonfiction Books
- *The Abolitionist Movement* (Cornerstones of Freedom) (Elaine Landau)
- *The Abraham Lincoln You Never Knew* (James Lincoln Collier and Greg Copeland)
- *A History of US: War, Terrible War: 1855–1865* (Joy Hakim) (E)
- *I Lift My Lamp: Emma Lazarus and the Statue of Liberty* (Nancy Smiler Levinson) (OOP)
- *If You Lived at the Time of the Civil War* (If You . . . Series) (Kay Moore and Anni Matsick)
- *If You Lived When There was Slavery in America* (If You . . . Series) (Anne Kamma and Pamela Johnson)
- *If You Traveled on the Underground Railroad* (If You . . . Series) (Ellen Levine and Larry Johnson)
- *Outrageous Women of Civil War Times* (Mary Rodd Furbee)
- *Sojourner Truth: Ain't I a Woman?* (Frederick McKissack and Patricia C. McKissack)
- *You Wouldn't Want to Be a Civil War Soldier: A War You'd Rather Not Fight* (You Wouldn't Want to . . . Series) (Thomas Ratliff and David Antram)
- *You Wouldn't Want to Be a Worker on the Statue of Liberty! A Monument You'd Rather Not Build* (You Wouldn't Want to . . . Series) (John Malam and David Antram)
- *Your Travel Guide to the Civil War* (Passport to History) (Nancy Raines Day)

### Speech
- The Gettysburg Address (Abraham Lincoln) (E) (Note: The Gettysburg Address is a CCSS exemplar text for grades 9 through 10.)

## ART, MUSIC, AND MEDIA

### Art

- Alexander Gardner, *President Abraham Lincoln in the Tent of General George B. McClellan After the Battle of Antietam* (October 3, 1862)

### Music

- Daniel Decatur Emmett, "Dixie" (1861)
- "Goober Peas" (Traditional)
- Julia Ward Howe, "The Battle Hymn of the Republic" (1861)
- Patrick S. Gilmore, "When Johnny Comes Marching Home" (1863)

### Media

- Civil War photographs

## SAMPLE ACTIVITIES AND ASSESSMENTS

### 1. READING INFORMATIONAL TEXT, READING LITERATURE, SPEAKING AND LISTENING

Start this unit by reading aloud a favorite picture book about the Civil War, such as *Follow the Drinking Gourd* or *Sweet Clara and the Freedom Quilt*, not only to start building background knowledge of the Civil War period but also to help your students understand what you will expect from them in journal entries and other assignments. (RL.5.2, SL.5.1, SL.5.3, W.5.4, W.5.8)

### 2. SPEAKING AND LISTENING

How do the symbols of America (e.g., the Statue of Liberty, the American flag, the bald eagle) provide strength during times of conflict? Discuss as a class, citing examples from the poems and stories you've read. (SL.5.1)

### 3. READING POETRY, WRITING POETRY, LANGUAGE USAGE

Continue the Poetic Devices Chart (begun in Unit One) that includes examples of similes, metaphors, alliteration, and onomatopoeia in poems from this unit. Write your own poem about America that uses at least two of the techniques found. Your teacher may ask you to type your poem and insert a relevant picture or illustration for publication on the class web page. (RL.5.4, L.5.5, W.5.4)

### 4. ART, SPEAKING AND LISTENING

How is war depicted through art? View one of the most famous photos of the Civil War, *President Abraham Lincoln in the Tent of General George B. McClellan After the Battle of Antietam*, and discuss what the image teaches viewers about the Civil War, even before learning facts and reading literature from that time period. (SL.5.1)

## 5. READING LITERATURE, READING COMPREHENSION

While reading a story such as *Bull Run* by Paul Fleischman, keep an ongoing list of words to describe the main character(s). Mark the text with sticky notes and write the adjectives on the notes. After finishing the book, you will be asked to choose the best adjectives to describe the character's internal responses and external behaviors in response to conflicts experienced. (RL.5.1, RL.5.2, RL.5.6, RF.5.4a, RF.5.4b, RF.5.4c)

## 6. READING LITERATURE, READING INFORMATIONAL TEXT, SPEAKING AND LISTENING

Read and compare what you learn about slavery in America from fiction and nonfiction text (e.g., *Dear Austin: Letters from the Underground Railroad* by Elvira Woodruff and Nancy Carpenter and *If You Lived When There was Slavery in America* by Anne Kamma and Pamela Johnson). How does knowing the historical information enhance your understanding of the fictional story? Talk with a classmate to share ideas prior to large-group discussion. (RL.5.9)

## 7. RESEARCH, INFORMATIVE WRITING, LANGUAGE MECHANICS

As a class, keep a chart of information about the Civil War period learned from a variety of fiction and nonfiction; the chart will track responses to the following questions:

- What is the conflict?
- Why does this conflict occur?
- Who is involved on each side of the conflict?
- How is the conflict resolved?
- How does this conflict affect our lives today?

Keep a list of your responses to these questions in your journal. Share thoughts with a partner who has read the same book you did, and collaboratively contribute to the class chart or a shared spreadsheet. After the class finishes the graphic organizer, individually write a summary explaining one of the conflicts studied. Your response should be a well-developed essay that includes at least three supporting details and a statement about how the event fits into the larger context of the Civil War. Check your writing for plagiarism. Edit your writing, especially for commas to set off the words *yes* and *no* and to indicate direct address (see Standards for more details). Your teacher may ask you to publish your essay on the class blog or the class web page. (RI.5.3, RI.5.5, RI.5.7, RI.5.9, RF.5.4a, RF.5.4b, RF.5.4c, W.5.2, W.5.4, L.5.1a, L.5.1b, L.5.1c, L.5.1d, L.5.2a, L.5.2b, L.5.2c)

## 8. SPEAKING AND LISTENING

At the end of the unit, compare the lives of different characters, real and fictional, during the Civil War and discuss how they grew because of the conflict they experienced. (RI.5.3, RI.5.5, RI.5.7, RI.5.9, SL.5.1 RF.5.4a, RF.5.4b, RF.5.4c)

## 9. INFORMATIVE WRITING, RESEARCH, LANGUAGE USAGE, LANGUAGE MECHANICS

Write a research essay about an event from the Civil War, highlighting the causes and effects of the conflict. Part of your essay should explain the relationship or interaction between individuals or events. Alternatively, choose a person to write about, noting how that person contributed to the cause or to the resolution of this historical conflict. The well-developed research essay should be logically ordered with at least two to three sources of information cited. Edit your writing, especially for commas to set off the words *yes* and *no* and to indicate direct address (see Standards for more details). Your teacher may ask you to draw and scan illustrations or insert relevant photos from the Internet for publication on the class web page. (W.5.2, W.5.7, RI.5.3, SL.5.4, SL.5.5, L.5.1a, L.5.1b, L.5.1c, L.5.1d, L.5.2a, L.5.2b, L.5.2c)

## 10. VOCABULARY

As an individual and as a class, keep an index card file of words studied (e.g., *secession, rebellion, abolition, confederate, rebel*). Keeping the words on index cards will help when you sort words by prefix, suffix, root words, meaning, and so on. How do word relationships (e.g., between *civil, civilization,* and *civilian*) help you understand the meaning of the words, while the prefixes and suffixes affect the part of speech and spelling? (Note: This will be an ongoing activity all year long.) (RI.5.6, L.5.4b, L.5.4c)

## 11. NARRATIVE WRITING, LANGUAGE USAGE, LANGUAGE MECHANICS, SPEAKING AND LISTENING

Write your own historical narrative that is set during the Civil War, includes a fictional character with a conflict to grow from, and incorporates authentic facts, photos, or artwork. Talk through your ideas with a partner before starting your first draft. You will have the opportunity to edit and revise your narrative with a partner, so that your final product is of the highest quality. The well-developed narrative should include ideas that flow logically, and at least five new vocabulary words or phrases that provide historical context. Edit your writing, especially for commas to set off the words *yes* and *no* and to indicate direct address (see Standards for more details). Publish your narrative on the class web page to encourage virtual conversation after the unit is over. (W.5.3, W.5.4, W.5.9a, W.5.9b, SL.5.5, L.5.1a, L.5.1b, L.5.1c, L.5.1d, L.5.2a, L.5.2b, L.5.2c)

## 12. LANGUAGE MECHANICS

As a class, continue adding to the Mechanics/Grammar bulletin board started in Unit One. Remember, once skills are taught in a mini-lesson and listed on the bulletin board, you are expected to edit your work for these elements before publication. (L.5.1, L.5.2, L.5.3)

## 13. VOCABULARY

As a class, continue adding to the Vocabulary Word Wall bulletin board where, throughout the year, you will add and sort words as you learn them in each unit of study. (L.5.4)

## ADDITIONAL ONLINE RESOURCES

- *Engaging Students in a Collaborative Study of the Gettysburg Address* (ReadWriteThink) (SL.5.3)
- *Using Historical Fiction to Learn About the Civil War* (ReadWriteThink) (RL.5.2, W.5.7)
- *Critical Perspectives: Reading and Writing About Slavery* (ReadWriteThink) (RL.5.2, W.5.7)
- *Strategic Reading and Writing: Summarizing Antislavery Biographies* (ReadWriteThink) (RL.5.2, RI.5.1)
- *Examining Plot Conflict Through a Comparison/Contrast Essay* (ReadWriteThink) (RL.5.9)

- *Civil War Music* (ArtsEdge, The Kennedy Center)
- *Pictures of the Civil War* (The National Archives)
- *The U.S. Civil War 1861–1865* (A History Place)

## TERMINOLOGY

Ballad

Cause and effect

Characterization

Conflict

Poetic terms: meter, rhyme scheme, metaphor, simile

Symbolism

## INTERDISCIPLINARY CONNECTIONS

This unit teaches:

- **History/Geography:** The Civil War (e.g., abolitionists, slave life, Abraham Lincoln, Gettysburg Address, Yankees and rebels, Blue and Gray, First Battle of Bull Run/First Battle of Manassas, Sojourner Truth, Harriet Tubman, Underground Railroad)

This unit could be extended to teach:

- **History/Geography:** Reconstruction (e.g., famous people, major events); Lincoln's assassination; slavery
- **Language Arts:** "O Captain, My Captain" (Walt Whitman)

# Grade Five, Unit Four Sample Lesson Plan

*"The New Colossus" by Emma Lazarus*

*I Lift My Lamp: Emma Lazarus and the Statue of Liberty by Nancy Smiler Levinson*

*(Please note that I Lift My Lamp is no longer in print. However, you can still use this lesson by utilizing another informational text in its place.)* In this series of five lessons, students read "The New Colossus" by Emma Lazarus and *I Lift My Lamp: Emma Lazarus and the Statue of Liberty* by Nancy Smiler Levinson, and they:

- Explore Emma Lazarus's place in history (RL.5.6, RI.5.1)
- Explore Emma Lazarus's Jewish identity (RL.5.6, W.5.4, W.5.7)
- Investigate the story of the Statue of Liberty (RL.5.6, RI.5.3, RI.5.9, SL.5.1)
- Probe the relationship between Emma Lazarus and Ralph Waldo Emerson (RI.5.3, W.5.4, W.5.7, SL.5.1)
- Examine the historical significance of "The New Colossus" (RL.5.2, SL.5.1, SL.5.2)

## Summary

**Lesson I: "Mighty Woman with a Torch" (Ch. 1 in *I Lift My Lamp*)**

- Critically read "The New Colossus" (RL.5.10, RF.5.4)
- Investigate the allusion to the "brazen giant of Greek fame" (RL.5.4, L.5.4)
- Explore the notion of "the golden door" (RL.5.4, L.5.4)
- Examine the theme of "The New Colossus" (RL.5.2)
- (While reading Ch. 1 in *I Lift My Lamp*) provide early information and lay a foundational, historical context to Emma Lazarus and the Statue of Liberty (RL.5.5, RL.5.6)

**Lesson II: Young Emma Lazarus and "A Monumental Idea" (Chs. 2–6)**

- Investigate the early life of Emma Lazarus (RL.5.6, RI.5.1)
- Explore the significance of America's idea of freedom (W.5.4, W.5.7)
- Conduct online/library research into the origins of the Statue of Liberty (RI.5.1, RI.5.7, W.5.4, W.5.7)
- Document findings of research (RI.5.9, W.5.4, W.5.7)

## Lesson III: Emma Lazarus and Ralph Waldo Emerson

Recall details of the relationship between Emma Lazarus and Ralph Waldo Emerson (in *I Lift My Lamp*) (RI.5.3)

Conduct online/library research on the relationship between Lazarus and Emerson (RI.5.3, W.5.4, W.5.7)

Explore details of the correspondence between Lazarus and Emerson (RI.5.3, W.5.4, W.5.7, SL.5.1)

## Lesson IV: Emma's Jewish Identity and the Statue of Liberty (Ch.7–End)

Explore the significance of Lazarus's Jewish heritage (RL.5.6, W.5.4, W.5.7)

Identify reasons for Jewish immigration to America (RI.5.7, RI.5.9, W.5.4, W.5.7, SL.5.4)

Probe the origins of "The New Colossus" (RL.5.2, RL.5.5, L.5.4, W.5.4, W.5.7)

Contextualize Lazarus's role in establishing the Statue of Liberty as a beacon of freedom (RL.5.6, RI.5.3, RI.5.9, SL.5.1)

## Lesson V: Lazarus, Emerson, the Statue of Liberty, and "The New Colossus"–Reflections

Recall how historical events, people, a monument, and a single poem all came together (RL.5.6, RI.5.3, RI.5.9)

Examine the lingering impact of "The New Colossus" (RL.5.2, SL.5.1, SL.5.2)

## Lesson IV: Emma's Jewish Identity and the Statue of Liberty
*Objectives*

Explore the significance of Lazarus's Jewish heritage (RL.5.6, W.5.4, W.5.7)

Identify reasons for Jewish immigration to America (RI.5.7, RI.5.9, W.5.4, W.5.7, SL.5.4)

Probe the origins of "The New Colossus" (RL.5.2, RL.5.5, L.5.4, W.5.4, W.5.7)

Contextualize Lazarus's role in establishing the Statue of Liberty as a beacon of freedom (RL.5.6, RI.5.3, RI.5.9, SL.5.1)

*Required Materials*

☐ Class set of "The New Colossus" by Emma Lazarus

☐ *I Lift My Lamp: Emma Lazarus and the Statue of Liberty* by Nancy Smiler Levinson

☐ Computers with Internet access

*Procedures*

1. Lead-In:

   Recall details of chapters 9 and 10.

2. Step by Step:

The progression of this part depends upon the previous lesson's homework. The assumption here is that the students will have read the final chapters of the book for homework. Adjust the lesson if you do in-class reading of these chapters instead.

   a. Discussion of chapters 9 and 10:

      ○ The persecution of European Jewry in the late nineteenth century

      ○ Lazarus's response

      ○ Jewish immigration to America

      ○ Lazarus's involvement with Jewish refugees

      ○ Lazarus's deep Jewish emotions as revealed in her poetry and letters

   b. Reread an informational text about Emma Lazarus and document the events that led to the composition of "The New Colossus."

3. Closure:

   Read aloud (or have a student volunteer read aloud) "Her Words Forever Sing," the final chapter of *I Lift My Lamp: Emma Lazarus and the Statue of Liberty*.

Differentiation

*Advanced*

● Students will create a concept map based on the word *inspiration*, either on paper or using concept map software.

● Students will explore the word *inspiration* by posting facets of the word's meaning to a physical cube (e.g., they can choose to describe it, compare it to the word *creativity*, illustrate its relationship to a musician or visual artist, apply it to a poet's work, analyze its root word and origin, or argue for or against it).

*Struggling*

- Provide students with an outline to guide the reading of chapters 9 and 10 for homework (or class work) or require them to use a particular number of sticky notes to mark important details in the text.

- Have the reading available for students to listen to on individual MP3 players.

## Homework/Assessment

Students write a two-paragraph composition in which they discuss the historical significance of "The New Colossus." (The paper will be used for class discussion in the final lesson of the unit.)

# Exploration, Real and Imagined

This five-week unit builds on the study of character development begun in Unit Four by having students articulate what we learn from real and fictional characters' experiences.

---

## ESSENTIAL QUESTION

What do people, both real and imagined, learn from exploring their world?

---

## OVERVIEW

Students choose an exemplar text with a dreamlike context—such as *Alice in Wonderland* or *The Little Prince*—to read with their peers and to examine what we can learn from the characters' experiences and development. If students have the opportunity to view performances of the books, they can also discuss how the performances are similar to and different from the book. In addition, students read informational texts such as *My Librarian Is a Camel: How Books Are Brought to Children Around the World* or biographies of explorers in order to apply lessons learned from literature to informational text. Students also create an individual semantic map of the word *exploration* in order to help their understanding of the real and fictional characters studied in this unit. Finally, this unit ends with an informative/explanatory essay in response to the essential question.

## FOCUS STANDARDS

These Focus Standards have been selected for the unit from the Common Core State Standards.

**RL.5.5:** Explain how a series of chapters, scenes, or stanzas fits together to provide the overall structure of a particular story, drama, or poem.

**RL.5.7:** Analyze how visual and multimedia elements contribute to the meaning, tone, or beauty of a text (e.g., a graphic novel, multimedia presentation of fiction, folktale, myth, poem).

**RI.5.8:** Explain how an author uses reasons and evidence to support particular points in a text, identifying which reasons and evidence support which point(s).

**RF.5.4:** Read with sufficient accuracy and fluency to support comprehension.

**W.5.3:** Write narratives to develop real or imagined experiences or events using effective technique, descriptive details, and clear event sequences.

**W.5.5:** With guidance and support from peers and adults, develop and strengthen writing as needed by planning, revising, editing, rewriting, or trying a new approach.

**SL.5.2:** Summarize a written text read aloud or information presented in diverse media and formats, including visually, quantitatively, and orally.

**L.5.5:** Demonstrate understanding of figurative language, word relationships, and nuances in word meanings.

## SUGGESTED OBJECTIVES

- Compare similarities and differences between two exemplar texts (e.g., *Alice in Wonderland* and *The Little Prince*).
- Respond to poetry, prose, and informational text in writing and in class discussions.
- Explain how poetry is used within prose.
- Discuss how illustrations in *Alice in Wonderland* and/or *The Little Prince* play a role in telling the story.
- Recite poetry for classmates—original and parody versions.
- Continue defining related words and identifying their parts of speech (e.g., *exploration, explorer, exploratory; character, characterization, characterize*).
- Interpret figurative language, including similes and metaphors.
- Research and report on an explorer.
- Write an exploration story.

## SUGGESTED WORKS

(E) indicates a CCSS exemplar text; (EA) indicates a text from a writer with other works identified as exemplars.

### LITERARY TEXTS

*Stories*

- *Alice in Wonderland* (Campfire Graphic Novel) (Lewis Carroll, adapted by Louis Helfand and Rajesh Nagulakonda)
- *Alice's Adventures in Wonderland* (Lewis Carroll) (E)
- *Down the Rabbit Hole* (An Echo Falls Mystery) (Peter Abrahams)

- *The End of the Beginning: Being the Adventures of a Small Snail (and an Even Smaller Ant)* (Avi and Tricia Tusa)
- *The Little Prince* (Antoine de Saint-Exupéry) (E)
- *The Nursery "Alice"* (Lewis Carroll and John Tenniel)

## Poems

- "Against Idleness and Mischief" (Isaac Watts)
- "How Doth the Little Crocodile" (from *Alice's Adventures in Wonderland*) (Lewis Carroll)
- "The Mouse's Tale" (from *Alice's Adventures in Wonderland*) (Lewis Carroll)
- "Queen of Hearts" (Mother Goose, anonymous)
- "The Spider and the Fly" (Mary Howitt)
- "The Star" (Ann and Jane Taylor)
- "'Tis the Voice of the Lobster" ("Lobster Quadrille") (from *Alice's Adventures in Wonderland*) (Lewis Carroll)
- "Twinkle, Twinkle, Little Bat" (from *Alice's Adventures in Wonderland*) (Lewis Carroll)
- "Words Free as Confetti" by Pat Mora (E)

## Quotations

- "Grown-ups never understand anything by themselves, and it is exhausting for children to have to provide explanations over and over again." (Antoine de Saint-Exupéry, *The Little Prince*)
- "It is only with the heart that one can see rightly; what is essential is invisible to the eye." (Antoine de Saint-Exupéry, *The Little Prince*)

# INFORMATIONAL TEXTS

## Nonfiction Books

- *Camels* (Nature Watch) (Cherie Winner)
- *Desert Mammals* (True Books) (Elaine Landau)
- *Deserts* (True Books: Ecosystems) (Darlene R. Stille)
- *Kids During the Age of Exploration* (Kids Throughout History) (Cynthia MacGregor)
- *My Librarian Is a Camel: How Books Are Brought to Children Around the World* (Margriet Ruurs) (E)
- *The United States of America: A State-by-State Guide* (Millie Miller and Cyndi Nelson)
- *Who Is Neil Armstrong?* (Roberta Edwards, Nancy Harrison, and Stephen Marchesi)
- *Who Was Daniel Boone?* (Sydelle Kramer)
- *Who Was Ferdinand Magellan?* (S. A. Kramer, Nancy Harrison, and Elizabeth Wolf)
- *Who Was Marco Polo?* (Joan Holub, John O'Brien, and Nancy Harrison)
- *Women Explorers in North and South America* (Capstone Short Biographies) (Margo McLoone-Basta)

## Biographies

- *René Magritte* (Getting to Know the World's Greatest Artists) (Mike Venezia)
- *Salvador Dalí* (Artists in Their Time) (Robert Anderson)

## ART, MUSIC, AND MEDIA

### Art

- Giorgio de Chirico, *The Disquieting Muses* (1916)
- Jean (Hans) Arp, *Mountain, Navel, Anchors, Table* (1925)
- Marcel Duchamp, *Bicycle Wheel* (1913)
- René Magritte, *The False Mirror* (1928)
- René Magritte, *Time Transfixed* (1938)
- Roberto Matta, *Psychological Morphology* (1938)
- Salvador Dalí, *The Persistence of Memory* (1931)
- Wilfredo Lam, *Untitled*, (1947)

### Illustrations

- Antoine de Saint-Exupéry, *The Little Prince* (1943)
- Sir John Tenniel, *Alice's Adventures in Wonderland*

### Music

- Danny Elfman, *Alice in Wonderland* [soundtrack] (2010) (Walt Disney Records)
- Steve Schuch, "The Little Prince" (1997) (Night Heron Music)

### Film

- *Lewis Carroll's Alice in Wonderland* (Broadway Theater Archive) (1983)
- Stanley Donen, dir., *The Little Prince* (1974)

## SAMPLE ACTIVITIES AND ASSESSMENTS

Note: Students should have the opportunity to choose a book to read and to discuss in groups. Whole-class activities are listed after the specific activities by text title (following). If both *Alice's Adventures in Wonderland* and *The Little Prince* are above some students' reading levels, you can add a third group that reads Avi's *The End of the Beginning*, an easier book with similar characteristics.

### 1. READING LITERATURE, SPEAKING AND LISTENING

Your teacher will introduce ways we can learn from characters' experiences in books by reviewing characters in some old favorites—such as *The Little Red Hen* and *Lon Po Po* or *The Three Little Pigs* and *The True Story of the Three Little Pigs*. You will start with some easier and more familiar stories in order to practice how to examine characters with more challenging and new texts. Talk about the character's point of view as well as the sequence of events experienced—the interrelationship among these and other elements in the story. (RL.5.1, RL.5.2, RL.5.3, SL.5.1, SL.5.3)

## ALICE'S ADVENTURES IN WONDERLAND

### 2. READING LITERATURE, OPINION WRITING

What does Alice think she will find when she jumps down the rabbit hole? If you were Alice, would you have done this? Why or why not? Write your response in your journal, share ideas with a classmate, and revise your response if you get additional ideas you would like to use. (RL.5.2)

### 3. READING LITERATURE, OPINION WRITING

Recall characters you have read about so far this year and compare them to characters from this text. For example, compare Alice's encounters in Wonderland with the Red Queen to another literary character that encounters a tyrant. What can you learn from Alice? Write your response in your journal, share ideas with a classmate, and revise your response if you get additional ideas you would like to use. (RL.5.3, SL.5.1)

### 4. READING LITERATURE

To see *Alice* and its illustrations in a different light, your teacher will introduce you to (1) *The Nursery "Alice,"* a version of the story that Carroll prepared for very young children; (2) *Down the Rabbit Hole* by Peter Abrahams; and/or (3) the graphic novel version of *Alice in Wonderland* (Campfire Graphic Novels). Discuss similarities and differences between these versions. (RL.5.7)

### 5. READING LITERATURE, READING COMPREHENSION

Summarize each chapter in your journal by answering the question "What does Alice learn from her experiences in *Alice's Adventures in Wonderland*?" Cite specific examples and/or mark the text with a sticky note to facilitate group discussion. (RL.5.5, SL.5.1a)

### 6. ART, SPEAKING AND LISTENING

Examine the work of two surrealist artists: Salvador Dalí and René Magritte. Compare the dreamlike state of the artworks to the experiences Alice has in Wonderland. In what ways are Alice's adventures similar to dreams (or nightmares)? To surrealist art? (SL.5.1)

## THE LITTLE PRINCE

### 7. READING LITERATURE, OPINION WRITING

What does the little prince or the pilot learn about himself by exploring the world and thinking about his adventures? Write your response in your journal (citing evidence from the text), share ideas with a classmate who chose the same character, and revise your response if you get additional ideas you would like to use. (RL.5.3)

### 8. READING LITERATURE, LANGUAGE USAGE

Symbols and metaphors are present throughout *The Little Prince*. Do these make it easier or harder for you to understand the story? Why? (RL.5.4, L.5.5a)

### 9. READING LITERATURE, READING COMPREHENSION, INFORMATIVE WRITING

Summarize every three to four chapters of *The Little Prince* in your journal by answering the question "What does the pilot learn from the little prince? What does the little prince learn from the pilot?" Cite examples from the text. (RL.5.5)

## 10. MUSIC, SPEAKING AND LISTENING

Listen to the song "The Little Prince" by Steve Schuch. Read the lyrics. Discuss similarities and differences between the song and the book. (SL.5.1)

## GENERAL

## 11. READING LITERATURE, SPEAKING AND LISTENING

At the end of your novel study, pair up with a partner who read a book that you did not. Share:

- What the character learned about himself or herself by exploring his or her unique world (RL.5.5, SL.5.2, SL.5.3, RF.5.4)
- How the illustrations are part of the story, showing specific pages (RL.5.7, SL.5.2)
- How the music/songs from this unit remind you of the story you read (if applicable) (SL.5.1)

## 12. DRAMATIZATION/FLUENCY

Choose a poem to perform interpretively from the suggested list, or write your own. Memorization is not required, but optional for this performance. (Alternatively, pair with a partner where one of you learns the Lewis Carroll version, and the other learns the original version. Perform both versions for the class, and then discuss how knowing the original helps us to appreciate the parody even more.) Record the readings using a video camera in order to share with others on the class blog. (L.5.5a, L.5.5b, L.5.5c, SL.5.6)

## 13. FILM, READING LITERATURE, SPEAKING AND LISTENING

How is reading *Alice's Adventures in Wonderland* or *The Little Prince* similar to or different from watching a DVD version? Which do you prefer? Why? Write your initial thoughts in your journal before discussing as a class. (RL.5.7)

## 14. READING INFORMATIONAL TEXT, INFORMATIVE WRITING

After reading *My Librarian Is a Camel* by Margriet Ruurs, has your perspective about the school library and access to library books changed? What are some ways that the author influenced your thinking? Cite specific examples from the text during class discussion. In your journal, write a response to this question: "What did you learn from this text?" (RI.5.8)

## 15. RESEARCH, INFORMATIVE WRITING, LANGUAGE USAGE, LANGUAGE MECHANICS

Not only do fictional characters learn from exploring their world, but real people do too. Research a famous explorer and his/her contributions to understanding of the world, and present your findings to the class. The research essay should be logically ordered with at least two to three sources of information cited. Edit your writing, especially correlative conjunctions, titles of works, and sentence variety (see Standards for more details). Your teacher may ask you to type your report and insert relevant visuals from the web for publication on the class web page. (W.5.7, L.5.1, L.5.2a, L.5.2b, L.5.2c, L.5.2d, L.5.3a)

## 16. NARRATIVE WRITING, LANGUAGE USAGE

Write your own exploration story about a real or fictional character. Your story should have a moral or a lesson you want the reader to learn from your character. You will have the opportunity to edit and revise your narrative with a partner so that your final product is of the highest quality.

The narrative should include ideas that flow logically and at least five new exploration vocabulary words. Edit your writing, especially for correlative conjunctions, titles of works, and sentence variety (see Standards for more details). Your teacher may ask you to type your story, add visuals, and possibly even record it as a podcast or using a video camera, for publication on the class web page. (W.5.3, W.5.4, W.5.5, L.5.1, L.5.2a, L.5.2b, L.5.2c, L.5.2d, L.5.3a)

## 17. VOCABULARY

As an individual and as a class, keep an index card file of words, literal and figurative, studied in this unit (e.g., *exploration, explorer, exploratory; character, characterization, characterize*). Keeping the words on index cards will help when you sort words by prefix, suffix, root words, meaning, and so on. How do word relationships help you understand the meaning of the words, while the prefixes and suffixes affect the part of speech and spelling? (*Note*: This will be an ongoing activity all year long.) In addition, you will create an individual semantic map of the word *exploration* in order to represent visually your understanding of the real and fictional types of exploration studied in this unit. (L.5.4a, L.5.4b, L.5.4c)

## 18. INFORMATIVE WRITING, LANGUAGE USAGE

Write an informative/explanatory essay in response to the essential question "What do people, both real and imagined, learn from exploring their world?" Your teacher may give you the opportunity to "give one, get one" before writing your response. Include at least three examples of things learned. Edit your writing, especially for correlative conjunctions, titles of works, and sentence variety (see Standards for more details) before sharing with your teacher. Your teacher may ask you to type your essay and respond to a poll about the unit on the class blog. (W.5.4, W.5.7, W.5.9a, W.5.9b, L.5.1, L.5.2a, L.5.2b, L.5.2c, L.5.2d, L.5.3a)

## 19. ART, NARRATIVE WRITING

Select any one of the suggested artworks and inventory the visual elements in the work. Consider what the artists might be trying to communicate about the figure(s) or the setting through their juxtaposition of imagery and/or use of distortion. What role does color play in the work? Use the list to write a short story based on the work, referring back to it as the story is developed. Is the story similar to a dream? (W.5.3, W.5.4)

## 20. ART, SPEAKING AND LISTENING

The suggested artworks in this unit belong to two related schools of art—Dadaism and Surrealism. Duchamp's *Bicycle Wheel* is considered a Dadaist work. Dadaists created "anti-art" that attempted to go against long-established ideas of what art looked like. Duchamp made a series of works he called "readymades," which paired or simply presented commonplace objects in an art setting. Jean Arp was also a Dadaist. Read the title of Arp's work out loud as you examine it. What do you see? Now, look at Magritte's *Time Transfixed*. Magritte worked as a Surrealist. Surrealism is an approach to art making that developed out of Dadaism. Much of Magritte's work is dream-like, featuring qualities found in Surrealism. Closely examine *Time Transfixed* and discuss as a class how Dadaism and Surrealism are similar and different. (SL.5.1, SL.5.5)

## 21. LANGUAGE USAGE

Your teacher will teach mini-lessons on the individual language standards. For example, he or she will explain correlative conjunctions. Then he or she will give you a set of sentences and ask you to insert the correct conjunction—for example, "Connor has not gone to school today, _____ [nor/or] has he done his homework." After the class understands this skill, you will select a piece of your own writing where you have used correlative conjunctions, or find part of your writing where adding these could enhance your writing. Edit to ensure that you used them correctly, and check your work with a partner. (L.5.1e)

## 22. LANGUAGE MECHANICS

As a class, continue adding to the Mechanics/Grammar bulletin board started in Unit One. Remember, once skills are taught in a mini-lesson and listed on the bulletin board, you are expected to edit your work for these elements before publication. (L.5.1, L.5.2, L.5.3)

## 23. VOCABULARY

As a class, continue adding to the Vocabulary Word Wall bulletin board where, throughout the year, you will add and sort words as you learn them in each unit of study. (L.5.4)

## ADDITIONAL ONLINE RESOURCES

- *Character Trading Cards* (ReadWriteThink) (RL.5.5)
- *Using Picture Books to Teach Characterization in Writing Workshop* (ReadWriteThink) (RL.5.2)
- *Book Report Alternative: Examining Story Elements Using Story Map Comic Strips* (ReadWriteThink) (RL.5.5)
- *The Original Alice: Alice's Adventures Under Ground* (The British Library)
- "Give One Get One" (RRISD Math Team)

## TERMINOLOGY

| | | |
|---|---|---|
| Metaphor | Paradox | Style |
| Nonsense literature | Parody | Symbol |

## INTERDISCIPLINARY CONNECTIONS

This unit teaches:

- **History/Geography:** Explorers (e.g., who they are, where/why they explored); geography of North and South America (e.g., fifty states, major oceans and rivers)
- **Science:** Camels (e.g., where they live, what is their habitat, what makes them suited for desert life)
- **Art:** Surrealism, Salvador Dalí, René Magritte, Roberto Matta, illustration

This unit could be extended to teach:

- **History/Geography:**
  - Explorers (e.g., Prince Henry the Navigator, Bartolomeu Dias, Vasco da Gama, Cabral, Christopher Columbus, Ferdinand Magellan, Balboa)
  - Deserts of the world (e.g., *Africa*: Sahara, Kalahari; *Asia*: Gobi; *North America*: Mojave, Death Valley; *South America*: Atacama Desert)
- **Science:**
  - Oceanography (e.g., surface, subsurface land features, ocean floor, composition of sea water, currents, tides, marine life)
  - Desert habitats (e.g., What lives in a desert? What adaptations would be needed by people to live in a desert?)

## Grade Five, Unit Five Sample Lesson Plan

*Alice's Adventures in Wonderland* by Lewis Carroll
*Alice in Wonderland: A Walt Disney Production*

In this series of four lessons (that begin after students have read *Alice's Adventures in Wonderland* by Lewis Carroll), students watch the film *Alice in Wonderland*, and they:

Note the differences between the novel and the movie (RL.5.1, RL.5.2, RL.5.7)

Analyze the impact of the differences between the novel and the movie (RL.5.2)

Articulate their observations in writing (W.5.1, W.5.4, W.5.9a, W.5.10, L.5.1, L.5.2, L.5.3)

### Summary

| Lesson I: *Alice in Wonderland*—The Movie | Lesson II: Alice's Adventures–The Novel and the Movie |
|---|---|
| Watch *Alice in Wonderland* (1951 Disney Production) (RL.5.7) | Reread assigned passage in *Alice's Adventures in Wonderland* (RL.5.1, RL.5.10, RF.5.4) |
| (Begin to) identify differences between the novel and the movie (SL.5.2, RL.5.7) | (In small groups) recall details of assigned scene in the movie (SL.5.1, SL.5.2, RL.5.5) |
| **Lesson III: Alice's Adventures–The Novel and the Movie** | **Lesson IV: Alice's Adventures–Assessing the Transition from the Novel to the Movie** |
| Analyze the movie's interpretation of the assigned scene (RL.5.5, RL.5.7, SL.5.2) | Recall ideas that were generated in Lessons II and III (W.5.8, SL.5.2) |
| Note the differences between the novel and the movie (RL.5.1, RL.5.2, RL.5.7) | Evaluate the impact that the differences between the novel and the movie have on the reader/viewer's understanding of Lewis Carroll's message (RL.5.2, W.5.1, W.5.4, W.5.9a, W.5.10, L.5.1, L.5.2, L.5.3) |

## Lesson IV: Alice's Adventures–Assessing the Transition from the Novel to the Movie

### Objectives

Recall ideas that were generated in Lessons II and III (W.5.8, SL.5.2)

Evaluate the impact that the differences between the novel and the movie have on the reader/viewer's understanding of Lewis Carroll's message (RL.5.2, W.5.4, W.5.1, W.5.9a, W.5.10, L.5.1, L.5.2, L.5.3)

### Required Materials

☐ Class set of *Alice's Adventures in Wonderland* by Lewis Carroll

☐ *Alice in Wonderland* (1951 Disney production)

☐ Students' notes

### Procedures

1. Lead-In:

   Students review their notes (from Lessons I–III).

2. Step by Step:

   a. Introduce the students to the in-class work. Students will create an outline in preparation for writing an essay. Their task is to evaluate the impact that the differences between *Alice Adventures in Wonderland*, the novel, and *Alice in Wonderland*, the movie, have on the reader/viewer's understanding of Lewis Carroll's message.

   b. Using their notes, students begin to work on the outline of their essays. They should follow the essay outline template shown here.

### Alice in Wonderland Essay Outline

*Introduction*

   Lead sentence: Introduces the text and the movie

   Contextualize: Introduces the specific passage on which the essay focuses

   Thesis statement: States the main point that the essay will make

*Body Paragraph I*

Topic sentence: supports the thesis statement

Support detail 1

Support detail 2

Support detail 3

*Body Paragraph II*

Topic sentence: supports the thesis statement

Support detail 1

Support detail 2

Support detail 3

*Body Paragraph III*

Topic sentence: supports the thesis statement

Support detail 1

Support detail 2

Support detail 3

*Conclusion*

The conclusion will:

Refer to the thesis statement (not repeat it)

Articulate a lesson that the essay teaches

Point to a possible greater idea, a special insight that the essay suggests

c. Students revise their outlines.

3. Closure:

Remind the students that for homework, they will use their outlines to write essays. Both the outline and the essays will be collected.

## Differentiation

### Advanced

- After writing the essay, students will rewrite the movie scene to be more in line with the author's message in the book. Supply students with a model of how movie scripts are written. As an extension, students may present their movie scene to the class, recorded on a video camera or created using video editing software.

- Students will research other movies that correspond to books they have already read this year. They may want to lead a series of class or lunch discussions (i.e., "The Book Is Better Club") based on the message in the movie versus the message in the book.

### Struggling

- Prepare pairs of movie scenes and passages for students to choose from for the focus of the essay. These can be collected for student review on portable media players.

- Students may work in small groups or with a partner to create outlines. Students can do this activity collaboratively on a shared spreadsheet.

- Give students the time they need to complete the essay, creating one paragraph each evening and reviewing/revising it with a partner and/or teacher the following day.

## Homework/Assessment

Write essay.

# Coming of Age

This final six-week unit focuses on the genre of the novel and uses "coming of age" as a unifying theme.

## ESSENTIAL QUESTION

How can literature help us understand what it means to "grow up"?

## OVERVIEW

In this unit, students choose one of many exemplar novels to study, using all the strategies and skills learned throughout the year. Coming of age is the recurring theme in the texts for this unit. Students compare and contrast characters' experiences in novels to develop their own definition for "coming-of-age novels." Students research the historical context behind a novel, such as the Great Depression as the historical context for *Bud, Not Buddy* by Christopher Paul Curtis. Striving to answer the essential question, students create multimedia presentations about coming of age.

## FOCUS STANDARDS

These Focus Standards have been selected for the unit from the Common Core State Standards.

**RL.5.3:** Compare and contrast two or more characters, settings, or events in a story or drama, drawing on specific details in the text (e.g., how characters interact).

**RI.5.6:** Analyze multiple accounts of the same event or topic, noting important similarities and differences in the point of view they represent.

**RF.5.4:** Read with sufficient accuracy and fluency to support comprehension.

**W.5.6:** With some guidance and support from adults, use technology, including the Internet, to produce and publish writing as well as to interact and collaborate with others; demonstrate sufficient command of keyboarding skills to type a minimum of two pages in a single sitting.

**W.5.8:** Recall relevant information from experiences or gather relevant information from print and digital sources; summarize or paraphrase information in notes and finished work, and provide a list of sources.

**SL.5.5:** Include multimedia components (e.g., graphics, sound) and visual displays in presentations when appropriate to enhance the development of main ideas or themes.

**L.5.3:** Use knowledge of language and its conventions when writing, speaking, reading, or listening.

**L.5.3(a):** Expand, combine, and reduce sentences for meaning, reader/listener interest, and style.

**L.5.3(b):** Compare and contrast the varieties of English (e.g., dialects, registers) used in stories, dramas, or poems.

## SUGGESTED OBJECTIVES

- Define the term *coming-of-age novel.*
- Compare the treatment of coming of age in a variety of novels.
- Compare and contrast novels and their film versions.
- Compare and contrast how characters in a story respond to challenges and what they learn from their experiences.
- Compare and contrast the experiences of real people during different historical time periods.
- Generate interview questions; interview people who can serve as sources of information on a research topic; relate their answers to research questions.
- Research the steps that would be involved in turning a hobby or interest into a career; communicate findings.

## SUGGESTED WORKS

(E) indicates a CCSS exemplar text; (EA) indicates a text from a writer with other works identified as exemplars.

### LITERARY TEXTS

*Stories*

- *Blue Willow* (Doris Gates)
- *Bud, Not Buddy* (Christopher Paul Curtis) (E)
- *Cat with a Yellow Star: Coming of Age in Terezin* (Susan Goldman Rubin and Ela Weissberger)
- *Christmas After All: The Great Depression Diary of Minnie Swift, Indianapolis, Indiana, 1932* (Dear America Series) (Kathryn Lasky)
- *Flying with the Eagle, Racing the Great Bear: Stories from Native North America* (Joseph Bruchac)
- *The Journal of C. J. Jackson: A Dust Bowl Migrant, Oklahoma to California, 1935* (Dear America Series) (William Durbin)
- *A Long Way from Chicago* (Richard Peck)
- *M. C. Higgins, the Great* (Virginia Hamilton) (E)

- *Native American Stories* (Joseph Bruchac)
- *Out of the Dust* (Karen Hesse)
- *Rose's Journal: The Story of a Girl in the Great Depression* (Marissa Moss)
- *The Secret Garden* (Frances Hodgson Burnett) (E)
- *Survival in the Storm: The Dust Bowl Diary of Grace Edwards, Dalhart, Texas, 1935* (Dear America Series) (Katelan Janke)
- *Then Again, Maybe I Won't* (Judy Blume)
- *Tuck Everlasting* (Natalie Babbitt) (E)
- *Walk Two Moons* (Sharon Creech)
- *The Wall: Growing Up Behind the Iron Curtain* (Peter Sis)
- *Where the Mountain Meets the Moon* (Grace Lin) (E)
- *A Year Down Yonder* (Richard Peck)

## Poems
- "Dreams" (Nikki Giovanni) (EA)
- "Freedom" (William Stafford)
- "I'm Nobody! Who Are You?" (Emily Dickinson) (EA)

## INFORMATIONAL TEXTS
### Nonfiction Books
- *Children of the Dust Bowl: The True Story of the School at Weedpatch Camp* (Jerry Stanley) (Read Aloud)
- *Children of the Great Depression* (Russell Freedman) (EA) (Read Aloud)
- *Dust Bowl Through the Lens: How Photography Revealed and Helped Remedy a National Disaster* (W. Sandler)
- *Dust to Eat: Drought and Depression in the 1930s* (Michael L. Cooper) (Read Aloud)
- *Getting Ready for a Career as . . .* (Series)
- *Gorilla Doctors: Saving Endangered Great Apes* (Scientists in the Field) (Pamela S. Turner)
- *The Great Depression* (Cornerstones of Freedom) (Elaine Landau)
- *The Kid's Guide to Money: Earning It, Saving It, Spending It, Growing It, Sharing It* (Steve Otfinoski) (E)
- *Kids During the Great Depression* (Kids Throughout History) (Lisa A. Wroble)
- *Quest for the Tree Kangaroo: An Expedition to the Cloud Forest of New Guinea* (Scientists in the Field) (Sy Montgomery and Nic Bishop) (E)
- *Setting Career Goals* (Stuart Schwartz and Craig Conley)

## ART, MUSIC, AND MEDIA
### Art
- Bernard Joseph Steffen, *Dusty Plowing* (ca. 1939)
- Blanche Grambs, *No Work* (1935)

- Conrad A. Albrizio, *The New Deal* (1934)
- Dorothea Lange, *Migrant Mother* (1936)
- Edward Hopper, *House by the Railroad* (1925)
- Hugo Gellert, *The Working Day, no. 37* (ca. 1933)

## Music

- Artie Shaw and His New Music, "Whistle While You Work" (no date)
- Duke Ellington and Irving Mills, "It Don't Mean a Thing (If It Ain't Got That Swing)" (1931)
- E. Y. "Yip" Harburg and Jay Gorney, "Brother, Can You Spare a Dime?" (1931)
- Jack Yellen and Milton Ager, "Happy Days Are Here Again" (1929)
- Jerome Kern and George Gard "Buddy" DeSylva, "Look for the Silver Lining" (1920)
- Marsha Norman and Lucy Simon, *The Secret Garden* (musical) (1991)

## Film

- Doug Atchison, dir., *Akeelah and the Bee* (2006)
- Robert Stevenson, dir., *Old Yeller* (1957)
- Victor Fleming, dir., *The Wizard of Oz* (1939)

# SAMPLE ACTIVITIES AND ASSESSMENTS

Note: Students choose a coming-of-age novel to read. Discussion groups are based on the novel chosen by each student.

## 1. READING LITERATURE, SPEAKING AND LISTENING

What is meant by the term *coming-of-age novel*? (Note: Prompting may be needed and answers could include: a story where a main character grows up by gaining knowledge or life experience; a story where I see a character transition from childhood to adulthood; a story where characters take on adult responsibility or learn a lesson, etc.) Create a class chart of characters read about and the ways they grow up in stories. After reading our novels, try to generate a definition of your own that will enable you to write your coming-of-age story. (SL.5.1)

## 2. READING LITERATURE, LANGUAGE USAGE

Keep a journal about your coming-of-age novel that specifies:

- The main character
- The obstacles faced
- The characteristics that enable him or her to overcome obstacles
- The character's internal responses and external responses to these obstacles
- The events that lead up to the climax and, ultimately, the character's growth
- Notes about varieties of English (dialects, registers) or other literary techniques used in the novel (L.5.3)

After reading your novel, create a coming-of-age comic strip that outlines the key events and supporting details that the main character went through to grow up. You may want to use comic strip software to publish your ideas. (RL.5.2, W.5.8)

## 3. READING LITERATURE, SPEAKING AND LISTENING

As a class, keep a chart with the following categories of the novels we've read, on paper or in a shared spreadsheet. As the chart is filled in, and at the end of the unit, use this information to make comparisons and generalizations about characters (and people) who undergo changes in their development:

- Setting
- Main character who undergoes a change, and adjectives that describe him or her
- Obstacles faced by the main character
- Climax (where the main character resolves the conflict)
- Resolution (how the story ends; what the character learns) (RL.5.2, RL.5.3)

## 4. READING LITERATURE, SPEAKING AND LISTENING

Be prepared to compare and contrast two or more characters, settings, or events across novels, drawing on specific information from each novel. What did you learn about yourself from these characters? Your teacher may ask you to write a personal response to this last question on a sticky note or in your journal before the class discussion begins. (SL.5.1, RL.5.3, RL.5.6, RL.5.9, RL.5.10, RF.5.4)

## 5. OPINION WRITING, LANGUAGE USAGE, LANGUAGE MECHANICS

Of the novels read in fifth grade, which was your favorite, and why? Write a convincing paper on why next year's fifth graders should be encouraged to read this novel. Write a well-developed essay that includes an engaging opening statement of your opinion, at least three supporting details, and a conclusion. Edit your work for all grammar studied this year, including language conventions (see Standards for more details). Your teacher may ask you to type your essay and draw or scan a favorite illustration for publication on the class web page. (W.5.1, SL.5.1, L.5.1, L.5.2, L.5.3a, L.5.3b, L.5.6)

## 6. FILM, READING LITERATURE, SPEAKING AND LISTENING

As an alternative means of examining the elements involved in coming-of-age stories, select a movie version of one of the stories to watch and discuss the elements from the chart (see Activity 3). Did the novel or movie address a question or issue with which you (or a friend) have struggled? (RL.5.7)

## 7. READING POETRY, SPEAKING AND LISTENING

Read and discuss the connection between the two people in Emily Dickinson's poem "I'm Nobody! Who Are You?" Relate the experience of the characters in the poem to the characters in your coming-of-age novel. Which characters can you see having a similar conversation? Justify your answer, citing specific details from the text. With whom has the main character in your book connected? Is the character an outsider? Your teacher may ask you to write a personal response to this last question on a sticky note or in your journal and share responses with a classmate before the class discussion begins. (SL.5.1, SL.5.2, L.5.6)

## 8. READING LITERATURE, SPEAKING AND LISTENING

Pair with a partner who read a different coming-of-age novel than you did. Collaboratively generate interview questions, keeping track of them in a shared spreadsheet, and then participate in mock interviews where you pretend to be the main character in the book you read (such as Mary Lennox from *The Secret Garden*, Sal from *Walk Two Moons*, or Mayo Cornelius from *M. C. Higgins, the Great*). Write about what you learned from your interview, and then have your partner check it for accuracy. (Alternatively, write interview questions for the author of your book and conduct research online to see if you can find answers to your questions for the author.) (RL.5.3, L.5.3a, L.5.3b, SL.5.6)

## 9. RESEARCH, READING INFORMATIONAL TEXT, INFORMATIVE WRITING, ORAL PRESENTATION, MULTIMEDIA PRESENTATION

Part of coming of age means moving into adulthood and getting a job. Read informational text about people who followed their interests and turned them into careers, such as Lisa Dabek in *Quest for the Tree Kangaroo*. What challenges did they encounter as part of their work? Conduct research about what steps you need to take to be ready for the profession(s) in which you are interested. Then write an essay about your research. Your research essay should be logically ordered and cite at least three sources of information. Edit your work for all grammar studied this year, including language conventions (see Standards for more details). Include visual displays in your presentation to the class as appropriate. Your teacher may ask you to type your essay and possibly add relevant visuals for publication on the class web page. (RI.5.6, RI.5.10, RL.5.6, W.5.7, SL.5.1, L.5.1, L.5.2, L.5.3a, L.5.3b, L.5.6)

## 10. RESEARCH, READING INFORMATIONAL TEXT, INFORMATIVE WRITING, ORAL PRESENTATION, MULTIMEDIA PRESENTATION

Read the biography of Peter Sis on his website and listen to the interview with Sis about his memoir, *The Wall: Growing Up Behind the Iron Curtain*. Read informational text about communism in order to better understand how the communist form of government under which Sis lived suppressed his personal and artistic freedom. Conduct research about what was involved in seeking asylum in the United States, and how that experience changed Sis in his mid-thirties. Your research essay should be logically ordered and cite at least three sources of information. Edit your work for all grammar studied this year, including language conventions (see Standards for more details). Include visual displays in your presentation as appropriate. Share your findings with the class. (RI.5.6, RI.5.10, RL.5.6, W.5.7, SL.5.1, L.5.1, L.5.2, L.5.3a, L.5.3b, L.5.6)

## 11. RESEARCH, READING INFORMATIONAL TEXT, INFORMATIVE WRITING, ORAL PRESENTATION, MULTIMEDIA PRESENTATION

Coming-of-age novels are "timeless" because they take place in a variety of contexts and settings. For example, *Bud, Not Buddy* by Christopher Paul Curtis takes place during the Great Depression. You have learned this year that knowing the historical context increases your understanding and appreciation for historical fiction. Research an event from the Great Depression, focusing on how that event affected people of the time. What lessons did people or society learn from the Great Depression? If possible, start by interviewing someone who lived during the Great Depression. (Your teacher may bring in a guest speaker with a personal connection to the Great Depression time period.) Present your findings to the class so that you can generate a better understanding of that historical period. Your research essay should be logically ordered and cite at least three sources of information. Edit your work for all grammar studied this year, including language conventions (see Standards for more details). (W.5.2, W.5.7, RI.5.3, SL.5.4, L.5.1a, L.5.1b, L.5.1c, L.5.2a, L.5.2b, L.5.3a, L.5.3b, L.5.6)

## 12. INFORMATIVE WRITING, LANGUAGE USAGE, LANGUAGE MECHANICS

Look back to what you learned during the America in Conflict unit (Unit Four) and compare it to what you learned about life during the Great Depression. Write an informative/explanatory essay about how life changed for African Americans from the start of the Civil War to the end of the Great Depression. How did it stay the same? Your response should be a well-developed essay that includes at least three supporting details. Edit your work for all grammar studied this year, including language conventions (see Standards for more details). (RI.5.2, W.5.2, W.5.4, W.5.8, L.5.1, L.5.2, L.5.3a, L.5.3b, L.5.6)

## 13. MUSIC, SPEAKING AND LISTENING

Listen to music from the Great Depression. Discuss how music can provide insight into historical events. What do you learn about these events by listening to music? How do the arts provide comfort and solace in times of conflict? Your teacher may ask you to write your own response on sticky notes, on a whiteboard, or in your journal before discussing as a class. (SL.5.1)

## 14. MULTIMEDIA PRESENTATION, LANGUAGE USAGE, LANGUAGE MECHANICS

A culminating project is for you to create your own coming-of-age multimedia presentation. You can create a movie or a keynote presentation, write a poem or a song, start a blog, and so forth. Create a character with an obstacle to overcome. How does he or she overcome it? The presentation should begin with an introduction that answers the essential question "How can literature help us understand what it means to 'grow up'?" Use at least ten new words or phrases that we've learned and studied throughout the year. Edit your work for all grammar studied this year, including language conventions (see Standards for more details) before publishing in an online format. (W.5.3, W.5.6, W.5.8, W.5.9a, W.5.9b, RI.5.10, SL.5.5, SL.5.6, L.5.1, L.5.2, L.5.3, L.5.3a, L.5.3b, L.5.6)

## 15. LANGUAGE MECHANICS

As a class, continue adding to the Mechanics/Grammar bulletin board started in Unit One. Remember, once skills are taught in a mini-lesson and listed on the bulletin board, you are expected to edit your work for these elements before publication. (L.5.1, L.5.2, L.5.3)

## 16. LANGUAGE USAGE, VOCABULARY

In small groups, select a passage from a book read in this unit, such as *Bud, Not Buddy* by Christopher Paul Curtis, that has a unique dialect. Discuss whether the use of slang-like language helped to add to the tone and authenticity of the book. Discuss 1930s slang words from the book *Bud, Not Buddy* and try to think of contemporary words that could replace the 1930s version. Remember—slang is acceptable to use in story dialogue, but shouldn't be used in formal writing. You will have the opportunity to rewrite a section of *Bud, Not Buddy* in contemporary language and compare the new presentation to the original version. (L.5.3b)

## 17. VOCABULARY

As a class, continue adding to the Vocabulary Word Wall bulletin board where, throughout the year, you will add and sort words as you learn them in each unit of study. (L.5.4)

## 18. ART, SPEAKING AND LISTENING

View Edward Hopper's *House by the Railroad*. Does the house appear occupied or abandoned? Does the railroad track appear to cut off access to the house, at least visually? What feelings do you get when you view this image? Note that Hopper claimed to try not to depict emotion in his paintings, only facts. Do you think Hopper was trying to depict the status of society at this time— or just a house? Would you describe this painting as happy, sad, or neither? (SL.5.1. SL.5.4)

## 19. ART, SPEAKING AND LISTENING

Compare the Dorothea Lange photograph with the drawing by Blanche Grambs. Can you still feel emotion looking at the drawing, even though you are not seeing the character's face? What about in Lange's photograph? What makes this image so powerful? (SL.5.1. SL.5.4)

## ADDITIONAL ONLINE RESOURCES

- *Once They're Hooked, Reel Them In: Writing Good Endings* (ReadWriteThink) (W.5.3, W.5.4)
- *Creating Family Timelines: Graphing Family Members and Significant Events* (ReadWriteThink) (RI.5.7)
- *Literature as a Jumping Off Point for Nonfiction Inquiry* (ReadWriteThink) (RL.5.9)
- *Actor Sidney Poitier Was Born in 1924* (ReadWriteThink) (W.5.1)
- "Web-Based Thematic Unit:" *Bud, Not Buddy* (Eduscapes)
- *The Impact of the Great Depression on Family and Home* (Novelguide.com)
- *A New Deal for the Arts* (The National Archives)
- Interview with Peter Sis about *The Wall: Growing Up Behind the Iron Curtain* (Book Expo America)
- Peter Sis's website

## TERMINOLOGY

| | | |
|---|---|---|
| Climax | Idioms such as "act your age," "at the tender age of . . .," "ripe old age" | Imagery |
| Dialogue | | Resolution |
| Foreshadowing | | Style |

## INTERDISCIPLINARY CONNECTIONS

This unit teaches:

- **Art:** Edward Hopper, Dorothea Lange
- **Economics:** Money (e.g., employment, private enterprise, banks, budgets, taxes, investments)
- **History/Geography:** The Great Depression (e.g., stock market crash, unemployment, "Hoovervilles," "Dust Bowl")

This unit could be extended to teach:

- **Science:** (as an extension of *The Secret Garden*) Plant structures and processes (e.g., vascular and nonvascular plants, photosynthesis, plant cell structures, classification)
- **Mathematics:** Money (e.g., solving multiplication problems with money, savings and checking accounts)

## Grade Five, Unit Six Sample Lesson Plan

### The Secret Garden by Frances Hodgson Burnett

*In this series of ten lessons, students read The Secret Garden by Frances Hodgson Burnett, and they:*

Annotate the novel for listed lessons' objectives (RL.5.1, RL.5.10, RF.4.4, W.5.8, W.5.9)

Identify the literary elements of the novel (RL.5.3, RL.5.5, RL.5.6, SL.5.5)

Follow the protagonist's evolution (RL.5.2, RL.5.3)

Investigate the plot of the novel (RL.5.3)

Probe the significance of the indoor and the outdoor settings (RL.5.3)

Identify key conflicts (RL.5.2)

Note the role of the minor characters (RL.5.3, L.5.3b)

## Summary

### Lesson I: Meet Mary Lennox (Chs. I–III)

(Begin to) discover the purpose of annotations (RL.5.1, RL.5.10, RF.4.4, W.5.8, W.5.9)

Note details of Mary's life before her departure for England (RL.5.1, RL.5.2)

Examine early presentation of Mary (RL.5.1, RL.5.2)

Explore Mary's arrival at Misselthwaite Manor (L.5.3b, RL.5.5)

Probe the emerging conflict (RL.5.2, SL.5.1)

### Lesson II: Mary's New Life Begins (Chs. IV–VI)

Explore Martha's perception of Mary (RL.5.1, RL.5.3)

Record early details of Dickon (RL.5.1, RL.5.3)

Note Mary's early attraction to the "mysterious garden" (RL.5.1, RL.5.5)

Follow Mary's explorations (RL.5.5)

Trace the mystery that unfolds (RL.5.1, RL.5.5)

## Lesson III: Discoveries (Chs. VII–IX)

Explore Martha's impact on Mary (RL.5.1, RL.5.3)

Examine the relationship between Mary and the robin (RL.5.1, RL.5.3)

Note Mary's early actions as she enters the garden (RL.5.1, RL.5.3)

## Lesson IV: Dickon (Chs. X–XII)

Explore Mary and Dickon's first meeting (RL.5.1, RL.5.3)

Examine the purpose of Dickon's mention of the "missel thrush" (RL.5.1, RL.5.3, L.5.4a)

Detail Mary's meeting with Mr. Craven (RL.5.1, RL.5.3)

Revisit Mary's evolving character (RL.5.3)

## Lesson V: Colin (Chs. XIII–XV)

Explore the first meeting between Mary and Colin (RL.5.1, RL.5.3)

Note Mary's growing influence over Colin (RL.5.1, RL.5.3)

Juxtapose Colin's and Dickon's personalities (RL.5.1, RL.5.3)

Examine Mary's relationship with the two boys (RL.5.1, RL.5.3)

## Lesson VI: Mary's Growth (Chs. XVI–XVII)

Note Mary's growing independence (RL.5.1, RL.5.2)

Explore the narrator's claim that Colin's fight with Mary (Ch. XVI) was "rather good for him" (RL.5.3)

(Continue to) juxtapose Colin's and Dickon's personalities (RL.5.3)

Note Mary's reaction to Mr. Craven's gift (RL.5.3)

## Lesson VII: "I shall live forever and ever and ever!" (Chs. XVIII–XX)

Note Colin's gradual transformation (RL.5.1, RL.5.3)

Explore Mary's role in Colin's transformation (RL.5.1, RL.5.3)

Examine the nature of Dickon's growing influence on both Mary's and Colin's transformations (RL.5.1, RL.5.3)

## Lesson VIII: Magic (Chs. XXI–XXIII)

Probe Colin's growing inner strength transformation (RL.5.1, RL.5.3)

Explore the relationship between magic and actions (RL.5.4)

Examine Colin's interpretation of magic (RL.5.4)

## Lesson IX: (Ch. XXIV–End)

Examine Dickon's mother's role in reaching the novel's climax (RL.5.2, RL.5.3, RL.5.5)

Explore the relationship among Mary, Martha, Dickon, and Colin (RL.5.3)

Probe the thematic strands in the novel (RL.5.2)

## Lesson X: Annotations Revisited

Revisit the objectives of the lessons

Explore the annotations (RL.5.1, RL.5.10, RF.4.4, W.5.8, W.5.9)

Revisit the themes of the novel (RL.5.2)

Trace a single theme (in the form of an argumentative essay) (RL.5.2, W.5.1, W.5.4, W.5.9, W.5.10, SL.5.4. L.5.1, L.5.2, L.5.6)

## Lesson I: Meet Mary Lennox (Chs. I–III)

### Objectives

(Begin to) discover the purpose of annotations (RL.5.1, RL.5.10, RF.4.4, W.5.8, W.5.9)

Note details of Mary's life before her departure for England (RL.5.1, RL.5.2)

Examine early presentation of Mary (RL.5.1, RL.5.2)

Explore Mary's arrival at Misselthwaite Manor (L.5.3b, RL.5.5)

Probe the emerging conflict (RL.5.2, SL.5.1)

### Required Materials

☐ Class set of *The Secret Garden* by Frances Hodgson Burnett

☐ Sticky notes

### Procedures

1. **Lead-In:**

   Introduce the lesson's objectives and instruct the students to reread the first three chapters (the assumption here is that students will have read those chapters for homework). Instruct the students to annotate the chapters for the lesson's objectives. (Students use the sticky notes to make the annotations.)

2. **Step by Step:**

   a. Students annotate chapters I, II, and III for the lesson's objectives. You may choose to provide the students with samples. Here are a few annotations for a description of Mary's early life:

   "She had not wanted a little girl at all, and when Mary was born she handed her over to the care of an Ayah *[Mary is not loved]*, who was made to understand that if she wished to please the Mem Sahib she must keep the child out of sight as much as possible. So when she was a sickly, fretful, ugly *[Her mother considers her "ugly"]* little baby she was kept out of the way, and when she became a sickly, fretful, toddling thing she was kept out of the way also. She never remembered seeing familiarly anything but the dark faces of her Ayah and the other native servants, and as they always obeyed her and gave her her own way in everything, because the Mem Sahib would be angry if she was disturbed by her crying, by the time she was six years old she was as tyrannical and selfish *[This is why she becomes so selfish]* a little pig as ever lived."

b. Lead a class discussion in which the students use their annotations to help explain their understanding of Mary's early life. Remind the students to continue annotating during the discussion.

3. Closure:

Explain the homework.

## Differentiation

### Advanced

• Working ahead of the class, students create digitized dramatic readings of chapters, recorded on portable media players or using video cameras. (These readings can be used to aid less advanced readers.)

• Choose a favorite chapter and create a script for a scene of a play. Follow a framework for script writing. As time allows, choose characters and direct the short play in rehearsals and performance. Record using a video camera.

### Struggling

• Students may need an audio text (CD, playaway, text-to-speech, portable media player) available to them to ease the volume of reading in this unit.

• Students will limit annotations to only one or two of the class objectives.

• Provide a graphic organizer to sort the annotations according to the lesson's objectives.

## Homework/Assessment

Read chapter IV through chapter VI and annotate (follow the class activity) for the objectives of Lesson II:

• Explore Martha's perception of Mary

• Record early details of Dickon

• Note Mary's early attraction to the "mysterious garden"

• Follow Mary's explorations

• Trace the mystery that unfolds

# Sample Text Study

To provide specific guidance about how educators might implement the instructional shifts called for by the CCSS-ELA, Common Core's teacher-writers have crafted a group of exemplar "text studies," a sample of which appears on the following pages. More text studies can be found at www.commoncore.org.

Our text studies begin with a selection of an "anchor text," and an explanation of how that text meets the new expectations for rigor and content richness. Next, we present a series of text-dependent questions based on both the words and (when applicable) illustrations in the text. The questions explore key components of the text as they address focus standards and help students to absorb essential knowledge. Exemplar answers are offered as guideposts for teachers as they move students toward a deep content understanding. Because students benefit from engaging with new and interesting words in context, certain text-dependent questions center on academic vocabulary. Opportunities to hone knowledge of grammar and conventions also are highlighted.

Each text study contains at least one culminating performance assessment that provides students an opportunity to demonstrate mastery of the skills under study and comprehension of the content in the anchor text. These performance tasks often ask students to write or present what they have learned, and thus offer an opportunity to gauge student comprehension and mastery of the identified standards.

We are excited about our text studies and hope you will join us at www.commoncore.org, where we will continue to share more of them.

# TEXT STUDY
## AMOS & BORIS BY WILLIAM STEIG

**Grade:** 3

**Unit:** 2

**Unit Title:** Inspired by the Sea

**Text Type:** Literary Text

**Lexile Level:** AD810L

**Rationale:**

This text was selected because of its superb literary quality. In particular, it exhibits engaging characterization, vivid descriptions of setting, a compelling plot, and an unmistakable theme. The book's purposeful cadence and supporting illustrations enhance all of these qualities. It could be compared to similar tales or fables, such as *The Lion and the Mouse*. In addition, it presents an opportunity for you to pair it with informational texts within an integrated science unit about mammals, oceans, or migration—or within an integrated social studies unit about survival.

## SUGGESTIONS FOR USE

Although *Amos & Boris* is an exemplar literary text for the 2–3 grade span, it is a challenging text for readers in the second unit of third grade. You may need to read it aloud with a document camera during the first read with students, then go back and reread with students closely, pausing to discuss each question. The vocabulary is challenging, but the story is engaging enough to provide a context for rich comprehension.

## COMMON CORE STATE STANDARDS ALIGNMENT

### FOCUS STANDARDS

Students will practice the following standards through the completion of the performance assessment task:

**RI.3.3:** Describe characters in a story (e.g., their traits, motivations, or feelings) and explain how their actions contribute to the sequence of events.

**W.3.1:** Write opinion pieces on topics or texts, supporting a point of view with reasons.

or

**W.3.2:** Write informative/explanatory texts to examine a topic and convey ideas and information clearly.

## ADDITIONAL STANDARDS

**L.3.1:** Demonstrate command of the conventions of standard English grammar and usage when writing or speaking.

**L.3.1(a):** Explain the function of nouns, pronouns, verbs, adjectives, and adverbs in general and their functions in particular sentences.

**L.3.1(c):** Use abstract nouns (e.g., *childhood*).

## VOCABULARY

Some words from this book may be unfamiliar to students or may be used in a different way than students have seen previously. Possible words for study include

| | | |
|---|---|---|
| Backwashes | Iodine | Sextant |
| Breakers | Mammal | Telescope |
| Compass | | |

## GRAMMAR EXTENSION

**Abstract nouns:** You could choose from among the abstract nouns, many of which may be new to third graders, for vocabulary and grammar work. Some of these are used more than once in the book. Students may do exercises–after mini-lessons–in which they

- Categorize nouns as abstract or concrete. (Remind students that some things you can touch, such as *boat*, and these are concrete nouns. Other nouns describe things you cannot touch, such as *strength* and *wonder*.)
- Recognize and practice the ways in which some words can be more than one part of speech, depending on their use.
  - Examples: *wonder, love,* and *touch*
- Recognize and practice different forms of these words.
  - Examples: *navigate/navigation; strong/strength; lonely/loneliness*
- Compare and contrast nouns used in association with Amos and Boris.

| | | |
|---|---|---|
| Admiration | Cheer | Grandeur |
| Adventure | Daintiness | Iodine |
| Agony | Delicacy | Loneliness |
| Ambitions | Enterprise | Love |
| Bulk | Friendliness | Navigation |

| Pity | Relief | Touch |
| Power | Secrets | Voice |
| Privilege | Situation | Warmth |
| Purpose | Strength | Wetness |
| Radiance | Tide | Wonder |

## TEXT STUDY

*Note to teachers: Words in **bold** below are featured in the Vocabulary and Grammar Extension sections above.*

1. According to page 1, who is Amos, and where does he live?
   - Amos is a mouse who "lived by the ocean."

2. On pages 1 and 2, how does the author convey that Amos was fascinated by the sea?
- The text says,
   - "He loved the ocean."
   - "He loved the smell of sea air."
   - "He loved to hear the surf sounds—the bursting breakers, the backwashes with rolling pebbles."

   *Note to teachers: Note that these are sensory details; you may also note the use of alliteration here.*
   - "He thought a lot about the ocean, and he wondered about the faraway places on the other side of the water."
   - Amos decides to build a boat to explore the "faraway places."
   - He works day and night on his project: he built the boat during the day, and he studied **navigation** at night.

3. According to page 3, how does Amos prepare for his journey?
- He loads the boat with supplies: food, water, tools, and "necessities such as **iodine**, a yo-yo, and playing cards."

   *Note to teachers: You might pause to discuss the meaning of the abstract noun* necessity *and compare it to the adjective* necessary.

4. Why do you think that Amos includes a yo-yo and playing cards as "necessities"?
- Amos was wise to realize that he might need things to do while sailing.
- Amos probably enjoys playing games.

5. When does Amos decide to set sail, and why?
- Amos waits until there is a calm sea and a high tide.
- According to the illustration, Amos had to push the boat with all of his strength into the water at the time when the water was closest to shore. He could not have pushed it into the sea without the tide to help him.

6. Does Amos enjoy the first part of his trip? Cite details that support your answer.

- Yes.
  - Amos overcame seasickness and "proved to be a natural sailor, very well suited to the ship."
  - He "was enjoying his trip immensely."
  - "It was beautiful weather."
  - Amos was "full of **wonder**, full of **enterprise**, and full of **love** for life."

7. What adjectives would you use to describe Amos, based on the first four pages?

Note to teachers: Answers may vary. The following are likely and acceptable responses. This is a good place to talk with students about shades of meaning.

- He is thoughtful and curious. (page 2)
  - "He thought a lot about the ocean, and he wondered about the faraway places on the other side of the water."
- He is enterprising. (page 2)
  - Instead of just wondering about "faraway places," he builds a boat and studies navigation so that he can go exploring.
- He is practical. (page 3)
  - He packs food, fresh water, tools, first aid supplies, and games to occupy him while he travels.
- He is optimistic, patient, and/or determined. (page 4)
  - He wisely planned his boat launch.
  - He used his "savage strength" to push it out to sea.
  - He worked through his seasickness and kept learning to sail.

8. In pages 7–9, how does the author highlight the ways in which Amos was "full of **wonder**, full of **enterprise**, and full of **love** for life," as he is described on page 5?

- "He marveled at the sight of some whales spouting luminous water."
  - The author could have said, "Amos watched whales spouting water," but instead he uses the word "marveled," which shows that Amos was fascinated by the whales (i.e., full of **wonder**, rather than fear).
  - He uses the word "luminous" to indicate that the spouting water was a beautiful sight to Amos.
- The author says that Amos was "a little speck of a living thing in the vast living universe," but also that "he felt thoroughly akin to it all."

Note to teachers: Students may need help understanding what it means to feel "akin" to something. Even this tiny creature felt connected to the universe, and that he was an important part of it.

- The author says that Amos was "overwhelmed by the beauty and mystery of everything," illustrating his love for life.
- Even after he falls off the boat and loses it forever, the patient and optimistic Amos considers his options calmly, and decides "just to keep afloat, treading water and hoping that something–who knows what?–would turn up to save him."

9.   What actually causes Amos to fall off the boat?

- Amos fell off the boat because he was distracted, "overwhelmed by the beauty and mystery of everything."

10.  How does the author show that Amos remains curious, optimistic, patient, and determined, despite his desperate situation?

- On page 9, Amos carefully considers how to solve his problem.

- On page 10, Amos is able to accept "a bit of cheer and warmth" that the sun gives him, despite his "vast loneliness."

- On page 10, Amos calmly wonders what it would be like to drown, what heaven would be like, and if there would be other mice there.

11.  How is Amos rescued?

- A whale named Boris finds him and agrees to take Amos back to his beach.

12.  Why do you think Boris is willing to go "out of his way" to return Amos to his home on the beach? Cite evidence from the text in your answer.

- On page 13, Boris says, "Not only would I not mind . . . I would consider it a **privilege**. What other whale in all the world ever had the chance to get to know such a strange creature as you!"

13.  Looking at pages 13–19, how would you describe Boris?

- Boris seems a lot like Amos, even though they are physically different.
  ○ Like Amos, Boris is ready for an adventure.
  ○ Like Amos, Boris is patient. When Amos gets upset about Boris's sounding, Boris decides to warn Amos when he is about to sound.
  ○ Like Amos, Boris is curious.
    – *He is curious about Amos, who is also a mammal, even though he is physically very different from himself.*
    – *He is "curious about life on land and was sorry he could never experience it."*

14.  What lines on page 16 best summarize Boris's attitude toward Amos?

- "Boris admired the **delicacy**, the quivering **daintiness**, the light **touch**, the small voice, the gemlike **radiance** of the mouse."

15.  What lines on page 16 best summarize Amos's attitude toward Boris?

- "Amos admired the **bulk**, the **grandeur**, the **power**, the **purpose**, the rich **voice**, and the abounding **friendliness** of the whale."

16.  Using evidence from pages 17–19, describe the friendship that develops between Amos and Boris.

- "They became the closest possible friends." (page 17)

- "They told each other about their lives, their ambitions." (page 17)

- "They shared their deepest secrets with each other." (page 17)

- When the time came to say goodbye, they told each other that they wished they could "be friends forever," even though they knew they would probably never see each other again; they said that they would never forget each other. (page 18)

- Amos offers to help Boris, as Boris has helped him. Boris and Amos both knew that little Amos could probably never help Boris, but Boris "knew how willing he was." Boris says, "Little as he is, he's all heart. I love him, and I'll miss him terribly." (pages 18 and 19)

*Note to teachers: You might help students understand the improbability of Amos helping Boris the way Boris had helped him, and what this relationship between them suggests about friendship—how friends are willing to help one another, no matter how difficult it might be to do so.*

17. Describe what happens to Boris many years later during a hurricane, and how his experience is similar to what happened to Amos.

- Both Amos's and Boris's troubles occurred in the sea.

- Boris was "flung ashore by a tidal wave and stranded" on land, where he could not survive, just as Amos had been stranded in the sea, where he could not survive.

- Like Amos, Boris felt scared and alone as he lay on the beach.

- "Just as Amos had once felt," Boris was "sure he would die." (page 24)

- Amos ultimately rescued Boris, as Boris had rescued him. (pages 26–27)

18. When Boris and Amos say goodbye on the last page (page 28), how is it similar to when they said good-bye the first time (on pages 18–19)?

*Note to teachers: You might take this opportunity to review the structure of the story and how the plot developed as a result of the characters' traits and motivations.*

- Both times, Boris and Amos are very sad.

- Both times, they think that they will never see each other again.

- Both times, the author describes how they will never forget each other.

  ○ The first time, each tells the other he will not forget his friend.

  ○ At the end, the author says, "They knew they would never forget each other."

## PERFORMANCE ASSESSMENT

### PART ONE

Ask students to fill in a chart that lists the characters' traits, motivations, and feelings in one column (you could fill in the first column) and their actions in second. In a class discussion, guide students to recognize that the events in the second column—read top to bottom—constitute the plot of the story. Help them to understand that it is the characters' traits, motivations, and feelings that determine the action of the story.

For example:

| Character Traits/Motivations/Feelings (CAUSE) | Actions (EFFECT) |
| --- | --- |
| Amos is curious about the sea | . . . so he builds a boat and learns navigation. |
| Amos is practical | . . . so he prepares carefully for his journey. |
| Amos is distracted by the beauty of what he sees at sea | . . . so he falls off the boat, loses it, and gets stranded in the middle of the sea. |
| Amos is optimistic and patient | . . . so he treads water, hoping that something will rescue him. |
| Boris is adventurous | . . . so he agrees to change his course and rescue Amos and ultimately bring Amos home. |

## PART TWO

Give students the following writing task:

Write an informative/explanatory essay that summarizes the plot of the story and describes what causes the main events of this story to happen. Be sure to cite three to four examples from the text that explain the connection between the characters' traits and their actions.

Your response should:

☐ Summarize the plot of the story.

☐ Tell how characters' traits and actions cause the main events of this story.

☐ Cite three to four examples from the text that explain the connection between the characters' traits and their actions.

☐ Have a sense of conclusion.

☐ Include proper punctuation, capitalization, and correct spelling in the final draft.

OR

Give students the following writing task:

Write an opinion essay in which you answer the question, "How do you think Amos and Boris became good and loyal friends?" Be sure to cite three to four examples from the text to support your opinions.

Your response should:

☐ Introduce the topic, including your opinion, of why Amos and Boris became such good and loyal friends.

☐ Include an organized list of reasons for your opinion.

☐ Provide three or four examples from the text to support the reasons for your opinion.

☐ Use linking words and phrases (e.g., *because, therefore, since, for example*) to connect opinion and reasons.

☐ Provide a concluding statement.

# TEXT FLUENCY

Read the following text out loud for students, demonstrating the elements of fluent reading: accuracy, prosody, and appropriate rate.

Fluent reading of the first passage will require students to relay a change of mood from Amos's absolute admiration of the beauty around him to the rolling off the deck and into the sea. The long phrases and effortless pronunciation of new vocabulary will take practice.

The second passage explores the ways Amos and Boris's differences deepened their mutual friendship.

## PASSAGE 1

(106 words)

One night, in a phosphorescent sea, he marveled at the sight of some whales spouting luminous water; and later, lying on the deck of his boat gazing at the immense, starry sky, the tiny mouse Amos, a little speck of a living thing in a vast universe, felt thoroughly akin to it all. Overwhelmed by the beauty and mystery of everything, he rolled over and over and right off the deck of his boat and into the sea.

"Help!" he squeaked as he grabbed desperately at the *Rodent*. But it evaded his grasp and went bowling along under full sail, and he never saw it again. (page 7)

## PASSAGE 2

(79 words)

Swimming along, sometimes at great speed, sometimes slowly and leisurely, sometimes resting and exchanging ideas, sometimes stopping to sleep, it took them a week to reach Amos's home shore. During that time, they developed a deep admiration for one another. Boris admired the delicacy, the quivering daintiness, the light touch, the small voice, the gemlike radiance of the mouse. Amos admired the bulk, the grandeur, the power, the purpose, the rich voice, and the abounding friendliness of the whale. (page 16)

# Who Is Common Core

Common Core is a nonprofit 501(c)3 organization that creates curriculum and promotes programs, policies, and initiatives at the local, state, and federal levels, with the aim of providing students with challenging, rigorous instruction in the full range of liberal arts and sciences. Common Core was established in 2007 and is not affiliated with the Common Core State Standards (CCSS).

Common Core has been led by Lynne Munson, as president and executive director, since its founding. In six short years, Lynne has made Common Core an influential advocate for the liberal arts and sciences and a noted provider of CCSS-based curriculum tools. Lynne was deputy chairman of the National Endowment for the Humanities (NEH) from 2001 to 2005, overseeing all agency operations. NEH is an independent agency of the federal government that funds scholarly and public projects in the humanities. Lynne was the architect of Picturing America (http://picturingamerica.neh.gov), the most successful public humanities project in NEH history. The project put more than seventy-five thousand sets of fine art images and teaching guides into libraries, K–12 classrooms, and Head Start centers. In 2005, Lynne led the first postconflict U.S. government delegation to Afghanistan to deal with issues of cultural reconstruction. In 2004, she represented the United States at UNESCO meetings in Australia and Japan, where she helped negotiate guidelines for cross-border higher education.

From 1993 to 2001, Lynne was a research fellow at the American Enterprise Institute, where she wrote *Exhibitionism: Art in an Era of Intolerance* (Ivan R. Dee, 2000), a book examining the evolution of art institutions and art education. Lynne served as a research assistant to NEH chairman Lynne Cheney from 1990 to 1993. She has written on issues of contemporary culture and education for numerous national publications, including the *New York Times*, the *Wall Street Journal*, *USA Today*, *Inside Higher Education*, and National Review Online's *The Corner*. She has appeared on CNN, Fox News, CNBC, C-SPAN, and NPR, and she speaks to scholarly and public audiences. She serves on the advisory board for the Pioneer Institute's Center for School Reform. Her degree in art history is from Northwestern University.

# Acknowledgments

It has been four years since Common Core's Curriculum Maps in English Language Arts were introduced. We have been thrilled to see how enthusiastically this work has been embraced. As of this date, more than 18,000 educators have become users of the online version of this work, while more than 100,000 own at least one of the print volumes.

Our teacher-writers have been in the field sharing their expertise and learning alongside our users. We have been gratified to have the opportunity to engage with teachers from Jordan, Utah to Rogers, Arkansas to Beulah, North Carolina and beyond. Each of these experiences—along with engaging with our users online—has contributed to our understanding of the future of this work. That future can be seen on our website, www.commoncore.org, where anyone can view a collection of "text studies" wherein we have taken a group of suggested works from our original ELA curriculum maps and created a series of text-dependent questions (and more) that illustrate how to engage students in the reading and interrogation of a high-quality text at a level that meets the expectations of the CCSS.

We've rebranded our ELA offering "The Wheatley Portfolio" in honor of the celebrated poet Phillis Wheatley, herself an example of stalwart excellence in the American canon. That work was crafted by many of the same teacher-writers who contributed to this volume, including Lorraine Griffith and Sheila Byrd Carmichael. We also are grateful for the many new friends we have made—including Caroline Schenk and Susan Hensley, district partners from Arkansas.

There are so many who deserve to be recognized for their contribution to the Maps' success. They include Emily Dodd, Hillary Marder, Alyson Burgess, Barbara Davison, Natanya Levioff, and Sarah Woodard. Diego Quiroga's relentless advocacy on behalf of our members led him to execute key improvements to our online and print resources. Chris Clary and Ed Alton undertook a revamping of our website that has made these materials easier and more pleasurable to use. Chris and Ed were aided by the creative writing genius of Peter Chase and the visionary images of Amy DeVoogd. And Russ Cohen and his team at Schoolwide, Inc., have been instrumental in assisting our teachers in the selection of superb texts, and our efforts to ensure that these excellent books reach thousands of students across the country.

Many people ask us what lessons we have learned since we started creating CCSS-based curriculum a few years ago. The list of lessons is, of course, too long to include here. But there is one top-level take-away that I must mention. We always suspected—and now know for certain—that teachers cannot be successful unless they are provided with (or are given the freedom to choose!) truly excellent books to use in their classrooms. You cannot build quality curricula, or even an effective single lesson, on books that are poorly written and devoid of knowledge and craft. Too many of our schools have invested fortunes in mediocre basals and numbing leveled readers that will prove to be of absolutely no use in meeting the expectations of the CCSS. What teachers and students need are beautifully written and illustrated books that celebrate the important stories they tell. We are glad to be part of an effort to put high-quality books into the classroom.

Again, thank you for your interest in what we do at Common Core. We are a small nonprofit, doing all we can to give teachers the content-rich materials they deserve and need. Thank you for supporting this work.

*January 6, 2014*                                                                                         Lynne Munson

# Index of Suggested Works